JOSEPH FIELDING SMITH

Joseph Fielding Smith, July 19, 1914, age 38

JOSEPH FIELDING SMITH
GOSPEL SCHOLAR, PROPHET OF GOD

FRANCIS M. GIBBONS

Deseret Book Company
Salt Lake City, Utah

Books by Francis M. Gibbons

Joseph Smith: Martyr, Prophet of God
Brigham Young: Modern Moses, Prophet of God
John Taylor: Mormon Philosopher, Prophet of God
Wilford Woodruff: Wondrous Worker, Prophet of God
Lorenzo Snow: Spiritual Giant, Prophet of God
Joseph F. Smith: Patriarch and Preacher, Prophet of God
Heber J. Grant: Man of Steel, Prophet of God
George Albert Smith: Kind and Caring Christian, Prophet of God
David O. McKay: Apostle to the World, Prophet of God
Joseph Fielding Smith: Gospel Scholar, Prophet of God

Photos on pages 334 and 379 are reprinted with permission from the *Deseret News*. All other photos are reprinted courtesy of the Historical Department Archives of The Church of Jesus Christ of Latter-day Saints. Used by permission.

Library of Congress Cataloging-in-Publication Data

Gibbons, Francis M., 1921–
    Joseph Fielding Smith : Gospel scholar, prophet of God / Francis M. Gibbons.
        p.   cm.
    Includes bibliographical references and index.
    ISBN 0-87579-537-4
    1. Smith, Joseph Fielding, 1876–1972.   2. Church of Jesus Christ of Latter-day Saints — Presidents — Biography.   3. Mormon Church — Presidents — Biography.   I. Title.
BX8695.S64G53   1992
289.3'092 — dc20
[B]   91-46965
                                                                        CIP

Printed in the United States of America

10   9   8   7   6   5   4   3   2   1

Contents

Contents

Preface

The author first met President Joseph Fielding Smith on Thursday morning, April 9, 1970, in a meeting of the First Presidency when he was called to succeed Elder Joseph Anderson as the secretary to the First Presidency. Thereafter, I served President Smith and his counselors during the remainder of President Smith's administration, which ended with his death on July 2, 1972.

The benign, white-haired man I met that morning was almost ninety-four years old. At the time he became the president of the Church on January 23, 1970, he had served as a member of the Twelve for almost sixty years, longer than any other person of this dispensation. During twenty of those years, he had been either the president or the acting president of the quorum. He had served continuously for almost sixty-four years either as the Church historian or assistant Church historian. And he had served for almost five years as a counselor in the First Presidency. Moreover, he had authored twenty-five books and was generally recognized as the leading scripturalist and interpreter of doctrine in the Church. Knowing all this, I was impressed. And on meeting and becoming acquainted with him, I was even more impressed, but in a way I had not expected.

The man whom I met in person was far different from the man I had thought him to be, gauged by his demeanor in the pulpit and his precise literary style. And in the months that followed, the difference became even more apparent. It is true, I suppose, that most people in the public eye act differently when they are offstage. That is to be expected. But to find in one an almost complete reversal of his public image when seen in his private circles is extraordinary.

What the public saw in President Smith was a seemingly stern, no-nonsense speaker who seldom if ever strayed from the strictures of the scriptures. He rarely used stories by way of illustration. Humor never found its way into his sermons. There are few instances when he even smiled in the pulpit. To think of him laughing there is beyond reason. He was always punctual, arriving early at meetings, where he would sit quietly and reverently on the stand, waiting for the meeting to start. And if he conducted, the meeting would always start on time—and it would, if at all possible, end on time. Such precision created the impression that his decisions would be made according to the strict rules of justice, unbending, unyielding, and unfeeling. But the reality is that no one was more charitable and more merciful than President Joseph Fielding Smith in rendering judgment on transgressors. As the Prophet, it was his responsibility to decide cases of cancellation of sealings and restoration of blessings. His decisions were always made in kindness and love and with the widest latitude of mercy that the circumstances could justify. It was not uncommon for him to say on learning the circumstances of an aggravated case, "Why don't people behave themselves?" This was not said accusingly or by way of condemnation but with sadness and regret.

President Smith's love and concern for others was evident in all of his relationships behind the scenes of his public ministry. His wife, Ethel, who bore him nine children, has described this quality and contrasted her husband's public and private images better than anyone else: "I have often thought," she wrote of President Smith, "when he is gone people will say, 'He is a very good man, sincere, orthodox, etc.' They will speak of him as the public knows him; but the man they have in mind is very different from the man I know. The man I know is a kind, loving husband and father whose greatest ambition in life is to make his family happy, entirely forgetful of self in his efforts to do this. He is the man who lulls to sleep the fretful child, who tells bedtime stories to the little ones, who is never too tired or too busy to sit up late at night or to get up early in the morning to help the older children solve perplexing school problems. When illness comes, the man I know watches tenderly over the afflicted one and waits upon him. It is their father for whom they cry, feeling his presence a panacea for all ills. It is his hands that bind up the wounds, his arms that give courage to the sufferer, his voice that remonstrates with them gently when they err, until it becomes their happiness to do the thing that will make them happy. The man I know is most gentle, and if he feels that he has been unjust to anyone the distance is never too far for him to go and, with loving words or kind deeds, erase the hurt. He welcomes gladly the young people to his home and is never happier than when discussing with them topics of the day — sports or whatever interests them most. He enjoys a good story and is quick to see the humor of a situation, to laugh and to be laughed at, always willing to join in any wholesome activity. The man I know is unselfish, uncomplaining, considerate, thoughtful, sympathetic, doing everything within his power to make life a supreme joy for his loved ones. That is the man I know." (*Improvement Era,* June 1932, p. 459.)

Here, then, was a gentle, kind, and loving man who reflected the best qualities of his upbringing in the home of a prophet. And here was a man who had been tried and tested for more than six decades in his service as a special witness. In the process, he had acquired a depth of knowledge and understanding of the Church, its doctrines and its procedures, superior to that of any other living person. In that sense, therefore, he was eminently qualified to be the president of the Church. But, you say, this man was almost ninety-four years old. Could he effectively be the chief executive officer of a vibrant, worldwide church of almost three million members? Some critics said no. That judgment was based on the false assumption that the role of a prophet is identical with the role of the chief executive officer of a business corporation. Such a judgment ignores the essential role of a prophet: to learn the will of God as to the direction of His earthly church and to transmit that to its members. To do this does not require the vigor of youth, the mastery of administrative techniques, or a vast knowledge of global politics and economics. Still less does it require an expertise in law, the arts, or the sciences. Admittedly, the possession of some or all of these qualities in whatever degree would be helpful; and this Prophet possessed a goodly share of them. But one could function effectively as a prophet though he had none of these, provided that he possessed the faith, the purity, and the spirituality necessary to receive divine revelation.

Joseph Fielding Smith possessed these qualities in rich abundance. He had available a host of able and dedicated men and women, prepared to perform the various duties necessary to bring his prophetic vision to reality. Chief among these were his counselors, Presidents Harold B. Lee and N. Eldon Tanner, experienced and gifted administrators, in whom he had complete confidence and to whom he made broad delegations of authority. Yet he retained the ultimate control, or the key, which he could turn at any time, either to reduce or to increase the authority he had delegated.

It was a constant source of interest and fascination to watch this Prophet at work. He listened more than he talked. And he listened with intensity. His basic mentality was sound, so that when he faced a decision only he could make, he made it firmly and unequivocally after listening to the discussion of his brethren. Because his life extended back to the administration of President Brigham Young, his mind was a rich treasure of historical facts. To hear him relate, for instance, how as a boy he had watched the workmen removing huge granite blocks from the mouth of Little Cottonwood Canyon to be used in building the Salt Lake Temple gave one a sense of intimate contact with the past. Indeed, he was a bridge between the pioneer past and the present. Stored in his mind were countless images and scenes of bygone days that he could often recall with greater clarity and ease than the events of the day before. These included personal recollections of the early leaders of the Church, whom we know only through the written word or by posed pictures that can never convey an accurate perception of what a person really was like. He was personally acquainted with John Taylor, Wilford Woodruff, and Lorenzo Snow, presidents of the Church, all of whom his father had served as a counselor. He had attended the dedication of the Salt Lake Temple, where he had seen and heard President Wilford Woodruff offer the dedicatory prayer. As a son in a polygamous family, he had poignant recollections of the trauma and terror of the underground years when his father was driven into exile in the Hawaiian Islands. He remembered Salt Lake City when its streets were lighted with gas lamps and when most of its homes lacked indoor plumbing. All this and much more President Smith carried around in the storehouse of his memory, facts that, if triggered by a question or an offhand remark, he could recall instantly and report with uncommon accuracy. What a treasure are the elderly in our midst! What a gold mine of memory they possess that we often fail to tap. And what is said here generally is also said especially of President Joseph Fielding Smith.

He was special because of his long life, his family connections, his apostolic and prophetic callings, and his careful training as a writer and a historian. It is unlikely there will ever be another like him.

It is risky for an author to intrude himself into the narrative. Yet he may have personal knowledge that could provide insights and a better understanding of his subject's character and motivations. On this account, I have elected in this preface to recount several anecdotes based upon personal contacts with President Smith or his immediate family or associates, hoping they will be interesting to the reader.

Joseph Fielding Smith was an avid sportsman, whether as a participant or a spectator. Knowing this, I said to him one day as we walked together toward the temple through the tunnel beneath Main Street, "President, I understand that when you were younger, you enjoyed playing hand-ball." After a pause, he answered in substance: "Yes. For many years three of my friends and I regularly played doubles together, and I enjoyed it very much. But twenty-five or thirty years ago, I gave it up. I did so because of the comments of a doctor friend. I was seated one day in front of my locker at the gym after a game, perspiring heavily and breathing hard, when the doctor stopped to visit. 'Joseph,' he said, 'you are too old to play so vigorously, and if you keep it up, you may fall dead on the court one day.' I said to him, 'Are you trying to tell me I should give up handball?' He answered, 'That's exactly what I am trying to tell you.' President Smith said that he followed that advice and that he never again played a game of handball. Then, after remaining silent for a moment, he added with a twinkle in his eye, "And I don't think my three friends ever forgave me."

While his participation in sports waned with the years, his role as an interested spectator continued to the end. This was especially true when members of his family were involved. It is reported that he never missed a game when a member of the family participated unless he was sick or out of town. Once his son Douglas, who played football at East High School in Salt Lake City, was injured during the first half of a game. His concerned father went to the locker room at halftime to inquire about him. Elder Smith entered while the coach was delivering a lively harangue to his players that was peppered with mild cuss words. Momentarily ignoring his son, who lay prone on the floor, the apostle proceeded to lecture the coach on the evils of profanity and the virtues of pure speech. During all this, Doug feigned unconsciousness to avoid having to provide commentary on his father's impromptu sermon, either to his embarrassed coach or his highly amused teammates.

Perhaps the most striking example of Elder Smith's loyalty to his athletic sons involved Mitt, who was a star on the University of Utah football team. One Saturday night the team had a crucial game that conflicted with the priesthood meeting of general conference. The father, who was torn between his church and family duties, devised a scheme by which he could fulfill both at least in part. He would attend the priesthood meeting and then, during the rest song, slip out to go to the stadium. He approached one of the other Brethren (who later told this story) to invite him to go along. He declined because he had a deacon-aged son at the meeting whom he felt might not understand. Under these special circumstances, however, Joseph Fielding Smith had no difficulty in justifying his actions. The son had to know where he stood in the order of his father's priorities. And to unobtrusively leave during the rest song, as he did, neither created an upset nor violated his apostolic creed.

His concern and love for the family lay at the root of his personal motivations. In them he saw the foundation of his future glory. Consistent with the tenets of the Church, he believed that the perfection he sought depended largely on the integrity of his immediate family circle, linked in an eternal bond with those who had gone before and those who would follow. Therefore, he sought constantly by word and by deed to cement family relationships. His door was never closed to a member of the family. When any of them came for counsel or conversation, he was available.

And he always greeted them in the traditional Smith way with a hug and a kiss. Even his strapping athletic sons received the same affectionate treatment. It was always a touching thing to witness such a demonstration of love, which was spontaneous and genuine and devoid of any self-consciousness or embarrassment.

There can be little doubt that the safety and welfare of his family occupied a central place in President Smith's private prayers and devotions — at least this was the conviction of his son Reynolds, who shared an unusual experience one day as we lunched together in the Lion House. As we discussed his father, Reyn confided that he had had a cigarette in his mouth only once in his life, and then for only a fleeting moment. It occurred when he was a student at the Roosevelt Junior High School in Salt Lake City. Those acquainted with this school know that its entrance was on a quiet side street that had very little vehicular traffic. On this day, Reyn had just walked out of the front entrance of the school with a friend who smoked who urged him, as he had often done, to "just try one." On this occasion, the friend succeeded. Reyn took one of the cigarettes and lit up. A few puffs later, who should pull up at the curb in his car but Reyn's father. Rolling down the window, Elder Smith said to his astounded son, "Reynolds, I want to talk to you tonight after dinner" and drove off. Reyn reported, "When my father called me Reynolds, I knew he meant business." Elder Smith let Reyn stew in his guilt the rest of the afternoon and during the evening meal, when he had surprisingly little to say. Afterward, seated uncomfortably in his father's study, that sacrosanct place that was strictly off limits when the children were young, Reynolds faced judgment. What he received was merely a kindly, loving lecture about the evils of "that filthy habit" and a reminder of who he was and how his conduct reflected on the whole family. It ended with the request that Reyn promise he would never again put a cigarette in his mouth. Reyn took the pledge. "It never happened again," he said. Through all the intervening years, including a stint in the United States Navy during World War II where smoking was endemic, he honored the commitment made to his father. And we do not doubt that Reyn went to his grave with the promise intact.

The odds against Joseph Fielding Smith appearing on that out-of-the-way street at the very moment his young son lit up his one and only cigarette are astronomical. Although he did not say it, Reyn's manner and tone implied that the incident convinced him of the extraordinary depth and power of his father's spiritual sensitivity, especially as it related to the welfare of his family.

The unstinting love President Smith always showed toward the members of his family was reciprocated by them in kind. Without exception, they were always solicitous of his welfare and desirous of doing what he wanted them to do and what would make him happy. In his later years, after it became difficult for Aunt Jessie to drive their little car on the rides around town they enjoyed so much, the sons alternated in serving as their chauffeur. It was one such an outing that produced wild excitement in the Gibbons household. One evening in the spring of 1971, our fourteen-year-old son, Daniel, came running into the study exclaiming, "Dad, Dad, come quick! President Smith is out front." My first impulse was to say to this creative jokester, "Yeah, and is President Nixon with him?" But the exuberance of his tone soon convinced me he was not joking. Hurrying outside, I saw President Smith's modest white Hornet parked in the driveway. At the wheel was Joseph Fielding, Jr., and in the back seat were his father and Aunt Jessie. For several minutes the entire family enjoyed the presence of the Prophet and his wife. Their gracious manner and thoughtful inquiries about our welfare put everyone at ease. There was no pretension or posturing but only a sense of friendship and love that was touching and reassuring.

Preface

After Aunt Jessie died, the solicitous love of President Smith's children toward him seemed to grow. They took turns going to Amelia's home in the evenings, where the Prophet had gone to live, to visit, to read to him, or to serve him in any other way they could. These occasions were not looked on as fulfilling a duty but as an opportunity to be near the man who had nurtured them physically through infancy and childhood and who now, in their maturity and his old age, fed them spiritually from the wealth of his accumulated knowledge and wisdom. I hope that through the pages of this book, the reader will derive some of the same spiritual nourishment, along with useful information and insights about Joseph Fielding Smith, the tenth president of The Church of Jesus Christ of Latter-day Saints.

Acknowledgments

Grateful acknowledgment is extended to many people for valued assistance in the preparation of this manuscript. Thanks are given to numerous associates and relatives of President Joseph Fielding Smith, who provided special insights into his life and work, and especially to Amelia Smith McConkie, Douglas A. Smith, and Hoyt W. Brewster, Jr. Thanks also to Ruth G. Stoneman for expert and extensive research assistance, to the staff in the Historical Department of The Church of Jesus Christ of Latter-day Saints, and to the executive and editorial staff of Deseret Book Company for their consideration and support. And, as always, thanks to the Mentor.

Chapter One

A Centennial Baby

The child was born July 19, 1876, only fifteen days after the one-hundredth anniversary of the Declaration of Independence. Once the officiating midwife announced that the baby was a boy, there was no doubt what his name would be. The mother, Julina Lambson Smith, the first plural wife of Joseph F. Smith, had been promised that her husband's full name would be reserved for her first son. The other two plural wives, Sarah Ellen Richards Smith and Edna Lambson Smith, Julina's younger sister, knew this and therefore were reconciled when their sons who were older than this baby did not receive their father's full name. At the time, Sarah Ellen had two boys, Joseph Richards and Heber John; and Edna also had two, Hyrum Mack and Alvin Fielding. But it was this centennial baby, Joseph F. Smith's fifth son, who would receive the father's full name, Joseph Fielding Smith.

The family into which this infant was born was one laden with tradition and distinction. The father, Joseph F., was the son of Hyrum Smith, who had shared a martyr's

1

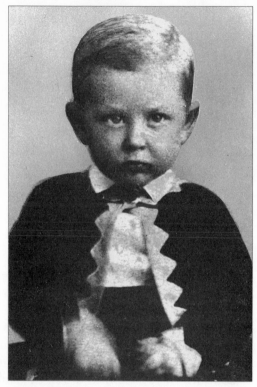

*Joseph Fielding Smith
as a child*

fate with his younger brother, the Prophet Joseph Smith, first president of The Church of Jesus Christ of Latter-day Saints. Joseph F. was born in Far West in 1838, across the street from the temple site, during the height of the Missouri persecutions against the Latter-day Saints. His first name, Joseph, was given in honor of his grandfather, Joseph Smith Sr., the first Patriarch of the Church, and his uncle Joseph, the Prophet. The middle name, Fielding, honored his mother, Mary Fielding, a native of England who had migrated to Canada, where she was converted by the preaching of Parley P. Pratt. After her conversion, Mary moved to Kirtland, Ohio, where she met and married the widower, Hyrum Smith, nurturing the five living children of her husband's first wife while giving birth to her only son, Joseph F.

At the time of the birth of Joseph Fielding Smith in the summer of 1876, his thirty-eight-year-old father was a member of the Quorum of the Twelve Apostles of the Church and was serving informally as a counselor to the First Presidency, a role he had played for ten years. His youth, his family ties, his eloquence, and his achievements as a missionary and an apostle, added to his close relationship with Brigham Young, the president of the Church, cast an aura of special distinction over Joseph F. Smith that inevitably extended to the members of his large and growing polygamous family. And the inheritance of the exact name of such a distinguished man set this centennial baby apart from the other children in the family. From the moment of his birth, therefore, Joseph Fielding Smith had an edge over his siblings and over all the other children born into Mormon families during this centennial year. And that edge became more evident as the father rose in the hierarchy of the Church and as the son's native abilities began to flower under the impulse of self discipline.

The sprawling two-story family home where this infant was born was located at 333 West First North in Salt Lake City, three blocks northwest of Temple Square. It was directly across the street south of the campus of the University of Deseret, whose name was changed to the University of Utah in 1892. This site was later relinquished to the West High School when the campus of the University of Utah was moved to its present location on the east bench of Salt Lake City. At the time, in addition to the new baby's four brothers, there were three sisters who lived there, Mary Sophronia (fondly called Mamie) and Donnette, Julina's daughters, and Sarah Ellen's daughter Leonora. Thus, Joseph Fielding Smith's arrival brought to twelve the number who occupied this house: the eight children, the father, and his three polygamous wives. But this was only the beginning. These three wives would later give birth to a total of twenty-one additional children; and two other polygamous wives whom Joseph F. Smith later married, Alice Ann Kimball and Mary Taylor Schwartz, would

3

give birth to a total of fourteen. Later on, other housing was provided for members of the clan; but this house on West First North where Joseph Fielding Smith was born would always be looked on as "the old family home" of President Joseph F. Smith and his wives and children.

It is apparent, therefore, that as he grew up, Joseph Fielding Smith never lacked for friends or company. He had all he wanted or needed within his own family. And it was a remarkable family, not only from the standpoint of sheer numbers, but also because of an unusual sense of love and unity among them and a uniform pride in the Smith ancestry. That ancestry extended back eight generations from Joseph Fielding Smith to Robert Smith, the first member of the family in America, who migrated from England in 1638. A tailor by trade, Robert eventually purchased a good-sized farm located partly in Boxford and Topsfield Townships, Massachusetts. His descendants occupied this farm for several generations, so they were known as "the Topsfield Smiths." Significantly, the first of the twenty-five books written by Joseph Fielding Smith was entitled "Asael Smith of Topsfield." He wrote it not long after he became a clerk in the Church Historian's Office. The book was based on extensive research he conducted in old records, wills, deeds, and minutes in the courthouse at Salem, Massachusetts. This was supplemented by numerous records provided by George Francis Dow, secretary of the Essex County Historical Society, at whose request Joseph Fielding wrote the sketch. It was later read by Mr. Dow at a meeting of the society.

Asael Smith, a great-grandson of Robert, was one of the first of the Smith ancestors to whom the family pointed as having had special spiritual endowments of the kind enjoyed so abundantly by his descendants. To some this is anomalous because of a widely held perception that Asael was irreligious, if not agnostic. This resulted from his independent turn of mind and his refusal to accept and follow some of the traditional teachings of protestantism. The most convincing evidence of his deep spirituality, however, is a remarkable document he wrote to his family on April 10, 1799. In it he invoked the blessings of God upon his family, admonishing them to put their trust in Him who, he said, would never forsake them. He affirmed the immortality of the soul and warned against trifling with the things of God. He said that in speaking to or about God to be "in good earnest" and to do everything in respect to deity "in a serious manner." In talking about religion, he did not recommend any particular sect but instead urged his family to search the scriptures and to "consult sound reason." In closing, he declared that Christ "is perfect" and would never fail them "in one circumstance." He also expressed a conviction about the reality of the resurrection, when his body would become like the Savior's "own glorious body." In Asael's eighty-eighth year, his son, Joseph Smith Sr., presented him with a copy of the Book of Mormon, which he read nearly through without the aid of glasses. He pronounced it authentic, declared that a new religious age was upon the world, and confided to members of his family that he always knew that God would raise up some branch of his family to be a great benefit to mankind.

Asael Smith's son, Joseph Smith Sr., father of the Prophet Joseph Smith, was a visionary man. Over a period of eight years, from 1811 to 1819, he received a series of seven vivid dreams which he shared in detail with his family and which were recorded by his wife, Lucy Mack Smith, in her biography of the Prophet Joseph Smith. These reveal the deeply spiritual nature of the Prophet's father (Joseph Fielding Smith's great-grandfather), who accepted his son's account of the origin of the Book of Mormon without question; who was one of the eight witnesses, having seen and handled the plates; and who became the first Patriarch to the church.

Hyrum Smith, another son of Joseph Smith Sr., was Joseph Fielding's grandfather. He was also one of the eight witnesses, succeeded his father as the Patriarch to the Church, and served as a counselor and an assistant to his brother, the Prophet, with whom he shared a martyr's death.

Joseph Fielding's father, Joseph F., was a teamster during the exodus, though but a boy; served as a missionary in the Hawaiian Islands while still in his mid-teens; became an apostle and a counselor to Brigham Young at age twenty-six; was sustained a member of the Twelve at twenty-seven; and before becoming the sixth president of the Church, served as a counselor to presidents Brigham Young, John Taylor, Wilford Woodruff, and Lorenzo Snow.

Besides these illustrious ancestors on his direct family line, Joseph Fielding claimed relationship to a host of Smith uncles and cousins who played vital roles in the development of the Church. A great-great-uncle, John Smith, Joseph Smith Sr.'s brother, was the first president of the Salt Lake Stake and later served as the Patriarch to the Church; a great-uncle, Samuel Smith, one of the Prophet's brothers, was one of the eight witnesses and is reported to have been the first missionary for the Church, distributing a copy of the Book of Mormon that is said to have been instrumental in the conversion of Brigham Young; a cousin, George A. Smith, who was a son of Uncle John, was ordained an apostle and inducted into the Quorum of the Twelve at age twenty-one, the youngest man in this dispensation to receive this distinction. And after Joseph Fielding's birth, other Smith cousins, John Henry Smith and George Albert Smith, a son and grandson respectively of George A., became members of the Twelve. Later still, John Henry became a counselor to President Joseph F. Smith, and George Albert Smith served as the eighth president of the Church. In addition to these high-profile members of the family, there were many other Smiths, some of them concealed under married names, who served faithfully in different organizations and in different communities.

All this created a widely held perception that the Smith family was the first family of the Church, endowed with special distinction—and with special responsibilities. These ideas were repeatedly impressed on the minds of the Smith children as they grew up: that they were descendants of the prophets and that as such, they had a special responsibility to live in a way that would add honor and luster to their ancestors and to the family name. Such was the practice of President Joseph F. Smith, the lingering effects of which were evident throughout the long life of his son and namesake. "Joseph Fielding Smith has never forgotten his heritage," wrote a grandson, Joseph F. McConkie. "He has constantly and consciously sought to walk in the footsteps of his father, not in the sense of aspiration to high position, but rather in dedication and zeal to the gospel cause. He has said that whenever he has passed the picture of his father that hangs in the Salt Lake Temple, his father seems to say to him 'Do your best.' The desire of his life has been so to live that he would be worthy to march at the side of his grand uncle the Prophet Joseph Smith in that last great battle with the adversary." (*True and Faithful* [Salt Lake City: Bookcraft, 1971], p. 99.) This grandson has also provided insight into the way Joseph Fielding Smith implanted the same ideas in the minds of his own family. "When you visit in President Smith's home," wrote this grandson, "you can sit in a wooden rocking chair which once belonged to his grandfather, Hyrum Smith. Doing so places you under the kindly and watchful eyes of a full-length oil painting of President Joseph F. Smith. And in those days when it was not so difficult for this venerable father and grandfather to rise, Joseph Fielding Smith would walk his grandchildren to the door, place his arm around their shoulders, and say, 'Remember that you have the blood of prophets in your veins.' " (Ibid.)

But pride in ancestors and their achievements was not the most significant thing Joseph Fielding Smith learned in the home of his father. There he also learned by word and deed the more important principles of love and unity. In his later years, Joseph Fielding Smith characterized his father as the most tender-hearted man he ever knew. The father lavished love and affection upon each of his many children, demonstrated not only by his words but by the well-known Smith family custom of kissing each other when they met, whether in public or in private. Perhaps this tender conduct toward the members of his family was caused in part by the fact that Joseph F. was only six years old when his own father was murdered; and he was orphaned eight years later when his mother died. Therefore, he never really knew the joy of a nuclear family, except during the first six years of his life. And even those years were abnormal as the Latter-day Saints were struggling to recover from the ordeals they endured in Missouri and to build a new city at Nauvoo, Illinois. The heavy demands upon the time of Hyrum Smith, who played a key role in these events, and the pressures that accompanied them prevented any real semblance of family life. So the extraordinary efforts Joseph F. made to create a sense of security and love among the members of his family no doubt traced in large part to a desire to provide them with something he did not have as a boy.

One should not think, however, that frequent expressions and demonstrations of love in this family eliminated the need for discipline. An illustrious heritage did not exempt the Smith children from occasional acts of disobedience nor from their consequences. Joseph F. loved his children enough that he was not reluctant to discipline them in cases of misconduct. And in rare instances, the discipline included mild physical punishment. Joseph Fielding always remembered the time when his father punished him physically because he thought the son had lied to him when, in fact, he had not. Years later when Joseph Fielding mentioned this to him, the father disclaimed any recollection of the incident, but he added in jest that if, indeed, it had occurred, the punishment then administered applied to other unknown infractions for which the son was not punished!

Chapter Two

The Growing Years

To understand Joseph Fielding Smith, one must understand the environment of his youth. His ancestral heritage and special family traits have already been sketched. These exerted a powerful influence on the boy as he grew. Carrying that name and being under the influence of the famous man who first bore it ensured that he would have a strong sense of identity and a powerful incentive for achievement. Yet the influence of the father on the growing boy, significant though it was, did not match the influence of the mother. The father's church and civic duties and his responsibility to the other wives and their children prevented him from giving special attention to any one child. It was the mother, therefore, who was the main source of training and discipline. And the father's frequent absences from home on church assignments, or because of pressures exerted by enemies of the Church, accentuated the mother's role.

An important but unexpected assignment came to the father less than a year after Joseph Fielding's birth. In April 1877, the general conference of the Church was held in St.

George, Utah, coinciding with the dedication of the temple there. Because of the event's historic significance, Elder Smith brought along several members of his family, including Julina and her nine-month-old baby. Years later, Joseph Fielding would refer to this as his first church "assignment," undertaken in company with the president of the Church, Brigham Young. On the second day of the conference, it was announced that Joseph F. Smith had been appointed to preside over the European Mission and that he would be leaving soon for his mission headquarters in Liverpool, England. As they had no foreknowledge of it, the call came as a great shock to Elder Smith and his family.

That the young father and husband had been called unexpectedly during a session of the general conference came as no surprise as this was a characteristic of President Young's administration. Nor was it unusual for Joseph F. to be called to leave his family in pursuit of his apostolic calling. The Smiths had long since become reconciled to the dominant influence exerted over the lives of the entire family by the father's role as a member of the Twelve. The charge he had willingly accepted upon his call to that quorum, and to which his wives and children were equally devoted, had imposed a lifelong obligation to subordinate his personal affairs to the demands of his office and to be prepared on a moment's notice to go where duty called. What was surprising, however, was the place to which this assignment would take him. Only three years before, he had received an identical call. At that time, he had left his three wives and their children and gone to Liverpool, where he remained for a year and a half before being summoned home. If it occurred to Joseph F. and his family that the blessing of serving in Merry Old England might well be shared more liberally with other members of the quorum, no one mentioned it. The decision was accepted silently, willingly, and uncomplainingly. All seemed to understand that such was the lot and the expectation of the Smith family.

When the family returned to Salt Lake City, they immediately began to prepare for the father's departure. Unlike his earlier call to preside in Liverpool when he went alone, this time Joseph F. was allowed to take members of his family with him. At a gathering of the clan, it was decided that Sarah Ellen and her four-year-old son, Joseph Richards, would accompany the apostle. The fact that Sarah was then grieving over the death of her baby, Heber John, who died a month before, weighed heavily in the decision for her to go along. To simplify the problems of travel and of living in a foreign land, it was also decided that Sarah's six-year-old daughter, Nonie, would stay in Salt Lake City with Julina.

So close were the children of the three wives and so interdependent were they upon each other, and upon their natural mothers and their "aunties," that Nonie settled into the routine of life under the direction of her surrogate mother, Julina, with no apparent difficulty or trauma. Repeated instances such as this tended to obliterate any lineal distinctions between the Smith children and to create the illusion that there was no such thing as a half-brother or half-sister among them. Indeed, in his maturity Joseph Fielding Smith would bridle at the suggestion that any of his father's children were half-brothers or sisters, regardless of the wife who gave birth to them. They were brothers and sisters, one and all, equally loved and admired.

Given the tenuous financial condition of the Church at the time, Joseph F. Smith's lack of independent means, and the slender living allowance then provided for the General Authorities, one may wonder how the two wives and their children who remained at home were able to survive. The answer is simple — they worked. Both Julina and Edna were trained midwives and continued to ply their obstetrical skills while their husband was away. The standard fee for a delivery was $5.00, paid either in cash or domestic commodities. The burgeoning polygamous population in the valley and the prominence and professionalism of Joseph F.'s wives assured a rather steady

11

though not rich income from this source. In addition to their midwifery, Julina and Edna supplemented their income by cooking at the Endowment House. These resources, with help from the neighbors in cultivating the family garden and in tending their domestic animals, enabled those who remained at home to live without want.

The death of President Brigham Young in late August 1877 unexpectedly shortened Joseph F. Smith's second tenure as the president of the European Mission. He was asked by John Taylor and the other brethren of the Twelve to return home early to participate in important decisions affecting the Church. The Brethren decided that the First Presidency would not be reorganized immediately and that the affairs of the Church would be temporarily directed by the Quorum of the Twelve, acting through an executive committee and various task committees. Obviously these steps could have been taken without the presence of Joseph F. Smith in Salt Lake City. However, subsequent events proved that his personal support and abilities were wanted and needed by John Taylor as the Twelve worked through the many difficulties that followed the death of President Brigham Young. That Elder Taylor selected him as his second counselor when the First Presidency was reorganized in October 1880 suggests the extent to which he relied upon Joseph F. Smith.

The main difficulty that faced the Church during this period and that heavily influenced the Smith family arose on January 6, 1879. On this date the United States Supreme Court upheld the constitutionality of the 1862 anti-bigamy act in *U.S. v. Reynolds*. This decision eroded away the main legal justification the Saints had had for ignoring this law. They had contended that the act was unconstitutional and that therefore it was not binding on them. For seventeen years the Latter-day Saints had squared their commitment to the twelfth article of faith, which enjoins obedience to law, with a deliberate noncompliance with the 1862 act on the ground that it violated their constitutional right to freedom of religion and therefore was void. The Reynolds

Joseph F. Smith and his family; note Joseph Fielding Smith, top row center

decision swept away that contention, leaving the Saints without a legal basis for ignoring the act. This put them in the position of asserting that God's mandate through the Prophet that the Saints live in plural marriage superseded the civil law. It was this irreconcilable conflict that so tragically affected the Latter-day Saints in the years that followed and, in a special way, cast a cloud of sorrow and gloom over Joseph F. Smith and his family.

The storm of public opposition to the Latter-day Saints that produced the 1862 act and other repressive legislation intensified following the Reynolds decision. Aggressive enforcement of that act and the later passage of the Edmunds Act and the Edmunds-Tucker Act in 1882 and 1887 applied additional pressure on the brethren who practiced plural marriage and drove them underground. A chief object of the effort to ferret out and prosecute Mormon polygamists was Joseph F. Smith, not only because of his position in the First Presidency but because he was the custodian of the Endowment House records, which contained incriminating evidence that some of the brethren had entered into plural marriages. Included among them was the record of Joseph F.'s last two polygamous marriages, to Alice Ann Kimball on December 6, 1883, and to Mary Taylor Schwartz on January 13, 1884.

At the time his father married Mary Schwartz, Joseph Fielding Smith was not yet eight years old. He was far too young to understand fully the theological and political implications of the events that dominated the life of his family. Nor could he understand why anyone would want to imprison his father or interfere with the orderly pattern of his family life. But he understood clearly the fear created in him by the federal officials who prowled the neighborhood seeking his father or asking questions as to his whereabouts. "We refused to even tell them our name," the son later wrote. "We lived a very peaceful and happy family life except when we became troubled and I became frightened by deputy marshals. In those early days they were always seeking to bring trouble upon the authorities of the church, and because of those conditions my father was sent away when I was a youth. . . . Both father and mother were in the [Hawaiian] Islands for a number of years." (Smith and Stewart, *Life of Joseph Fielding Smith*, pp. 38–39.)

The departure of Joseph Fielding Smith's parents for the Hawaiian Islands occurred in January 1885 while he was eight years old. The father had to leave because of the increased tempo of the efforts to find, try, and imprison him and to exact from him evidence about plural marriages performed in the Endowment House. This information would then be used to prosecute other Mormon leaders. Actually, young Joseph's parents made an abortive attempt to leave for Hawaii the previous month. On December 18, 1884, the apostle, his five wives, and all the children gathered furtively in the Smith home. There, in a tearful and tense atmosphere, the family was told about the father's need to flee and about the decision that Julina and her baby girl of the same name would accompany him. After making necessary explanations and after imparting counsel to guide the family during his absence, Joseph F. blessed each wife and child who would remain behind. It was hardly the ideal scene one would envision to usher in the season of joy and peace. And it was especially poignant for young Joseph Fielding, both of whose parents were to go away, leaving him in charge of his "aunties." In his maturity, he recalled the emptiness that engulfed him as he watched the receding horse-drawn sleigh that carried his parents and sister to the train depot, his mother waving forlornly until the sleigh was out of sight.

A heavy winter snow storm that blanketed the inter-mountain area stalled the Smiths' train in southern Idaho, making it necessary to return to Salt Lake City. This brief reunion of the family, which added a glimmer of joy to the holiday season, made their final parting even more poignant when, later, Joseph Fielding's parents and his sister Julina left again for Hawaii.

The eight-year-old boy had difficulty adjusting to the absence of both parents. Although he received loving care from his aunties and was buoyed up by the friendship of his brothers and sisters and assorted relatives, they could hardly substitute for the bonding influence of his mother and father. After two years, his mother returned, bringing with her his sister, Julina, and a new brother, Wesley, who was born in the islands during her absence. His father remained in Hawaii for some time afterward; but even when he returned to Utah, he was seldom able to visit his family because of the incessant pressures exerted by the federal officials. Thus, for a period of seven years, from ages eight to fifteen, Joseph Fielding Smith was essentially fatherless.

In reflecting on this period of his life, he observed: "People will say 'Well you ought to be good, having the father to train you that you had.' But, they don't know all the circumstances. My father was a busy man, away from home in those years a good part of the time. In fact, during the years when a boy needs the counsel of his father the most, I had no father, because he was sent away because of difficulties with the government and spent his time with my mother on the Islands of the Pacific, which were called the Sandwich (now Hawaiian) Islands. So, during those years when a boy needs his father's help and counsel, I had no father." (Ibid., p. 39.)

Yet, there were offsetting compensations for the loss of his father's companionship. The most important of these was the development of a strong sense of independence and responsibility. Being his mother's eldest son, Joseph Fielding became, in a way, the man of that branch of his father's family. He took the role seriously and he devoted himself to it with uncommon diligence. Although very young at the time, Joseph Fielding did a man's work. His father owned a farm at Taylorsville in the western part of the Salt Lake Valley. There the son became proficient in all farming chores—planting, irrigating and harvesting hay, and caring for the livestock. As in all things, that proficiency was not gained without much effort and not a little trauma. He once broke a leg when he was swept off a load of hay by a bar atop the gate to the Church tithing yard. Later, he was thrown from a load of hay when the team was spooked, landing on the double tree between the horses, which bolted down an embankment into the canal. Terrified that he might be killed or maimed, Joseph was finally able to break clear of the animals and load and escaped unhurt. A neighboring farmer helped him and his brother, George, retrieve the wagon and horses from the canal. In the city was a family garden plot, which, in season, always needed tending; and chickens and a cow near the family home required attention all year around.

At age ten, when his mother returned from Hawaii, Joseph Fielding began his most unusual work career as a youth—he served as his mother's driver on her calls as a midwife. His task was simplified when a delivery occurred during the daytime and in good weather; indeed, under such circumstances, his work was enjoyable. Nighttime calls, however, especially during bad weather, were unpleasant. "I marvelled that so many babies were born in the middle of the night," wrote he, "especially on cold winter nights." On these occasions, he "fervently wished that mothers might time things a little better." (Ibid.,

p. 53.) It was not so much the driving he objected to, for that was usually quite enjoyable, regardless of the weather. What he disliked were the preparations to get under way and the waiting when he got there. To roll out of a warm bed at night during the winter months; corral his horse, Meg; harness the horse; drive to the home of his mother's patient; and then wait, sometimes for hours, first tried and then developed his own patience. And following a delivery, his mother would return daily to the home of the patient for five or six days to make certain that everything was all right. Considering that Julina Lambson Smith delivered almost a thousand babies and needed chauffeuring services for the initial and follow-up calls, one gains an insight into the heavy involvement of Joseph Fielding Smith in his mother's obstetrical practice. And considering that Julina never lost a mother or a baby during the years of her midwifery, one also gains an appreciation for her skill and professionalism.

The horse, Meg, which usually provided the transportation for Julina and Joseph, was a gentle mare, obedient and reliable. However, her stable mate, Junie, was just the opposite. Junie was feisty, temperamental, and disobedient, albeit funny, likeable, and smart. "Junie was one of the most intelligent animals I ever saw," Joseph Fielding said of her. "She seemed almost human in her ability. I could not keep her locked in the barn because she would continually undo the strap on the door of her stall. I used to put the strap connected to the half-door of the stall over the top of the post, but she would simply lift it off with her nose and teeth. Then she would go out in the yard." (*New Era*, January 1971, p. 4.) Once in the yard, Junie would turn on the faucet that fed water into the animal's drinking trough. But she would never turn it off. Instead, she would wander aimlessly around the yard, trampling the lawn or the garden, or generally making a nuisance of herself. However, she never ran away. She always stayed close to home, so the family had the exclusive enjoyment of her high jinks. At times during the day, her antics were a source of amusement and were passed off with good-natured tolerance. But it was different at night. It was a source of great irritation to Joseph Fielding to hear the water running in the drinking trough in the middle of the night. Then, because he had charge of the horses, he had to get out of bed, turn off the water, corral Junie, and try to lock the gate in a way to prevent her escape.

The contest between the mare and his son did not go unnoticed by Joseph F. "My father suggested that the horse seemed smarter than I was," reported Joseph Fielding. "One day he decided that he would lock her in so that she could not get out. He took the strap that usually looped over the top of the post and buckled it around the post and under a crossbar, and then he said, 'Young lady, let's see you get out of there now.' My father and I left the barn and started to walk back to the house; and before we reached it, Junie was at our side, somewhat to my delight. I could not refrain from suggesting to Father that I was not the only one whose head compared unfavorably with the mare's." (Ibid.)

While the chief function of the horse Meg was to transport members of the family in their buggy on business or errands, she, as well as Junie, could be saddled for recreation like a ride up the canyon for sight-seeing or fishing. There were also horses at the Taylorsville farm, and Joseph and the other Smith children rode them for fun when their chores were finished. And swimming was a favorite recreation, as was baseball. During Joseph's youth, each ward had its own school whose curriculum included sports, especially baseball. There were spirited competitions between ward teams. "Our chief 'enemies,' " he wrote, "were the boys of the Fifteenth Ward, which adjoined the Sixteenth Ward, to which I belonged." These "enemies" included George Q. Morris, with whom Joseph Fielding would later share the apostleship. This early exposure to competitive sports was the beginning of a lifelong interest that he savored, whether as a participant or a spectator. This interest was transmitted intact to each of his sons.

Joseph Fielding had no interest in hunting, which was a popular sport in his day, as it is now. This resulted from a natural repugnance toward killing and from a shocking experience he had as a boy when some friends persuaded him to go hunting. During the hunt he shot a rabbit, whose cries of anguish sounded almost human. He was so devastated by the experience that he never again used a gun.

The ward schools provided Joseph Fielding Smith with his only formal education as a boy, except for two years in a "college," which was the equivalent of high school. In the Church schools he was drilled in the basics of reading, writing, and arithmetic. His elegant signature and cursive script attest to the thoroughness of his training in penmanship. And his voracious appetite for books and the written word, an appetite that was never satisfied, says much for the effectiveness of these rudimentary schools. While they were short in the scope of their curriculum and the technical training of their teachers, they were long in the motivations for excellence implanted in their students.

Joseph's favorite reading was always the scriptures. If given a choice between them and any other literature, classical or modern, he would always select the Standard Works. "From my earliest recollection," he told a Tabernacle audience, "from the time I could first read, I have received more pleasure and greater satisfaction out of the study of the scriptures, and reading of the Lord Jesus Christ, and of the Prophet Joseph Smith, and the work that has been accomplished for the salvation of men, than from anything else in all the world." (*Conference Report,* April 1930, p. 91.)

There can be little doubt that President Smith's preoccupation with the scriptures, which he read repeatedly and thoughtfully from his youth, had a predominant effect on his literary style. That style was precise, taut, and unadorned. It aimed for accuracy and brevity. It sought to convey ideas and facts with a minimum of words in a vocabulary that was understood by the ordinary reader. It is seldom, if ever, necessary to use a dictionary in reading the writings of Joseph Fielding Smith. It was not that his vocabulary was limited in scope; in fact, it was rich and extensive. But, in writing or speaking, he always opted for words that were frequently used and well understood. Betraying his British heritage, he preferred to use short, descriptive, Anglo-Saxon words that carried a punch and drove home his meaning without doubt or equivocation. He seemed wary of words with more than two or three syllables, and he shied away from the frequent use of words derived from the Romance languages. In a sense, his literary style was a reflection of his character—clear, uncomplicated, honest and forthright, free of subtlety, familiar and comfortable as an old friend.

The young Joseph Fielding Smith was encouraged and guided in his reading by his mother. In later discussing the influences that shaped his life, he said, "I am grateful for the training that I received and I tried to follow the counsel that was given to me by my father. But I must not give him all the credit. I think a good part of it, a very great part of it, should go to my mother whose knee I used to sit by as a little child and listen to her stories about the pioneers. My mother deserves a great deal of credit so far as I am concerned because she used to teach me and put in my hands, when I was old enough to read, things that I could understand. . . . I had a mother who saw to it that I did read, and I loved to read." (Smith and Stewart, *Life of Joseph Fielding Smith,* p. 56.)

While the scriptures formed the bulwark of his reading in the early years, his mother later led him into reading the history of the Church as recorded in the *Millennial Star.* Given his mother's intimate involvement in the preservation and recording of Church history during her youth and his own later distinction in that field, it is easy to surmise that Joseph Fielding Smith's career as a Church historian was shaped and fueled in large part by Julina Lambson Smith. It would not be an exaggeration to say

Julina Lambson Smith, mother of Joseph Fielding Smith

that Julina was reared on Church history. At age nine, she went to live with her Aunt Bathsheba, who was married to George A. Smith. At the time, George A. was the Church historian. The Smith home was on East South Temple across the street south from the present Church Administration Building at 47 East South Temple, and a wing had been added to the Smith home to house the Church's historical archives. Julina lived in this house for nine years and intermittently helped her uncle and his assistants with various archival tasks. One of these assistants was young Joseph F. Smith, a cousin of her uncle George, who at age twenty-six was a veteran of three missions to Hawaii. As they saw each other in the Historian's Office over the months, love bloomed. "I often saw him and admired him," wrote Julina in her later years. "I thought he was the most handsome and finest man I had ever seen. I didn't think for a moment he had ever really noticed me but later I learned he had watched me for some time and had fallen in love with me. When he proposed marriage, I was somewhat frightened and also happily surprised. I answered him by saying, 'I will not marry anyone unless my Uncle George approves.' Joseph went immediately to Uncle George A. . . . and asked for my hand. He said, 'Joseph, there isn't a young man in the world I would rather give her to.' " (Julina Lambson Smith, "Family History," Church Archives.) Joseph F. and Julina were married in 1866 when he was twenty-eight and she was eighteen. That same year Joseph F. was ordained an apostle and designated as a counselor to President Brigham Young. The following year he was set apart as a member of the Quorum of the Twelve Apostles.

This, then, was the environment into which Joseph Fielding Smith was born ten years after his parents were married. Under their tutelage, especially that of his mother, he became imbued with a love for the scriptures and for the history of the Church. It was in the realm of these two subjects that the mature Joseph Fielding Smith would carve out a special niche for himself.

Chapter Three

The Maturing Years

T he patterns of one's life emerge only in retrospect. As we look back now, it is easy to trace the parental and environmental influences of his infancy and early youth that helped shape the man Joseph Fielding Smith ultimately became. But as he actually lived those years, young Joseph may have wondered now and then whether there was any symmetry or overriding purpose in his life. He endured so much confusion and uncertainty. The years when his parents lived in Hawaii were especially upsetting for the boy. While his aunties and his brothers and sisters were good to him and loved him, this did not compensate fully for the absence of his parents. In these circumstances, he reached out to other adult relatives for support and direction, especially his Uncle Albert, his Aunt Melissa Davis, and his great-aunt, Mercy Thompson. The Davis family lived on a farm west of the Jordan River. Whenever Joseph felt lonely or in need of encouragement, he could always find a listening ear at the home of this saintly couple. Moreover, the Davis's horses were always available for a ride without the constraints sometimes imposed, or at least felt, on his father's farm, where horseback riding was usually a reward for work performed, not an activity of sheer recreation as it was at Uncle Albert's.

Aunt Mercy Thompson was the sister of Joseph Fielding's grandmother, Mary Fielding Smith. Mercy and her sister, Mary, and their brother, Joseph Fielding, were converted at Toronto, Canada, by Elder Parley P. Pratt in the 1830s and soon after moved to Kirtland, Ohio, where they became personally acquainted with the Prophet Joseph Smith. Later, Mercy married Robert B. Thompson, one of the Prophet Joseph Smith's personal secretaries, who died at Nauvoo in 1840 before the exodus. Aunt Mercy migrated west with her sister, Mary Fielding Smith. After Mary's death, her son, Joseph F. Smith, prepared a small home for Aunt Mercy only a block from the Joseph F. Smith family home on West First North. There he was able to help take care of her needs. Young Joseph Fielding Smith was a frequent visitor there, especially while his parents stayed in Hawaii. He never knew his grandmother, Mary Fielding Smith, who died shortly after coming to the Salt Lake Valley, long before Joseph Fielding was born. "I have always regretted that," he told a Tabernacle audience, "because she was one of the most noble women who ever lived; but I did know her good sister, my Aunt Mercy Thompson, and as a boy I used to go and visit her in her home and sit at her knee, where she told me stories about the Prophet Joseph Smith. And, oh, how grateful I am for that experience." (*Conference Report*, April 1962, p. 44.)

The boy's anxieties were eased when his mother returned from Hawaii in March 1887. And four months later he and the rest of the family were overjoyed when the father also returned. It was originally intended that President Joseph F. Smith would remain in Hawaii longer than this. However, he was summoned home earlier than was expected by George Q. Cannon, First Counselor in the First Presidency, when President John Taylor's condition became critical. He arrived in Utah on July 18, 1887, the day before Joseph Fielding's eleventh birthday, and went directly to President Taylor's hideaway in the home of Thomas F. Roueche in Kaysville, several miles north of Salt Lake City. There he found President Taylor sitting in a chair in a semiconscious condition with his feet and legs much swollen. When the counselors entered the sick room together, President George Q. Cannon roused the Prophet and said to him that it was the first time the members of the First Presidency had been together for two years and seven months. When asked how he felt about that, President Taylor answered weakly, "I feel to thank the Lord."

Because he was still much sought after by federal officials, Joseph F. Smith was unable to visit his family in Salt Lake City openly. So, shortly after returning to Utah, he went there under cover of night for a brief but joyful reunion. He then returned to the Roueche home in Kaysville, where he remained until July 25 when President John Taylor quietly passed away.

To Joseph F. Smith, John Taylor was the "Great Martyr." He noted the Prophet's death in his journal: "He rallied for a few moments, but precisely at 5 mts to 8 p.m. the Great Martyr breathed his last. Thus what the deadly bullets of the Carthage assassins failed to do 43 years ago the 27th of last June, the malignant persecutions of their successors have accomplished, by driving him into exile to avoid falling into their murderous hands." These harsh words were summarized in a phrase often heard among the Latter-day Saints: "In Utah was finished what Carthage began." (CHC 6:188.)

Later Joseph F. Smith collaborated with George Q. Cannon to compose an official statement that assessed the blame for President Taylor's death. It recounted the murders of Joseph and Hyrum Smith in the Carthage jail, where John Taylor was critically wounded. The blood he then shed, wrote they, mingled with the blood of the slain Prophet and Patriarch to make him "a living martyr for the truth." His death on the underground, they concluded, made him a double martyr. "President John Taylor has

President Joseph F. Smith, father of Joseph Fielding Smith

been killed by the cruelty of officials who have, in this territory misrepresented the Government of the United States. There is no room to doubt that if he had been permitted to enjoy the comforts of home, the ministrations of his family, the exercise to which he had been accustomed, but of which he was deprived, he might have lived for many years yet. His blood stains the clothes of men, who with insensate hate have offered rewards for his arrest and have hounded him to the grave. History will yet call their deeds by their right name." (In Roberts, *Life of John Taylor,* pp. 413–14.)

The bitter feelings this statement reveals were especially poignant to Joseph F. Smith, feelings he often expressed to his family and which were shared by his son, Joseph Fielding. As the statement implies, President Taylor's death was linked in Joseph F. Smith's mind with the martyrdom of his father Hyrum Smith and his uncle, Joseph Smith, in the Carthage jail on June 27, 1844. At that time, Joseph F. was a few months less than six years old. He was, therefore, too young to have understood the complicated religious, political, and social issues that underlay the Carthage jail murders. These he would learn later. But he was old enough to understand the meaning of his father's death and to remember vividly in later years the terrible impact it had upon him. In 1906, when he was sixty-eight years old, President Joseph F. Smith visited Nauvoo with a party from Salt Lake City. As the group visited various places of historic interest in the city, President Smith shared his personal recollections of the events that preceded and followed the murder of his father and uncle. Stopping on one of Nauvoo's streets, he pointed to a spot where he had stood when the group of horsemen passed on their way to Carthage. His father stopped, and, without dismounting, picked the boy up, kissed him, and then put him back on the ground. Joseph never saw his father alive again. He also recalled the night of the martyrdom. After the family had retired, someone knocked on the window to tell Mary Fielding Smith that her husband had been killed; and he recounted how, as the bodies of the two brothers lay in state, someone lifted him up so he could look upon the faces of his father and uncle for the last time. These terrible events were the sad legacy of the Smith family and were kept alive by their periodic retelling within the family circle. And now as the mature Joseph F. Smith faced further harassment at the hands of the federal officials following the death of President John Taylor, his wives and children would become personal witnesses and, to some extent, participants in still another chapter of family woe.

Soon after President Taylor's death, the Twelve met to discuss their next move. It was decided to follow the precedent set after the deaths of Joseph Smith and Brigham Young, with the Twelve temporarily administering the affairs of the Church through an executive committee and task committees. On February 2, 1888, Joseph F. Smith received an assignment from Wilford Woodruff, president of the Twelve, that would again take him away from his family. He was asked to go to Washington, D.C., as the Church's representative in the Eastern States. A written commission given to him eight days later more fully defined his responsibilities. He was to take charge of all the business affairs of the Church in that region; to preside over the Church branches and over all the proselyting missionaries there; to direct the immigration of new converts; and to act as the Church's political agent. In this last capacity, he was to direct and correlate the activities of all Church members in the east who had been or would later be appointed to work toward statehood for Utah.

After being set apart for his new assignment by President Wilford Woodruff and Elders Franklin D. Richards and George Q. Cannon, Joseph F. did something that had become a ritual in the Smith family. He called all his wives and children together, gave them counsel and instructions about their activities and conduct during his absence, and then laid his hands on their heads to bless them. One can imagine the impact such an incident had upon eleven-year-old Joseph Fielding Smith who would reach age twelve within a few months, the age at which Latter-day Saint youths pass into manhood and receive the Priesthood of Aaron. It is one thing to learn about patriarchs and prophets from the scriptures and ecclesiastical literature. It is quite another to witness a scene such as this, in which the role and function of a family patriarch is demonstrated in a way that the participants will never forget. From such incidents, it is easy to see why the family of Joseph F. Smith was always held up as a model for the Latter-day Saints to emulate. And it is also easy to see the origin of the life-style Joseph Fielding Smith followed in rearing and instructing his own family.

The day after blessing his family, Joseph F. Smith left for the East in company with London convert Charles W. Penrose, who, just a week before, had celebrated his fifty-sixth birthday. Sixteen years later when his friend was seventy-two, President Joseph F. Smith would call Elder

Penrose to the Twelve; and seven years after that, when the Englishman was seventy-nine, he would call him as a counselor in the First Presidency, where he would serve during the last seven years of President Smith's administration. He was selected to accompany Joseph F. on this mission to the East because of his good judgment and his negotiating and literary skills.

Had one checked the passenger list of the train that carried this pair, he would not have found the names of Joseph F. Smith and Charles W. Penrose. Instead, he would have found the names of Jason Mack and Charles Williams, pseudonyms they used to mask their identity from their enemies. This was a mark of the times for Latter-day Saint polygamists, who, during the underground years, were constantly on guard, furtive about their movements and secretive about their purposes. And to add another layer of protection, some of the brethren occasionally changed pseudonyms. Joseph F. Smith, for instance, used the name of J. F. Speight during his exile in the Hawaiian Islands.

The effect on Joseph Fielding Smith of this subterfuge and of his father's deliberate refusal to obey the antipolygamy laws is impossible to ascertain. It did not create in him a sense of rebellion against civil law, since throughout his life he was a model of conservatism and good citizenship. Still less did it create any personal ambiguity about the uniform application of Church doctrine and policy since Joseph Fielding Smith was without peer in insisting that they be obeyed by all and in obeying them himself. It can be assumed, therefore, that when he matured to the point where he understood the issues involved, he accepted the views of his father and other Church leaders as expressed by President John Taylor—that since the law directly conflicted with revelation, the Saints were justified in violating the law and also in taking the steps necessary to avoid being caught doing it.

When his father went east with Elder Penrose, Joseph Fielding Smith had not matured to the point that he could have articulated his reasons for endorsing what his father said and did. It was sufficient for him that his father said it and did it. He relied unquestioningly on his words and actions. To the little boy, his father could do no wrong, and the son did whatever the father asked. It was his father, for instance, who had introduced Joseph Fielding to the Book of Mormon and given him the incentive to read it. "When I was a small boy, too young to hold the Aaronic Priesthood," he reported later, "my father placed a copy of the Book of Mormon in my hands with the request that I read it. I received this Nephite record with thanksgiving and applied myself to the task which had been assigned to me. There are certain passages that have been stamped upon my mind and I have never forgotten them." (Smith and Stewart, *Life of Joseph Fielding Smith*, p. 57.) By the time he was ten years old, young Joseph had read the book through twice. So diligent was he in following the direction of his father that he would hurry to finish his chores, or sometimes even leave a ball game, so he could go and read the book.

This copy of the Book of Mormon was defective — some of the pages were out of sequence. Young Joseph learned later that because of this defect, his father was able to buy it at a reduced price. Money was scarce for a man with such a large and growing family. Therefore, economy and frugality were watchwords in the Smith household. And sometimes, even with the most rigid budgeting, there was not enough to go around. Joseph F. remembered one dreary Christmas when there was no money at all with which to buy gifts for his children. "Under these spiritless conditions, one day just before Christmas," he wrote, "I left to do something for my chicks. I wanted something to please them, and to mark the Christmas day from all other days — but not a cent to do it with! walked up and down Main Street, looking into shop windows — into Amussens Jewelry store, into every store — everywhere — and then slunk out of sight of humanity and sat down and wept like a child, until my poured out grief relieved my aching heart; and after a while returned home, as empty as when I left." (*Improvement Era*, July 1966, pp. 615–16.)

The father remained in the East for several months, directing the lobbying efforts for statehood, supervising the local branches, and overseeing the immigration of European converts. Even though he had a drawing account for his expenses, he lived with the most exacting frugality, mending his own clothes, sewing on lost buttons, and guarding every penny with utmost care. On February 17, 1888, for instance, the day of his arrival in Washington, D.C., he noted in his diary: "My expenses today were, porters fees 50 cents, cab 50 cents = $1.00." The following day, after noting that he had had an oyster lunch with L. John Nuttall, he recorded, "I took a dozen raw — 40 cents." And on the first day of a trip to New York, he noted these expenses: "Cab fare 37 1/2 cents [he had shared a cab with Elder Penrose] provisions 85 cents, telegram 25 cents, Railway fare $6.50, cash paid to Bro. Penrose, $1, total = $8.97 1/2 cents." Later on a trip to Newport News, where he inspected ships he had engaged to bring converts from abroad, he and his companion put up at the Hotel Warwick, where he found everything "first class . . . especially prices." At the day's end, Joseph F. tabulated his expenses, exclusive of the "exhorbitant" hotel bill of $4.00, which he paid the next day: "Breakfast $1.00, cab 25 cents, bus 10 cents, railway 30 cents, porters fee 37 1/2 cents, total $2.17 1/2 cents."

At home during his absence, Joseph F.'s family practiced the same rigid economy. Nothing was wasted around the Smith household. Clothes were continually being altered or mended or were laid aside until another child grew into them. Seldom was new clothing purchased. And when a garment had absolutely passed the stage of usefulness, the worn fabric was saved in a cache for a future rag rug. The rule of the house on clothes was capsulized in a simple couplet that reportedly originated with Brigham Young: "Use it up, wear it out; make it do, or do without."

Not only were *things* not wasted, but neither was time.

In such a household where the family lived constantly on the edge of want, everyone capable of working had their assigned tasks. It was during this period that Joseph Fielding came into his own as his mother's chief obstetrical aide. In between calls, he and his brothers who were old enough had literally endless chores with the barnyard animals and, in season, with the family garden near the home and with the Taylorsville farm. Meanwhile, the girls in the family were occupied with numerous household tasks, sewing, mending, cleaning, baby-tending, and cooking, although, as will appear later, cooking was not the exclusive domain of the girls, since Joseph Fielding became particularly adept in the culinary arts.

As for the mothers and aunties, they expertly juggled their time between duties in the home and their employments outside it so that the children were adequately supervised, motivated, and trained, and the skimpy household budget was augmented with money earned from midwifery or from cooking at the Endowment House. In such a communal environment, any lines of distinction between the children of the different wives were practically erased so that the children willingly and without thought took direction from the wife who happened to be in charge at the moment.

While the chores and tasks were endless, the family's application to them was not. There were interludes of play and recreation, especially when the children were toddlers. And when they reached school age, they regularly engaged in sports and cultural activities, which were part of the curriculum.

The father returned temporarily to Salt Lake City in June 1888, having spent four months in his assignment in the East. The federal officials still sought his arrest, so he had to lay low. But by now, he was expert enough in avoiding detection by using disguises, or by moving about after dark, that he was able to meet periodically with his family. Joseph Fielding reported later that on such occasions, his father "spent his time instructing his children

32

in the principles of the gospel. They one and all rejoiced in his presence and were grateful for the wonderful words of counsel and instruction which he imparted on these occasions in the midst of anxiety. They have never forgotten what they were taught, and the impressions have remained with them and will likely do so forever. . . . Among my fondest memories are the hours I have spent by his side discussing principles of the gospel and receiving instruction as only he could give it. In this way the foundation for my own knowledge was laid in truth." (Smith and Stewart, *Life of Joseph Fielding Smith,* p. 40.)

President Joseph F. Smith was able to remain in Salt Lake City through December 1888, furtively meeting with his family on occasion and counseling behind the scenes with his Brethren of the Twelve. Because he stood at or near the top of the government's arrest list, he never attended public meetings during this time, nor appeared on the streets unless it was dark or he was in disguise. Because of this, he was unable to attend the October general conference, though he was in town, and learned about the proceedings only by reading summaries of the sermons in the newspapers or by receiving briefings from those who did attend.

Joseph F. left Salt Lake City on December 30, 1888, to return to Washington, D.C., after having enjoyed the companionship of his family during the Christmas season. Before boarding the train, he went through the usual ritual of meeting with, counseling, and blessing his wives and children. At Ogden, as a precaution against detection, he left the north-south feeder train before it entered the station, was driven around the business district in a buggy, then boarded the Union Pacific east-west train after it left the station.

He remained in the nation's capital for only another three months before returning to Salt Lake City to stay. During this time, he continued to direct the lobbying effort out of public view, concealed behind his pseudonym and sending and receiving messages in cipher. He helped polish a detailed presentation made to the Senate Committee on Territories by U.S. Congressman from Utah, John T. Caine, and others, which pleaded Utah's case for statehood. Because it was detailed and convincing, Elder Smith had 15,000 copies printed and mailed to influential people around the country, including government officials and secretaries of bar associations.

Another project of Elder Smith and his lobbying committee was to endeavor to obtain presidential pardons for convicted or indicted polygamists. Before returning home to stay, two cases were successfully concluded, those of George Q. Cannon and Charles W. Penrose. On February 21, 1889, he wired congratulations to Elder Cannon: "While deeply regretting the circumstances which have kept you so long confined, I rejoice that today will see you comparatively free once more. I congratulate you and thank God. All here join." These were among the first of many presidential pardons granted to Latter-day Saint polygamists, arranged for by the lobbying machinery Elder Joseph F. Smith helped to perfect. Many months later, following the publication of the Manifesto, that machinery was instrumental in obtaining a general amnesty for all Mormon men who had previously engaged in plural marriage.

Since he had fulfilled the main purposes for which he had been sent East, Joseph F. Smith was permitted to return to his family in March 1889, a few weeks after the success in obtaining the presidential pardons for Elders Cannon and Penrose.

Chapter Four

Into Manhood

On his return to Salt Lake City, Joseph Fielding's father was home, yet not at home. What he was able to do for his friends, he had been unable to do for himself. Therefore, he came back under the same cloud of illegality that had covered him when he left. He was still being sought by federal officials for violation of the polygamy laws and was unable, therefore, to live openly with his family. Under these circumstances, space was made available to him in the Gardo House, east of the Historian's office on South Temple across the street from Brigham Young's Beehive House. There in the Gardo House, on April 5, 1889, Wilford Woodruff raised the question about reorganizing the First Presidency. All the members of the Twelve were present except Francis M. Lyman, who was still in the penitentiary for polygamy. After discussion, it was decided to reorganize, and on motion unanimously approved, Wilford Woodruff was ordained and set apart as the fourth president of the Church. According to the usual procedure, President Woodruff nominated his counselors. They were George Q. Cannon and Joseph F.

Smith, who were then approved by the Twelve and set apart by him.

At the time, Joseph F., although only fifty-one years old, had held the apostleship for twenty-three years, during most of which time he had served as a counselor to the president of the Church. It was that office, and the responsibility it entailed, that had made him a principal target of the federal officials. Therefore, his selection as a counselor to President Woodruff, while accepted willingly and without reservation, was not a cause of rejoicing but of deep reflection and of some misgivings. "I would rather have taken a mission to Vandeman's land as an elder," he confided to his diary, "than to be called to the responsibilities of a counselor in the First Presidency if my own choice was to be consulted. But inasmuch as the President had expressed his mind upon it—and had given us the 'will of the Lord' on the subject—so far as I was concerned, that was the end of the matter with me." Yoked as he was to the apostleship, he was not at liberty to consult his own desires but was under covenant to follow the direction of the Prophet without question.

We are left to conjecture about the effect of such an example of faith and fidelity upon President Joseph F. Smith's young son and namesake who was then almost thirteen years old. Given the boy's adulation of his father, his obedient nature, and his serious turn of mind, it is reasonable to assume that the impact on Joseph Fielding was powerful and lasting.

Living in the Gardo House, under the threat of indictment and conviction, was akin to imprisonment for Joseph F. Smith. He was unable to appear in public except in disguise or at night; therefore, he did not attend the October general conference. His papers and books were moved to the Gardo House, where, behind the scenes, he was able to confer regularly with the Brethren, handle paperwork, and receive some selected visitors whose reliability in keeping confidences was unquestioned. So, on the day after the conference, he received Francis M. Lyman, who brought with him a gift from a fellow prisoner who was still at the penitentiary. It was a carved oak walking stick that had been made for President Smith by his longtime friend, William H. Maughan, bishop of the Wellsville ward in Cache Valley, whom Joseph F. had called to preside over the Birmingham England conference in 1875.

As indicated, what little walking President Smith did at this time was at night or when he had on a disguise. He became quite adept at concealing his identity. Shortly after the general conference where he was sustained again as a counselor in the First Presidency, he walked in disguise to the First North home. "After a short visit with my family I returned to the Gardo, meeting only three persons on the trip . . . B. Young, C. O. Card and Geo. W. Thatcher," he wrote. Then with a certain sense of pride, he added, "They did not know me."

At the time of this visit in April 1889, only Julina and Sarah and their children, including Joseph Fielding, were living in the old family home. Because of the dangers threatened by the federal officers, the other wives and their children had been dispersed to different locations. Edna, for instance, was then living at a hideout called "Camp Solitude"; and the others were located temporarily in different places in the valley. In view of subsequent events, this dispersion of the family seems to have been a prelude to the historic action taken the following year. For some time, the leaders of the Church had been quietly discussing alternate solutions to the problem of plural marriage. The lobbying efforts for statehood that Joseph F. Smith had directed were part of this process. Yet they knew that the ultimate solution lay in the spiritual realm, which they could not control. It was to this principal source that the Brethren turned for relief from the burdens that had been imposed upon the Latter-day Saints by the antipolygamy acts. These burdens had affected them both collectively and individually. Collectively, these acts had effectively dismantled the Church as an operating entity. The Edmunds Tucker Act, passed in March 1887, had provided for the disincorporation of the Church, for the dissolution of the Perpetual Emigration Fund Company, and for the escheatment of Church properties to the government of the United States. Subsequent legal action taken under the act implemented these severe provisions, resulting in the confiscation of Church properties and the appointment of a receiver to control them. And the burdens on the individual members of the Church were demonstrated by the upset to family life typified by what had happened to the family of President Joseph F. Smith.

In a search for a solution to these complex problems by spiritual means, the First Presidency proclaimed December 23, 1889, the eighty-fourth anniversary of the birth of the Prophet Joseph Smith, as a general fast day throughout the Church. To end this fast, the First Presidency and the Twelve held a special prayer circle in the Gardo House, where Joseph F. Smith was still living. He later noted in his diary specific things the brethren had focused on as they implored the Lord for guidance out of the difficulties that had engulfed them. "Among the subjects prayed for," wrote President Smith, "were the following: 1. That the plots and schemes which are being framed for the purpose of robbing us of our civil and political rights and obtaining control of our cities, counties and territory, might be confounded. 2. That all who conspire in any manner to injure or destroy the work of God or take from the people their rights and liberties be defeated. 3. That the unfavorable actions of courts and of officials might be overruled in such a manner that no injury will be done to Zion. 4. That the executive of the nation, the cabinet, the senate, the house of representatives, the judiciary and the people of the nation might be so influenced and controlled that their hearts may be softened towards the people of God, and not inclined to listen to the slanderous reports and falsehoods circulated concerning us, and which may be brought before them; and that all officers of our nation may be inspired with such wisdom, justice and mercy that they may gain the love and esteem of the people and the approbation of the Lord. 5. That the supreme court should be so moved upon and strengthened and filled with courage as to render a righteous decision in our causes before them. 6. That the eyes of the nation might be opened to see us in our true light, and be inclined to trust us with kindness and consideration due to fellow citizens who are loyal and true to the constitution of our country. 7. For the Lord to come to our help and deliver us from the many snares spread around us for our overthrow and destruction, to make our path plain before us, and to lead us to escape the pits dug for our feet. 8. That the Lord will pour out in great power His Holy Spirit and the gifts thereof upon his servants that they may be filled with qualifications and power necessary to enable them to magnify their offices acceptable to Him, and to fill the hearts of the Saints with comfort and peace, witness unto them that he has not forgotten and does not neglect Zion. And to pray for such other things as the Saints saw and felt that we needed."

By degrees, and over a period of years, these fervent prayers were answered. And in some instances, the answers came in ways the Brethren had not expected or foreseen. Their own attitudes and actions played an important role in the changes that occurred. Thus, during the early part of 1890, the First Presidency and the Twelve quietly took steps toward a suspension of the authority to perform plural marriages. In early September, Joseph F. accompanied Presidents Woodruff and Cannon to San Francisco, where they stayed for over two weeks as the guests of Colonel Isaac Trumbo. Away from the pressures of day-to-day administrative work at headquarters, the members of the First Presidency were able to counsel in a leisurely way. The arrangements were ideal for this, as they had a large suite in the Palace Hotel with separate bedrooms for each and with a large, common parlor. The party returned from San Francisco on September 20. Three days later, slanderous and distorted reports were circulated about steps allegedly taken by the First Presidency looking toward the cessation of plural marriage. This prompted

President Woodruff to make the following entry in his journal on September 25, 1890: "I have arrived at a point in the history of my life as the President of the Church of Jesus Christ of Latter-day Saints where I am under the necessity of acting for the temporal salvation of the church. The United States Government has taken a stand and passed laws to destroy the Latter-day Saints on the subject of polygamy or patriarchal marriage, and after praying to the Lord and feeling inspired, I have issued the following proclamation which is sustained by my counselors and the Twelve Apostles." He then set out in its entirety what has since been referred to as the Manifesto, by which the teaching and practice of plural marriage was suspended.

While the revelation was recorded in President Woodruff's journal, the proclamation was a formal document dictated by him and edited by Joseph F. Smith, President Cannon, and others. The final draft was carefully reviewed and approved by President Woodruff and his counselors. On September 24, it was given to W. B. Dougall, who was in charge of the *Deseret Telegraph* office, for transmission through the Associated Press. The following day when the AP dispatch arrived from the East, the statement had been severely edited, much to the annoyance of President Woodruff. He then directed that the entire proclamation be sent out over the AP wire

As expected, the document created widespread discussion outside the Church and not a little consternation within it. Although it was not wholly unexpected, either by the enemies or the members of the Church, the reality of it required some radical readjustment in thinking. The enemies, for instance, suddenly found themselves bereft of the main focus of attack upon the Mormons. And the members were left to sort out the meaning of an action suspending a principle given to the Saints by a prophet.

As the leaders counseled before the October general conference, weighing the impact of the Manifesto on the faithful members of the Church, there was extensive discussion whether it should be presented to the conference for formal acceptance. Joseph F. Smith spoke strongly in favor of doing this at a meeting of the First Presidency and the Twelve held on Thursday, October 2, 1890. But there was a difference of opinion that caused the Brethren to lay the matter aside for the time being. The issue arose again three days later when a wire from congressman John T. Caine reported speculation among the national leaders as to whether President Woodruff's Manifesto "stood alone, unsupported by authority from the church." This, with conflicting statements made by Utah's governor and others, caused the Brethren to decide to present the document for action by the conference. This was done on Monday, October 6, 1890, when Bishop Orson F. Whitney read the "Official Declaration" or Manifesto to the general conference assembled in the Tabernacle. Then, on motion of Lorenzo Snow, president of the Twelve, the document was unanimously accepted as "authoritative and binding" on the Church.

This historic action had little immediate impact on President Joseph F. Smith and his family. He was still under indictment for past violations of the antipolygamy laws. And though he had begun to disperse his various families, establishing them in different homes, he continued to cohabit with his wives. This constituted a continuing violation of these laws, which still remained in effect. Therefore, it was necessary for Joseph Fielding's father to remain on the underground despite the Manifesto. He continued to live in the Gardo House, venturing out only at night or when he had on a disguise.

Yet the Manifesto had a restraining influence upon many nonmembers, especially those whose opposition to the Church had been based solely on a philosophical rejection of polygamy as a marital institution. Such as these took a liberal and forgiving view toward the Latter-day Saints who had practiced plural marriage, urging either that the laws not be enforced or that they be applied with leniency. These relaxed attitudes even affected members of the judiciary. Non-Mormon judge Charles S. Zane was a prime example of this shift in emphasis. Before the Manifesto, he interpreted the law rigidly. Afterward, he applied flexible standards of equity in deciding unlawful cohabitation cases. He even went so far as to sign a petition asking that polygamists be given an official pardon. Another judge, James C. Miner, reacted similarly when in one case he dismissed a suit against a polygamist who said he accepted the Manifesto, imposing a fine of only six cents. Adopting this new attitude also, local prosecutors were less inclined to press charges vigorously. This wise policy of compromise and accommodation received executive confirmation when, in January 1893, President Benjamin Harrison granted amnesty to all Saints who had observed the law since the Manifesto, and when, in September 1894, President Grover Cleveland issued an even broader decree of amnesty.

Before these general actions were taken, however, Joseph F. Smith received what he had hoped and prayed for over many years—a presidential order of personal amnesty. He had been under a cloud for seven years, living furtively, shielded by pseudonyms and disguises, secretive about his movements, constantly on guard against federal officials, and anxious about the possibility of arrest, conviction, and imprisonment. With the Manifesto in place, and sensing the changed attitudes among the federal officialdom at all levels, he applied to President Benjamin Harrison for amnesty on July 20, 1891. There was a twenty-five day delay in sending the application to Washington, D.C., because of a desire to obtain the endorsement of prominent Utah officials who were not Latter-day Saints. Among the nonmembers who endorsed the application were territorial governor Arthur L. Thomas and chief justice Charles S. Zane. President Harrison, who was on vacation at the time, received the application at Cape May, New Jersey. A press release from there on September 7, 1891, announced, "Amnesty has been granted to Joseph F. Smith." Two weeks later the official document arrived in the mail bearing the signature of President Harrison and

William F. Wharton, acting secretary of state. "I thank God," wrote President Smith in his journal on September 21, 1891, "and am grateful to the President of the United States." The Sunday following the arrival of the certificate of amnesty, President Smith openly attended worship services in the Salt Lake Tabernacle for the first time in seven years. "The house was full to the galley," he wrote. "I spoke briefly, for I was so overcome by my feelings that I could scarcely restrain them. A good spirit was present. . . . This is a memorable day for me, and no words at my command can express my gratitude to God."

These events were the cause of great rejoicing in the family of President Joseph F. Smith. At last the father and husband could return openly to the old family home on West First North. He could again walk the streets of Salt Lake City in broad daylight without fear, using his own identity. He could again mingle with his children in public, work with them around the home and on the farm, and teach and train them, both in the privacy of the home and in his office in the First Presidency's suite.

However, life in the Old Home was not quite the same when President Smith took up residence there again after receiving amnesty. Only Julina and her children then lived there. Separate permanent homes for the other four wives and their children had been established at other locations within easy walking distance from 333 West First North. Even at that, there were enough children living there that Joseph Fielding never wanted for companionship. At the time, Julina had nine living children, ranging in age from twenty-two to ten months. The oldest, Mamie, and her nineteen-year-old sister, Donnie, were old enough to assume many of the household responsibilities previously borne by the other wives. Moreover, fifteen-year-old Joseph Fielding pitched in to help with the house work. It was during this period that he learned his way around the kitchen, helping to prepare meals and mixing and baking bread. He also learned how to make a good pie. And he did his share of washing and ironing clothes for himself and for his six younger brothers and sisters: David, age twelve; George, ten; seven-year-old Clarissa; Wesley, five; Emily, three; and Rachel, ten months. One other child, Edith, would be born later. These household duties were in addition to Joseph Fielding's outside chores at the house and on the Taylorsville farm and to his responsibilities to chauffer his mother on her obstetrical calls. But David and George were now old enough to help with all these duties, so that the full load did not fall solely on Joseph Fielding.

The financial burden on Joseph F. Smith to maintain five separate households was overwhelming. Since his own sources of income were severely limited, he had to look within the family for help. The answer was for the older boys to find employment outside the home. This was the incentive for Joseph Fielding to obtain employment at ZCMI as a stock clerk and "cash boy." He began working there in his late teens and continued at it until he left for the mission field in the spring of 1899. The demands of this employment made it necessary that he completely shift his obstetrical chauffering duties to his younger brothers, David and George.

The work at ZCMI was a drudge. "I worked like a horse all day long," he later reported to his family, "and was tired out when night came, carrying sacks of flour and sacks of sugar and hams and bacons on my back. I weighed 150 pounds, but I thought nothing of picking up a 200 pound sack and putting it on my shoulders. I was a very foolish fellow, because ever since that time my shoulders have been just a little out of kilter. The right one got a little more 'treatment' than the left." (Smith and Stewart, *Life of Joseph Fielding Smith,* p. 65.)

Before commencing this employment, Joseph Fielding completed his formal education with two years of study at the Latter-day Saint College, which provided high-school level training. There he had taken the main courses offered by the school's narrow curriculum — mathematics, geography, history, basic science, and penmanship. He was a solid, careful student, more interested in substance than in form, independent and analytical in his thinking and not easily swayed from conclusions to which his reasoning had led him. Valuable as this formal schooling was, it was during his years at the college, and throughout his employment at ZCMI, that Joseph Fielding Smith received an extracurricular training that, more than anything else, helped prepare him for the prophetic role he would play later in life. It was during these years that his father began to use the son as an unofficial, unpaid secretary. And it was a service Joseph Fielding would render intermittently during the remainder of his father's life.

As Joseph Fielding worked with his father, handling correspondence, conducting research, taking dictation, preparing documents, carrying messages, or serving as a sounding board and confidant, he acquired an insight into the structure and operation of the Church and a close view of a prophet of God at work, things he could never have learned in a book or from a lecture. The father, while lauding education and encouraging Church members to become well educated, was convinced that learning by experience and observation was superior to book learning. "The best school I ever attended is the school of experience," he wrote to Joseph Fielding while he was in the mission field. "There are some things that seem difficult for me to learn. One thing is english orthography and I see you are a little like me in this regard." He then listed several words the son usually spelled wrong, gave the correct spelling for them, and expressed confidence that when writing in the future he would spell them correctly. (This and other quoted correspondence to or from Joseph Fielding Smith is located in the Church archives.) In other similar ways, the father taught the son many things of a technical, procedural nature that enabled him to function ably in his personal, church, and other employments. These were important to Joseph Fielding who, throughout his long life, acknowledged his debt to his father for the practical training he had received from him.

Of all the things his father taught him, however, nothing was more important or of more lasting value than the instruction he received about gospel principles and their application to daily life. "Among my fondest memories," he reported later, "are the hours I have spent by his side discussing principles of the gospel and receiving instruction as only he could give it. In this way the foundation for my own knowledge was laid in truth, so that I too can say I know that my Redeemer lives, and that Joseph Smith is, was, and always will be a Prophet of the Living God." (*Improvement Era,* June 1932, p. 459.) The son left this account of the impact on him of his father's powerful testimony: "As a preacher of righteousness, the sincerity of his words penetrated the souls of men. He spoke as one having authority and with a firmness, conviction and confidence begotten of a knowledge of the truth. There was no element of doubt or uncertainty in his testimony. Especially was this so when he spoke of the divinity of the Savior or the mission of the Prophet Joseph Smith. It has sunk deep into my heart; it fills every fibre of my soul; so that I say before this people, and would be pleased to have the privilege of saying it before the whole world, that God has revealed unto me that Jesus is the Christ, the Son of the Living God, the Redeemer of the world." (Ibid.)

During the early years of service as his father's volunteer secretary, Joseph Fielding had an insider's view of many significant events in Church history. None of these was more impressive to him than the dedication of the Salt Lake Temple, which took place in April 1893. From infancy, he had seen this building in a half-finished state of construction. The work on it was torturously slow, occasioned by the difficulty of moving and fashioning the huge granite blocks used in building the walls and the periodic stoppages or slow-downs in the work caused by a lack of money or pressures exerted during the underground years. As a young boy, Joseph Fielding had watched with fascinated interest as the workmen chiseled the unwieldy granite blocks into shape and hoisted them into place. He had also seen how cast-off stones were used in constructing the nearby Assembly Hall, which, though started many years after the temple, was completed more than ten years before it. To see all the debris, machinery, and workmen's tools removed from the square, leaving the completed temple standing stately and tall near the Tabernacle and the Assembly Hall, undoubtedly created a sense of pride and thanksgiving in Joseph Fielding and all other Latter-day Saints. And such feelings would have been greatly accentuated as they entered the temple to see the dignified beauty of its interior appointments. No expense or effort had been spared to make the sacred building a fit abode for the Savior of the World, whose house it is.

Joseph Fielding was present in the temple when President Wilford Woodruff dedicated it to the Lord. Seated in the large assembly room of the temple that day, from where he could see his father on the upper level of the stand at President Woodruff's left, little did seventeen-year-old Joseph Fielding Smith realize that in his old age the prophetic mantle then worn by Wilford Woodruff would rest upon his shoulders.

Joseph Fielding saw President Woodruff later in 1893 under very different circumstances. In September of that year, the Prophet invited his counselors and members of their families to join him and his family on a trip by special train to Chicago, Illinois, to attend the World's Fair.

Joseph Fielding was one of the members of his father's family privileged to go. Significantly, it was his first trip outside Utah. That alone was enough to make it one of the most memorable experiences of his life. But the attraction of the fair, the invitation extended to the Salt Lake Tabernacle Choir to participate in a choral contest there, and the privilege of traveling as the guest of the Prophet in his private cars added special meaning to the occasion. "I had the privilege of sitting in the state room or the room that was given to President Woodruff," Joseph Fielding reported later, "and listened to his counsel and advice." (Smith and Stewart, *Life of Joseph Fielding Smith*, p. 63.)

The apparent awe young Joseph had for the Prophet

and his sense of gratitude at being present in that intimate setting worsened the impact of an unhappy incident that occurred during the trip. "We got scolded by President Woodruff," he reported in his old age. The "we" referred to himself and a son and daughter of President Woodruff who were Joseph Fielding's good friends. The three teenagers had gone to the open platform at the rear of the train, where they were eating watermelons and throwing the rinds over the low railing that enclosed the platform. Their youthful exuberance and apparent obliviousness to the dangers involved apparently worried President Woodruff. "When we came in we got a scolding. We were told that if that train had gone with speed around a corner we could have been swept off, which was absolutely true, and I remember that very keenly." (Ibid.)

That Joseph Fielding Smith remembered this reprimand with such vividness over such a long period of time, as he also remembered so poignantly the occasion when his father punished him for something he did not do, implies an extraordinary tenderness and sensitivity of spirit. There was no rebellion or obstinacy on his part on either occasion. Nor is there any indication that he became sullen or self-pitying as a result of the treatment he received. Still less is there any hint that he sought to retaliate or to defend or justify his conduct. He merely took the rebukes in silence. The impact they may have had upon his thinking or future conduct is, of course, a matter of conjecture. But it is not unreasonable to infer that these and other similar incidents helped develop the quality of character referred to by his wife Ethel: "If he feels that he has been unjust to anyone, the distance is never too far for him to go and, with loving words or kind deeds, erase the hurt."

While Joseph Fielding had no apparent inkling of his prophetic future when he heard President Woodruff offer the prayer at the dedication of the Salt Lake Temple, he received special insight about it less than three years later when he was given his first patriarchal blessing. It was on

January 19, 1896, that he went to the Patriarch to the Church, John Smith, for this purpose. The Patriarch, who was Joseph Fielding's uncle, was the oldest son of Hyrum Smith by his first wife, Jerusha Barden, who died in Kirtland in the mid 1830s, leaving several children. John was five years old when, in 1837, his father, Hyrum Smith, married his second wife, Mary Fielding, who bore her only son, Joseph F. Smith, in 1838. So Mary Fielding raised these two boys and the other children sired by Hyrum Smith as a unified family, making no distinction between her own children and those to whom Jerusha had given birth.

When, therefore, John Smith laid his hands on the head of his nephew to bless him, he did so not only with full knowledge of their relationship and of Joseph Fielding's relationship to the martyrs Joseph and Hyrum Smith, but also with the spiritual power and insights gained during more than forty years of service as the Patriarch to the Church. He was ordained to that office on February 18, 1855, by President Brigham Young when John was only twenty-two years old. Over the intervening forty-one years, he had given hundreds of patriarchal blessings. It is unlikely, however, that he ever gave one of greater significance than the one he conferred on his nephew. In addition to the usual preliminaries, the declaration of lineage (Ephraim), and promises about his status and blessings in the eternities, it contained these special provisions about his earthly role and mission: First, the man who lived to age ninety-six was told: "It is thy privilege to live to a good old age." Second, his role as the head of the Church was foreshadowed: "It is . . . the will of the Lord that you should become a mighty man in Israel" and "It shall be thy duty to sit in counsel with thy brethren and to preside among the people." Third, he was given insight into the half-nomadic kind of life he would lead during his apostolic ministry: "It shall be thy duty to travel much at home and abroad, by land and water, laboring in the ministry." Fourth, he was admonished about things that were essential to enable him to fulfill his role in life: "Thou hast much to do in order to complete thy mission in life. . . . Reflect often upon the past, present and future . . . hold up thy head, lift up thy voice without fear or favor, as the spirit of the Lord shall direct . . . strive to inform thy mind and be prepared for events to come, and remember the instruction of thy parents and honor the Priesthood. . . . Remember also that he [God] will reward thee according to merit." Fifth, he was promised certain spiritual gifts and blessings: "The blessings of the Lord shall rest upon thee. His spirit shall direct thy mind and give thee word and sentiment, that thou shalt confound the wisdom of the wicked and set at naught the counsels of the unjust. . . . It shall be thy duty to be a peacemaker wheresoever thou shalt sojourn . . . and peace shall be in thy circle. . . . Thou shalt find friends among strangers. . . . Thou shalt lay hands upon the sick and they shall recover for this shall be one of thy gifts."

Reading this blessing in the light of Joseph Fielding Smith's life confirms that the patriarchal mantle worn by his father, Hyrum Smith, and his grandfather, Joseph Smith Sr., had fallen on John Smith. It proved to be an accurate and valuable blueprint for the man destined to become the tenth president of The Church of Jesus Christ of Latter-day Saints.

Later the same year in which he received his patriarchal blessing, two other events occurred that had an important influence on Joseph Fielding Smith's future in the Church. On September 8, 1896, he received the Melchizedek Priesthood and was ordained an elder by Charles Seal. He was then received into the Sixth Quorum of Elders in the Salt Lake Stake. His certificate of ordination was signed by Z. C. Mitchell, the president, and Frederick A. Fish, the secretary. Two days later, Joseph Fielding received his endowments in the Salt Lake Temple.

Ordinarily, a young man of twenty does not receive his endowments unless he is planning to leave on a mission or to get married. Neither of these events was in the offing for Joseph Fielding when he went to the temple in September 1896. His mission was nearly three years away, and his marriage would not take place for eighteen months. But he was seriously interested in a young lady at the time, Louie Shurtliff, the daughter of Lewis Shurtliff, who was the president of the Weber Stake in Ogden, Utah. Louie was boarding at the Smith home while she attended the University of Utah across the street. Her distinctive name was a contraction of "Louisa," the name of Lewis Shurtliff's first wife, who died before he married Louie's mother, Emily Wainwright.

President Joseph F. Smith had been well acquainted with Lewis Shurtliff since their boyhood days in Nauvoo. When it was learned, therefore, that his daughter Louie planned to attend the University of Utah, she was invited into the Smith home, which had ample room for a boarder since at that time only Julina and her children occupied it.

Louie Shurtliff was the same age as Joseph Fielding Smith. At eighteen, when she first came to live in the Smith home, she was a tall, attractive young lady, well bred, studious, and musically talented. Her only purpose in coming to live with the Smith family was the convenience of having accommodations near the university. During the three years of her residence there, she discovered a more important and enduring purpose.

Her relationship with Joseph Fielding seems to have remained on a strictly platonic level for many months. He was shy and reticent and quite unskilled in the nebulous realm of dating and romance. Of course, having been raised around a troop of girls, he pretty well understood them and their winning ways. But these were his sisters, with whom he felt perfectly at ease. But with a girl outside the family circle, it was different. Therefore, in keeping with his conservative, cautious character, Joseph was apparently quite formal if not distant toward Louie. He was exceedingly busy at the time, working at ZCMI and in his spare moments in the evenings or on weekends, assisting his father. Besides, at age eighteen he was too young to give any consideration to a serious relationship with a girl.

But even if he had wanted to develop such a relationship with Louie in the beginning, it is doubtful that Joseph Fielding would have been successful. She had come to Salt Lake City for an education, not for romance. She was a serious student who applied herself with discipline to the requirements of university-level study. While the University of Utah was comparatively small at the time, still it had a faculty of distinction that demanded high performance from the students. Its new president, James E. Talmage, who also taught courses in geology, was even at that early time highly regarded in academic circles. The faculty also included the likes of George M. Marshall, an honors graduate of Cornell University who was professor of English literature; George R. Mathews, a Yale graduate, professor of modern languages; and Byron Cummings of Rutgers, professor of ancient languages and literature. The director of the school's speech and drama department at the time was Maude May Babcock, one of Utah's most noted actresses. These and other professors, and lecturers like Joseph F. Merrill in physics and chemistry and Richard R. Lyman in engineering, kept Louie and her fellow students challenged and occupied. And if in the beginning of her career at the university she had been interested in serious socializing, she would likely have been more inclined toward the students with whom she was thrown into contact each day, such as J. Reuben Clark, Stephen L Richards, and George Q. Morris, who were key members of the staff of the *Chronicle,* the school's newspaper; or David O. McKay, who was prominent in school athletics.

So, in the beginning it seems that the relationship between Joseph Fielding and Louie, although cordial and friendly, was nothing special and certainly nothing that hinted they would be man and wife. Over a period of months, however, their relationship changed. They found that they had much in common, including a pioneer heritage extending to the earliest days of the Church. They shared the background of having been reared in homes where the fathers were heavily preoccupied with Church responsibilities. And although Joseph Fielding was not a university student, he was studious and analytical, which gave him and the Smith's attractive boarder another plank of common interest. In the end, however, the thing that radically altered their platonic relationship, was that they fell in love! Joseph Fielding was never able to explain or define exactly what happened. He only knew that at some point, months after Louie Shurtliff came to live in the Smith home, he was certain he wanted to marry her, to share children with her, and to spend his life and eternity with her.

In time, Louie became convinced of the same things. Exactly when is a matter of speculation, as neither one later attempted to pinpoint the date. Clearly, however, they had reached an understanding by the end of her second year at the university. Persuasive evidence that Joseph's intent and commitment were more than transitory is seen in the fact that in the summer of 1896 he rode his bicycle to and from Ogden twice to see Louie, who had gone home for the summer. This was two round trips of a hundred miles each over unsurfaced, rutted roads—on a bicycle! Obviously, the young man was hopelessly hooked.

Louie's last year as a boarder at the Smith home passed swiftly and pleasantly. We can imagine with what alacrity Joseph left the drudging work at the store and hurried home to clean up so he could spend time with Louie. He enjoyed listening to her play the piano. And occasionally she could coax him into singing a duet. They had little money and little spare time, so their courting consisted almost entirely of visiting in the family parlor in the evenings, attending social events at their ward or at the university, and, when the weather was good, strolling.

What little time they spent together in the parlor was well chaperoned; in addition to his parents, there were Joseph Fielding's seven younger brothers and sisters who trooped in and out at will.

Louie Shurtliff, first wife of Joseph Fielding Smith, in her wedding dress

Louie graduated from the University of Utah on June 7, 1896, with a three-year teaching certificate. Her parents had bought her a stunning white brocaded satin gown for the occasion. It is not unlikely that they had something other than graduation in mind when they bought it — with its dainty lace stand-up collar, the dress was ideally suited for use as a temple wedding gown.

Although Joseph Fielding and Louie and both of their families knew by now that marriage was in the offing for the young couple, there were convincing reasons why it should be delayed for a while. In the first place, they had no money and no home and no immediate prospects of getting one. And second, Joseph Fielding was now twenty-one years old, the age at which many Latter-day Saint young men had already completed their missions. Indeed, as already mentioned, at the same age his father was already a seasoned missionary, having served several years proselyting in the Hawaiian Islands during his mid teens. Everyone had assumed from the beginning that Joseph Fielding would one day fill a mission as his father had done. The question was not whether he would go, but when. He was prepared to leave at any time.

Meanwhile, he continued to work at ZCMI. Louie returned to her home in Ogden, where she held two jobs, teaching school and, in the off hours and on Saturdays, clerking in her father's store. The young couple carried on their courtship the following year through regular correspondence and periodic personal visits. They alternated in traveling to and from Salt Lake City and Ogden, staying overnight in the homes of their parents. Whenever Louie went to Salt Lake, she would stay in the same room she had occupied for three years, feeling as much at home there as she had in her parents' home in Ogden.

By early spring in 1898 Joseph Fielding had not received a call to the mission field, so the couple decided not to delay the marriage longer. And it was not uncommon in those days for young married men to be called on missions. Therefore, there was no thought that marriage would preclude Joseph Fielding from later serving as a missionary. He explained the circumstances of the nuptials: "When she finished and graduated from her school," he wrote, "I did not permit her to go home and stay there, but I persuaded her to change her place of residence, and on the 26th day of April, 1898, we went to the Salt Lake Temple and were married for time and all eternity by my father, President Joseph F. Smith." (Smith and Stewart, *Life of Joseph Fielding Smith,* p. 75.)

The couple joined in marriage that spring day was one of great promise. The patriarchal blessing Joseph Fielding had received two years before portended a future life of significant service in the Church. And his new bride harbored the feeling that her quiet and faithful young husband was destined to become one of the high leaders of the Church. It was, therefore, with great hopes and expectations for the future, with little money and an abundance of love for each other, that they set up housekeeping in the Smith's old family home, where a small apartment was prepared for them. By living there, they hoped to save money toward the purchase of their own home. The expenses and duties in maintaining the house were shared so that while living there was an economy to the newlyweds, it did not impose an added burden on President Smith's already overloaded budget.

The young couple lacked the means to travel on a honeymoon. So, they settled down immediately into a pleasant domestic routine with Joseph Fielding working at ZCMI and Louie involved with the customary household duties. Their religious and social life revolved around the Sixteenth Ward, whose chapel was located a few blocks west of the old family home. Joseph had played a key role there in the past, serving for a time as the superintendent of the Sunday School. Within six months of the marriage, however, he was called to serve as a member of the Salt Lake Stake YMMIA Board, being set apart by two members of the stake presidency, Angus M. Cannon, president, and Joseph E. Taylor, counselor, and by Richard R. Lyman, a future member of the Twelve, who was then the superintendent of the stake YMMIA. Since there was only one stake in the Salt Lake Valley at the time, this assignment brought Joseph Fielding into personal contact with leaders of the Young Men throughout the area, entailing as it did speaking and training assignments in the various wards that dotted the valley. Meanwhile, Louie became active in the auxiliaries of the ward, where her musical talents and her professional training as a teacher made her much in demand.

It was an exciting time for a young couple to begin their married life in Salt Lake City. Much of the trauma and bitterness caused by the conflicts over plural marriage had disappeared. Statehood for Utah, which became a reality on January 4, 1896, had removed the irritation that federal dominance over local governmental affairs had created for so long. Utahns now felt that they were in charge of their own destiny; and that feeling had released the pent-up energies of the people. A sense of forward motion, of enthusiasm, self-confidence, and creativity permeated the state.

Joseph Fielding and Louie partook of these feelings. Theirs was a favored and promising position. Sharing the house of a member of the First Presidency, a man whom both Lorenzo Snow and Wilford Woodruff had prophesied would one day be the president of the Church, they were accorded privileges and opportunities few Church members enjoyed. They had reserved seating at the general conference sessions, occasionally received passes to various entertainments, and were given discounts on some purchases. Because of their family status and especially because of Joseph Fielding's name, they were accorded a special deference and respect quite apart from their own achievements and good qualities of character. That "the blood of the prophets" flowed in the veins of Joseph Fielding Smith was a powerful psychological factor that not only motivated him to high achievement but also exerted a potent influence on all who knew him, setting him apart in a special circle of distinction.

In the first few months of their marriage, this young couple enjoyed a freedom and exhilaration that would never be surpassed during their life as man and wife. They were not encumbered with the responsibility of caring for babies. The little apartment they had in the old family home was easy to maintain, so they were free to come and go at will. Various inexpensive amusements and recreations were available to them, such as occasional plays at the Salt Lake Theatre, outings and picnics at Saltair on the lake, Tabernacle choir rehearsals, and, of course, the frequent, continuing round of social events at the ward. And across the street were the library facilities of the university and the attraction of the periodic athletic events in which the university teams were engaged. Most important to them, however, was the excitement and sweetness of conjugal love that they experienced for the first time after their temple sealing. Life was indeed rich and rewarding for Mr. and Mrs. Joseph Fielding Smith Jr.

A few months after their marriage, an important change in Church leadership occurred when President Wilford Woodruff died. He and his first counselor, George Q. Cannon, had gone to San Francisco to recuperate from health problems, leaving Joseph F. Smith in charge of affairs at home. At the time the Prophet's condition was not considered serious. It therefore came as a surprise when on September 1 President Joseph F. Smith received a wire from George Q. Cannon advising that President Woodruff was critically ill with a uremic infection, that he was unconscious and was not expected to recover. The next day he was dead, at age ninety-one. The Church marveled that President Woodruff had lived so long in good health. The patriarchal promise to Joseph Fielding Smith that it would be his "privilege to live to a good old age" would cause him to exceed that record by five years.

Because of instructions given by President Woodruff, there was little delay in reorganizing the First Presidency following his death. Eleven days later, on September 13, 1898, eighty-four-year-old Lorenzo Snow was ordained as the fifth president of the Church. At his side were the same counselors, George Q. Cannon and Joseph F. Smith, who had served his two immediate predecessors, Wilford Woodruff and John Taylor.

As far as the Smiths were concerned, this change in Church leadership had little impact on their lives. Joseph F. played essentially the same role he had played under Presidents Taylor and Woodruff, retaining the same responsibilities and enjoying the same privileges. Although he did not speak out about it as he had done at the death of President Taylor, he undoubtedly would just as soon not have continued to bear the crushing burdens this position entailed.

Chapter Five

The Missionary

J oseph Fielding Smith was not as well acquainted with
Lorenzo Snow as he had been with his predecessor,
Wilford Woodruff. He remembered President Snow
as a somewhat reserved man, "loyal and true to the
Gospel of Jesus Christ." This lack of close acquaintance
was because Lorenzo Snow served as president of the
Church for only three short years. And during most of
that time, Joseph Fielding was out of the country, serving
as a missionary in Great Britain. Therefore, he was not
involved in special events with President Snow, such as
the trip to the Chicago World's Fair, where members of
the families of the First Presidency came together in a
personal, intimate setting.

The call to the mission field signed by President Lor-
enzo Snow was dated March 17, 1899. That it designated
Great Britain as his field of labor was mildly surprising to
Joseph Fielding. During a preliminary interview with him,
Franklin D. Richards, president of the Twelve, had asked
Joseph where he would like to serve. Giving the expected
answer, he said he wanted to go to the place where he

Elder Joseph Fielding Smith, missionary, 1900

was sent. "But, you must have some place you would prefer to go to," persisted the apostle. Gauging from this that his own feelings might be given weight in the decision, he said he would really prefer to go to Germany. "So they sent me to England," wrote the missionary jokingly. The reason for this stated preference was never explained. Given his name and strong family orientation, one might have expected the prospective missionary to have opted for Hawaii or England, where his father had served. Such an expectation was no more valid, however, than was Joseph Fielding's hope that he would be sent to Germany.

Joseph's brother, Richards, Sarah's son, who was three years older than he, was also called to England at the same time, as was a neighbor, William Armstrong. The three young men were given two months to prepare for their departure. Joseph Fielding's first concern was to provide for Louie's care during his absence. One idea was that she continue to reside in the Smith home, where she had already lived for four years, including one as a young bride. The couple finally decided, however, that she should return to Ogden to live with her parents. There she could resume her teaching and her work in the Shurtliff store to help maintain her husband in the mission field.

With this major decision out of the way, the missionary turned to other less important yet essential things that had to be done before he could leave. There was the purchase of necessary clothing, luggage, toiletries, and writing materials. The latter included a diary, a four-by-six-inch leatherbound notebook, the first of dozens of similar diaries that Joseph Fielding Smith filled during the remainder of his long life. To protect them from moisture and to prevent undue fraying of the pages at the edges, this one had a fold-over, snap-on cover. Motivated by the instructions of the modern prophets about keeping personal diaries, the training of his historically minded parents, and his own sense of history, Joseph Fielding faithfully recorded the significant events of his subsequent life in these diaries. They provide the core of the remaining portion of this biographical sketch.

On April 22, 1899, a month before his departure, the missionary received his passport from the U. S. Department of State. It described him as a light-complexioned, brown-haired, twenty-two-year-old man, five feet nine inches tall with bluish-gray eyes. In three months he would turn twenty-three. The document could not describe the conflicting joy and sorrow that agitated "Jos. F. Smith, Jr." as he prepared to leave family, friends, and country for the first time.

On May 12, 1899, the day before they left Salt Lake City, Joseph Fielding and Richards and the other departing missionaries received their formal pre-mission training— brief instructions from President Joseph F. Smith and Elder George Teasdale and Heber J. Grant of the Twelve about the policies, procedures, and pitfalls of missionary work and the joys, sorrows, and rewards it entailed. Afterward, they were set apart. Both of the Smith boys were blessed and set apart by their father who, at the same time, ordained them to the office of seventy.

Joseph Fielding finished packing the next day; and that evening, Saturday May 13, 1899, he left for the mission field. "At six o'clock told all the folks goodbye," he wrote under that date in his first diary entry, "and left for the depot with feelings that I never felt before, because I was never away from home more than one month in my life, and to think of going away for two years or more causes very peculiar feelings to take possession of me."

Missing from those who met at the old family home to bid the missionary good-bye was his eleven-year-old sister, Emily. Irritated because Joseph had often sent her and the other younger children to bed early during the months of his courtship and marriage with Louie, Emily had prayed that the Lord would call her brother to the mission field speedily. Now that her prayers had been answered, she felt guilty and ran to a neighbor's house to hide so she wouldn't have to face him.

The first leg of the journey, from Salt Lake City to Ogden, was pleasant, although filled with nostalgia, as the local train sped by scenery that was familiar to Joseph Fielding and his companions. At Kaysville a fellow missionary, Fred Williams, boarded the train as did Joseph's father-in-law, Lewis W. Shurtliff, who wanted to spend some time alone with his son-in-law before he caught the mainline train in Ogden. More than most, Lewis Shurtliff understood the peculiar feelings Joseph Fielding was experiencing. Over thirty years before, shortly after the death of his first wife, he had been called on a mission to England, leaving four small children behind. Now he wanted to buoy up his young son-in-law, to share counsel that might be useful in the mission field, and to assure him that Louie would be well taken care of during his absence.

The Union Pacific eastbound mainliner the missionaries boarded in Ogden had originated in the Bay Area near San Francisco. There and at intervening stops it had taken on an almost full load of passengers. Those who boarded at Ogden created an overload. The chair car to which the missionaries were assigned was a scene of bedlam. "We could not sleep," Joseph confided to his diary, "for the car was so crowded and we were cramped in our seats and there was great confusion." A cloud of tobacco smoke that filled the car worsened the conditions, inflaming the eyes of the missionaries and causing them to cough and wheeze. It is not unlikely that Joseph Fielding Smith's long war against "that dirty, filthy habit" began this miserable night. Never before had he been subjected to heavy tobacco smoke over such a long period of time. His only previous lengthy trip on a train was the one to Chicago to attend the World's Fair. Then, however, he had traveled in President Woodruff's chartered cars, which were notably free of tobacco smoke. In the years ahead, his duties required frequent long trips on public conveyances where smoking was allowed, and Elder Smith became outspokenly militant in condemning it. He was never known to be reticent or diplomatic in voicing his outrage at having to breathe someone's tobacco smoke. And more than once he was even heard to mutter words of disapproval when he passed a smoker on the street.

In these conditions, the night seemed endless as the train rocked and lurched its way through the canyons and valleys of northeastern Utah up to the Wyoming plateau. There, when it became light, the situation improved, with new and interesting scenery to distract his attention from the conditions inside the car. Joseph Fielding's interest in the Wyoming landscape did not arise from its beauty; in fact, it was uniformly dull and in some places just plain ugly. But perhaps the young missionary reflected on events of long ago that had occurred in that bleak place, events that had involved his father and other relatives who had struggled there under far worse conditions than those in Joseph's chair car.

On reaching Cheyenne, Wyoming, late Sunday afternoon, the missionaries were transferred to a cleaner, less crowded car. "I washed myself for the first time since leaving home," Joseph wrote, "for I had not had a chance before then, there being no water on the car we were on." Moreover, the scenery had improved around Cheyenne with the appearance of some perennial trees, like those in the canyons east of Salt Lake City.

By Monday the train reached Omaha, Nebraska, where the missionaries switched to another railroad line for the more pleasant trip across Iowa and Illinois to Chicago. Here Joseph Fielding and his brother, Richards, temporarily parted with the other missionaries going to England in order to travel to Buffalo, New York, from where they took a side trip to see Niagara Falls. This was done not only with their father's approval but at his suggestion. President Joseph F. Smith felt that while the chief object of a mission was to preach the gospel, another less-important though vital purpose was to educate the missionary and to give him a broader understanding of people and places.

"It is the greatest sight that I ever saw," wrote Joseph Fielding with a sense of awe following a four-hour inspection of the falls. The brothers rented a hack that took them to all of the main view points on both the American and Canadian sides. Conscious of the need to economize, Joseph wrote with apparent satisfaction, "There are very many schemes to get a man's money from him, but we did very well as the entire trip cost us less than four dollars each."

On Thursday, May 18, Joseph and Richards rejoined their companions in New York City, where they spent two days absorbing its sights and sounds. Keyed in by their sisters Mamie and Donnie, who had lived in New York while studying at the Pratt Institute in Brooklyn, the Smith brothers, accompanied by some of their companions, made the grand tour. Before beginning it, however, there was an essential ritual for Joseph Fielding to perform. "The first thing I did when I reached here," he wrote, "was to take a good bath. . . . I feel like a new man now."

The elders did most of their sightseeing on foot. They walked all through Central Park and down to the Battery, from where they could see the Statue of Liberty. The canyon-like aspect of New York's streets created by today's skyscrapers did not exist then. Still, the missionaries were duly impressed with the city's tall buildings. "Saw the largest building in New York (thirty stories) but do not know its name," wrote Joseph. However, since this was not much higher than the top of the Moroni statue on the Salt Lake Temple, the missionaries were not as impressed with New York's buildings as they were with its harbor and rivers and with its infinite variety of ships, boats, tugs, barges, and ferries. Standing in South Ferry Park, they were fascinated to watch the seagoing ships enter the harbor and move slowly up the Hudson River to dock. A ride on the ferry gave them a better perspective of Manhattan Island as well as a tame prelude to the exciting ocean voyage ahead of them. And for young men who had never before visited a sea port, New York's bustling waterfront with its crush of passengers, porters, baggage carts, stevedores, and cabs was an unbelievable sight. Walking across the Brooklyn Bridge, the visitors were impressed with the flow of traffic, counting as many as twenty cars in a minute's time, one every three seconds! In Brooklyn the thing that interested them most was the Navy Yard, where they were permitted to board and inspect several of the ships in dry dock.

On Saturday morning, May 20, the elders traveled to Philadelphia, their port of embarkation. During the afternoon they had time to take in the main historic sites of the city—Independence Square, the Liberty Bell, and Carpenters Hall, the meeting site of the First Continental Congress. Here the elders were intrigued with the Declaration of Independence and with the signatures of the founding patriots, especially the flamboyant script of John Hancock.

Saturday evening at the conference headquarters, Joseph Fielding found an unexpected gift waiting for him—a letter from Louie! He wrote, "It was a very agreeable surprise to me to receive a letter from home as I did not expect one until I reached Liverpool."

There were nineteen missionaries in Joseph Fielding's group who boarded their ship Saturday night at the Philadelphia pierhead. She was a Belgian liner named the *Pennland,* a ship of somewhat ancient vintage, seaworthy, but very slow and lacking in many of the amenities found on the faster and newer ships. This was the maiden voyage for all of the missionaries except Joseph's brother, Richards, who had accompanied his parents to Liverpool as a little boy. But Richards had little recollection about that trip; and so he shared with the others romanticized ideas about ocean travel as, with gaiety and anticipation, the Mormon elders boarded the *Pennland* Saturday night. They came aboard early so as to be ready for an early departure Sunday morning.

One night aboard this ship, even though she was secured at dockside and was therefore free from the turbulence of the open sea, dispelled most of the myths the Mormon missionaries had heard about seagoing ships. Inside, the *Pennland* was dingy, stinky, and stuffy. The ventilation was poor, and odors accumulated and preserved over the years had become so intermingled as to produce a new, peculiar odor that was distinctively "The Pennland Smell." Moreover, their sleeping accommodations were cramped and crowded. These conditions, and the natural excitement they felt about their departure, guaranteed that the elders would be up and dressed and in the open air topside to see the hawsers cast off shortly before 6:00 Sunday morning, May 21, 1899.

A pilot was taken aboard the *Pennland* to guide her out to the open sea. Whether it was through the pilot's ineptness or because she was simply a bad-luck ship, the *Pennland* found herself stuck on a sand bar within a short while after leaving the Philadelphia pier. Reluctant to dislodge her by reversing and racing the engine, the captain merely dropped anchor and waited for a team of tug boats to come and pull her off. This procedure took seven long hours, during which the missionaries joined the other passengers for lunch and later attended a worship service conducted by the *Pennland*'s chaplain. Joseph showed little enthusiasm for what he saw and heard there, reporting only that he found the service to be "very peculiar." In the late afternoon, the ship was finally freed from the sand bar. "By 6:00 we were on our way toward the mighty deep," he reported. "We remained on deck until the ship's pilot left. We then went to our rooms."

The following day, the elders learned their first nauseating lesson about the sea. "Most of our company were sick," wrote Joseph Fielding. However, neither then nor later was he troubled with seasickness. "I had to be practically alone for a number of days," he noted later, "as all the other missionaries remained in their cots."

The *Pennland* took thirteen days to make the trip from Philadelphia to Liverpool, almost twice as long as for newer ships. The passengers did not really become conscious of the snail's pace of their ship until other ships began to pass them. The incident that finally convinced the competitive elders that they were definitely not riding on a winner involved the steamship *St. Louis*. Joseph Fielding Smith told the humiliating story: "On the way we saw the smoke from the steamship St. Louis, which left a day or two after we did from New York. It came in sight, passed us, and went out of sight inside of one hour." For ambitious young men who wanted to get ahead in the world, repeated instances such as this, which demonstrated the inferiority of their ship, were distressing. So, when at last the *Pennland* passed another vessel, it was cause for mild rejoicing. "It is good to think that we can move faster than *some things*," wrote Joseph. And yet, even that victory was tinged with an element of defeat. In reporting the incident, Joseph Fielding noted that it took almost six times as long to pass this slower ship than it had taken for the *St. Louis* to pass the *Pennland*.

Despite his preoccupation with the slowness of his ship and its shabby accommodations, Joseph enjoyed his first sea voyage. Since he was not plagued with seasickness, he was able to enjoy every novel experience to the fullest.

The sight of a whale, an iceberg, a flying fish, or a gliding albatross was an exciting experience for this untraveled and unsophisticated young man from Utah. And occasionally Joseph remained on deck at night, gazing for hours at the heavens through an atmosphere so clear that the stars and galaxies seemed to be multiplied in their numbers and brilliance.

One advantage of the *Pennland*'s slower pace was that it afforded an opportunity to become better acquainted with the other passengers and to try to plant a few gospel seeds. So a day or two after their ship was under way, Joseph and his companions who were not down with seasickness began to circulate among the passengers, talking to them and distributing tracts to those who showed an interest. "We hope they will read them," he wrote. With the captain's approval, the elders scheduled their own worship service the second, and last, Sunday they were aboard ship. Joseph, who was one of the two speakers, recounted events of Church history, showing that the Saints had been treated unjustly. The audience was unimpressed; and later most of the passengers seemed to avoid the elders when possible. So, even before reaching his field of labor, Elder Smith began to sense a feeling of rejection that was to shadow him throughout his stay in England. And yet, occasional comments or questions from the passengers implied that they were favorably impressed with the appearance and deportment of the missionaries, which reflected favorably on the Church and, the elders hoped, would help tear down the barriers of prejudice and misunderstanding that impeded their work.

The *Pennland* made landfall midmorning, Friday, June 2, as the southeast coast of Ireland came into view — a blessed sight for the seasick elders. Chief among these was Joseph Fielding's brother, Richards, who had few moments of comfort during the long voyage. Joseph had been very solicitous of him and had tried to help; but there was little that could be done since there was no place to go to avoid the constant rocking of the ship. But as the *Pennland* made its way up the St. George's channel and rounded Carmel Head, the turbulence subsided.

After sailing into the harbor, the *Pennland* moved up the Mercy River toward the Liverpool wharf. As the ship moved slowly along, Joseph Fielding had his first close-up view of the land of his forefathers. Here civilization had existed for centuries. Long ago, Roman legions had dominated the land, bringing with them their government, architecture, and language, all of which, in diluted form, were still to be found in England. But what drew his attention was the ancient appearance of the buildings at dockside, long rows of weathered warehouses, begrimed with layers of soot and smoke left by pollution, which hung like a pall over the waterfront.

On the pier waiting to welcome the new elders were members of the staff of the European Mission headquarters. After exchanging greetings and collecting their baggage, the new elders were taken by cab to the mission headquarters at 42 Islington.

While Richards had no clear recollection of it, this was the same place he had lived with his parents for a few months during 1877. It was once a proud and respectable neighborhood, but it had almost become a slum. Even during the 1870s, it had begun to deteriorate. The father, President Joseph F. Smith, reported that during a stroll he and his assistant, L. John Nuttall, took through the neighborhood in January 1875, they counted fifty pubs or "gin palaces" within a mile's radius of 42 Islington. At that time, the father had written that "liquor in some form has become an indispensable necessary to the English people." (Joseph F. Smith Diary, January 5, 1875.) And during the intervening twenty-four years, the conditions around the mission headquarters had deteriorated even further, so much so that shortly after Heber J. Grant was called as the mission president in October 1903, 42 Islington was sold by the Church.

This, then, was the place to which Joseph Fielding and Richards and their companions were welcomed on

June 3, 1899. It was far removed from the old family home on West First North, both in terms of the seven thousand miles that separated them and of the vastly different environments that surrounded them. Although the elders knew they were far from home, yet inside the mission headquarters, they found a touch of home in the mission president and the office elders, all of whom were from in and around Utah.

The mission president who greeted them was Platte D. Lyman, who but a short time before had replaced Rulon S. Wells, a member of The First Council of the Seventy. President Lyman's counselors, James L. McMurrin and Henry W. Naisbitt, were away from Liverpool at the time on an assignment in Scotland. That assignment, which had taken them to Glasgow for meetings of the Scottish Conference, demonstrates the truism that history deals in surprises and coincidences. It was at a priesthood meeting in Glasgow on May 29, 1899, that James L. McMurrin uttered the well-known prophecy that young David O. McKay, the conference president, would one day sit in the leading councils of the Church. Five days later, there appeared at 42 Islington a new, untried missionary, Joseph Fielding Smith, who, seventy-one years later, would succeed David O. McKay as the president of the Church.

President Lyman lost no time in assigning the new missionaries to their fields of labor. The next day, Sunday, June 4, Joseph Fielding boarded a train headed for Nottingham, the city to which he had been assigned. He was alone. Richards was on his way to Leeds, while the other elders had left, or would soon leave, for their assignments in different parts of Great Britain or Continental Europe, all of which was under the jurisdiction of the mission presidency in Liverpool.

The three-hour train ride to Nottingham took Joseph into the heart of the East Midlands coal fields and into one of the most highly industrialized areas of England, famed for its manufacture of hosiery and fine lace. Although he could understand the language of the people, their customs and attitudes were strange, making the missionary feel ill at ease. "The railroads in this country," he mused in his journal, "are so different from those in our own country that a person must keep his wits about him. I travelled alone, in a strange land, and among a strange people, where I would have little or no sympathy if I were known." This last statement was a veiled reference to the deep antagonisms that had developed toward the Church in England. The name *Mormon* had become a word of bitter derision there. Indeed, it was libelous to falsely accuse a person of being a Mormon. These attitudes sprang chiefly from the practice of polygamy and the distorted publicity given to it by the English press and clergy. Despite the Manifesto, there was a widespread belief that the Church still taught and practiced plural marriage. And this created a suspicion in many that the missionaries sought only to lure women to Utah, there to subject them to a life of debauchery. On this account, Joseph Fielding believed he would receive no sympathy from the other passengers were it known that he was a Mormon missionary. So, he withdrew within himself and made no effort to engage those around him in conversation. "My thoughts were continually turning towards home," he wrote.

Through miscommunication, the missionaries in Nottingham had not been advised of Elder Smith's arrival, so no one came to the train station to meet him. Since he had been furnished with the address of the conference headquarters, Joseph collected his baggage and hired a cab to take him there. He found the missionary quarters locked and empty. The elders had gone to afternoon worship services at the branch. Putting his trunk and grip in the doorway, Joseph began walking back and forth in front of the building to stretch his legs and case the neighborhood. He was careful not to walk beyond the view of his gear, because many rough-looking boys were playing in the street. Joseph questioned their intentions, and they returned the favor. "[They] eyed me with curiosity," wrote the new missionary, "and sang a parody on one of our mountain hymns for my own personal benefit." Joseph found the serenade amusing. "Chase me, girls, to Salt Lake City, where the Mormons have no pity,", they sang with gusto. "If I approached them, they would run from me," he wrote, "which amused me as much as I amused them." Such a reception the first day in his first field of labor boded ill for the future. The attitudes of derision and unfriendliness shown by these boys likely reflected attitudes they had learned at home, attitudes that would not be conducive to missionary work.

Joseph Fielding was welcomed warmly and apologetically by the missionaries when they returned from church. Had they known he was coming, they would have met the elder with the famous name and accompanied him home, avoiding the confrontation with the urchins in the street.

Elder Smith was made acquainted with his new companions and the digs that would be his home for several months. All the missionaries laboring in Nottingham shared the same house, which included their living quarters and the conference office. They did most of their own laundry, all of their own sewing, and some of their own cooking. Some meals were prepared for them by hired cooks, and their shirts were usually washed and ironed professionally. Each elder contributed a proportional amount to a common fund that was drawn on to pay for food and housing. Having come from a large family, such communal living was nothing new to Joseph Fielding Smith. Indeed, he felt right at home.

The conference president, George Ruff of Coalville, Utah, was not in Nottingham when Joseph arrived, so the new elder did not immediately learn what his first assignment would be. The following day, Monday, being the usual preparation day for the missionaries, no proselyting was done. Instead, one of the elders, George F. Ashley, accompanied Elder Smith to a shopping district downtown where he bought a hat, which was then part of the standard gear for missionaries, and some writing paper and envelopes. On the way home, the elders visited Arboretum Park, where "all kinds of birds" were kept. In the months ahead, Joseph would visit here periodically as a diversion to study the wide variety of birds that had been gathered for the enjoyment of the people of Nottingham.

Upon the return of President Ruff, Joseph was assigned to labor in Nottingham, an assignment that would keep him at conference headquarters for the first five months of his mission. Tuesday, June 6, 1899, was his first day of actual proselyting. "This has been a very important day in my short life," he wrote enthusiastically. "I came from my home less than a month ago for the purpose of preaching the gospel of our Lord." His day's work consisted of the two main kinds of proselyting engaged in by British missionaries at that day — tracting and street meetings. As to the first, he and his companion distributed twenty-five tracts. "It did not come to me very easy," he reported frankly. And as to the street meeting he and two other missionaries held, he wrote: "I bore my testimony to the world for the first time today, but I will be able to do so better. With the help of the Lord, I shall do his will as I was called to do."

It had been sixty-two years since the first Latter-day Saint missionaries, Heber C. Kimball and his companions, had commenced proselyting in England. Within a few days after their arrival in Preston in 1837, they had baptized their first converts in the River Ribble. During the next several decades, thousands of converts were baptized in the British Isles and Europe. In the early years, especially, the harvest was plentiful. The stories of the baptism of whole congregations by Wilford Woodruff had become part of the folklore of the Church, well known to Joseph Fielding and all the other British missionaries.

This and other examples of unusual proselyting success in England created unreasonable expectations in the minds of many missionaries. The assumption was that if the earlier missionaries had enjoyed such phenomenal success, so could they. But there was a vast difference between the two eras. Wilford Woodruff, for instance, was thirty-three years old when he worked in England the first time, a veteran of several previous missions and of Zion's Camp, a member of the Twelve and a personal confidant of the Prophet Joseph Smith, whose testimony of the events in the Sacred Grove had imbued him with a fiery fervor that would never be quenched. He and the other missionaries of his day brought a new and startling message of the appearance of Gods and angels on the earth in modern times and of a new sacred record of ancient peoples who once inhabited the American continent, translated from golden plates by a young man, a modern prophet, who then lived in the United States. The startling effect of such a message and the eloquence and spirituality that surrounded these men gained widespread attention, attracting large groups of people who wanted to hear and see them. In such a context, tracting of the kind performed by Joseph Fielding and his companions was almost unknown to the earlier missionaries. The tracts they had published were used chiefly for distribution at their meetings to elaborate on subjects covered there or to lead the audience into a study of other gospel principles. They relied mostly on word of mouth or newspaper advertising rather than on tedious tracting to create teaching situations. And in the beginning, widespread opposition from the press and the clergy had not developed, and the minds of the people had not been poisoned against the Mormon missionaries, especially in reference to polygamy, whose practice by the Latter-day Saints was not publicly acknowledged until the 1850s. The hardening of attitudes during the intervening sixty years had created a rock-like resistance to Mormonism that the missionaries found almost impossible to penetrate. Nor was their task made easier by the existence of strong local units of the Church. The routine practice of the early missionaries to encourage new converts to migrate to the United States had regularly creamed off most of the ablest converts. This, with the widespread practice of having missionaries preside over local Church units, had stunted the growth of the Church in England, preventing the development of a thriving Mormon community to which the missionaries could point as evidence of the fruits of their message and on which they could rely for help in their work.

All these conditions combined created an almost impossible proselyting task for Joseph and his companions. It was tough sledding all the way. Just how tough is seen in the fact that during his two-year mission, Elder Smith did not convert and baptize a single person. He did confirm one member, but that was the full extent of his proselyting harvest.

It took Elder Smith only a few days in the field to conclude that his efforts in bringing new members into the Church would not be crowned with much, if any, success. But being young and inexperienced at the time and being unaware of the great convert harvest that would take place in England a few decades later, he ascribed this to the wrong reason. "The blood of Israel has almost been gathered," he confided to his journal a week after commencing his labors in Nottingham. As later events proved, the blood of Israel was still there in large numbers; but their eyes had been so blinded by the lies and distortions circulated about the Latter-day Saints, or by their own misconduct, that they failed to see and refused to hear.

One must not think that because of a lack of converts Elder Smith's mission was a failure. Quite the contrary. He worked hard during the months of his service. In a letter to Louie after he had been in the field for several months, Joseph reported that he and the other missionaries distributed 10,000 tracts each month, either through door-to-door contacting or at street meetings, and that they visited about 4,000 homes each month. It is impossible to gauge what the ultimate results of such a vast amount of work was or might be. An impression made at a door or on a street corner, or a tract picked up and read months, or even years, after it was delivered might be the seed that would ultimately grow into a conversion. Therefore, the number of converts a missionary baptizes can often be a misleading criterion as to the success or failure of a mission. The true test is whether one has worked hard and consistently and done his best under the circumstances. Judged by that standard, Joseph Fielding Smith was eminently successful.

But the flip side of missionary work pertains to the training and discipline of the missionary. It was here, perhaps, that the value and "success" of Elder Smith's mission can best be seen. It was in England that he received his first detailed training in the organization and development of the Church at the grass-roots level. It was here, through constant study and prayer, that his understanding of the doctrines of the Church flowered. It was here that his personal discipline was improved through faithfully following the missionary regimen of early rising, regular study, persistent work, and fervent prayer. Here he learned greater self-reliance and self-confidence by living and working under difficult circumstances in a foreign land. Here he learned humility when any thought or hope of a great harvest of converts was dashed. And finally, it was here that Joseph received his first intimate view of the ways of the world, a view that was vital in his understanding of the weaknesses and frailties of men and women and therefore of their need for the saving principles of the gospel he taught.

The polygamous community in which Joseph Fielding Smith was born and reared lived by a strict code of morality and sobriety. Sexual relations outside the marriage covenant, once known, were dealt with severely. There was a single standard of morality for both men and women, and the violation of marital covenants by persons of either sex was not tolerated. And the Word of Wisdom imposed upon the Latter-day Saints a code of abstinence from the use of alcohol, tea, coffee, and tobacco. There were, of course, saloons in Salt Lake City, but they were clustered in a small section of the downtown area that residents like Joseph Fielding seldom if ever passed through. Any incidents of public drunkenness or brawling in Salt Lake City usually occurred in this small area, and seldom were women involved. Moreover, the information about what went on in the saloon district was skimpy as far as most residents of Salt Lake City were concerned, seeping out only occasionally by word of mouth or, in aggravated cases, by articles in the local newspapers. Having been reared in such a sheltered environment, twenty-three-year old Joseph Fielding Smith was hardly prepared for what he found in Nottingham. "On our way home," he recorded in his diary soon after arriving there, "we saw more drunken men and women than I ever saw before in my life, and the women I believe outnumbered the men. I have seen more wickedness here in two weeks than I have seen at home in all my life." Later on a July afternoon, Elder Smith and a companion went to study in the city's spacious park, reputedly the scene of some of the exploits of Robin Hood and his men of the Sherwood Forest. The elders very soon had to abandon the idea. "The Spirit of God is not on that piece of ground," he wrote emphatically, "for it is a wicked spot. We saw things there in broad daylight that we could not imagine if we had not seen." And he learned of astonishing things that he did not see when the relatives of one of his companions told the elders that "it was a common thing for men to exchange wives for a week at a time."

The loose morals among the adults was reflected in a lack of proper training and supervision of the young people who congregated aimlessly in the streets or parks on weekends and holidays. "Coming home from Arnold Sunday night," Joseph wrote in a letter to Louie, "for a distance of almost five miles the streets were so full of young people that I could hardly work my way through, and a good part of the time had to take to the road. You could not imagine what it is like hardly without seeing it for yourself."

Such were the conditions Joseph found among the people of Nottingham. They were good people of the same stock as Joseph's ancestors, people with potential who sorely needed the truths the elders taught. But their attitudes and life-style caused them either to ignore the missionaries or to summarily reject their message when it was presented to them. To be subjected to such indifference and rejection day after day was discouraging. In these circumstances, encouraging letters from home were a main source of motivation for the missionary to continue with the work and not to give up. Louie was Joseph's most faithful correspondent. Her frequent letters, always upbeat and positive, were filled with expressions of love and support, news about family and friends, and anxious inquiries about Joseph's health and diet. As to the latter, he assured Louie in a letter written a month after he arrived in Nottingham that he and his companions ate "very well" although their menus were conspicuously lacking in variety. "We have the same thing every day of the week," he wrote. "The elders speak of it as the one mush, one meat, and one jam. Every morning we have mush made from graham flour, never a change, for the law is as strict as that of the Medes and Persians. For dinner we have meat . . . and for tea ham and canned tomatoes or some lettuce. . . . I do not starve by any means. I can eat plenty."

Joseph Fielding's parents also were faithful in writing to him, although because of the many demands on their time from the other children, they did not write as often as Louie. Julina, like Louie, seemed preoccupied with Joseph's health and asked many searching questions about his diet, rest, and hygiene. The father, on the other hand, seemed most interested in his son's finances and his spiritual growth and development. On June 22, 1899, five weeks after the son left home, President Smith sent Joseph Fielding a "receipt" for five dollars, which was a medium of exchange used by the Church to enable missionaries in the field to draw money from mission headquarters that had been deposited to their credit in the United States. "While you and Buddie [Richards] will no doubt be as economical as you can be," wrote President Smith in the letter with which the receipt was transmitted, "I do not want you to go hungry, naked, or without shoes, and I hope to be able to supply you what you may actually need over and above your own resources." In acknowledging the gift, Joseph told his father, "I shall be very careful of the means you send me. I do not spend anything unless I have a good reason for it." Perhaps to underscore just how careful he was to economize, he told his father that he even refrained from buying the delicious English toffee that was such a favorite of the missionaries. He went on to say things that must have been especially pleasing to the father. "I am here to preach the gospel," wrote Joseph, "and I hope I will be able to do that well." In doing that, he expected not only to confer a blessing on those whom he taught but also to reap a personal blessing that would help qualify him for future service. "It is my desire to improve my mind and talents while I am here," he continued, "that I may always be useful for something in life." Finally, he shared with his father the earnest desire of his heart. "I want to be right on all things," he confided, "and nothing gives me more pleasure than to learn something about the gospel. My desire is to become acquainted with it and gain wisdom." It is not difficult to see how this desire of the earnest young missionary found fulfillment in the future when he became the Church's most prolific writer on doctrine and the General Authority to whom doctrinal questions were most often referred for answer.

"I like your spirit," President Smith wrote in answer to his son's letter. "I have faith in your integrity and I have pleasure and satisfaction in you." He then set up some personal goals for Joseph to strive toward. "I want you to cultivate wisdom and deliberate judgment and patience as well as the Holy Spirit and the love of God," he counseled. He also shared some of the things that troubled the Brethren at home. "*The Salt Lake Tribune* and the hireling priests," he wrote, "have stirred up a hot wave of persecution against the elders in the Southern States Mission. They have mobbed and beaten a number of our elders and have burned and destroyed a number of our meeting houses. It is all in the democratic South."

Such news enabled Joseph Fielding to make comparisons between the conditions in his own mission and elsewhere. The British missionaries were sometimes subjected to mob action, usually as the result of controversies arising at street meetings. Then, in the heat of the moment, it was not uncommon for drunks in the audience to abuse them verbally, or sometimes to throw things at them. But it was not in the British character to beat, tar and feather, or kill missionaries as was sometimes done in the United States. In a talk delivered in the Kenwood II Ward of the Wilford Stake, June 26, 1960, Elder Smith told of an experience he had in England when a butcher grabbed a knife and threatened to kill him because Joseph had offered him a tract. "I knew in England he wouldn't do that," he told the audience. "If he had been in the United States, I don't know what he would have done, but English people don't do that." (Tape in possession of the family.) So with all their faults and failings, Elder Smith recognized a certain gentility and tolerance among the English that minimized any real concern about being harmed.

As to possible damage to chapels, there was no concern because the Church owned no chapels in England. The members met in small, rented halls whose quality ranged from tolerable to disreputable. Because of the poor reputation of the Mormons in England, landlords in middle or lower middle class neighborhoods would not rent to the Church. Therefore, the leaders, desperate for some place to hold meetings, took anything that was available. As a result, the mission had acquired a collection of crummy halls situated in shabby neighborhoods whose appearance repelled investigators and embarrassed the missionaries. After a year in the field, and with things looking up a bit after acquiring something a notch better, Joseph Fielding described the meetingplace of the Nottingham Saints for Louie: "Ever since I have been here and for a long time before," he wrote, "the Nottingham Saints have been meeting in a sort of suspension shanty over a stable almost three rods back from the street — the last place on earth a person would look for a meeting room, and a place that would frighten away a timid investigator. . . . We have had hard work to get a hall anywhere else, for everyone will not receive the 'Mormons.' They have paid about $1.75 a week for the old room that is not worth ten cents. But at last we have found another room and moved into it yesterday. It is an improvement on the other, but still is not the best on earth but as good as we can get, I suppose."

It was in the old room over the stable that Joseph Fielding and the other missionaries met each Sunday with the Nottingham Saints, and an occasional investigator, during the first several months of his mission. It was here, with an occasional assignment to speak or teach, that he enjoyed a change from the dreary sameness and discouragement of tracting and street meetings. It was something to look forward to. Despite the dingy surroundings, it was a joy to meet with the Saints and elders, to sing the songs of Zion, to share testimonies and insights into the gospel, and to partake of the sacrament. These unchangeables glossed over any defects in the quality of the meeting place.

After several months in the field, Joseph Fielding was transferred to nearby Derby, a city founded a thousand years earlier by the Danes that was noted for the manufacture of fine porcelain and textiles. Here, as in Nottingham, the young missionary, whose hometown was less than thirty years old when he was born, stood in awe at the ancient appearance of the city's streets and main buildings. He found the people much the same as in Nottingham, indifferent to his message and antagonistic because of misconceptions about the Latter-day Saints.

In Derby, Joseph was the senior companion to Elder Stephen W. Walker, who was nine years older than he. Elder Walker is reported to have written home, observing that his new companion was very young and a little green but that he would "leave his mark upon the world."

The routine in Derby seldom varied. The elders were up early to shave, study, pray, and breakfast. When the weather permitted, they left their apartment in midmorning to tract or visit members. Later in the day, after "tea" and more tracting, they would often hold a street meeting, which usually commenced with the pair singing a Latter-day Saint hymn, followed by a prayer and talks by both elders. While one was speaking, the companion would circulate among the listeners or passers by, distributing tracts and, where possible, engaging in gospel conversations. The meeting ended with a closing prayer. The elders never knew, and never would know, whether the meetings had any beneficial effect upon those who listened to them or who accepted their literature. But they had a therapeutic effect upon the missionaries, deriving from a sense that they were preaching the gospel and therefore were doing their duty. Moreover, there was a certain exhilaration that attended the speaker as he lifted his voice and gave expression to his thoughts and bore his testimony. And at the end of the meeting, there came a feeling of satisfaction, or at least a sense of relief that the ordeal was over.

However, there was nothing exhilarating about tracting. For Joseph, it was hard, discouraging, and mostly unproductive work. Too often the conversations at the door were mere monologues. Those who answered the knock would usually clam up when they saw who it was. "I visited 81 houses with tracts," he recorded one depressing day, "but could not get the people to talk. . . . I find it very difficult to get the people to talk either for or against us. Most of them are silent unless it is to say, 'Good afternoon.' " On the same day he wrote, "One or two tracts were refused and one door was slammed in my face." Occasionally Joseph shared his distaste for tracting, explaining to Louie his frustration when people refused to talk to them: "I would rather have someone accuse us of almost anything so long as he will talk than to have them keep as mum as an oyster."

Once in a while, however, the elders found an exception—someone who talked, perhaps too much. Such was a Catholic woman who gave Joseph "a thorough roasting." She reversed the usual roles with the missionaries and did most of the talking. "She could not say anything mean enough about the 'Mormons,' " Joseph told Louie. "She said they were the vilest people on the earth." And being an orthodox Catholic in Victorian England, the little lady fired off what she probably thought was the ultimate insult when she charged that "Brigham Young was the twin brother of Henry the Eighth."

Those few who did talk were an incentive for the missionaries to learn the doctrines of the Church. Since they never knew what points might be raised by the few talkative ones, the elders had to be prepared for anything. So Joseph Fielding acquired a thorough knowledge of the gospel through regular, concentrated study. His hours spent reading the scriptures formed the foundation of his vast knowledge of the doctrines of the Church. In a letter to Louie in November 1899, not long after being transferred to Derby, Joseph commented on his diligent efforts to learn the doctrine and to memorize key scriptures. "I am trying to learn something while I am here," he wrote. "Since I left Nottingham I have put my time in to study and I feel that I can hardly find a minute when I do not feel that I ought to be preparing my mind with useful knowledge." Then indicating that these preparations were intended as much for the future as for his present work, he added: "I feel that when I come home that more will be expected of me than I am capable of as it generally is with returned missionaries. They are generally supposed to have learned all that the Bible contains or else they have neglected their duties." Reflecting feelings of inadequacy in this effort, he frankly confided to his wife: "But it must not be expected of me for I am rather dull of comprehension. I have tried all day to learn a passage of scripture and have not got it yet. But I am determined to learn it before I am through. It is the 9, 10 and 11 verses of the second chapter of 1st Cor[inthians]."

Because the biased attitudes of the people prevented a logical, consistent presentation of gospel principles, Elder Smith ordinarily had to use his gospel knowledge as a tool to refute unfair charges against the Church. "The only way to meet these people," Joseph wrote in his diary, "is to ask them if they believe the Bible and when they say yes you can soon make them wiggle." He told of one particularly combative woman whose criticisms were answered one by one from the scriptures, "until she began to abuse our people and tell me how wicked they are, etc. When she got through I spoke to her in such a way that she became ashamed of herself and began to beg my pardon without telling me so in that many words."

So throughout his mission, Joseph's relationship with his contacts was essentially an adversarial one. Notwithstanding, Joseph and his companions continued day after discouraging day with their rounds of tracting and street meetings. Their tracting efforts took them all over Derby. And some of the neighborhoods were tracted more than once, something that had been done by scores of missionaries who had preceded them. The townspeople generally had become so accustomed to seeing the missionaries that their minds had been closed to the message, and their negative responses had become automatic. Given these circumstances, one can understand what prompted diary entries such as this one: "I am of the firm opinion that this nation among others is almost gleaned. I went tracting this afternoon and delivered over 100 tracts with little success."

The elders walked to and from their tracting areas and anywhere else they wanted to go. Only in an emergency or dire necessity would they take a cab or bus or train. And when they had to consult with conference headquarters in Nottingham, they usually walked there and back. In March 1900, for instance, having heard that packages from home had arrived there, Joseph and his companion walked the twelve miles to Nottingham to pick them up. They stayed overnight at conference headquarters and returned the following day. "This morning Brother Walker and I left Nottingham for Derby carrying our bundles with us," wrote Joseph in his diary. "They weighed altogether about thirty pounds. The snow made it very bad under foot and increased the difficulty of walking." On opening his package at Derby, he found that it included a fruit cake. "I had used the bundle as a seat while we ate our lunch," he wrote in dismay. "But the cake tasted just as good for all that, and ten times better because it was made by my sister at home."

Joseph Fielding's most ambitious walk during his mission was from Ultoxeter in Staffordshire, through Derby, to Nottingham. "I left at 6 A.M.," he wrote, "and I arrived in Nottingham at 12 at night, travelling on foot all that distance." He could not recall ever riding on a bus during his mission. "I walked," he wrote, "I didn't have the money to take street car rides."

Long and frequent walks in the open air, an adequate diet, and sufficient rest combined to keep Joseph healthy throughout his mission. He was seldom sick and was hospitalized only once, and then not for illness. Following Joseph's transfer back to Nottingham, one of the office elders caught smallpox and was put in the hospital. So were the other five office elders, who were quarantined for two weeks in an isolation ward to restrict the spread of the disease. Ironically, it proved to be the most enjoyable proselyting experience of Joseph's mission. "We have made friends with the nurses and others who visited us during our imprisonment," he wrote in his diary. "Many times we have had talks with them about the gospel; also left with them books to read." When they were released from the hospital, the elders sang several hymns, leaving the staff "with tears in their eyes." He felt the experience had broken down many barriers and that the missionaries had planted many seeds that would later bear good fruit. "I think we have made an impression at the hospital for good, especially with the nurses who confess that we are not the people they thought we were and they will now defend us at all times."

In June 1900, after six months of service in Derby, Elder Smith was transferred back to Nottingham. There he would serve as the clerk of the conference during the remainder of his mission. At the same time, his junior companion, Stephen W. Walker, was appointed as the conference president, replacing George Ruff. Joseph did not receive this transfer with enthusiasm. "I am thankful I do not have to stay here at this more than a year," he wrote to Louie. "That is just about 12 months more than I care for." Later he confided to her, "If I am here in the field two years, then 18 months of that time will be 'killed' in the conference house."

Two main factors lay at the root of Joseph's dissatisfaction. First, his clerical duties severely limited his proselyting activities. He had come to England to preach the gospel, something he could not do while chained to a desk. There his days would be spent mostly in what to him were routine and uninteresting activities. The second factor was one he did not discuss openly but that was hinted at broadly in his diary and correspondence. That was the sense of disappointment or even failure he experienced when his junior companion was called as the conference president in preference to him. And that sense was compounded by being relieved of full-time proselyting duties and assigned to subordinate, routine tasks under the direction of the one who had previously looked to him for leadership. Joseph was mature enough and sufficiently schooled in Church doctrine and procedure to know that one's position in the Church and before God is much less important than his performance and character. Yet he was human enough to wonder whether the reversal of positions between him and Elder Walker reflected a defect in the quality or the strength of his leadership. Whatever were his thoughts about the matter, there can be little doubt that it was a growing experience for him and taught a lesson that was essential for the future Prophet to learn.

Although they were not to his liking, Elder Smith settled into his new duties with the determination to make the best of a bad situation. His work in the office was generally divided among three areas: clerical duties, which took most of his time; some proselyting in the afternoons and evenings; and personal and housekeeping chores. Intermixed with these were study, personal and official correspondence, and occasional recreational activities. Also, at times when the conference president was away from Nottingham, Elder Smith assumed his responsibilities as necessary.

The elders who worked in Nottingham shared the same living quarters, as already noted. They alternated in handling the cooking, shopping, and housekeeping chores. The other elders must have looked upon the arrival of Elder Smith as a gift from heaven. Because of his orderly habits and the training he had received from his mother and aunties in cooking and housekeeping, Joseph soon brought about a revolution in the way the elders lived at the Nottingham conference house. "This morning I got up early," he wrote in his diary, "as I am on the committee preparing breakfast this week. . . . The quarters we occupy are not the cleanest in the world. . . . I went through the cupboard this morning and tried hard to straighten it up a little for it was in a terrible condition. After I had thrown away a large number of tin cans etc., and emptied a dozen or more papers of mush into one and after throwing many other papers away and cleaning a few dishes that were covered with dirt and grease, the place looked somewhat respectable."

But an orderly, more sanitary kitchen was only a small part of the contribution Joseph made to the cleanliness and well-being of the elders living in the conference house. He soon introduced the brethren to an entirely new diet. During his first stay in Nottingham, he deplored the menus that were served. He noted in his journal, "I have had to eat things since I have been here that would turn almost any Utahn's stomach." Especially repugnant to him was the meat usually served for dinner that had been "dead many days." Within a few months after returning to Nottingham as the conference clerk, all this had been changed. "We buy in for ourselves and cook for ourselves," he wrote to Louie in November 1900, "so we have just what we want and plenty of it. We are not starving ourselves now. We live almost entirely on vegetables and fruit. We seldom see meat unless we get a piece to make soup with. . . . All the elders here say they never felt better in their lives. I feel well, and I think the way we are living has a great deal to do with it."

Joseph, the old groceryman, also introduced his companions to the miracle of the bean and the economies that came from bulk buying. He wrote, "I taught them some things that they did not know. One was that navy beans were very good. You could eat them boiled or in soup. I went to the store one day to get some navy beans. . . . The man reached down off the shelf a one pound package and handed it to me. I said 'I don't want just one pound; I want eight or ten pounds.' He looked at me in astonishment. He went to his shelf, looked up, and he took down eight one-pound packages and said, 'This is all I've got.' I took the eight packages home. We lived on beans boiled and bean soup. You don't know how good it is if you haven't tried it."

When Joseph's mother learned of the extent to which he had become involved in cooking for the elders, she was annoyed. "I do not think I will ever teach another boy to cook," she wrote. "You made a mistake. You should have spoiled everything you tried to cook."

Joseph's positive influence upon the other elders extended far beyond the kitchen. He was a model of self-discipline, worthy of emulation by all. He was usually the first one out of bed in the morning. If ever one of the other elders wanted to arise before the usual hour, he needed only to ask Elder Smith to arouse him. He knew Elder Smith would already be up, poring over the scriptures. And the wisdom and insights he gained by this means, added to the rich store of doctrinal knowledge he had acquired before his mission under the tutelage of his father, magnified his stature in the eyes of the others. When questions of doctrine or procedure arose, he was usually looked to as the final arbiter. This also included the conference president, Stephen W. Walker, who, although nine years older than Elder Smith, was always willing to defer to his younger companion in doctrinal matters. On one occasion, for instance, Joseph and President Walker were engaged in a conversation about religion with their landlord, Mr. Blood. "I was somewhat backward at first about speaking," Joseph Fielding noted in his diary, "and only did so when I saw it was necessary." He soon found it necessary to intervene when the landlord said that while they believed differently as to matters of church government, all Christian sects were in agreement about the fundamental doctrines of the church. "We drew the line at this," wrote Joseph, "and by request of President Walker I took the argument off his hands." In a lengthy diary entry, Elder Smith traced the broad outlines of the conversation that followed, which demonstrated his precise understanding of the gospel and the facility with which he cited the key scriptures to support his contentions. When Elder Smith referred to the principle of continuing revelation as a main feature that distinguished the restored church from all others, the landlord was "horrified." "He began to take me in hand as a youth," wrote Joseph, "whose knowledge of the scriptures had been sadly neglected and perverted to ever think of such an idea." Mr. Blood cited the curse of John, invoked upon all who "shall add unto these things" as negating the idea of continuing revelation. But when Elder Smith logically explained that John wrote his gospel after this statement was made and that the Bible, as such, did not then exist, the landlord "changed the subject" immediately, shifting to a concept that he thought was unassailable—that salvation comes only by faith, works being unessential. On being questioned, he first conceded that one would have "to keep the counsel of God" to be saved, which is a kind of work. But he rejected the idea that baptism is necessary. "No," he said emphatically. "Where do you get such a doctrine as that? . . . Not in *my* Bible." At that, he went to get his Bible, and on returning he demanded, "Now show me where God says baptism is essential to my salvation." When Joseph read from the third chapter of John what Jesus said to Nicodemus and from 1 Peter 3:18–21, Mr. Blood, completely unhinged, "danced up and down shouting . . . Christ or baptism? Which is it? Does Christ save us or does baptism? . . . It is either Christ that saves us or baptism. Which is it? If we are saved by baptism we have no need of Christ." When asked about the scriptures he had just read in his own Bible, he answered hotly, "I won't believe Paul or Peter." The session went on for nearly two hours, during which Joseph answered all of the questions the landlord raised, covering a broad range of gospel subjects. It was a remarkable performance by one so young to call up by chapter and verse the numerous scriptures necessary to answer the questions randomly raised by the landlord. There can be little doubt that the disciplined training Joseph Fielding Smith received in the mission field, during an era when the elders were constantly attacked for their beliefs, helped prepare him for the key roles he would play during his apostolic ministry, his roles as a defender of the faith and an answerer of gospel questions.

Notwithstanding the hours of careful study Joseph had spent in acquiring the knowledge necessary to answer Mr. Blood's questions, there was no sense of conceit at the accomplishment, nor did he ascribe to himself any special qualities of intelligence. "Never before was I assisted through the power of God than at the time," wrote he of the incident. "It was due to his assistance that we were successful."

Joseph understood well the difference between winning an argument and gaining a convert. So, as the combative, adversarial attitudes toward the Church changed in Great Britain, the role and focus of the Mormon missionaries changed also. A key figure in that change was Joseph Fielding Smith. It is significant that during the 1950s and 1960s, when the church reaped such a great harvest of converts in the British Isles, Joseph Fielding Smith, in his role as the president of the Twelve, was also the chairman of the General Church Missionary Committee. During these critical years, when the foundations of the Church were so significantly strengthened and extended there, the notions of arguing or debating with nonmembers had disappeared entirely. Indeed, missionaries were then instructed to avoid argumentative confrontations and to move on to others when someone like Mr. Blood was encountered. During Joseph's missionary days, however, such a policy would have deprived the elders of almost all proselyting contacts because of the deep-seated antagonisms toward the Church and its representatives.

While Elder Smith freely acknowledged divine help in the discussion with the landlord, as he always did in performing his missionary labors, he nevertheless was conscious of his own abilities and was never reluctant to express his views openly and with self-confidence. He once told of a gospel conversation he had with another elder who, exasperated by Joseph's insistence that he was right on a point of doctrine, blurted out, "Joseph Fielding Smith, if you don't repent, you're going straight to hell." (Joseph F. McConkie, *True and Faithful*, p. 26.) Joseph Fielding always expressed his views calmly and precisely without heat or rancor, but with a certitude that was sometimes unsettling or annoying to those who disagreed with him, as it was in the case of this missionary companion.

With so little time for proselyting and because the neighborhood near the conference house had been saturated with tracting, the office elders often had trouble finding something to do. Street meetings were always an option, and the elders held many of them. Yet this was an unsatisfying and largely unproductive activity. "This is a very poor place for open air work at best," Joseph wrote to Louie shortly after being transferred back to Nottingham, "as we can only go in some out-of-the-way place to hold meetings and then to talk to lamp posts and dirty youngsters who never saw a bathtub nor heard of an article called soap." In these circumstances, the elders occasionally attended the meetings of other religious groups, hoping either to make acquaintances that might open the door to teaching situations, or to receive permission to speak at their meetings. One such group was the "Brethren's Bible Class," whose meetings Elder Smith attended on several occasions. At first he was optimistic that this would open new teaching opportunities. He wrote to Louie, "They have partly offered us the use of their hall if we would go and talk to them. But they want to question us as they feel led. If we get the chance we will go, for there may be some among them who are seeking for light and we may be able to do some good." Joseph and the other elders were disappointed when they met with this group, who simply called themselves the Brethren. They found that their "offer" for the elders to come and speak was an apparent device to get the missionaries into their midst so the Brethren could convert them to their beliefs. Disappointed, Joseph reported the results to Louis: "They muzzled us and did not permit us to speak. They spent all the time on the subject of 'saved by grace' believing that all who call on the name of God shall be saved, no matter what their works may be." This was a doctrine prevalent in England at the time, and Joseph was not allowed to respond or to ask questions, as he had done with his landlord.

Another group whose meetings the elders once attended was a spiritualist cult that used the same hall the Latter-day Saints used for their meetings. Present was a clairvoyant, a Mrs. Peters from Manchester, who, in attempting to demonstrate her powers, questioned a young man who was seated directly in front of Elder Smith and his three companions. When Mrs. Peters failed in her attempt to describe an acquaintance of the young man, she discontinued questioning him and turned to someone else. "The woman then suddenly left him," Joseph Fielding explained in his journal, "and declared to the congregation that the four men who were sitting just back of the young man to whom she had been giving the description had a great deal of power and for that reason she had failed." Joseph later decided it was a waste of time to attend these meetings. "I do not care to go see them any more," he confided to his diary. "I am satisfied."

The incident about attending the spiritualist meeting was recorded in Joseph's diary in great detail, as were many of his other experiences. Although he may not have consciously done so for that purpose, this habit was an excellent exercise to help hone his writing skills, which were to play such a key role in his apostolic ministry. And the numerous letters he was required to write as the conference clerk and those he wrote to Louie and other members of the family for his own enjoyment served the same purpose. Had Elder Smith seen clearly what the future held for him, he likely would have felt less concerned about the eighteen months he "killed" in the conference headquarters, for that service provided an important ingredient in shaping the man young Joseph Fielding Smith was to become.

As Elder Smith searched for different ways to use his time profitably, he hit upon an idea that again called his writing skill into play. He drafted a letter that was mailed to about two hundred ministers who lived in the Nottingham and Derby area. An LDS pamphlet was sent with each letter. Joseph's objective in doing this was clearly set out in the diary. "They are teachers of the people," he wrote, "and the people naturally follow them. I feel that they are in need of warning if anyone is, and they ought to have it. I want them to have it, too . . . for they should be left without excuse . . . [so] they cannot say the gospel was never presented to them." In the hope of opening a correspondence with them, Joseph Fielding wrote to each minister: "I desire that you kindly forward to me a pamphlet setting forth the fundamental principles of your faith, which, I promise you, I shall carefully read." He then added a statement that sounds like modern ecumenism: "My sole desire being that we might come to a 'unity of the faith.' " What Elder Smith did not tell the ministers was that the unity he had in mind was the unity that would prevail when they joined The Church of Jesus Christ of Latter-day Saints! Although young and relatively inexperienced, Joseph was not lacking in self-confidence or in the scriptural knowledge that would have enabled him to hold his own in discussions about doctrine with even the most learned among the professional clergy in England.

Elder Smith was not surprised by the minimal response he received from the local clergy to his letter, although he may have been a little disappointed. "The ministers do not answer us now," he wrote to Louie. "I think they have had their heads together to see what they could do in order to put down this strange doctrine. I think they must have come to the conclusion that the best thing to do is to ignore us, to let our letters go unanswered."

Two of the three ministers who did respond seemed to be concerned about the serious drain on membership that had been suffered by the Church of England. Both also seemed to attribute this to unimportant differences in detail and not to any fundamental differences in doctrine. "The differences which separate us are so slight," wrote the Reverend Perry Holbrook, "and the division among Christians causes such untold harm that I earnestly wish that good and true people would be content to hold their little notions private." The Reverend S. Arthur Berry expressed essentially the same view. "It is much to be deplored," he wrote, "that men should have severed themselves from the national church and so pandered to their own wishes that we find today several hundred different sects in England all divided rather by circumstantials than essentials." And Reverend Berry, reflecting an attitude that anyone who entertained views different from those taught by his own church was apostate, harumphed, "I certainly will read the pamphlet you so kindly sent, although I must confess that it seems to be published without authority."

Another minister who responded to the letter was even less cordial. "Some years ago," wrote Reverend George Hill, "I looked into the doctrines of the Mormons, and found them so utterly incredible that they cease to interest me. I have perused the pamphlet you sent to me and find that my early judgment is well warranted." Joseph Fielding's judgment of the ministers was no less explicit. "These men do not want the truth," he told Louie. "They are ministers by trade, because it is money in their pockets."

Whatever disappointments Joseph experienced in his work, whether in the rejection from the British clergy or in the abrupt, discourteous treatment he received in tracting, were soothed by the loving letters he received regularly from Louie. "My own precious Joseph," began a typical letter, "I do love you so much that I could not possibly tell you because it grows greater with each day that comes." Louie then identified one of the chief characteristics — trustworthiness — that distinguished Joseph from so many young men. "I do trust you so entirely," she wrote, "and have such perfect confidence in you that I am more happy in leaving you and being left than I could possibly be if you were as giddy as some young men are. But I know that you love duty far more than you do pleasure and so I have so much love and trust that I feel as though you are about as near being a perfect young man as could be." Often Louie enclosed pressed flowers with her letters as tokens of her love, a practice Joseph reciprocated. "Thank you for the flowers you sent," wrote Louie on another occasion. "You did not tell the names but the pansies I knew and Mama knew the others." But neither had to rely on pressed flowers to know of the mutual love they shared, for their words left no room for doubt. "There are a great many things to write about," she continued, "but somehow I like best to write 'I love you'. I sometimes think I could write it over, a thousand times, and still wish to write it again." And Joseph was also buoyed up by letters from his parents as well as from Louie's father. "I have always felt," wrote Lewis Shurtliff on one occasion, "that you would fill a glorious mission and gain an experience that will fit you for the exalted station that you are destined to fill in the future."

Not all news from home was good news. "I received letters from my father and my wife this evening containing the sad information of the death of my sister Alice," he wrote on May 11, 1901. "It is a dreadful blow to us all. I did not realize the seriousness of her illness, although I knew she was sick." After commenting on the hope for a reunion hereafter, which the gospel provides, Joseph, as he often did, offered a prayer in his diary: "May I always walk in the path of truth and honor the name I bear, that the meeting with my kindred may be to me indeed most sweet and everlasting, is my humble prayer."

About the same time Joseph received word of Alice's death, he learned that President George Q. Cannon had passed away April 12, 1901, in Monterey, California. With the passing of President Cannon, Joseph Fielding's father had become the ranking apostle behind President Lorenzo Snow and the one next in line for the prophetic office. The last step to that high place would be taken by President Joseph F. Smith only a few months after the release of his son and namesake from the British mission.

Meanwhile, Elder Smith continued to plug away at his clerical and missionary work. To go month after month without a convert was depressing. Neither his diary nor his letters home revealed the depth of his discouragement. Only years after his release did he disclose the extent of his sense of futility and failure at the time. He once told his son Joseph that conditions were so bad and the people so uninterested that he reached a frame of mind where he thought that he could not continue. One night he lay awake thinking of the need to work for passage home." (Smith and Stewart, *Life of Joseph Fielding Smith,* p. 92.) He never allowed such a thought to take root, however, and soon dismissed it as being unworthy of one who bore the name Joseph Fielding Smith.

As Elder Smith and his companions considered ways to make their work more effective and enjoyable, they hit upon the idea of organizing a quartet. And to give the quartet a touch of distinction, they gave it the name "The Sagebrush Singers." While Joseph Fielding had a good singing voice, he was always self-deprecating about it. So when Louie inquired about his singing, he painted a dark picture. "Well, I have no voice in the first place," he explained to her, "and what I have . . . is like a file." As to the performance of the quartet, he later explained, "After listening to us *sing,* people were glad to hear us *talk.*"

Despite Elder Smith's comments, the quartet undoubtedly enlivened their street meetings and added entertaining variety to the meetings of the Nottingham branch. And singing the songs of Zion with his missionary companions could not have failed to lift his spirits.

Other diversions broke the monotony of their seemingly unproductive proselyting work. The elders competed now and then in sports activities and occasionally attended English football or soccer games. And in September 1900, Joseph joined his brother, Richards, and seven other British missionaries on a two-week "vacation" to visit the world's fair then in progress in Paris, France. This diversion may be surprising to those who are acquainted with the present restrictive policy governing missionary travel. The change in policy results mainly from the changed circumstances. In the earlier days, when international travel was so difficult and expensive and when such a relatively few traveled abroad, it was felt to be wise to allow missionaries to see things of historic or cultural importance, things they might never again have the chance to see and that would broaden their understanding. That rationale applied with added force to this outing, since the world fair in Paris was a once-in-a-lifetime event.

Because London was on the route to Paris, the elders were also allowed to spend some time there, visiting the sites of historic interest. For someone like Joseph Fielding, whose ancestry traced to England and who had such a lively interest in history, the visit to London may well have been more significant to him than the visit to the Paris world fair. Here he was excited by Westminster Abbey, where he "saw the graves and tombs of many of the rulers and prominent men and women of England." Of special fascination in the Abbey was the ancient coronation chair on which the monarchs of Great Britain had been crowned for centuries. And beneath it was the famous Stone of Scone, reputed by ancient legend to have been the "pillow upon which the Patriarch Jacob rested at Bethel when he beheld the vision of angels." According to the legend, the stone was brought to the British Isles about 700 B.C. by an Israelite prophet, was first used in Ireland and then in Scotland in the coronation of their kings, and finally was brought to England and used for the same purpose. The stone, lying beneath the coronation chair, was said to symbolize the union of the Scottish and English kingdoms.

The predominant impression of Westminster Abbey on the elders was one of age and tradition. Salt Lake City's most prominent building, the temple, was dedicated only seven years before. But here was a more ornate building that counted its age in centuries, not years. And that same impression remained as other old buildings and sites were visited. At the White Tower they inspected a vast array of ancient armor, helmets, breastplates, greaves, cuirasses, shields, and gauntlets used by combatants of old to protect the vulnerable parts of the body. Here too were numerous artifacts and displays featuring significant campaigns or incidents in British military history. "We saw the blanket," wrote Joseph in his diary, "upon which General Wolfe died at the Heights of Abraham in Canada."

Leaving the White Tower, the elders walked through the storied parade grounds where for centuries royal troops, attired in their military regalia, had passed in review or engaged in jousts for the entertainment of the monarch and the royal entourage. At the nearby Beauchamp Tower, Joseph and his companions inspected the quarters where persons of rank were once imprisoned; and just outside they were shown the site of the old scaffold and the spot where Anne Boleyn and other persons of royalty had been beheaded.

At the Wakefield Tower, the elders saw the crown jewels of many of the monarchs of England, "including Victoria's, the grandest of all." The queen passed away only a few months after Elder Smith visited London. "We received the news tonight" he wrote on January 22, 1901, "of the death of Queen Victoria which occurred at 6:30 this evening. The newsboys are shouting and running to and fro selling their papers." In appraising the impact of her long reign, Joseph believed that under it England had "reached to the height of her glory" in "her Golden Age."

Crossing the channel, the missionaries traveled by train to Paris through the countryside of Picardy, dotted with prosperous farms whose well-tended fields had been cultivated for centuries. Many had a picture postcard beauty, bordered with neatly trimmed hedges or attractive stone walls. In the French capital, the missionaries were surprised to find many other elders from Utah who were serving in different parts of Europe. Among those from Germany was Elder Thomas E. McKay, a future General Authority and a younger brother of David O. McKay.

The fair that had attracted the elders to Paris showcased the scientific, technological, industrial, and artistic development of the French nation. On display in the numerous pavilions and halls were examples of French ingenuity and skill. After spending many hours looking at the various exhibits and displays, Joseph Fielding expressed satisfaction at what he had seen and pronounced the fair to be a huge success. Then, perhaps betraying a trace of national bias, he wrote that while the Paris World Fair was outstanding, "it was not as grand as the Chicago Fair."

While the fair was the main object of interest for the missionaries, there were many other things in beautiful Paris to claim their attention. Because the automobile was still in its infancy, the streets were not crowded with the crush of honking, hurrying taxis that in the decades ahead would give Paris still another claim to fame. Automobiles there had reached only about the same minimal level of density that the elders had observed on the Brooklyn Bridge. In the place of the cabs they found numerous carriages drawn by horses, whose rhythmic clopping on the paved or cobbled streets added an interesting and not unfamiliar din to the hum of the city. And while such a horde of horses created some problems of metropolitan pollution unknown in Paris today, they eliminated the blighting blanket of automobile exhaust that now chokes the world's major cities.

Joseph and his companions were impressed with the city's broad, tree-lined boulevards, the languid yet effusive manner of Parisians seen in the numerous sidewalk cafés that dotted the city, and the beauty of the Seine River as it flowed majestically through the capital. Because Joseph had never before been among people who spoke a language other than English, he was both amazed and mystified by the ability of Frenchmen to understand each other. "It seems strange," he wrote, "to be in a land where you cannot understand anyone or make them understand." And he was delighted with the numerous fruit and flower stands that seemed to be everywhere. "I have eaten more fruit today," he wrote the day of his arrival in Paris, "than I have had all the while I was in England."

The elders walked whenever possible, but they soon found that the things they wanted to see were scattered over a wide area of the city. So Joseph and the other British missionaries and sixteen elders who were working on the continent pooled their money and "hired a 'drag' for the day and visited points of interest in Paris."

While Paris, like London, impressed the elders with its age and traditions, the most pronounced impression it left upon them was the influence of the River Seine that snakes its way through the center of the city for eight miles. For young men raised in the desert, the sight of so much water with the surrounding greenery—the trees and shrubs bordering the cobbled quays at the water's edge and the line of graceful trees at the street level—impressed an image not to be forgotten.

Among the first stops on their tour was a visit to the Ile de la Cité, the small, ship-shaped island in the middle of the river. Here, at the heart of the ancient city, the early Roman governors had built their palace and their administrative offices. And here the Gallo-Roman boatmen had

100

built an altar to Jupiter. The site of this ancient pagan altar later became the site of the famous Cathedral of Notre Dame, which Joseph and his companions inspected with great interest. Like Westminster in London, this impressive chapel counted its age in centuries, not in years, like the Salt Lake Temple with which the elders were prone to make comparisons.

In turn, the elders visited, among other landmarks, the site of the Bastille, the ancient prison whose capture on July 14, 1878, became the symbol of the French Revolution; the Eiffel Tower; the Arch of Triumph, commissioned by Napoleon in 1806; the vast museum at the Louvre, which contained such masterpieces as the Venus de Milo and the Mona Lisa; and Napoleon's tomb, located in the Chapel of Saint Louis, part of the Hotel of the Invalids, founded by Louis XIV to shelter aged or crippled veterans.

During the day, the elders crossed many of the bridges that span the river, including the 200-year-old Pont Neuf, which is decorated with numerous grotesque masks and on which street vendors had set up their stands as they had done for many decades. They also rode through many of the parks that dot the city, whose thousands of trees, added to those bordering the river and lining the streets, created a luxuriant garden effect.

On another day, Joseph and several of his companions traveled to Versailles, a short distance from the city, to tour the ancient palace that had been occupied by many of France's monarchs and by Napoleon.

Leaving Paris, Joseph and the other British elders retraced their steps, returning to England and their respective conferences where they again took up their missionary labors. For Joseph, the two-week interlude was a time of refreshment and renewal. He returned to his duties with new enthusiasm and a sense of purpose. By this time, he had begun the last leg of his mission, which would end within a few months. During that time, he busied himself with the daily office duties, preparing correspondence, managing the conference office, handling and receipting for the tithing paid by members in the conference, preparing reports, shepherding the elders who passed through Nottingham, and acting for the conference president when he was out of the city. Interspersed with these duties was the usual round of tracting, street meetings, and supervision of activities in the Nottingham Branch. In all of this, much was simply boring routine, made worse by the absence of baptizing success. Yet, in the resolute discharge of his duties, performed under difficult circumstances, Elder Smith developed qualities of character that were vital to the prophetic role he would ultimately play, the qualities of discipline, patience, and persistence. And with these came a greater spirituality, enriched by the emergence and growth of the gift of healing, which had been promised to him in his patriarchal blessing. The members of the Church in the areas where he served, perhaps sensing this special quality in Elder Smith, called on him for blessings of health or comfort. The most dramatic example occurred in the case of Georgie Lord. This young English boy was seriously ill with a respiratory infection that so constricted his breathing that his face had turned a bluish red. Following the administration, he was restored to health, suffering no ill effects from his illness. At that time, and in that place, where medical skills were either minimal or unavailable, members were more inclined to seek divine help in time of illness than to turn to medical doctors.

As Elder Smith's term of missionary service wound down in the spring of 1901, word was received in Nottingham that Elder Francis M. Lyman of the Twelve had been appointed by the First Presidency to replace Platte D. Lyman as the mission president. Later Elder Stephen Walker and Joseph were invited to attend a special meeting on May 25 at Bradford in the Leeds Conference, where the outgoing and incoming mission presidents counseled with the leaders from several conferences about the change in administration. Joseph's brother, Richards, who had served his entire mission in the Leeds Conference, was present, as was their friend William Armstrong, who was then president of the Grimsby Conference.

While at Bradford, Joseph received a letter from his father asking that before leaving for home, he go to Toppesfield in Essex County, the ancient home of the Smith clan. There he was to search for genealogical information about his ancestors. Since President Lyman had informed Joseph he would sail for home on June 20, there was no time to waste. He hurriedly returned to Nottingham, where he spent several days training Elder J. S. Dixon, his replacement, in the duties of conference clerk, packed a few clothes in his stick grip, and caught the train to London.

What a difference two years can make! The well-dressed, dignified man who traveled alone by train from Nottingham to London in early June 1901 differed markedly from the frightened, homesick young elder who had traveled alone from Liverpool to Nottingham two years before. Now Elder Joseph Fielding Smith was quite at home among these strangers who spoke English with such a curious accent. Nor did he seem intimidated by them nor reluctant to identify himself to them. Having experienced almost every known form of verbal abuse and personal rejection for two years on the doorsteps and street corners of England, Joseph was prepared to deal with any contingency that might arise between him and his fellow passengers. Moreover, the errand that would take him to Toppesfield was cause for exhilaration, as was the knowledge that within a matter of weeks he would be reunited with Louie and other members of his family.

Joseph easily made the transfer in London to the train that took him eastward to the quiet village that had nurtured his ancestors for generations. There he presented himself at the rectory of the parish priest, the Reverend H. B. Barnes, requesting permission to examine his parish records. The priest granted the request, and Joseph spent many hours poring over these old records, extracting names, dates, and places that helped fill the gaps in his family pedigree. This valuable information would later be used by members of the family to perform vicarious ordinance work for these ancestors.

Little did Joseph Fielding realize that in fulfilling this assignment made by his father, he had been introduced to an aspect of Church work that would loom large in his future apostolic career; for thirty years he would serve as the president of the Genealogical Society of Utah and in the presidency of the Salt Lake Temple, either as a counselor or as the president.

It is easy to surmise that the short time Elder Smith spent in Toppesfield on this occasion was, perhaps, the high point of his two-year stay in England. To visit the ancient church where his ancestors had worshiped, or had been christened, baptized, and married, or where their funeral rites had been performed likely gave him a new feeling of kinship toward them. And to see their names in the old church registers, written long ago by ancient scriveners who knew these forebears, who were acquainted with their appearances and personalities, doubtless converted them in his mind from mere names on paper to real people to whom he owed a debt for his very physical existence.

When Elder Smith returned to Nottingham from his short stay in Toppesfield, he was ready to go home. Only a few things remained to be done. He carefully cleaned, ironed, and packed his clothes; delivered a farewell address to the members of the Nottingham Branch; and, on June 19, 1901, left for Liverpool. There, later in the day, he met Richards, who had traveled there from Leeds. The following afternoon, Thursday, June 20, the Smith brothers were accompanied to the Mersey River pierhead by members of the mission office staff. There they boarded their ship, the *Commonwealth*, which was destined for Boston. The return voyage differed little from the one that had taken them to England, except that the *Commonwealth* had considerably more zip than the *Pennland* and covered the distance in only eight days.

The missionary brothers were greeted at Boston by

their father, who had adjusted his busy schedule to be there when they arrived. With him were Richards' mother, Sarah, and two sisters, Minerva and Ina. The decision to allow Sarah rather than Julina to accompany President Smith on this trip likely was dictated by a desire to help ease Sarah's grief at the recent death of her daughter, Alice.

The Boston area held a special attraction for the Smith family. Five ancestors, on lines other than the Smiths, were aboard the *Mayflower*, which landed at nearby Plymouth in 1620. And, as already noted, the first Smith ancestor, Robert Smith, arrived only eighteen years later to establish the family name and reputation on New England soil. So while they were there, President Smith and the other members of the family toured the area for several days, visiting places of historic interest. The party then traveled to Buffalo, New York, where they visited the Pan American Exposition that was in progress there. Since Buffalo was so close to Niagara, the party made a side trip there and spent several hours viewing the falls before catching a train west. They arrived in Salt Lake City on Tuesday, July 9.

Chapter Six

Foundations for Family and Career

The Salt Lake depot was more crowded than usual this July 9, 1901. The increment was caused chiefly by the presence of the numerous Smith clan, which had turned out en masse to welcome home President Joseph F. Smith and the family members traveling with him. Most conspicuous among these were the two returning missionaries, Richards and Joseph Fielding, who were special objects of the ritualistic hugs and kisses for which the family had become so widely known. The Smith who especially caught Joseph Fielding's eye, however, and who received more than a perfunctory embrace and kiss on the cheek was Louie Smith, who was there with a contingent of Shurtliff in-laws from Ogden.

After visiting briefly with his mother and other members of the family in Salt Lake City, Joseph accompanied Louie to Ogden, where she had been living with her parents. There they spent a few quiet, unhurried days, enjoying each other's company, catching up on the news, and laying their plans for the future.

As they assessed the situation, two items emerged at

106

the top of their agenda of needs: housing and a job. The first was easily solved when Joseph's parents invited the young couple to take up residence again in the Old Family Home on West First North in Salt Lake City. Donnie and David A. had both married while Joseph was in England, so there was ample room in the house. The second was more difficult. Job hunting first took Joseph back to ZCMI, where he had worked for several years. The only job available was in the wholesale department doing the same kind of drudging work he had done before. This he declined. Since no other prospects opened up immediately, he gratefully accepted a temporary job in the Salt Lake County Clerk's office, which he obtained through the influence of his new brother-in-law, Alonzo Pratt Kesler, Donnie's husband. While working there, he received an offer of permanent employment as a collector of excise taxes in several western states; this would have required periodic visits to establishments that sold beer and liquor. In thinking over this offer, Joseph conferred with his father, who counseled against accepting it. "Remember this, son," he told Joseph, "the best company is none too good for you." Soon after came a job offer that was ideally suited to Joseph Fielding Smith's temperament and interests. Anthon H. Lund, a member of the Twelve who had succeeded Franklin D. Richards as the Church historian while Joseph Fielding was in England, offered him a job as a clerk in his office. Joseph accepted with alacrity and soon became absorbed in a work that would dominate most of the remaining years of his long life.

In the Historian's Office, Joseph Fielding found himself surrounded by a group of men who would challenge his abilities and discipline to the utmost. The first, of course, was the fifty-seven-year-old historian, Anthon H. Lund, who had been a member of the Twelve for twelve years. A kind, scholarly man, who would later become a counselor to Joseph Fielding's father in the First Presidency, Elder Lund took a paternal interest in his new twenty-five-year-old employee, going out of his way to

train and motivate him as if he were a son. Joseph reciprocated these feelings and, in demonstration, once forcibly
removed a man from his home who persisted in berating
his benefactor. By way of explaining or, perhaps, justifying
this unusual conduct, Joseph said afterward, "I would not
listen to any criticism of my beloved President Lund." Next
was forty-six-year-old Orson F. Whitney, an assistant historian and longtime bishop of the Eighteenth Ward in Salt
Lake City, who, within five years, would be called to the
Twelve. Elder Whitney, who was the author of a multivolume history of Utah, stood foremost among the literary
stylists of his day. He later composed a Mormon classic
entitled *Elias,* an epic poem in the style of Homer and Virgil,
which portrays the plan of salvation in dramatic form. He
was also a biographer, having written a biography of his
grandfather, Heber C. Kimball.

Another assistant historian, Brigham H. Roberts, forty-
four at the time, was an even more prolific writer than
Orson F. Whitney. A member of the First Council of Seventy, Elder Roberts left a rich literary legacy in his major
contributions to the compiling and writing of both the
Documentary History of the Church and the *Comprehensive
History of the Church*. He was also a biographer, having
written a biography of one of his heroes, President John
Taylor. Finally, there was assistant historian, Andrew Jenson, the compiler and writer of the monumental multivolume *LDS Biographical Encyclopedia.*

One can imagine the excitement and enthusiasm with
which Joseph Fielding took up his new duties, surrounded
by men of such character and accomplishment. There can
be little doubt that the example of these men and the stim-
ulus of working with them day by day provided a powerful
motivation to Joseph Fielding Smith to improve his skills
and to increase the volume of his own literary output.

It is not often that a man is so blessed as to make his
living doing the thing he enjoys most and for which he
has a natural aptitude. Joseph was one of these fortunate
ones. From the time his mother introduced him to the

Millennial Star when he was only a boy, he had loved Church history. Now he had access to all of the original documents and the artifacts pertaining to the history of the Church from the very beginning. He was studious and analytical, and he knew how to work. The habits of discipline and patience he had developed in the mission field would now be valuable tools in the career that lay ahead of him, as would his clear and precise literary style, honed as he had faithfully kept his diary and struggled with the voluminous correspondence in the Nottingham Conference House. The promising young man with the famous name was now on the path that would ultimately lead him to the prophetic office as president of the Church.

Within days after Joseph Fielding began working in the historian's office, an event occurred that made his name even more famous. On October 6, 1901, his father was sustained as first counselor to President Lorenzo Snow, filling the vacancy created by the death of George Q. Cannon. At the same time, Rudger Clawson was sustained as the Prophet's second counselor. But neither counselor was ever set apart. On October 10, 1901, eighty-seven-year-old Lorenzo Snow quietly and unexpectedly passed away. His death dissolved the First Presidency, which had been sustained only four days before, and resulted in the automatic release of his two counselors. His death also left Joseph F. Smith as the ranking apostle and, therefore, the actual head of the Church. According to precedent that was by then well established, Joseph F. Smith was ordained soon after as the president of the Church at a meeting of the Twelve in the upper room of the Salt Lake Temple. That action was later ratified at a Solemn Assembly on November 10, 1901.

Because of these historic actions taken within weeks after Joseph Fielding Smith began working as a clerk in the Historian's Office, his father and namesake stood as the sixth president of The Church of Jesus Christ of Latter-day Saints. The father's change in status cast a reflected prominence on the son and opened many doors of opportunity to him that otherwise would have been closed. And, judging from diary entries that expressed concern about living up to his name, it imposed powerful pressures upon him to conduct himself in a way that would reflect nothing but credit on his father and on other ancestors who bore the name Joseph Smith.

But other important changes at this time also affected Joseph Fielding Smith. Joseph Fielding's friend and benefactor, Anthon H. Lund, was sustained as the second counselor in the First Presidency; and his brother, Hyrum Mack Smith, only four years older than he, was sustained as a member of the Twelve. These circumstances, added to the fact that his cousin, John Henry Smith, was already a member of the Twelve, were calculated to give Joseph Fielding a sense of security, freeing his mind of any concern about his employment and opening the way for him to establish his family life on a solid foundation.

With an assured income, Joseph's and Louie's most pressing need was permanent housing for themselves and the children whom they confidently expected would be added to their family. That expectation took on more meaning when, a few months after Joseph Fielding began to work in the Historian's Office, Louie conceived her first child. The knowledge that fatherhood was imminent spurred Joseph Fielding into activity to make his and Louie's dream of owning their own home a reality.

At the time of their marriage, Joseph's parents gave him and Louie a lot at 165 North Second West as a wedding gift. It was just around the corner from Joseph F. Smith's home at 333 West First North. Such close proximity would make it convenient for Joseph to work on the new home while he and Louie continued to live in the Old Smith Family Home. They were comfortable there, more so than before, because after Joseph F. Smith became president of the Church, he and Julina and their unmarried children vacated the old home and moved into the Beehive House, then the official residence of the president of the Church. But Joseph and Louie felt the need for a place of their own where they could live independently and establish their own agenda and family traditions.

To reduce expenses, Joseph Fielding did much of the work himself, contracting out, piecemeal, the kind of work he felt incompetent to perform or did not want to perform. Since there was an old foundation on the lot where a previous home had stood, it was necessary to clear this away before the work on their own home could commence. Joseph did most of this preparatory work himself, laboring in the evenings or on Saturdays as time would allow. He then contracted with George Nebeker to help prepare a cellar, purchased a set of architectural plans, and employed Mathew Noal to do the carpentry work. The building permit was issued on June 17, 1902. The house was sufficiently completed in a year so that Joseph and Louie could move in. "Today is Louie's 27th birthday," Joseph wrote in his diary on June 16, 1903. "I moved the cook stove into the new home this evening; David and Wesley helping me. The carpet men from the Co-op Furniture Company also laid a carpet." It took only three days to complete the move so that the Smiths were able to celebrate Independence Day in their new home.

It was a two-story brick house that faced east. In the style of the day, it had a large front porch. On the main floor were a parlor, dining room, kitchen, pantry, bedroom, and bath. Aside from the cellar, this was the only part of the house that was finished off; the second floor was uncompleted. Later, additional bedrooms, a study for Joseph, and another bathroom were added there.

By the time Joseph and Louie moved into their new house, their family had grown to three. Their first child, Josephine, was born September 18, 1902, in the old Smith home just a few months after work on the new home had commenced. Louie had had a difficult time carrying her baby, and the birth was prolonged and complicated. She had spent many weeks of her pregnancy in Ogden, where her mother could take care of her. At times they feared she might die or suffer a miscarriage. But she had endured

111

the pain and discomfort and was rewarded for her suffering with the gift of a bright and beautiful baby who was given the female version of her father's name.

The move into their new home did not entail a transfer to another Church unit, so the Smiths retained their membership in the Sixteenth Ward of the Salt Lake Stake. Here the young couple became exceedingly active again as they had been in the early months of their marriage. Because of his experience in Nottingham, Joseph Fielding was called as a home missionary soon after his return from England, a position in which he served for nine years, being released only because of his call to the Twelve in 1910. His orientation toward missionary work also resulted in his call as one of the presidents of the Twenty-fourth Quorum of Seventy in the same year he and Louie moved into their new home. His duties there included service as the quorum instructor. About the same time, he was called as a member of the general board of the YMMIA, a call for which he was well qualified because of his service on the Salt Lake Stake YMMIA board prior to his mission. In this position, which he filled for sixteen years, he would work closely with his father, who was the general superintendent of the organization, and with Elder Heber J. Grant of the Twelve and Elder B. H. Roberts of the First Council of Seventy, who were his father's assistants in the superintendency. And as a guarantee that he wouldn't get into mischief in his off hours, Joseph Fielding was also called as a member of the high council of the Salt Lake Stake in 1904, the year following his and Louie's move into their new home. His brother, Hyrum, set him apart to this position and at the same time ordained him a high priest.

With these significant ecclesiastical responsibilities at the general, stake, and ward levels, and with his role in the Historian's Office, Joseph Fielding Smith was in the process of receiving a thorough, overall training and indoctrination in the policies and procedures of the Church and in the practical application of its doctrines, a training that was vital for him to receive. And perhaps more important to him than any of these in terms of the role he ultimately played was his continuing behind-the-scenes role as his father's unofficial secretary and confidant. As his letters to Joseph Fielding in the mission field indicated, the father appreciated the son's spirit and attitude. He seemed to have no sense of pride or arrogance, nor did he seem to have any aspiration to office. Instead he showed a modest deference to his father's wishes and an eager desire to serve and to please him. Notwithstanding these qualities of character, Joseph Fielding had a healthy desire to become better qualified to serve in whatever position he might be called to fill. He also had a healthy self-confidence, was not reluctant to express his views, and openly manifested a desire to gain more wisdom and understanding. Given such a combination of characteristics and circumstances, President Smith seemed completely comfortable in taking the son into his confidence and making him privy to the inner workings of the Church at the highest level.

But the Prophet used his son not only to handle his official and personal correspondence and as a sounding board for his ideas and plans but also as an emissary in conveying or receiving messages. Occasionally Joseph Fielding was even sent to fill speaking assignments for his father. One notable example occurred when the Prophet, unable to fill a commitment to dedicate a chapel in Brigham City, Utah, sent Joseph Fielding as a substitute without telling the stake president, Oleen H. Stohl, of the change. There are differing versions of President Stohl's reaction and comments when he met the train to find that the Joseph Fielding Smith who had arrived was not the Joseph Fielding Smith whom he expected and wanted. The version most often told, and certainly the funniest, has President Stohl saying, "I could bawl. We were expecting the President of the Church and we get a boy instead." Flashing his wry sense of humor, Joseph, in another version, is reported to have answered, "I could bawl too."

Many of the assignments Joseph Fielding received from

his father were strictly personal and pertained only to him or the family. Apparently satisfied with Joseph Fielding's genealogical research in Toppesfield, England, President Smith also sent him to Essex County, Massachusetts, to gather further information. The son left in July 1902, when Louie was having great difficulty carrying her first baby. With him was Licurgus A. Wilson, whom President Joseph F. Smith had employed to help compile the family genealogy. The pair was gone for almost a month. In addition to searching records at Salem, Massachusetts, they visited Robert Smith's old farm at Boxford and the Asael Smith farm near Topsfield. While browsing through the Topsfield cemetery, they found a monument honoring early Smith ancestors erected in 1873 by George A. Smith, then a counselor to President Brigham Young. George A. was a descendant of Asael Smith through "Uncle John" Smith, a brother of Joseph Smith Sr.

The information gleaned during this trip not only formed the basis for Joseph Fielding Smith's first book but also confirmed or corrected basic facts necessary to link up branches of the Smith clan that had grown from their first American ancestor, Robert Smith. And that record, added to the information Joseph Fielding Smith uncovered at Essex County, England, further fleshed out the family tree.

This trip was the first of several Joseph Fielding took in the early years of his employment in the Historian's Office. The next one, in the summer of 1904, was to Missouri to gather data for the Church archives. He was accompanied on this occasion by his father-in-law, Lewis Shurtliff. The pair met James G. Duffin, president of the Central States Mission, at Independence, Missouri; he served as their guide. Between Independence, the location of the temple site, and Adam-ondi-Ahman to the north, were places of great historic interest, both to the Church and to Joseph Fielding Smith personally. As he visited them, the future Church historian made copious diary entries about the things he saw and the people he interviewed. It was at Richmond that his grandfather Hyrum

Smith and the Prophet and others were temporarily imprisoned in a home before being moved to the nearby Liberty jail. At that house occurred the well-known incident when Joseph Smith rebuked the vulgar soldiers who were guarding them. And in Richmond were to be seen the graves of Oliver Cowdery and David Whitmer, two of the three witnesses who were shown the golden plates by the Angel Moroni.

At Liberty was the cramped and dingy jail where Joseph and Hyrum had been illegally incarcerated for many months. There the Prophet Joseph demonstrated his family deference to Joseph Fielding's grandfather by insisting that Hyrum, the eldest of the two, always sit at the head of the dining table at mealtime. And it was there the martyrs received a visit from their wives, Mary Fielding Smith and Emma Hale Smith, who traveled in a springless wagon from Far West while Aunt Mercy Thompson tended Mary's baby, Joseph F.

Joseph Fielding's visit to Far West was especially significant. As he stood on the temple site, he could see the lot just across the street where once had stood the house in which his father was born. "My father was born there November 13, 1838," wrote he, "just 11 days after his father was carried off a prisoner by the mob." It was a source of amazement that there were no buildings in sight to identify this place as the site of a once-thriving community. "Today the evidence of a settlement has all disappeared," he noted, "and the land has been converted into farms and pastures." Notwithstanding, Joseph Fielding recognized its potential as the site for a city. "It is one of the most beautiful spots for the location of a city in the world," he wrote. With the customary care of a historian, he also noted that the temple lot stood "on the highest rise," that the cornerstones were still in place, and that the public square was "now a field." "It was on this square," Joseph continued, "that the Saints were forced at the bayonet point to sign away their property to defray the expenses of the mob which drove them from the state."

These and other similar events imbued Joseph Fielding with a sense of outrage that was never completely extinguished. He could not speak or write about them without showing the contempt and disdain he had for those who had so brutally treated his people.

At Gallatin, Joseph Fielding interviewed blind, eighty-three-year-old Joseph McGee, a lifetime resident, who was seventeen years old at the time of the Mormon expulsion from Missouri. He remembered many of the events during that dark period and, responding to questions, related them in detail. He saw Joseph Smith before his imprisonment, whom he characterized as "a powerful man," and told of a wrestling match he had witnessed when the Prophet defeated John Brassfield, "the champion wrestler of the county" in the first two falls of a three-fall match. He also said John Brassfield was one of the guards at the Liberty jail accused of aiding the Smith brothers when they escaped in the spring of 1839. He reported the locals were so angered by the escape that they rode the chief jailer, sheriff William Morgan, on an iron bar "so violently that he died shortly after."

Mr. McGee served as a major in the union army during the Civil War until 1864, when he was blinded. With such a background, he provided interesting commentary about the residents of Missouri. "The Missourians were mostly from the Southern States," he reported, "principally Kentucky and Tennessee. They were hospitable and would feed a stranger and lodge him, yet they were a rough, uneducated class, very quarrelsome and delighted in fighting even among themselves." During the war, therefore, he said "the whole section of country in and around Missouri was terribly divided, neighbors fighting neighbors, sons against fathers, in opposing armies. Especially in Jackson County was the suffering great." In this, Joseph Fielding saw a fulfillment of predictions made by the Prophet about retributions that would be visited upon Missouri and its people for wrongs committed against the Latter-day Saints.

At Adam-ondi-Ahman, Joseph Fielding found that the altar of stones there had been partially destroyed by some of the local residents while digging for gold, which, according to false reports, had been buried there by the Latter-day Saints. He noted that this altar "was built on the highest portion of a bluff or mound on the north bank of the Grand River." From that vantage point, he and his companions could see the fertile valley of Adam-ondi-Ahman, lying to the southwest, through which the river lazily snaked its way. This valley was sacred to Joseph Fielding and the Latter-day Saints as the place where Adam convened a family council before he died and where, as part of the winding-up scenes, a grand priesthood council would meet under Adam's direction. While in Missouri on this occasion, Joseph Fielding took in still another fair when he and his father-in-law went downriver to visit the exposition and fair then in progress at St. Louis.

On returning to Salt Lake from Missouri in the late summer of 1904, Joseph Fielding took up a task that had occupied much of his time during the previous months. He helped gather material to submit to the United States Senate Committee on Privileges and Elections, which was then holding hearings to determine whether Reed Smoot should be allowed to continue to serve as U.S. senator from Utah. Senator Smoot, who was a member of the Twelve, was elected to the Senate in January 1903. He took his seat two months later. In noting that fact, Joseph wrote in his diary on March 5, 1903: "Honorable Reed Smoot took his seat as United States Senator from Utah today." He added that the ministers of Salt Lake City had "tried to stir up an opposition that he may be denied his seat," and that "many false reports" had been circulated. Indicating he felt nothing would come of these charges, Joseph Fielding noted that they were "all to no effect." This feeling that the controversy would blow over was buttressed when on May 29, 1903, President Theodore Roosevelt visited Salt Lake City to appraise the situation, following which he spoke out openly in favor of Senator Smoot. However, even the support of one as popular and influential as President Roosevelt was insufficient to thwart the campaign of vilification mounted by the senator's enemies.

Since Reed Smoot had never been a polygamist, that charge, which had been successfully used to deny B. H. Roberts a seat in Congress several years before, was unavailable to his detractors. Nor did there appear to be any character flaws or lack of personal qualification that would disentitle him to serve. In these circumstances, the thrust of the senator's enemies was to attack the Church, attributing to him as a member of the Twelve any supposed shortcomings of the Church and its hierarchy. It was charged, among other things, that the Church had taught disloyalty to the government and its laws and was therefore treasonous. Moreover, it was asserted that the Church, through its leaders, continued to teach and sanction plural marriage. Because of the broad nature of these charges, the implications of which extended to almost every aspect of the controversies between the Church and its enemies from the beginning, the Historical Department was asked to ferret out any documentary evidence that would help answer them. And so, Joseph Fielding and the other clerks in the Historian's Office had been busily involved searching through the records to find anything that might assist those who were defending Senator Smoot before the committee.

The work of this committee became very personal to the Smith family when, in February 1904, President Joseph F. Smith was subpoenaed to testify before it. Joseph Fielding carefully followed the news reports of the proceedings, making pointed diary entries about them and about his father's interrogators. While the questions delved into many aspects of President Smith's career as a General Authority, they focused chiefly on his role as a polygamist and on whether he had continued to teach plural marriage or to perform or authorize the performance of plural marriages after the Manifesto. President Smith openly admitted that he had continued to live with his wives after 1890.

He denied, however, that he had taken other plural wives after that date, or had performed plural marriages thereafter, or had authorized others to do so, and he denied that he had continued to teach or advocate polygamy. Some of the questions that elicited these denials were very personal and suggestive. Joseph Fielding was infuriated by them and by the lack of respect shown toward his father. "The 'siege' in Washington continues," he wrote on March 4, 1904, "with my father on the stand. He has been forced to answer all kinds of questions which have been asked by moral lepers who are unworthy to unloosen his shoes, and some of these vile creatures are, too, members of the committee."

The committee continued its hearings for more than two years after President Smith testified, and in June 1906, by a vote of eight to five, it recommended that Senator Smoot be deprived of his seat. However, the full Senate rejected this recommendation several months later, which allowed him to continue to serve, a distinguished service that would extend another twenty-five years.

In the aftermath of his testimony before the committee, President Joseph F. Smith, with the concurrence of his brethren, issued what has since been known as the Worldwide Manifesto. Its purpose was to make clear that the original manifesto of 1890 was intended to apply to all members of the Church in all lands and to eliminate any questions of the kind raised during the lengthy Smoot hearings.

When he wrote his father's biography many years afterward, Elder Joseph Fielding Smith analyzed the Smoot hearings and his father's participation in them. There he pointed out that the chairman of the Committee on Privileges and Elections, Senator Julius C. Burrows of Michigan, who was among the most biased of its members, was the nephew of Sylvester Smith, an excommunicant from the Church. Sylvester Smith, no relative to Joseph Smith, was once a secretary to the Prophet as well as a member of Zion's Camp. He later became embittered toward the

119

Church and made scurrilous accusations against the Prophet and other leaders. It was Joseph Fielding's belief that Senator Burrows had been strongly influenced in his attitudes by the example of his uncle, and that his rough-shod treatment of President Joseph F. Smith during the Smoot hearings was a kind of unreasoning attempt to strike back, through a descendant, at those whom he believed had wronged his uncle.

In the forefront of the public media that drummed up opposition to Reed Smoot during the Senate hearings was the *Salt Lake Tribune*. Owned by Thomas Kearns, a wealthy Utahn who had made his fortune through mining, the Tribune carried on a relentless smear campaign against Senator Smoot and other Church leaders, chiefly President Joseph F. Smith. The blunt articles and editorials in this paper, which reflected the hatred of its owner, were mostly written by a skilled and bitter apostate, Frank J. Cannon. Both Thomas Kearns and Frank Cannon were former United States senators from Utah. Both seemed to feel that their fall from political prominence was the handiwork of the hierarchy of the Mormon Church. And both seem to have selected President Joseph F. Smith as the chief target of their animosity. So angered were Joseph Fielding and other sons of President Smith at the treatment their father received in the columns of the *Tribune* that they once decided to go down to the Tribune office and give Frank Cannon a good "thrashing." They were stopped by their father, who had learned about the plan. Joseph Fielding then turned to a more peaceful and effective way to respond. He wrote an article defending the Church and President Smith that was published in the two major newspapers in Ogden, Utah. In explaining his actions, Joseph wrote on March 18, 1905: "For a long time past a very bitter anti-Mormon feeling has existed against the President of the Church, and the 'Mormon' people. Frank J. Cannon is the most bitter anti-Mormon . . . and as an editor of *The Tribune* made many vicious assaults on the presidency of the church."

These attacks by the *Tribune* coincided with similar attacks made by leaders of the Reorganized Church. On January 28, 1905, the *Daily Star* of Toronto, Canada published an interview with Richard Evans, a counselor in the presidency of the Reorganized Church, which, Joseph Fielding wrote, was a "wilful misrepresentation of the doctrines of the Latter-day Saints." In response, Joseph again took up his pen to write another letter, this one to the editor of the *Daily Star,* answering point by point the charges made in its article. He also wrote directly to Mr. Evans, which opened up a correspondence between the two, in which they discussed the differences of interpretation and understanding between the two churches. The main point of difference that emerged was that of plural marriage. It was the contention of Mr. Evans and the Reorganized Church that the practice of plural marriage among the Latter-day Saints was commenced by Brigham Young, not the Prophet Joseph Smith.

The manner in which Joseph Fielding went about responding to this issue demonstrates a key quality of his character that would appear frequently throughout his life. Since this involved only an issue of fact, he wanted facts to support his position. This led him to conduct a series of personal interviews with women then living in Salt Lake City who had been polygamous wives of Joseph Smith or who knew of his involvement in plural marriage; the researcher obtained many statements or affidavits from these women. In late May 1905, he visited Peter Lott with his uncle, John Smith, the Church Patriarch. There they examined the family Bible of Cornelius P. Lott, which contained an entry showing that the Prophet Joseph Smith was married to Melissa Lott. A month later he interviewed his aunt, Lucy Walker Smith, who confirmed that she, too, was married to the Prophet and also said she "knew personally and positively that the Partridge sisters and Sarah and Maria Lawrence were also the Prophet's wives." Finally, in late September of the same year, Joseph Fielding and his mother visited Catherine Phillips Smith, who affirmed that the Prophet Joseph Smith sealed her as a plural wife to his brother, Hyrum Smith, Joseph Fielding's grandfather.

Armed with these facts obtained from original sources, Joseph Fielding wrote and had published a booklet entitled *Blood Atonement and the Origin of Plural Marriage.*

During this same period the other counselor in the presidency of the Reorganized Church, Frederick M. Smith, became involved in the controversy. Frederick was a grandson of the Prophet Joseph Smith and a counselor to his father, Joseph Smith III, the president of the Reorganized Church. Frederick visited Salt Lake City in the summer of 1905 at the invitation of President Joseph F. Smith to attend a Smith family reunion, held in conjunction with a celebration commemorating the 104th anniversary of Hyrum Smith's birth. While he was in Salt Lake City, Joseph Fielding served as Frederick's host, showing him around the city and inviting him to his home for dinner. During this visit, Frederick added fuel to the controversy and greatly annoyed Joseph Fielding when he published an open letter in the *Salt Lake Tribune* addressed to the people of Royalton and Sharon, Vermont, protesting the plan of the Mormon Church to construct a monument there in memory of the Prophet Joseph Smith, Frederick's grandfather. In it, according to Joseph Fielding's diary entry of June 30, 1905, "He accused the leaders of the church of all manner of wickedness, called them law breakers and declared that they . . . were not worthy the fellowship of honorable people."

After such a scathing denunciation, Joseph Fielding was surprised when Frederick called on him the next day "to see how he felt about his article in the morning paper." Joseph minced no words in telling his cousin he was annoyed, especially because no mention was made of these charges when Frederick was a guest in his house. There followed a spirited discussion about the introduction of plural marriage among the Latter-day Saints. Joseph showed his cousin writings from his own church publications that admitted that the Prophet Joseph Smith had introduced this doctrine. At this, Frederick "became very excited and had to retract some statements that he made." He also "declared that if his grandfather introduced plural marriage — which he practically admitted that he did — that it only lessened him in his [Frederick's] estimation."

Following this confrontation, the dialogue between Joseph Fielding and his cousin heated up. In collaboration with Frank J. Cannon, Frederick later wrote an article published in the *Saints Herald,* the Reorganized Church's newspaper, in which he repeated and embellished the charges made in the *Tribune* article. Joseph Fielding responded promptly. "I wrote a reply to a vicious attack on the authorities of the church," he noted in January 1906, "which appeared in the *Saints Herald.* Again, he supported his arguments with a citation of facts that could not be denied or ignored.

Undoubtedly, Joseph Fielding's spirited and able defense of the Church and its leaders loomed large in the action taken at the general conference in April 1906. At that time, he was sustained as an assistant Church historian. This advancement elevated him to a level of official prominence that lifted him from the ranks of clerical anonymity, added weight to his words, and opened doors to research and writing opportunities that had previously been closed. The appointment coincided with the call of Orson F. Whitney to the Quorum of the Twelve which, in terms of authority and responsibility, placed Joseph on a par with B. H. Roberts, Andrew Jenson, and Amos Musser, the other assistant historians, all four of whom reported directly to the Church historian, Anthon H. Lund.

Because of his new position, the notoriety he had received from his writings, and the multiple positions he had held at the ward, stake, and general levels, Joseph Fielding came to be much in demand as a speaker. Not long after the controversy between him and Frederick M. Smith arose, he was invited to give a lecture at a special meeting in Ogden, Utah. In preparation, he assembled the pertinent facts about the schism that had resulted in the creation of the Reorganized Church. He then wove them into a clear and convincing narrative. Later, encouraged by his father-in-law and others, he expanded the scope of the subject treated at the lecture and prepared a booklet for publication entitled *Origin of the Reorganized Church: The Question of Succession.* Still later, he broadened the scope of this booklet and published a second edition that received a wide distribution.

In preparing the booklets on plural marriage and succession in the presidency and the earlier one about Asael Smith, Joseph Fielding proved himself to be an able, articulate advocate for the Church and its leaders and a convincing exponent of Church history and doctrine. This, added to his name and important family connections; his solid service as a missionary; his exemplary role as a son, husband, and father; and his penchant for hard work gave him an aura of success and an expectation of future prominence. It also increased confidence from others, who sought his assistance in matters of sensitivity and importance. These factors were doubtless influential in his appointment in January 1907 to a prestigious committee whose purpose was "to prepare data for a defense of the church against assaults made upon it by its enemies." Included in the membership of this committee were three General Authorities, Elders Orson F. Whitney and David O. McKay of the Twelve and Elder B. H. Roberts of the First Council of Seventy. Others of special prominence on the committee were James E. Talmage, president of the University of Utah and a future member of the Twelve, and General Richard W. Young, a son of Brigham Young. Over the long period this committee functioned, Joseph Fielding Smith, its junior member, was in frequent contact with these men of prominence and ability who were able to gauge his character and competence and the depth of his knowledge and commitment. He seems to have been accepted by them as an equal, as one qualified to stand with them in the front ranks of Church leadership. His service on this committee also led Joseph to an even more detailed study of the voluminous documents in the Church's historical archives, a study that helped fill any gaps in his knowledge about the origin and the development of the Church and the character and accomplishments of its leaders. All this would be of vital importance in fulfilling the heavy responsibilities that would come to him in the future.

Meanwhile, in addition to these responsibilities and many others, Joseph continued to serve his father in the unofficial capacity of a private secretary. Indeed, his expanded knowledge of Church doctrine and history and his understanding of the critical issues facing the Church better equipped him to render such service. So, the Prophet began to look more and more to his son and namesake to handle both his private and official correspondence and to serve as a personal emissary, as a sounding board, and as a traveling companion. As to the latter, Joseph Fielding accompanied his father on an extended trip into Old Mexico in September 1905. There they visited the Mormon colonies in Dublan and Juarez, holding meetings with the members and leaders of the Church in this remote area. This was the first time Joseph Fielding met Anthony W. Ivins, the stake president in the Mexican colonies, who, two years later, would be called to the Twelve and who, later still, would be called as a counselor to President Heber J. Grant. Judging from favorable diary references made to him, Joseph Fielding had great admiration for President Ivins, with whom he would share the apostleship in the years ahead. And, of course, Joseph Fielding would later share this special status with his father, as during this trip he shared the pulpit with him. This was the first time President Smith and his son Joseph Fielding had been together, speaking to the Saints in an official capacity, the father as the president of the Church and the son as a member of the general board of the YMMIA.

There were two main purposes for this trip to the Mexican colonies. The first was to dedicate an LDS academy at Juarez. This was another of a string of similar Church-owned schools that extended from Canada to Old Mexico. The second was to confirm the scope and the effect of the World-wide Manifesto, which had been published the previous year following the Smoot hearings. Because the original manifesto of 1890 had grown out of restrictive legislation enacted in the United States, some members and leaders had erroneously assumed that it was not intended to apply to areas outside the United States. Thus some plural marriages had been performed in Old Mexico after 1890. During this trip, the Prophet made it plain that all plural marriages were unauthorized and void. It is significant that two members of the Twelve, John W. Taylor and Mathias F. Cowley, who had mistaken views about the manifesto, resigned from the Twelve on October 28, 1905, the month after President Joseph F. Smith and his son visited the Mormon colonies in Old Mexico.

President Smith again demonstrated his philosophy about the education of his children when he took Joseph Fielding to California on the return trip to Salt Lake City. There the son saw the Pacific Ocean for the first time. He and his father also visited Santa Catalina Island, a resort lying several miles off the Pacific coast.

Less than three months after the trip to Mexico, Joseph Fielding joined his father and a large group on a chartered train to New England for the dedication of the new monument at Sharon, Vermont. The party left the Salt Lake City depot on Monday, December 18, 1905, and arrived at South Royalton, Vermont, on Friday. The dedication was scheduled the following day, which would mark the one-hundredth anniversary of the Prophet's birth. Since the visitors arrived early on Friday, Joseph Fielding and other members of his family had time to travel to nearby Tunbridge, where his grandfather Hyrum Smith was born. The area was covered with a heavy blanket of snow, so they had to travel by sleigh. With his father and his older brother Hyrum, Joseph Fielding visited the Tunbridge town clerk's office to check for genealogical information. In a few hours they were able to gather valuable data that enabled them to fill gaps in their family records and to tie into information Joseph Fielding had obtained in Toppesfield, England. Especially important was confirmation of the dates of the marriage of Joseph Smith Sr. and Lucy Mack Smith and the births of Alvin, Hyrum, and Sophronia.

On Saturday, the visitors were driven to the monument. The day was gray and cold, and its bleakness accentuated the rugged appearance of the surrounding terrain. The monument and a modest bungalow that had been constructed nearby stood in a sheltered cove that had once been part of a farm owned by Solomon Mack, Lucy Mack Smith's father. The Church had purchased the site in May 1905. Pursuant to a resolution adopted at the general conference in April 1904, the original plan was to erect a monument honoring both Joseph and Hyrum Smith. Later considerations caused a change in plan to commemorate only the Prophet Joseph Smith, although a plaque on one side of the monument alluded to the martyrdom his brother had shared.

Many local leaders and curious residents were present to witness the unveiling of the monument. Joseph Fielding likely expressed the feelings of the family and other Church members who were there: "I felt that I was on sacred ground," he wrote, "a place dear to me, one which I had desired to see." The brief services, which were conducted by President Smith, included remarks by Junius F. Wells, who chaired the planning committee, and by the Prophet, who then offered the dedicatory prayer. After the congregation joined in singing "Praise to the Man," Edith A. Smith, the oldest member of the Smith family present, unveiled the monument. The solid granite shaft, thirty-eight and a half feet high to symbolize the years of Joseph Smith's life, and the two granite bases on which it stood weigh almost a hundred tons.

After the formal ceremony, Joseph Fielding joined other members of the family and a few close associates in the cottage, where President Anthon H. Lund presented the Prophet with a gold watch, chain, and locket. In a rare show of emotion in public, Joseph Fielding's father wept as he accepted the gift. "My heart is like that of a child," he said. "It is easily touched, especially with love. I can much easier weep for joy than for sorrow."

After the dedication, some members of the official party from Salt Lake City returned home while Joseph Fielding and his father and several Smith relatives left South Royalton to visit other places in New England of significance to the family. They traveled first to Boston, where meetings in Deacon Hall were attended by members and missionaries. On Christmas day, they went to nearby Topsfield and Boxford to visit Robert Smith's farm, where many of his children were born. While there, they refreshed themselves with a drink from the old well, whose water, Joseph Fielding reported, was "clear and cool."

Next on the itinerary was a stop in Palmyra, New York, and nearby Manchester Township, where they visited the farm and home owned by Joseph Fielding's great-grandfather, Joseph Smith Sr. Seeing the rooms where Joseph Smith Jr. had lived and the grove where he had received the vision of the Father and the Son brought into clearer focus events in the early history of the Church. Other early events seemed clearer too when the party visited the Hill Cumorah, where President Smith offered a special prayer and the group sang *An Angel from on High*.

Leaving Palmyra, they traveled to Cleveland, Ohio, by train and on to Kirtland by team. Here the temple and the old home of Hyrum Smith were of special interest. Seeing the inscription on the temple that the Reorganized Church was in succession "by decision of the court. February 1880," President Smith is reported to have said, "No order of the court could transmit the succession of the Holy Priesthood or of the spirit and power and religious rights of the church established by revelation from God."

Joseph Fielding traveled East again in May 1907. With him was his younger brother, David A. Smith. Their purpose was to meet four other brothers who were returning from missions abroad. Alvin and Chase had served in Great Britain, while George and Willard had been sent to Scandinavia. During George's two-year absence, Joseph Fielding had substituted for him as the treasurer of the Salt Lake Tabernacle Choir. After meeting in Boston where the returning missionaries landed, the six brothers duplicated the tour that had been made by President Smith's party in December 1905.

Six months after the return of the six brothers, another of President Smith's sons was called to the ranks of the General Authorities when, on December 11, 1907, David A. was set apart as the second counselor in the Presiding Bishopric. Three years younger than Joseph Fielding, this brother had shown unusual skill in business matters. So Charles W. Nibley had selected him to serve as his second counselor when Bishop Nibley was called to replace the ailing William B. Preston, who had served as the presiding bishop for twenty-three years. David A. Smith's service in the presiding bishopric would cover thirty-one years, spanning the entire tenure of Bishop Charles W. Nibley and Bishop Sylvester Q. Cannon.

At the time of Joseph Fielding's return from the trip to meet his missionary brothers, an epidemic of spinal meningitis was raging in Utah. Only two months before, the daughter of his cousin, Albert J. Davis, had died of the disease. Joseph and Louie were concerned for their two young daughters, four-and-a-half-year-old Josephine and her fifteen-month-old sister, Julina, who had been born February 5, 1906. The parents were anxious to provide security and opportunity for their children in the same way their parents had provided for them. This desire had led Joseph and Louie to commence a renovation project on their home three months after Julina was born. It entailed finishing the second story to provide an extra bath, additional bedrooms, and a private study for Joseph. The project was necessary because of the growth of the family, which the couple expected would continue, and it became financially feasible when Joseph received a modest increase in salary at the time of his appointment as an assistant historian in April 1906. The private study for Joseph was becoming an urgent necessity as his personal library grew and as he required the space and seclusion necessary for his research and writing projects. Here, in the early morning hours, or at night after the children were in bed, he could work without interruption, leaving his papers on his desk or working table, ready for easy access when he returned. He soon learned that his young children had little regard for the importance of his working tools. If the door to the study was open or unlocked, they felt no reluctance to enter and to handle or even carry away his papers and writing equipment. This created special problems when the father occasionally brought home documents from the Historian's Office. On this account, Joseph soon began to lock the door to his study, allowing the children to enter only when he was present. To youngsters growing up, this practice cast an aura of secrecy, even of mystery, around this room. Only when they married and had inquisitive children of their own and appreciated better the significance of their father's work did they fully understand why that part of their home was off limits.

With a lovely home, two beautiful daughters, supportive families, a host of friends, rewarding church activities, and secure, enjoyable employment for Joseph, this young couple seemed to have everything necessary for supreme happiness and contentment. That this was a reality for them is suggested by Joseph's diary entry of November 1, 1907. "With Louie, I spent the greater part of the day in the Salt Lake Temple," he wrote, "one of the happiest days of our lives and the most profitable to us."

Chapter Seven

Shadow and Light

T he cyclical nature of life was demonstrated to Joseph Fielding the month following his happy experience in the temple with Louie. On December 23, 1907, his great happiness was replaced by deep sorrow when his sister Leonora Nelson died from complications of a stillborn birth a few days before. The unexpected passing of this beloved sister, fondly called Nonie, cast a shroud over the holiday season. "Christmas day was spent by the family in sorrow," Joseph noted in his diary. The funeral was held the day after Christmas.

Nonie's death reminded the entire family of the tenuous nature and short duration of life and doubtless prompted the action taken the following month. On January 21, 1908, Joseph Fielding and his brother David A. went to the city cemetery to look for a Smith family burial plot that, Joseph wrote, "would be of use for at least a century where all our dead could be buried together." Later President Smith went to the cemetery with his sons to help decide which plot to purchase. When the decision had been made, David A., who had recently been called as a coun-

*Louie Shurtliff Smith
later in life*

selor in the Presiding Bishopric, was asked to petition the
city council for a reduction in the price of the plot selected.
Joseph Fielding noted that the site consisted of fourteen
lots, "one of which belongs to Joseph Nelson and it is there
that my sister Leonora is buried."

Little did Joseph Fielding realize that in less than three
months his wife and sweetheart would be buried there
also. Louie was expecting again at the time and was having
difficulty carrying her third child, just as she had had in
carrying Julina. The main problem was her inability to keep
anything on her stomach. Those with medical skills whom
she consulted, including her mother-in-law, Julina Smith,
diagnosed her ailment as "pernicious vomiting." But the
diagnosis did not include a prescription for her recovery.
As a result, she became progressively weaker as her system
was regularly robbed of the nutrients so necessary for the
health of herself and the baby she carried. Lacking a medical solution for Louie's problems, the concerned couple
resorted to the only other source of help they knew – they

prayed. They prayed separately and together, both vocally and in secret. They enlisted family and friends to join them in their fervent pleadings. Louie received priesthood administrations, all to no avail. In mid February, her name was placed on the prayer role in the Salt Lake Temple, where the First Presidency and the Twelve offered up special prayers in her behalf. Nothing happened except that her condition continued to worsen. By March the situation was critical. "During the remainder of the month," wrote Joseph, "I spent my time . . . principally at home where I felt that I was needed." Then betraying the highly developed sense of responsibility he felt toward his work, he added, "I felt also, that I was justified in neglecting all other duties and in devoting my time and attention so far as possible to my sick wife and our babies."

The vigil was "one of constant anxiety and worry." Joseph's principal concern was for Louie, who suffered "most excruciating pain for three or four weeks." And the ordeal took an enormous emotional toll on her husband, who had to stand by helplessly as he watched his sweetheart dwindle toward death. "I have passed through trials and experiences of the deepest and most painful kind," wrote he.

The end came on Monday, March 30, 1908, when Louie Shurtliff Smith slipped quietly away, leaving behind her husband of ten years and two small daughters, Josephine and Julina, ages five and two. The funeral service was held on April 2. The speakers Joseph Fielding invited to participate were John Watson — Louie's former bishop in the Ogden Fifth ward — and three members of the Twelve, his cousins John Henry Smith and George Albert Smith and his friend David O. McKay, who had been one of Louie's classmates at the University of Utah.

His wife's death was a terrible blow to Joseph. He had depended on her for so many things. She had made their home a haven from the storms of life. There he had always found peace and contentment and encouragement. Above all others, Louie was confident that in the future her husband would occupy a high place in the leadership of the Church. She seems to have devoted herself to help him prepare for the day when the call would come. This willingness to subordinate her personal desires and aspirations to the mission of her husband was, no doubt, a source of great strength to Joseph. And the loss of that constant support left a great void. Yet these were not the main reasons why Joseph mourned Louie's passing; he mourned mainly because he loved her dearly. In a real sense, she was part of him. Their unity was symbolized in the two little girls who derived qualities of character and appearance from each of their parents. To sever that relationship caused grievous wounds that time would heal but that, for the moment, brought deep mourning. Joseph turned to his diary to express his sense of loss, his feelings of love and admiration for Louie at her passing, and his need for help to continue without her. "With a sick heart," he wrote, "I acknowledge the Lord and trust in Him for His help and comfort, for in Him only can I trust securely." He then offered this eulogy: "A purer, nobler, truer companion and mother there is not to be found in the whole earth. . . . She was constantly engaged in doing good. She loved her husband and babies dearer than her life and for them she laid it down. . . . She sacrificed self and her own comfort for those she loved and her example is one to be emulated by her children and all her loved ones." Then looking to their future, he implored, "O my Father in Heaven, help me, I pray Thee, to so live that I shall be worthy to meet her in eternal glory, to be united again with her, never again to be separated, throughout the countless ages of eternity." Finally, the future prophet turned to matters of an entirely personal nature. "Give me wisdom and knowledge of heavenly things," he wrote, "that I may have power to resist all evil and remain steadfast to Thy *truth*. O Lord, help me, grant unto me eternal life in Thy Kingdom. Guide my footsteps in righteousness, give unto me Thy Whole Spirit."

What Joseph Fielding aimed for here was nothing less

than perfection. And twenty-three years after being called to the Twelve, he would publish a book entitled *The Way to Perfection,* in which he clearly outlined the path to be followed by anyone who aspired to reach that goal. To fully understand the life and works of President Joseph Fielding Smith, one must realize that to him this was a realistic, attainable goal, worthy of one's best efforts applied consistently throughout life. It was no passing fancy. Nor was it something deserving of only lip service. This was the lodestar of his earthly existence, the ultimate goal toward which he strove and around which he ordered every aspect of his life.

It is doubtless true that Louie's death, which followed so soon after the death of his sister, Nonie, was the first time in his young life that Joseph Fielding Smith fully grasped the meaning of the principle he had often taught, that it is necessary that there be an opposition in all things. The reality of death and the short duration of life brought into clearer focus, and made sweeter, experiences such as the one he had had with Louie in the Salt Lake Temple the previous November. And now that she was gone, he wanted to build on that sacred relationship through the lives of the daughters who had blessed their home. "Help me to rear my precious babies," he pleaded, "that they shall remain pure and spotless throughout their lives, and when we have finished our course, take us unto Thy Celestial Kingdom, we pray Thee."

Joseph Fielding soon learned that rearing two little girls alone while holding down a full-time job was an impossible task. He tried it with the aid of a babysitter during the day, but that didn't work for long. The little girls sorely missed their mother and seemed to cry almost incessantly for her. This robbed the father of much needed sleep, which reduced his efficiency at the office and created additional tension at home. A few weeks of this convinced Joseph of the need to accept the invitation of his parents to move into the Beehive House to live with them. So, he closed his home temporarily and for several months lived in

Brigham Young's old home across the street from the Historian's Office. Being so close to the girls, he was able to stop to see them during the day and to help his mother and sisters in their care. But while Grandma Smith and their aunties were kind to the little girls and did everything possible to comfort and help them, it was not like home where all of their playthings were nearby and where they were the center of attention of their solicitous mother, the mother whom they at last began to realize would not return. Under these circumstances, the girls never really settled comfortably into the routine of their grandparents' home. They were often cross and moody, given to frequent crying and to persistent pleading to be taken to their own home.

Joseph soon saw that the best solution lay in his remarriage. Yet he was reluctant to take steps in that direction too soon after Louie's death out of concern that it might be misinterpreted as a sign of disloyalty. Apparently sensing Joseph's reticence to take an action that was essential to the well-being of all, President Smith finally counseled his son that he take steps promptly to find a wife. When Joseph learned that Louie's parents were of the same opinion, he resolved to do it.

Making the decision to find a wife was easy. The hard part was how to go about it. Yet it turned out not to be difficult at all. By now, Joseph was a mature man of thirty-two who had been trained and disciplined in the principles of his religion. It was only natural, therefore, that he would rely on those principles in making what would be one of the most important and far-reaching decisions of his life. Therefore, Joseph prayed. He prayed that the Lord would indicate to him the one who would be a congenial and loving companion and also a kind and caring mother for his children. His prayers were answered.

It is somewhat incredible that Joseph Fielding Smith, bearing the name of his father and working in the Historian's Office, as his father had done, would find his wife there as President Smith had found Julina. The answer to

Ethel Georgina Reynolds, second wife of Joseph Fielding Smith

Joseph's fervent prayers came in the person of Ethel Georgina Reynolds, an attractive eighteen-year-old girl who was employed as a clerk in the Historian's Office. Aside from her physical beauty, Joseph Fielding seemed to be attracted to Ethel chiefly because of her kind and gentle nature, her keen intelligence, and her industrious habits. Moreover, she belonged to a prominent and dedicated Mormon family, which was of critical importance to Joseph Fielding, who was anxious that his children be well born. Ethel's middle name, Georgina, was given to her in honor of her father, George Reynolds, who was a member of the First Council of Seventy. Elder Reynolds's distinguished career had included service as a private secretary to President Brigham Young, as a longtime member of the Sunday School general board, as a legislator and editor, and as the author of a concordance of the Book of Mormon. He wrote this monumental work over a period of more than twenty years, including several months of incarceration in the Utah penitentiary under the Federal anti-bigamy law of 1862. His case had been deliberately structured to test the constitutionality of that law. The supreme court's affirmance of his conviction in the landmark case, *U.S. v. Reynolds,* had memorialized Elder Reynold's name among the Latter-day Saints for his courage in volunteering to serve as the sacrificial lamb in this famous litigation.

All these circumstances were important to Joseph in his decision to seek Ethel's hand, although the final and determining factor was the spiritual impression that he should do so. But after that critical decision had been made, there still remained the delicate task of how to go about it. His strategy of courtship began when he invited Ethel to join him and the two little girls on an outing at Wandamere Park on July 6, 1908. He was anxious to make sure that the personal chemistry was right between her and his daughters as it was with him. The outing proved to be a huge success. It was the final day of a three-day holiday to celebrate the Fourth of July. A festive aura filled the park, where the midway rides, the food stalls, and the side shows were a delight to the little girls. Meanwhile, the relaxed atmosphere afforded opportunity for Joseph and Ethel to visit companionably, to exchange ideas, and to explore areas of common interest and concern.

With this ice-breaker out of the way, Joseph felt more comfortable and confident about how to proceed in courting Ethel. Consistent with his conservative character, however, he proceeded with caution, waiting ten days before making his second move. Then he invited her on a date, just the two of them. His niggardly diary entry provides little insight into how things were developing. "Spent the evening with Miss Ethel G. Reynolds," he wrote succinctly. And they were together again three days later, July 19, Joseph Fielding's thirty-second birthday. That evening, a Sunday, Ethel accompanied the assistant Church historian to a sacrament meeting of the Murray Second Ward. There he answered the recent charges of a minister of the Reorganized Church that The Church of Jesus Christ of Latter-day Saints had deviated from the doctrines taught by the Prophet Joseph Smith. Afterward the couple went to the Reynolds home for refreshments. There in the family parlor, Ethel gave Joseph a two-volume set of the essays of Ralph Waldo Emerson as a birthday gift.

During the following month, the courtship followed a normal course with the young couple spending much time together in the evenings and working together at the Historian's Office during the day. In the process, they came to know each other very well, reaching a common ground of understanding on vital issues and, presumably, developing a romantic involvement about which Joseph furnished little detail. A diary entry of August 20 clearly indicates that the couple had reached an understanding and that their marriage was imminent. "Ethel G. Reynolds went through the temple for her endowments today, at my request," wrote Joseph significantly. Two days later he took Ethel and the two little girls to the cemetery to visit Louie's grave.

Although fourteen years separated the couple in age, in maturity and perception Ethel seemed more nearly the age of Joseph. She was musically talented, having served as ward organist since age eleven; was well read; possessed poise and self-confidence beyond her years; and shared Joseph's convictions about the Church. Having been raised in the home of an author, Ethel was aware of the time demands involved in literary pursuits. And because her father was a General Authority, she shared with Joseph an understanding of the special challenges and restrictions such a status entailed. Moreover, Ethel's employment at the Historian's Office gave her a good insight into Joseph's work and a shared knowledge about the foundations and the growth of the Church. In retrospect, this combination of circumstances, added to their congenial personalities and physical attraction for each other, suggests that it would have been difficult to find a couple more ideally suited for each other. Years later, Joseph confirmed this when he wrote to Ethel: "You do not know how often I have thanked the Lord that I made no mistake when I needed a companion. You were sent to me. You just had to come for I know you belonged to me."

The marriage and sealing were performed in the Salt Lake Temple on November 2, 1908. The brief report Joseph made of the event hardly revealed the love and gratitude he had for his new bride: "This forenoon, in the Salt Lake Temple at 11:30, Miss Ethel G. Reynolds was sealed to me for time and all eternity, by my father."

Under the circumstances, the happy couple decided to forgo a honeymoon. So they moved into the home at 165 North Second West, where they began their married life together. The two little girls, Josephine and Julina, seem almost instantly to have developed a bonding love for Ethel. Shortly after the marriage, while Josephine was in school, Ethel took Julina to the Beehive House to be tended while she went to a shower in her honor. But Julina would have none of it. She cried and clung to her and refused to be comforted by her grandmother and aunties. At last, Ethel gave up the idea of leaving the little girl at Grandma's and took her along to the shower. And Julina's attitude toward her new mother was shared by Josephine. They both stuck to her like glue, following her everywhere. They were seemingly concerned that if she got out of sight, she might disappear as Louie had done.

Once the courting and nuptials were behind them and they had made the personal adjustments that are always entailed in a new marital relationship, Joseph and Ethel settled into a happy, rewarding routine. Ethel's musical ability, intelligence, gospel knowledge, and family connections smoothed the way for her enthusiastic acceptance into the life of the Seventeenth Ward. As for Joseph, his schedule was already filled with family and church responsibilities. But there was still room for a little more. This year he became the librarian and treasurer of the

Genealogical Society of Utah, adding to his responsibilities as a member of the board, a position to which he had been appointed the previous year. Following his appointment as librarian and treasurer, he and a companion made a tour to inspect libraries in the eastern United States to generate ideas for the development of the society's library, which was then in its incipient stages. Out of this tour came several important recommendations that were adopted by the board. One of Joseph's key suggestions was that the society publish a genealogical magazine similar to the one published by the New England Society. When this proposal was discussed and approved, the board decided that the person best qualified to spearhead the work was Joseph Fielding Smith, who, accordingly, was appointed as the first editor and business manager of the *Utah Genealogical and Historical Magazine.*

Building a new publication from scratch was no easy task, especially for an editor on a limited budget and with no previous experience. And the ideas obtained in New England were of limited value and application because of the different focus of the Utah Society, whose purpose was to advance the aims of the Church in its mission to help redeem the dead, a concept that likely had never occurred to the New England editors. So, Joseph plowed ahead with his project, gathering or writing informative or inspirational articles designed to stimulate members of the Church to perform the labor called by Church leaders the most important work of all. When unexpected problems arose, he improvised and maneuvered around them. In the process, he learned many valuable lessons about organization and management that he had never encountered before. Previously his assignments had been in structured situations where his duties and goals had been carefully defined by others. Now he had to strike out on his own, charting the course for the infant publication and bearing ultimate responsibility for any success or failure it might realize.

There can be little doubt that this represented one of the most critical challenges Joseph Fielding had faced in his career. In a sense, his reputation was on the line. Failure would convey the negative idea that in a difficult and stressful situation, he lacked the will or the capacity to perform, illustrating the maxim that there are many thoroughbreds who never win races. On the other hand, success would mark him as a young man of promise who could be relied on in the crunch, and who would bear watching as a future leader.

Joseph acquitted himself well in this test. While he was completing the first issue of the magazine, his family was placed in quarantine because Julina had contracted scarlet fever. Working alone and under time pressures, he completed the manuscript in his study at home, applied an antiseptic to the document to guard against transmitting the disease, and left it in the mailbox by his gate. There it was picked up and taken to the printer, who set it in type and returned galley proofs to Joseph for final editing. That completed, he fumigated them and returned them for publishing. Under these difficult circumstances, the new magazine was launched. For the next thirty years, it was published regularly, providing helpful hints and suggestions for those engaged in genealogical research. In 1940, the magazine was discontinued as part of a revision and consolidation of Church programs and publications.

Chapter Eight

Call to the Twelve

Although the Church genealogical magazine continued for thirty years, Joseph Fielding Smith's direct connection with it continued only a few months. A series of events after the first issue was published created a major revolution in his life, changing forever the direction in which it would go. The first of these was the death of John R. Winder, first counselor in the First Presidency, on March 27, 1910. The second was the call of Anthon H. Lund as the new first counselor. And the third was the call of John Henry Smith, a member of the Twelve, as the new second counselor. Joseph Fielding did not learn about the last two events until later. Their effect, of course, was to create a vacancy in the Twelve.

As always, there was much speculation among members of the Church about who the new member of the Twelve would be. And there was much discussion among the First Presidency and the Twelve about the same subject. Prior to the April general conference in 1910, President Joseph F. Smith had invited members of the Twelve to make nominations about filling the vacancy. As the Breth-

Joseph Fielding Smith

*Joseph Fielding Smith,
April 26, 1910, a few
days after his appoint-
ment to the Twelve*

ren met in council in the upper room of the temple to discuss the matter, there was no clear indication as to who the new apostle should be. At length, President Smith excused himself from the meeting and retired to a private room, where he implored the Lord for guidance in making the choice. At that time it was revealed to him that his son, Joseph Fielding Smith, was to be called to the Twelve. But while the revelation was clear, it was not an easy step for the Prophet to take. His son Hyrum and a cousin George Albert Smith were already members of the Twelve; his son David A. was a member of the Presiding Bishopric; his brother, John Smith, was Patriarch to the Church; and his cousin John Henry Smith was now his counselor. There had been a furor when the other sons were called, and he knew an even greater hue and cry would be raised with the call of his namesake. Nevertheless, he presented the matter to his brethren, who unanimously approved.

According to the procedure followed at that day, Joseph Fielding was not informed of his call prior to the time it was announced from the stand of the Tabernacle. The April general conference in 1910 started on April 3 and continued through April 6 with a recess on Tuesday the 5th. Joseph Fielding was pleased that at the morning session on Wednesday, his father-in-law, Lewis W. Shurtliff, offered the invocation. Also at that session, his friend Ben E. Rich, whose brother was the first husband of President Joseph F. Smith's wife Alice Kimball Rich Smith was the first speaker.

Between the morning and afternoon sessions, Joseph Fielding went to his office on East South Temple to eat a sandwich and to check on some of the matters pending there. Shortly before 2:00 P.M., and as yet unaware of what would take place at the afternoon session, he left the Historian's Office and walked west on the south side of South Temple until he reached the middle of the block across from Temple Square. As he started across the street to enter the south gate of the square, Ben E. Rich approached him and, putting his arm around Joseph's shoulder, asked whether he would "take his place on the stand" that afternoon as one of the Council of the Twelve. Caught off guard, Joseph responded as best he could, explaining that his brother was already a member of that quorum and that he had no expectation of being called. He had barely recovered from the shock of Ben Rich's embarrassing question when a doorkeeper at the entrance to the Tabernacle said to him in an insinuating way, "Well, Joseph, who is the new apostle to be?" Somewhat irritated by the implication of the question, Joseph answered abruptly, "I don't know. But it won't be you and it won't be me." Entering the Tabernacle, Joseph took his seat on the lower level of the stand reserved for him as an assistant Church historian.

Still oblivious to what lay ahead, Joseph heard his father call the meeting to order, announce the opening hymn "We Thank Thee, O God, for a Prophet," and designate Elder Brigham H. Roberts to offer the invocation. The

Prophet then announced a special number by the Tabernacle Choir, "The Spirit of God Like a Fire is Burning," following which Elder Heber J. Grant of the Twelve was designated to present the General Authorities of the Church for sustaining vote. As Elder Grant stood to read the names, an air of quiet expectation settled upon the audience. Still, Joseph Fielding was unaware of the coming announcement that would change his life forever. But, as the speaker read down the list of names of the members of the Twelve, there suddenly came to him the strong impression that the new name to be added to the roster of the Twelve was his own. Nevertheless, when, following the name of Anthony W. Ivins, Elder Grant read "Joseph F. Smith, Jr.," Joseph Fielding was completely incredulous. "I was so startled and dumfounded," he wrote later, "I could hardly speak." And when Joseph was invited by Elder Grant to take his place with the Twelve, he rose from his seat at the side of Andrew Jenson and, with all eyes riveted upon him, walked self-consciously up the stairs and took his place at the side of Anthony W. Ivins, who would be his seat-mate for eleven years until Elder Ivins was called as the second counselor to President Heber J. Grant in 1921.

No mention was made of the new apostle during the remainder of the meeting, nor was he given the opportunity to respond to his call. His maiden address in the Tabernacle as a member of the Twelve would be delayed until the following October. But while Joseph Fielding was not mentioned directly during the remainder of the meeting, the sermon of Elder David O. McKay seems to have been directed toward the consequences that might be expected to follow from Joseph's call. Elder McKay took as his text the admonition of James about the evils of gossip and a loose tongue. "And the tongue is a fire," read he, "a world of iniquity; so is the tongue among our members, that it defileth the whole body, and setteth on fire the course of nature, and it is set on fire of hell." (James 3:6.) In commenting on this scripture, Elder McKay said, "My

brethren and sisters, let us go from this conference determined to control our tongues. That isn't much, is it? And
yet James says that he who can control that little member
has control over his whole body." (*Conference Report*, April
1910, p. 110.)

Most members heeded Elder McKay's admonition and
remained silent, even though privately the thought might
have occurred that having seven Smiths among the twenty-
six General Authorities was extreme. Yet any such
thoughts would have been stifled by the faithful members
because of their conviction that the Church was led by a
Prophet. Such as these would have seen divine purpose
in this anomaly. And any members who continued to harbor negative thoughts about the matter likely would have
been placated to learn that within ten years, death would
reduce the seven to three, and that two of these three
would ultimately be elevated to the prophetic office.

It is ironic, though not surprising, that the loudest
criticism of what took place came from nonmembers and
apostates, those who had no vested interest in the outcome. And the most shrill and articulate of the critics were
the *Salt Lake Tribune* and its acerbic editor. In an editorial
entitled "The Church of the Smiths," Frank J. Cannon gave
full sway to his fertile talent for vituperation and insult.
"Joseph F. is losing no time unnecessarily in his well defined purpose and process of Smithi-sizing the Mormon
Church," he began. After referring to Joseph Fielding's call
and "the brilliant galaxy of Smiths that now adorn the
controlling body," he wrote: "One may turn to the right
or to the left, move to the front or back up, and one will
bump into an official Smith. Gaze where one may in the
hierarchy and the sight taken is a front or rear elevation
of a Smith." From ridicule and mockery, the writer then
turned to bitter accusation of fraud and thievery. "There
isn't a single Mormon pie but there is a Smith finger in
it," he continued. "The Saints pay allegiance to Smiths,
they contribute money to Smiths, the Smiths spend that
money and they are Smiths who tell tithe payers to mind

their own business if asked what they do with the funds. It is a system of nepotism seldom witnessed in history — everywhere the omnipresent, robbing, non-accounting, lawbreaking Smiths, until the Mormon people actually begin to look and feel Smithy."

Joseph Fielding recognized this as the bitter railing of a man who had been disappointed in his expectation of personal preferment and gain. Once a United States senator from Utah and an agent for the Church in Washington, D.C., Frank J. Cannon, a son of President George Q. Cannon, became embittered after Church leaders withdrew their political support and denied him rich fees from a Church bond issue that he had expected would be handled by Eastern financiers with whom he was affiliated. He blamed President Joseph F. Smith for the loss of the bonding fees; as a counselor to President Lorenzo Snow, Joseph F. persuaded the Prophet to negotiate the bond issue through Western bankers. Senator Cannon also appears to have been angered by the decision to terminate the lease of the *Deseret News* to President George Q. Cannon and his sons. These incidents alienated Frank Cannon from the Church and its leaders. And following the death of his father in 1901, this alienation flowered into a consuming hatred that found expression in vicious *Tribune* editorials like the one that followed the call of Joseph Fielding Smith to the Twelve.

As an assistant Church historian, Joseph was well acquainted with these and other facts that helped explain Frank J. Cannon's motivation for attacking the Church leaders and especially the Smith family. Between the April conference in 1910 when he was called to the Twelve and the October conference that year when he delivered his first apostolic address in the Tabernacle, Joseph Fielding had ample opportunity to mull over the serious charges that had been made, charges he obviously felt should not go unanswered. So in his maiden address in the Tabernacle, he undertook to respond to Frank Cannon and the *Tribune,* although he did not mention them by name. "It seems to be the heritage of the ungodly, of the bigoted, and of those who love iniquity," said Joseph Fielding, "to sit in judgment and to place themselves as dictators, saying what shall be done and what shall be said by the authorities of the church. They accuse the brethren of all manner of iniquity, dissimulation, falsehood and try to cause a division between them and the people over whom they preside. They take unto themselves the prerogative of saying what shall and what shall not be the doctrines of the church, what shall and shall not be the government of the church, when it concerns them not at all." (*Conference Report,* October 1910, p. 39.)

Whatever else Frank J. Cannon and the *Tribune* learned from this speech, they surely learned that Joseph Fielding Smith was his own man, that he was articulate, and that he was bold and fearless. In it, he served notice that any attack upon him, his family, or the Church would not go unchallenged. Here was a young warrior, a defender of the faith, a combatant who had the temperament and the skills to act as a Church spokesman and advocate. Indeed, this speech of itself did much to confirm the inspiration of his call to the Twelve. And behind the speech was a man of substance and promise. Here was a man, reared in the home of a Prophet, schooled in Church doctrine and procedure through service abroad and at home, steeped in the knowledge of Church history, clean in thought and deed, and tested in the crucible of personal trial and tragedy. There can be no doubt that he was prepared and worthy for the call that came to him, and that the call was based upon his own merit and upon inspiration to the Prophet. The fact that the one who called him happened to be his father is irrelevant, especially in view of the long and distinguished apostolic service he later rendered, culminating in his succession to the prophetic office.

Joseph's call to the Twelve effected a major change in his life, heavily influencing his wife and the children. The manner in which he broke the news of his call to Ethel best demonstrates this. He told her, "I guess we'll have to sell the cow." When asked why, he explained, "I haven't time to take care of it anymore." The accuracy of this statement would soon be borne out as Joseph was indoctrinated into his new duties.

It took some time for Joseph to fully grasp the impact of his call to the Twelve. Days later, in lengthy diary entries, he attempted to articulate the feelings it evoked. "The reading of my own name as an apostle," he wrote, "came to me, as to the entire assembly, as a most sudden and to me unexpected shock, and left me in complete bewilderment from which I have not in days recovered. I feel extremely weak and pray to my heavenly Father for strength and guidance in my great responsibility that I shall not falter nor fail to perform all that is required of me." Then followed another of the personal, fervent prayers often found in Joseph Fielding's diaries, prayers that reveal the depth and sincerity of his character. "Oh my father," he pleaded, "help me, guide me in Thy truth and fit and qualify me, for I am weak, that I may indeed be Thy servant and have Thy Holy Spirit to guide me and direct my feet in the path of wisdom as one of the special witnesses of Thy Beloved Son, who died that I might live and be numbered among His chosen people through faithfulness to His Gospel and obedience to His laws. Give me strength and courage and buoy me up that that I may be worthy to bear Thy name and labor in Thy Kingdom and in the knowledge and testimony of the truth for I know the gospel is true and through obedience thereto is salvation through the name of Jesus Christ whose servant I am called to be."

Here we find a window into the heart and soul of a man destined to become God's mouthpiece on earth. Here we find no evidence of vanity or pride at having been elevated to such an exalted station. Here we see no posturing, no pretense or dissembling, and no boastfulness. We see only a sincere, humble man, convinced of the reality and power of God and desiring to receive the spiritual light and strength that would enable him to measure up to the requirements of his apostolic office.

Many people had sensed that Joseph Fielding Smith would one day be called to the Twelve, and some had expressed that feeling to him. He had always found it difficult to respond to such an expression. To brush it off abruptly would offend one whose mention of it showed a special love for him. But to acknowledge it, or to imply by word or action that Joseph expected it, might be misinterpreted as a presumption. So he usually responded in a neutral or jocular way as he had with Ben E. Rich and the doorkeeper at the Tabernacle. And, now that he had been called, confirming the predictions of these well-wishers, Joseph pondered over them and commented on some of them in his diary: "At the close of the afternoon session of conference and the adjournment of six months," he wrote, "I received the following note from Sister Susa Young Gates, who has always been a true friend to me and for years has hoped and prayed for me that I might some day be an apostle. 'My Beloved Joseph F. Jr. Let me ease the fulness of my joy by telling how grateful I am to God for this beautiful thing. Don't you see now that God is pleased with your earnest, modest labors—and most especially has He not thus indicated His own approval of the grand cause which you have so eloquently espoused? I have felt this coming for some time. I am so happy. Your Aunt Susa." After noting that he had received many other letters and telegrams of congratulation, he added: "Ben E. Rich, President of the Eastern States Mission, who has always been a friend to me, and one who years ago predicted that I should be called to this great responsibility, was one of the first to give me the hand of fellowship and his blessing, faith and constant prayers. May the Lord bless him." Joseph also reported in some detail on a conversation he had had with Francis M. Lyman, who was then president of the Twelve: "He said he had watched me for a number of years and while on the trip to Vermont, both going and coming and while there, he had watched me and felt at that time in his heart that I should some day be an apostle." Joseph added that similar predictions had

151

been made by others, which, he wrote, "I received lightly and without thought of their fulfillment."

The day after he was sustained, Joseph went to his office early to handle some of the matters that had accumulated during the conference. Then shortly before ten, he walked to the temple, going directly to the fourth floor, where he entered "the upper room," where the Brethren meet regularly in their council meetings. Assembled there were the First Presidency and all the members of the Twelve except Elders Reed Smoot (who was in Washington, D.C., serving as a United States senator), George Albert Smith (who lay gravely ill in St. George), and Charles W. Penrose (who was in England serving as president of the European Mission). Also present was Patriarch John Smith, Joseph Fielding's uncle, who, fourteen years before, had given him the blessing whose promises were now beginning to unfold.

Joseph had seen the upper room many times during the nine previous years as he had attended President Anthon H. Lund's prayer circle that was held in an adjoining room on the fourth floor of the temple. But he had never seen it as he did on this day with the leading brethren who were in attendance, attired in their temple robes. As Joseph Fielding was welcomed into this select circle, a circle to which he would return regularly during the next sixty-two years, he was given the apostolic charge by his father. In accepting the charge, the new apostle committed himself to a lifetime of dedicated service as a special witness of the Lord Jesus Christ, agreed to subordinate all other responsibilities to those of the apostleship, promised to hold in confidence the sensitive matters discussed in the council meetings, and obligated himself to uphold and promote all the decisions of the council, even though during the discussions leading up to them he may have expressed a contrary view. As to this last matter, he was encouraged to express his views freely so that the council could enjoy the benefit of his experience and wisdom.

Following Joseph's acceptance of the charge and prayer

at the altar, he was seated in a chair at the center of the room. All of the other brethren gathered around him in a circle, placed their hands on his head, and, with his father acting as voice, ordained him an apostle and set him apart as a member of the Quorum of the Twelve Apostles. In that ordination, as with the other apostles, he was also given all the keys and authority necessary to serve as the president of the Church should that calling someday come to him.

Chapter Nine

Early Apostolic Service

Joseph Fielding's jocular statement to Ethel that he no longer had time to milk the cow had more truth in it than he had imagined. Until he was indoctrinated into his apostolic duties, he had no conception of the demands on his time, energy, and emotional resources they would entail. When he was called to the Twelve, the Church had sixty-two stakes and twenty-one missions, with a total membership of less than four hundred thousand. Compared to today's church of more than seven million members in more than sixteen hundred stakes and two hundred missions, this would not appear to have been an overwhelming assignment. Yet in appraising the load borne by the General Authorities in that day, we must remember that four instead of two stake conferences were held each year and that the Brethren attended these conferences in pairs instead of singly. Moreover, the slow and often tedious means of travel added immeasurably to the burden. Automobiles were hardly more than a toy at the time, and trains reached only the communities that lay directly on the line of the railroad. So when a General

Authority received an assignment to visit a stake in a remote area, the time spent in teaching and training local leaders and members often represented only a small part of the time he was away from home. And when Joseph Fielding was at home, he had a full agenda of headquarters assignments. He continued to serve as an assistant Church historian, was the secretary and a member of the board of the Genealogical Society, and served on the General Board of Religion Classes. Moreover, his new role as a member of the Twelve made Joseph Fielding even more valuable to his father as he could now help with various sensitive and confidential matters. All this left little time for personal writing projects or his family.

Ethel, too, was now almost overburdened. Notwithstanding the joy with which Josephine and Julina had welcomed her into the family, there had been a period of readjustment during which Ethel became accustomed to being an instant mother and the girls adjusted to the different ways in which their new mother did things. Following closely on this period, Ethel became pregnant with her first child, Emily, who was born August 9, 1909. And at the time of her husband's call to the Twelve in April 1910, even though Emily was hardly toilet trained, Ethel was carrying her second child, Naomi, who would be born in November 1910. Added to her motherly duties, Ethel continued to serve in the auxiliary organizations of the Church and now assumed responsibility for many family matters that had previously been handled by her husband or shared with him.

In time, as other children joined the family, Ethel developed a marvelous skill in directing and nurturing her children and in managing the Smith household. She bore a total of nine children, raised Josephine and Julina, and, years later, took into the home and raised a young boy, the son of a man who had been killed while washing windows. When someone asked how it was possible for her to assume the responsibility for still another child when she had so many of her own, Ethel responded simply that "one more does not make any difference," thereby defining her relaxed and effective philosophy of child-rearing.

As Joseph Fielding prepared to attend stake conferences and conduct mission tours, he received special instruction from the president of his quorum. "President Francis M. Lyman instructed me in the duties of my calling," wrote Joseph Fielding, "and told me that I had been called by revelation from the Lord." President Lyman, who had been a member of the Twelve for thirty years, was a close friend of Joseph Fielding's father, having served under him as a missionary in England when Joseph F. presided over the European mission in the mid 1870s. President Lyman, whose father, Amasa, had also been a member of the Twelve, was serving as the president of the Tooele Stake when he was called to the Twelve in 1880. Therefore, he was well schooled in Church organization and procedure and eminently qualified to give pertinent instruction to the new member of the Twelve. During the remaining six years of President Lyman's life, Joseph Fielding had many opportunities to travel with him and to observe in practice the principles of leadership he had taught. And in the process, he also had many memorable experiences with him, some poignant and sad, others amusing and lighthearted. Of the latter, Joseph Fielding remembered two in particular. Once while the two were traveling to a conference assignment in a springless wagon, President Lyman asked the driver several times to avoid the ruts in the road, which severely jolted the passengers. Soon afterward, the wagon struck an especially large rut, giving the apostles a severe jolt and almost throwing them off the wagon to the ground. President Lyman looked accusingly at the driver who, not quite knowing how to respond, said half apologetically and half triumphantly, "Well, I hit it didn't I?" The other experience involved President Lyman's love for thick cream, which he used liberally on almost any food. On the occasion that gave rise to the story, Joseph Fielding had accompanied his quorum president to a stake where lived a family who, in the past, had furnished President Lyman with an abundance of thick cream. Remembering this, the president insisted that Joseph stay at the home of the stake president while he would go to the other home where he expected to again be given his favorite delicacy. He was bitterly disappointed. The next morning, he asked Joseph whether he had had cream for breakfast. When he said yes, President Lyman complained that he had had none and insisted that they trade places the next night! In the interest of priesthood subordination, Joseph complied.

The new apostle's first stake conference assignment was to accompany Elder George F. Richards to the Bear River Stake, whose headquarters were at Garland, Utah, a small farming community about eighty miles north of Salt Lake City. On Saturday morning, April 16, 1910, the two apostles traveled by train to their assignment, where they were met by the stake president, Milton H. Welling, who, prior to the creation of the Bear River Stake in 1908, had served as the president of the Malad, Idaho, stake. An educator by profession, President Welling, who was the same age as Elder Smith, became the patriarch of a large and distinguished family.

The visitors were driven directly from the train depot to the chapel in a horse-drawn carriage. There they commenced a procedure that Joseph Fielding would follow hundreds of times in the future. They first met with the stake presidency, high council, and bishoprics to receive reports and give instruction. It was in this meeting that the visitors were able to make a real impact on the administration of the Church in the area, for there were assembled all of the key priesthood leaders in the stake. Later in the day, quorum and group leaders also came for instruction. Saturday evening Joseph remained in Garland to counsel with local leaders and members, while Elder Richards traveled by carriage to nearby Fielding, a small community named after Elder Smith's maternal relatives, to visit a sister. The following day, the apostles joined to hold three major meetings: two general sessions, one in the morning and one in the afternoon, and a special meeting for auxiliaries held Sunday evening. Joining them was Lyman R. Martineau, a representative of the MIA general board.

Elder Smith delivered his main discourse Sunday morning when he and President Milton H. Welling were the only speakers. "He reported conditions in the stake," Joseph wrote, "and I spoke on the sacrament meetings and temple work including the genealogical society." It is a safe assumption that on this, Joseph's maiden apostolic speaking assignment at a stake conference, he relied heavily on the scriptures. This would have been consistent with his usual speaking style as it developed over the years and would have affirmed a statement attributed to him: "I never did learn to deliver a discourse without referring to the scriptures."

With variations, Elder Smith's first stake conference at Garland, Utah, was a prototype for the hundreds of stake conferences he would attend during the following six decades. Their value was incalculable. They provided a mechanism to train and direct local leaders, to receive input from those on the firing line, and to provide motivation and uplift to the members. They also served an important personnel purpose by bringing him into frequent contact with leaders throughout the Church in a setting where their character and personal life, their skills, and their potential for future service could be appraised.

During the remainder of 1910, Elder Smith attended twenty-four of these stake conferences in various parts of Utah, Idaho, Colorado, Wyoming, and Oregon. This represented almost 40 percent of all the stakes in the Church at the time. Thus, within a very short while after his call, he had become personally acquainted with all of the principal leaders of the Church serving in organized stakes. This provided him with an important insight into the mechanics of the Church, the spiritual and intellectual qualities of its members, the physical conditions under which they lived, and their social and cultural development. It also gave him an intimate knowledge of the physical environment in which Mormon communities were located, given the means of transportation he sometimes had to employ. Typical of some of the assignments he received during the first year of his service in the Twelve was the one to Castle Dale, Utah, in August 1910. His companion was Elder Orson F. Whitney of the Twelve. The pair left Salt Lake City by train Friday morning, August 5, and arrived at Price in mid-afternoon. They were met at the depot by their teamster, a Brother Leonard, who drove them in a buggy to the town of Huntington, where that evening they held a meeting with the Saints living there and nearby. Early Saturday morning, they were driven by team to Castle Dale, where, during the remainder of the day and Sunday morning, several meetings were held. On Sunday afternoon, Brother Leonard drove them to Cleveland, where an evening meeting was held. And at 4:00 Monday morning, they left by team for Price, where they arrived in time to catch the 8:00 train to Salt Lake City. The leisurely means of travel between these towns provided an insight and perspective into the area one could never gain driving at high speed over surfaced highways.

The continual round of these trips, some taking as long as ten days, left little time at home. And when Joseph Fielding was at home, his agenda of official and personal responsibilities was overcrowded. His historical and genealogical responsibilities were never ending. And those responsibilities multiplied the number of people who came to him for counsel or instruction. So, on Monday, August 15, 1910, Joseph spent most of the day with John R. Haldeman of Independence, Missouri. Mr. Haldeman was president of the Hedrikite Church, also called the Church of Christ, and he had come with his wife to obtain information about the early history of the Church. The following day, Elder Smith had a clerk in the Historical Department help Mr. Haldeman in getting excerpts from *The Evening and Morning Star* for his use and information.

The meetings of Joseph's quorum, and of the Council

of the First Presidency and Quorum of the Twelve, while serving as a forum of instruction and inspiration, required a substantial investment in time and sometimes imposed heavy and unwanted burdens of trauma and responsibility. Within months after his call to the Twelve, for instance, Elder Smith participated in two cases that resulted in the excommunication of prominent Church members for their involvement in plural marriage. The first was the scion of a family prominent in Church history whom the Twelve excommunicated on September 28, 1910, for "illegally entering into a plural marriage contrary to the rule of the church." Three days later, Joseph spent another full day with the Twelve considering the second case, which involved a patriarch who lived in northern Utah who was excommunicated on October 3 "for violating the rule and regulation of the church in that he performed plural marriages since the Manifesto." That it had been twenty years since the Manifesto was issued and six years since President Joseph F. Smith had published the World-wide Manifesto suggests the great inertia of a small minority of the Latter-day Saints in accepting and following the admonitions of the Church leaders.

This internal inertia was more than matched by the external pressures that were being exerted on the Church at this time. Mention has already been made of the incessant attacks upon the Church by the *Salt Lake Tribune*. This was accompanied by subtle and sometimes not-so-subtle attacks by the local protestant clergy, which for decades had carried on a campaign of criticism and verbal abuse. All this had stirred up such bitter antagonisms and resentments that less-stable members of the community were occasionally led to make actual physical assaults against the Church. Joseph Fielding recorded one such incident the day after returning from his first stake conference assignment. "This morning we returned home," he wrote on Monday April 18, 1910, "and I spent the afternoon at the Historians Office and learned that early this morning an attempt was made by dynamiters to blow up the steel work of the Utah Hotel; great damage was done and the windows in the neighborhood were broken. This is the second attempt of this kind."

Meanwhile, there were occasional agitations both on earth and in the heavens that drew Elder Smith's special attention. "This morning about 7:30," he wrote on May 22, 1910, "a severe earthquake shock was felt throughout Salt Lake City. My house was shaken violently, but no damage was done." And nine days earlier, while in Durango, Colorado for a stake conference, Elder Smith noted that he "had a good view of Halley's comet which extended over one-third of the heavens." Joseph Fielding was specially interested in physical phenomena of this kind as it related to signs in the heavens or movements of the earth that would precede the Millennial reign.

As Elder Smith settled into his new responsibilities, grasping for the first time the full scope of them, he did not neglect what he knew was the responsibility of greatest personal importance. This, of course, was his family. Like his father, Joseph loved his family above all else on earth. Although he was now severely limited in the time he could spend with them, he made that time count. He and Ethel were careful to note each birthday and other special event affecting the children and to celebrate them with appropriate gifts. Sunday, September 18, 1910, marked a signal day in the life of Elder Smith and his family. "This morning at 9:15," he wrote on that day, which was Josephine's eighth birthday, "I baptized Josephine in the Salt Lake Tabernacle font and confirmed her. My mother and my wife and babies were present, also Joseph S. Peery." The "babies" to whom he referred were four-year-old Julina and thirteen-month-old Emily. What the proud father did not mention was that Ethel was then carrying her second child, who would be born within two months.

Because Ethel worked hard in managing the household and caring for the three little girls, while carrying still another one, Joseph was solicitous to give her a respite whenever possible by attending social functions with her. The

kind they preferred above all others was to mingle with
the leaders of the Church and their wives, or with other
members of their families. An event that gave them special
pleasure was a dinner party at the residence of the Prophet
following the October general conference in 1910. "In the
evening," wrote Joseph under date of October 10, "The
First Presidency, the Apostles, the Patriarch and Presiding
Bishopric and their wives met at the Beehive House where
they spent a very enjoyable evening and partook of an
excellent supper. Remarks were made by each of the brethren and the Spirit of the Lord was with them." In November, Joseph and Ethel returned to the Beehive House for
another party when, during the afternoon and evening of
Monday the 14th, the entire Smith family gathered to celebrate President Joseph F. Smith's seventy-second birthday. Two days later, Ethel gave birth to her second child,
another daughter, who was named Naomi. The birth had
complications, and for a while the parents feared she would
not survive. Joseph noted gratefully that the little one "was
saved through the power and prayer and administration
after it appeared that breath could not enter her body." In
gratitude, Joseph and Ethel chose Thanksgiving Day,
Thursday, November 24, as the day for her blessing. "This
afternoon," Joseph noted on that day, "at my request, my
father blessed our baby. We gave her the name of Naomi."

Elder Smith's last conference assignment for the year
1910 was to the Sevier Stake on the weekend of December
16. His companion was President Francis M. Lyman. The
pair traveled to Richfield, Utah, the headquarters of the
stake, on Friday the 16th, where they were met by the
stake presidency. They were then taken to the home of a
counselor, James M. Peterson, where they stayed over the
weekend. After freshening up following their long train
ride, the pair went immediately to a meeting with the stake
presidency and high council where they heard reports and
gave instruction until a late hour. On Saturday, lengthy
report meetings were held, both in the morning and the
afternoon. In the evening, the Primary presented an en-

tertainment at Richfield's Opera House. On Sunday, general preaching sessions were held in the morning and the afternoon; the attendance, respectively, was 825 and 788. A special MIA session was held in the evening. And in between the sessions Sunday, the visiting apostles ordained seventies and high priests and set apart members of a bishopric. Exhausted from a full weekend of wall-to-wall meetings, the pair spent most of Monday traveling back to Salt Lake City. On his arrival home, Joseph found his family in turmoil with little Emily sick and Ethel weary from nursing her new baby around the clock while taking care of the home, supervising the older children, and doctoring Emily.

By now, Joseph understood that being a member of the Twelve involved much more than the public perception of that office. It meant much more than having a reserved place at general conference on those upholstered red seats in the Tabernacle, more than giving sermons and traveling to new places, and certainly more than receiving the admiration and respect of Church members everywhere. What it meant was a total subordination of himself and his family to the demands of his calling. It meant constant and often uncomfortable travel in every kind of weather. It meant irregular meals and diet, different beds at night, and sometimes the uncomfortable feeling of imposing on generous Saints who wanted to give the visiting apostle the best of what they had, regardless of the deprivation it might cause them. It also meant imposing on the family heavy burdens of responsibility that ordinarily would have been borne by a husband and father who was not constantly on the road. These burdens could have been mitigated had Joseph Fielding possessed independent means, or had his living allowance been sufficiently large to enable him to provide household help for his family. But neither of these conditions existed. As a result, Ethel was forced to struggle alone in her husband's absence to care for the household and their young family with only such help as relatives and neighbors might voluntarily provide.

As traumatic as these things might have been, there were other aspects of his calling that likely influenced Joseph Fielding's peace of mind. There was the constant pressure of preparing for the seemingly endless train of meetings and interviews. And aside from the strictly intellectual demands these imposed, there was also a spiritual dimension that was sometimes unsettling. This was a subtle, satanic influence he saw at work in various aspects of his ministry, an influence he persistently sought to combat by his teaching and example. He was fearless in speaking out against any words or conduct that were contrary to the doctrines and the policies of the Church.

As Christmas approached in 1910, Elder Smith enjoyed the first let-up in his hectic schedule since his call eight months before. He took advantage of it to relieve Ethel of some of the household chores that had become more burdensome with the arrival of Naomi. He revived his cooking skills, which had largely fallen into disuse since his missionary days, preparing meals for the family. He also helped with the housecleaning and child tending, providing Ethel with the chance to get away from the house to visit her family and friends. And he helped comfort and nurse the children when they were sick. "My baby Emily is not well," he wrote on Tuesday December 20, 1910. So he stayed home all morning to tend her and to help bathe and diaper baby Naomi. Three days later, Joseph Fielding took Josephine and Julina Christmas shopping; and that evening, he and Ethel attended a party at the Social Hall — a reunion of those who had gone to Vermont five years earlier for the dedication of the Joseph Smith monument. Although it was a special evening, the infirm condition of the family robbed it of much of the joy it would otherwise have brought. "I am suffering from a cold," Joseph wrote on December 23. "Ethel is also, and all the children have been ailing with colds." Emily seems to have been worse than the others; and the poor little girl had hardly recovered from this ailment when she was stricken with another. "Emily now has the measles and is quite sick," her father wrote on February 11. "I have held her most of the day," he wrote the following day. And on Monday, February 13, he noted, "I was home nearly all day nursing my baby Emily who seems to have a hard case of measles. She did not break out well at first and has suffered considerably."

Meanwhile, following the none-too-peaceful respite during the Christmas holidays, Joseph Fielding returned to the routine of attending stake conferences. Several assignments in January, February, and March took him into northern Utah and southern Idaho, where heavy snowstorms made it necessary to travel by horse-drawn sleigh. So in mid-February, Elder Smith, accompanied by Elder Joseph W. McMurrin of the First Council of Seventy, traveled to the Bannock Stake. "We were met at Oxford, Idaho, by a young man named Bevins," he wrote on Friday, February 17, 1911, "who drove us in a sleigh to Thatcher where we arrived in the evening, a distance from Oxford of 25 miles." Sunday afternoon, after holding meetings in Thatcher, the visitors were driven by sleigh to Grace, Idaho, where another meeting was held in the evening. The following morning, their hosts drove them by sleigh to a rural station at Alexander, where they flagged a train that took them home via McCammon, Idaho.

Two weeks later, Joseph returned to Idaho for a conference at Preston. He took his brother Wesley with him. At Logan, Utah, the Smith brothers were joined by Elder Charles H. Hart of the First Council of Seventy; he also accompanied them to Preston for the usual round of stake conference meetings. The following weekend found Joseph at the Bear Lake stake in southeastern Idaho, where again most of the travel was by sleigh. On this occasion, his brother David A. Smith of the presiding bishopric was his traveling companion. Elder Smith's experiences during this his first winter as a General Authority may have convinced him there was a germ of truth in the rumor that junior members of the Twelve were always assigned to the cold places in the winter and the hot places in the summer.

Occasionally when they were well enough to go and

when the distances made it feasible to do so, Elder Smith took Ethel and the children with him on stake conference assignments. Such an incident occurred on March 26, 1911, when the entire family went by train to nearby Ogden, Utah, where Joseph presided at the conference of the North Weber stake. "We had a very pleasant and instructive conference," he wrote. An apparent reason why the family accompanied him on this occasion was to enable the Shurtliffs to see their granddaughters, Josephine and Julina, who were fast growing into young womanhood, and to visit with Joseph and Ethel and their other children. The Shurtliff family continued to show a keen interest in Joseph Fielding's career.

On Tuesday, April 4, 1911, Elder Smith received still another assignment when he was sustained as the secretary to the Council of the Twelve "in the stead of Hyrum M. Smith, who was honorably released from that position." As its secretary, Joseph kept the minutes of the meetings of the Twelve and followed up as to matters decided by the quorum. Because he occasionally served his father in a similar capacity, Joseph Fielding thereby became even more intimately acquainted with the inner workings of the Church, which not only enabled him to perform his apostolic duties more effectively but also served as a valuable preparation for the later roles he would play, either as the president of the Twelve, or as the head of the Church.

The eighty-first annual general conference of the Church convened on Thursday, April 6, and continued through the following Sunday, with a break on Saturday. The general priesthood meeting was held on Friday evening. During the Sunday morning general session, Joseph Fielding presided over an "overflow" meeting held in the Assembly Hall. He was the concluding speaker, having been preceded by two stake presidents, John F. Tolton of the Beaver Stake and Alonzo A. Hinckley of the Millard Stake, and two mission presidents, John I. Herrick of the Western States Mission and Charles A. Callis of the

Southern States Mission. In his remarks, Elder Smith admonished those present to keep the commandments. Specifically, he focused on the need to observe the law of tithing, to obey the Word of Wisdom, to pray always, and to keep the Sabbath Day holy. As to the latter, he deplored the proliferation of Sunday amusements and chastised elected officials for their failure to adopt appropriate restrictive ordinances. He alluded to an "aviation meet" then in progress near the Great Salt Lake where "men with machines of marvelous construction [were] flying in the air." He expressed the hope that no Latter-day Saint would be found there on Sunday and noted that two of the principals involved in the meet, Orville and Wilbur Wright, "will not take part nor permit those who represent them to take part in any such exercise on the Sabbath day, thus setting an example to others." (*Conference Report*, April 1911, p. 87.) Perhaps to support the Wright brothers and to satisfy their curiosity about these newfangled machines, Joseph Fielding and others had gone to the lake the previous day to see the air show. "Saturday afternoon with the presidency and a number of brethren and sisters," he wrote on April 8, 1911. "I went out to the lake and saw four biplanes, or flying machines, manipulated by Eugene B. Ely, Charles Willard, Philip Phormlee and Walter Brookin, perform remarkable feats in the air. Two of the machines were of the Curtiss type and two were Wright machines." With this experience, Joseph Fielding Smith's interest in aviation was irrevocably kindled, an interest that, more than fifty years later, would culminate in his becoming an honorary brigadier general in the Utah National Guard. Joseph loved flying, and from the time of the first tentative flights of the Wright Brothers and other pioneers until his death during the jet age, he was an enthusiastic supporter of aviation and air travel.

But the comfort, convenience, and speed of air travel lay in the distant future as Joseph Fielding began the second year of his apostolic service. A three-and-a-half week trip he took into remote areas of Colorado, New Mexico, and Arizona, during May and June underscored the crude nature of transportation facilities that existed then compared to the sophisticated aircraft that would exist fifty years later. The trip commenced on May 17, 1911, when Joseph Fielding and his companion, George F. Richards, left Salt Lake City. The first part of the trip was comparatively peaceful and easy as they traveled by train through Denver and the San Luis Valley in Colorado and Santa Fe, New Mexico, to the little town of Bluewater, New Mexico. There they were provided with a wagon and horses to begin a two-week trip through desolate parts of New Mexico and Arizona to hold meetings with the Saints who lived there in isolated communities. The first day, the party traveled twelve miles to a campsite in the mountains. "Here we had the misfortune to lose one of our horses," Joseph wrote, "which I had ridden most of the way." Since a brother Tietjen took the horse Elder Richards was riding to try to find the lost horse, the apostles transferred to the springless wagon for the trip on to Ramah, New Mexico. They had traveled but a few miles when they "lost a wheel and were consequently delayed and under the necessity of obtaining another wagon." Joseph explained that this was a farm wagon, "which was too heavy for our harness, and the horses were small." Later, as they went down the west side of the Continental Divide, Joseph explained that "the road was very rough and rocky; at places there was no road at all, the bed of the canyon stream — now dry — being used, and barely wide enough for our wagon, managed to break our tugs, which caused another delay, while we wired them up." Arriving at Ramah in the late afternoon, the apostles "had a chance to clean up a little" before holding a meeting that lasted until ten o'clock. Among those present were David K. Udall, the president of the St. Johns Stake, and his second counselor, William D. Rencher, who had come to meet the visitors and to accompany them to St. Johns.

The travelers left Ramah early the next morning. "We had a good team and spring wagon with which to complete the journey," wrote Joseph. These had been provided by President Udall. But he failed to provide suitable weather for the two-day trip. "All day Thursday the wind blew fiercely in our faces," Elder Smith noted. And with the wind came clouds of dust that blinded and choked the travelers and saturated their clothing and bedding. "We have had a difficult time trying to get the dust out of our clothes," Joseph wrote on Saturday May 27, the morning after their arrival in St. Johns.

The affairs of the stake were no less chaotic. "There were not many present," Joseph wrote of the Saturday morning meeting. "Many stake and ward authorities were absent and those who came were not on time." Among the absentees were seven members of the high council who were in town but who failed to attend. The attendance at the afternoon session was also sparse. And afterward a controversy surfaced in which several members had petitioned for the removal of the local magistrate from his Church position. These circumstances prompted Elder Richards to mildly reprove the brethren at an evening meeting "for their indifference and apparent lethargy so apparent during the conference."

Wanting to get at the root of the problem, the two apostles met with the stake presidency and high council the following morning where it was learned that several of them did not observe the Word of Wisdom and that animosities had developed over a dispute involving the construction of a reservoir and canal. "We labored with them until meeting time," wrote Elder Smith, "and again after meeting until nearly two o'clock and again in the afternoon at the close of meeting until 7:00 P.M. before matters were adjusted." Because of their efforts to resolve these difficulties, the apostles were ten minutes late for the evening meeting, which was to have been devoted to the MIA. It suddenly ended shortly after they arrived. "The MIA meeting in the evening was adjourned after a very brief session," explained Elder Smith, "because the gas light failed us."

In the experience of Elder Smith and his companion at St. Johns, one sees how the leaders of the Church were able to maintain a spirit of unity and cohesion among the Latter-day Saints in remote rural communities extending from Canada to Old Mexico. Since they recognized and were submissive to the ecclesiastical authority the General Authorities possessed, the local leaders were amenable to the instruction and counsel the visitors gave. In this manner, through frequent, periodic visits, the Salt Lake brethren were able to monitor local conditions, to detect and resolve problems as they arose, to instruct the Saints in the doctrines and policies of the Church, and to motivate them to attain the objectives defined by the leaders.

After leaving St. Johns, the two apostles visited a string of other small communities that contained clusters of durable Latter-day Saints who lived tenaciously on the outer fringes of the Church: Eager, Lund, Nutrioso, Alpine, Luna, Snowflake, Taylor, Woodruff, and St. Joseph. Transportation between these towns was by horse-drawn wagons or buggies. Usually, the hosts of the next town would meet halfway to pick up the visitors and then, after meetings were held, take them halfway toward their next destination. At each stop, the travelers counseled with local leaders, laid at rest any difficulties, and preached to the members.

St. Joseph, the last stop on their itinerary, was on the main line of the Santa Fe railroad. There the two apostles caught a train to Williams, Arizona, a distance of about a hundred miles. Their purpose was to enable Elder Smith to see the Grand Canyon for the first time. Traveling several miles through a sparse pine forest, they suddenly came in view of this wonder of the world. The only words Joseph could find to explain this phenomenon and the impression it made on him were "a remarkable and awful chasm." Returning to Williams, the apostles took the Santa Fe train west to Los Angeles, where they made connection for the trip to Salt Lake City. As they had several hours before their train left Los Angeles, the travelers "went out to Long Beach and had a bath in the ocean."

One might have thought that after an arduous three-and-a-half week trip away from home, sleeping in a different bed almost every night, traveling much of the time on horseback or in horse-drawn conveyances, and under the pressure of numerous, sometimes stressful meetings, that Joseph would have taken off a day or two to recuperate and recharge his batteries. But what do we find? "Arrived home Friday morning at 6:30, June 9th," he wrote, "and was home all forenoon. In the afternoon I was at the Historian's office, also the president's office." The next day, Saturday, he spent all morning in the Historian's Office. In the afternoon, he went to the farm with David, George, and Wesley "and worked weeding beets." Finally, on Sunday, he got a day of rest—of sorts. "I tended the babies," he wrote, "while Ethel went to meeting." This would have included four-year-old Emily and seven-month-old Naomi.

While this kind of a schedule may seem hectic, if not exhausting, to others, Joseph seems to have taken it in stride and, indeed, to have thrived on it. At the time he was only thirty-five years old and in the prime of health. Therefore, travel of this kind would not have been a burden. On the contrary, it would have been interesting if not exciting to him as he saw new places and met new friends. This reaction is suggested by an entry he made in his diary on May 25 during the two-day trip from Ramah to St. Johns. "On our way," he wrote, "we spent a short time at the Zuni Pueblo Village, which was quite a sight." This was the first time Joseph had visited an Indian village, and the experience was fascinating to him, as this brief entry clearly implies.

On the other hand, the circumstances that provided Joseph Fielding with the opportunity to see and learn new things, to grow in his knowledge of people and events, and to increase in spiritual stature were the very circumstances that imposed heavier burdens of household and family responsibility upon Ethel. She was thereby deprived

of needed assistance she would otherwise have had around
the home. And it prevented her from devoting any ap-
preciable time toward self-development or caring for her
own needs. Such conditions provide greater understanding of diary entries such as this one made by Elder Smith
on September 2, 1911, during his visit to Lovell, Wyoming,
for a stake conference. "I received a letter from Ethel of a
rather gloomy nature," he wrote, "but informing me that
the children were all well."

Both Joseph and Ethel were fully aware of the strains
on the family, and especially upon Ethel. And they were
aware also of any subtle, perhaps unexpressed, anxieties
Josephine and Julina may have had, knowing that their
natural mother was dead. So, the parents made special
efforts to bridge over these difficulties and concerns,
thereby increasing the love and unity in the family.

On Friday, June 16, 1911, Joseph noted, "Today being
Louie's birthday anniversary . . . with Ethel and the children, I went to the cemetery with flowers." A month later,
on July 14, the whole family went to Liberty Park for an
outing. And the next Sunday, Joseph attended sacrament
meeting with the family at the 20th ward. "The babies,
Emily and Naomi," he explained, "would not permit me
to remain inside, they disturbed the meeting, so I remained
on the outside most of the time and let Ethel attend the
meeting as she gets fewer chances than I do."

It addition to allowing Ethel to enjoy sacrament meeting whenever possible, unencumbered with tending the
children, Joseph accompanied her to the occasional social
functions held by the family, the ward, or his quorum and
occasionally attended the theater. The plays seen there
were usually staged by traveling dramatic companies that
would come to town with their own cast and scenery,
remaining for a few days or weeks depending on the popularity of the show. So on September 29, 1911, Joseph and
Ethel went to the theater to see Henry Miller in *The Havoc*.
A few months later, they attended a comedy entitled *Get
Rich Quick Wallingford*. And on Ethel's twenty-third birth-

day, October 23, 1912, the Smiths celebrated by attending a play at the new Colonial Theatre—"The first time I was ever there," Joseph reported in his diary.

By now, it was even more difficult for the couple to get away for an evening of entertainment, since their family had grown to five girls with the birth of Lois on March 26, 1912. Ethel experienced some difficulty in giving birth to this her third child, who was several weeks premature. Relieved that both mother and child were healthy and strong, Joseph poured out his gratitude in this diary entry: "The Lord bless her and her mother and preserve them both from harm. May our little one and all our children grow to be good, honorable, Latter-day Saints, to labor in the service of their Heavenly Father, be protected from all harm, and be an honor to the name they bear. May I and their mother be blessed to teach them the truth that they may walk in the ways of the Lord and never depart from the truth which has been revealed. The Lord has been merciful to me—may I be worthy of all his blessings."

Only a few months before the birth of this newest member of the Smith family, another member of it died, full of years and crowned with accomplishment. On November 6, 1911, Church Patriarch John Smith passed away. "Uncle John was born in Kirtland, Ohio, September 22, 1832," Joseph Fielding noted in his diary on that date, "and was ordained to the office and priesthood of Patriarch by President Brigham Young, February 18, 1855. His first blessing was given August 17, 1856, to Samuel Knight, son of Newel and Lydia Knight, and his last patriarchal blessing was given October 30, 1911, to Alma Joseph William Gardner, who was born July 19, 1862, in Yorkshire, England. He commenced recording his blessings in book 'A' and went through the alphabet and was recording in book 'BB', in which there were 47 blessings at the time of his death. In all he gave 20,659 blessings."

Included among this vast number of blessings, of course, was the one given to Joseph Fielding in 1896, fifteen years earlier. Already the promises made there were beginning to unfold since from the time of his ordination to the apostleship he had been fulfilling his "duty to sit in counsel" with his brethren. The fulfillment of the promise that he would "live to a good old age" still lay far in the future, as did the one that he would "preside among the people." And one as obedient and faithful as was Joseph Fielding Smith would not have failed to take to heart the significant reminder in that blessing that God "will reward according to merit" and the admonition that he should "strive to inform thy mind and be prepared for events to come." As the grandson of the patriarch and martyr, Hyrum Smith, and the great-grandson of Joseph Smith Sr., the first Patriarch to the Church, there can be little doubt that Joseph Fielding was profoundly influenced by this blessing and would have been anxious to do everything necessary to obtain the promises it contained.

In time, indeed, within three years after his call to the Twelve, Joseph Fielding felt the need for more patriarchal guidance than was contained in the blessing given him by his Uncle John. Perhaps he had become more acutely aware of the vast scope and demands of apostolic service and the reality that the crowded schedule of travel, conferences, and consultations would dominate the rest of his life. Also there are hints that another circumstance weighed heavily in his quest—the blatant charges of nepotism that had surrounded his call to the Twelve. For one as sensitive, serious, and sincere as Joseph Fielding Smith, such charges would have wounded deeply. And while the loud furor over his call had subsided, lingering remnants of the feelings it had produced were manifested in snide remarks made by some, or in patronizing words or attitudes that implied that Joseph occupied his office only through the influence of his powerful father. Such attitudes would have been intensified after Joseph's call when his father began to use him in a consulting capacity in preference to others with greater seniority and experience than he. It is easy to understand, therefore, why this sensitive, able young man would have wanted to receive some spiritual clarification about his status and the role he was destined to play in the Church.

For whatever reason he sought it, Joseph's desire for a second patriarchal blessing was fulfilled at the little town of Scipio, Utah, on May 11, 1913. He and his companion, Joseph W. McMurrin, had traveled there two days before in connection with a conference of the Millard Stake. Joining them in Scipio was stake president Alonzo A. Hinckley, who, twenty-one years later, would join Elder Smith as a member of the Twelve. Also present for the conference was the stake patriarch, Joseph D. Smith, a native of England, who apparently was not related to the Asael Smith family. The only reference Joseph Fielding made to the incident that would have such a profound influence upon him was this short sentence: "While in Scipio, I received a blessing from Patriarch Joseph D. Smith."

The opening sentence of the blessing confirmed the reasons why it was sought and given. "I seal upon you a patriarchal blessing," it reads, "as it is the desire of your heart to know what the Lord requires of you." After declaring Elder Smith's lineage and referring to his convictions about the divine mission of the Prophet Joseph Smith, the patriarch made a statement that was to have a lasting effect upon Joseph Fielding. Said he, "You have been blessed with the ability to comprehend, to analyze, and defend the principles of truth above many of your fellows, and the time will come when the accumulative evidence that you have gathered will stand as a wall of defense against those who are seeking and will seek to destroy the evidence of the divinity of the mission of the Prophet Joseph Smith: and in this defense you will never be confounded, and the light of the Spirit will shed its rays upon your heart as gently as the dews that fall from heaven, and it will unfold to your understanding many truths concerning this work that have not yet been revealed." (Copy of blessing in Church Archives). That Elder Smith attached special significance to this statement is evident from the fact that he copied it verbatim in the back of his journal

175

for the year 1937. Nor is it coincidental that during this year he was compiling the material for his book *The Teachings of the Prophet Joseph Smith,* which was published the next year.

Other key provisions of this second patriarchal blessing provided Elder Smith with important insights: "You were called and ordained before you came in the flesh as an Apostle of the Lord Jesus Christ," said the patriarch, "to represent his work in the earth." And as to the ultimate role he would play during mortality, the blessing was no less explicit: "You will indeed stand in the midst of this people a prophet and a revelator to them for the Lord has blessed you and ordained you to this calling, and it will come upon you as naturally as the night shall follow the day." And on a purely personal level, the blessing contained these words of comfort and solace: "Your family will grow up and bless your name, and your influence with your sons and daughters, in connection with your wife, will hold your children in the gospel path and not one shall be lost."

Chapter Ten

Gaining Apostolic Stature

The receipt of his second patriarchal blessing seems to have marked the end of Joseph Fielding Smith's introduction to the work of the Twelve and to have opened the door to the remaining fifty-seven years of apostolic service that lay ahead. During the first three years, he had visited most of the stakes in the Church, thereby becoming acquainted with its principal leaders personally. In turn, the general Church membership had been exposed to this the youngest apostle and had been able to gauge the depth of his knowledge and his spirituality. They had found in him an earnest, sincere young man, well informed about Church history and doctrine, precise and analytical, who chose his words with care and who was deliberate and unemotional in his delivery. And those who had mingled with him personally had found him friendly and approachable, interested in the welfare of others — even sometimes jovial, though never loud or intrusive. At the same time, they detected in him a certain reserve tinged with self-confidence, although it lacked any arrogance or self-importance. Rather, his demeanor conveyed an inherent nobility of character as one who was precisely where God had always intended him to be.

After the incident in Scipio, Joseph Fielding seems to have pursued his calling with increased enthusiasm and diligence, although on the face of it the routine appears unchanged. The two succeeding weekends found him in Idaho, first at Blackfoot and then at Malad, farming communities where he found the winter wheat and spring plantings growing profusely. Although he was born and reared in the city, Joseph felt a special affinity for farmers because of the work he had performed on his father's farm over the years and because his ancestors for generations back had tilled the land. There was a faith and toughness about these people that commanded admiration. They planted in full confidence that the seeds would sprout and grow. And the intermittent ravages of flood, drought, and insect invasion, or the perverse fluctuations of the market, did not deter or dishearten them in their persistent plantings.

The week following the Malad conference provided Joseph with an interesting variation in his customary routine. On Thursday, May 29, 1913, he and Ethel traveled to Provo, Utah, to attend the graduation exercises at Brigham Young University. It was the first time he had attended such a convocation since Louie graduated from the University of Utah several years before. On this occasion, however, he was more than a mere spectator. A few months before, he had been appointed as a member of the Board of Trustees of BYU. So he and the other board members had an official function to perform. And following the exercises, he participated in a board meeting where a variety of matters affecting the university were handled. This was the beginning of a fruitful relationship between Joseph Fielding Smith and Brigham Young University that would extend for many decades. By 1939, he had been elected chairman of the executive committee of the board, a position he would hold until 1970 when, as president of the Church, he became chairman of the board. In these positions, Joseph exerted a dominant influence on the philosophy, policies, and procedures governing this distinctive institution. His views carried great weight in matters of finance, administration, faculty, athletics, student affairs, and the religious curriculum. It was his influence that swung the pendulum in favor of a new science building when others on the board felt it was too expensive. It was Joseph Fielding Smith who broke ground for the new fieldhouse on campus; and it was he who dedicated the beautiful building of fine arts. And whenever his busy schedule permitted it, he could be found at athletic events, enthusiastically cheering on the BYU teams, or at cultural or social programs on campus. He became one of the university's most vocal, enthusiastic, and influential supporters, never missing an opportunity to plug, publicize, or promote it. His aspirations for BYU were outlined in a letter to university president Ernest L. Wilkinson: "Brigham Young University [will] grow and become very great," he wrote on December 4, 1951, "with an expansion that will cover all fields that are of value to the members of the church, including, of course, the teaching of faith in God, and in the mission of our Redeemer, also that of the Prophet Joseph Smith. I can see where this school can become a great power for good, not only to members of the church but to all good people throughout the world." (Wilkinson Presidential Papers, BYU.)

Joseph's unabashed boosterism for BYU may be traced in part to the fact that he never had the opportunity to attend a university, let alone graduate from one. In a sense, therefore, his avid support of the school may have represented, in part, a vicarious attempt to compensate for his youthful deprivation of the chance for higher education. And later, at age seventy-five, any suppressed desire he had for a diploma, the symbol of academic achievement, was satisfied when in 1951, Brigham Young University awarded him an honorary Doctor of Letters for "Spiritual Scholarship."

This academic honor lay almost forty years in the future

179

when Joseph Fielding attended his first BYU convocation as a member of the school's board of trustees. The day was special, not only because of the events pertaining to the university but also because Ethel was with him. It was a rare occasion when she was able to accompany him on a trip out of town. So the young couple savored the day as they enjoyed the hospitality of the president of the university, who hosted the board members and their wives at the special functions connected with the graduation.

This delightful interlude ended two days later when Joseph hit the road again on the stake conference circuit. He first went north to Garland and then south to St. George, the scene of his first "church assignment." It had been thirty-six years since his last visit, when, as an infant, he had accompanied his parents there for the dedication of the temple. With no recollection of that first visit, Joseph really saw this charming community for the first time, the heart of Utah's "Dixie," set in the midst of rainbow-hued hills. Even then, St. George had become a favorite hideaway for many from up north who sought refuge from the snow, ice, and biting winds of winter. But now in mid-June, it was unpleasantly hot for Elder Smith and his companion, Joseph M. McMurrin, who, following a successful though poorly attended conference, left for home. "Bro. McMurrin and I returned," reported Joseph, "leaving at 4 A.M. Monday morning and arriving home Tuesday morning June 17th after a very dirty ride." The following weekend found Elder Smith in Ogden with Elder George F. Richards. There the two apostles organized the Ogden 11th Ward, which was carved out of the old Ogden 1st Ward. They installed Nathan A. Tanner as the ward's first bishop.

Joseph's last stake conference assignment before the summer break was to the Salt Lake Stake. "In the morning," he wrote on Sunday July 6, "I attended the opening session of the Salt Lake stake conference and the balance of the day I spent with my father." These private sessions with the Prophet became ever more frequent as Joseph Fielding matured and became better acquainted with the

*Joseph Fielding Smith
with his father, Joseph
F. Smith, May 2, 1914*

inner workings of the Church. His principal function in the role of a confidant to his father appears to have been to serve as a sounding board for the Prophet's plans and ideas. The father had full confidence in the son, and knew he would not divulge to others the things they discussed. That this confidence was not misplaced is seen in the fact that Joseph Fielding Smith's diaries and journals do not appear to contain a single reference to sensitive matters he had discussed with his father.

During the last part of July, Joseph enjoyed a respite from his demanding labors. He took advantage of the opportunity to strengthen his family ties, spending as much time as possible with Ethel and the children and enjoying some diversions. Not all of their outings were recreational, however, as on July 17 Joseph took his family to Holladay to pick fruit. The day following this outing, he accompanied his mother to Ocean Park, California, to help his sister Donnette and her children move back to Salt Lake City. They had spent some time in a beach cottage there for the health of one of Donnette's children who was "afflicted." On returning home, Joseph spent the rest of July following a relaxed schedule at the office and at home.

August 1 found Elder Smith on the road again when he and Elder David O. McKay traveled to St. Anthony, Idaho, for a conference of the Yellowstone Stake. This pair also teamed up the following week when they attended the Ogden stake conference together. Since the stake included wards in the Upper Ogden Valley, Huntsville, Eden, and Liberty, the apostles split up on Sunday, Joseph attending a meeting in Huntsville Sunday morning while David O. was in North Ogden. Then in the afternoon they switched, with Joseph speaking at the chapel in North Ogden while Elder McKay spoke in Huntsville, the place of his birth, where his father had served for so many years as a bishop.

The following week found Elder Smith in Bancroft, Idaho, for a stake conference. His father accompanied him, and it was one of the few times they attended a stake conference together in an official capacity. Also with them was Elder Charles H. Hart of the First Council of Seventy. One can imagine the stake president's anxiety at having three General Authorities attend his conference, including the president of the Church and his son and namesake who was a member of the Twelve. And one can also imagine the mutual sense of pride and joy father and son would have felt in each others' presence as they bore testimony and instructed the people.

The instructions the General Authorities gave at stake conferences in outlying areas varied according to the local conditions. They focused on the things they felt the people needed, not only to satisfy their spiritual needs but also to enable them to live happier, healthier, and more productive lives. Typical was the instructions Joseph Fielding gave at Escalante, Utah, in August 1913. "During the conference," he reported, "we spoke of ward teaching, missionary work, tithing [and] the need of [a] water system for the town of Escalante and other towns." Elaborating on this last item, he added, "The people in those towns in the eastern part of Garfield County live in rather primitive conditions in some respects which are unnecessary. Their water facilities are very poor."

Two days later in nearby Tropic, he "spoke of sanitary conditions, etc." By way of explanation, he added, "Here the people dip up water from the ditches for culinary purposes, pour it into barrels, let it settle, and then use it. When they dip it up it is like chalk in color, due to the clay." Elder Smith was quite astonished at the reason given by local leaders about why they did not remedy this situation. "Only three miles away there is a good spring from which water could be piped to town," Joseph recorded, "but it is not done for lack of enterprise and for fear the water would 'corrode the pipes.'" The regular instruction and encouragement given by Joseph Fielding and other leaders to the Saints living in remote rural areas helped unify the Church organizationally, preserve its doctrinal integrity, and help lift the members to a higher level of social and cultural development.

While at Escalante on this trip, Joseph Fielding had an experience that occurred with increasing frequency as he traveled around the Church. He met another cousin! And as it often happened, this one was concealed under a different name. This new-found cousin was Ernest A. Griffin, bishop of the Escalante Ward, whose mother was Sarah Smith Griffin, the daughter of the Patriarch Hyrum Smith by his first wife, Jerusha. Jerusha bore six of Hyrum's children, five of whom lived to maturity. The numerous progeny of these children, added to the progeny of Joseph Smith Sr. and uncle John Smith, provided Joseph Fielding with an extended family of almost astronomical proportions. He loved and cherished all these cousins and was always happy to find a new one, as he was happy to find Bishop Griffin.

Bishop Griffin's ward had a baseball team that had challenged the brethren from Panguitch to a game on Saturday afternoon during the stake conference. Apparently short-handed, the Panguitch team was bold enough to recruit one of the visitors from up north to fill in. "Between meetings in the afternoon," wrote Joseph Fielding on August 30, 1913, "I played ball with the Panguitch brethren against Escalante." That the new recruit was an apostle presumably was a matter of indifference to these brethren from Panguitch, so long as he knew how to play the game. They would soon learn that this agile, thirty-seven-year-old was no slouch with either the bat or the glove. The skills he had acquired while he was a mainstay on the old Sixteenth Ward team years before were intact, albeit a little rusty. And the Escalante team may have been surprised to find that the competitive fires still burned brightly in this mild-mannered apostle, who liked to win. Indeed, the fact that he neglected to mention the score may imply that his team did not win!

The backward conditions Joseph Fielding found in Escalante and Tropic may have been magnified in his eyes because of their contrast with the progressive spirit of enterprise and development that infused Salt Lake City at the time. The new Bishops' Building and Deseret Gymnasium were completed during the year Elder Smith was called to the Twelve; the Hotel Utah was completed the following year; the Latter-day Saints Hospital was doubled in size in 1913, the year of his visit to Escalante; and at that time, the new Church Administration Building was in the planning stage and would be completed in four years, thereby providing the General Authorities with quarters some thought were unnecessarily lavish. The wide disparity between these modern facilities and the primitive kind found in communities like Tropic was a chief factor in the thrust of Elder Smith and the other General Authorities to stimulate a more forward-looking attitude among the Saints in these rural areas.

With the completion of the Hotel Utah, Joseph Fielding and Ethel periodically enjoyed the luxury of its appointments. In defending the decision to allow a bar in the hotel on the ground that nonmembers who visited Salt Lake

Group photo at Deseret Gym, 1913; note Joseph Fielding Smith, no. 17

City would "want something to 'wet up' with once in a while," President Joseph F. Smith called the Hotel Utah "one of the most magnificent hotels that exists on the continent of America, or . . . the old continent either." (*Conference Report,* October 1911, p. 129.) This attitude seems to have been shared by most members of the Church, so that an evening out at the Hotel Utah was considered a signal event, deserving of special note. Such an occasion occurred two weeks after Joseph returned from Tropic when he and Ethel were the guests of Bishop Charles W. Nibley at a dinner in the hotel given in honor of Hyrum M. Smith, who had been called to preside over the European Mission. Also present were most of the other General Authorities and their wives. They enjoyed this special occasion with good food and conversation interspersed with musical numbers and remarks by the guests of honor and others called on by the host, Bishop Nibley.

On the day of Hyrum's departure for England, two days after the banquet, Joseph Fielding noted in his diary,

"I was appointed to take charge of his prayer circle during his absence." This entry reflects a practice followed by some members of the Twelve for many years. An apostle would invite selected persons to join him in a prayer circle that would gather periodically in the Salt Lake Temple. There doctrinal instructions and briefings about current Church affairs would be given as a prelude to a special prayer in which, in addition to the customary subjects of a prayer, there would be pleadings for guidance in particular problems or for blessings of health and protection. It was not uncommon when a prominent person was ill that all of the prayer circles would be asked to join in imploring God for a blessing of health upon the one afflicted. Special loyalties and common interests were nurtured by membership in these prayer circles. And it was these Hyrum sought to keep alive by asking his brother to carry on the meetings of his circle during his absence.

A few days after Hyrum's departure for England, the eighty-fourth semiannual general conference of the Church convened on Temple Square in Salt Lake City. On Sunday afternoon, October 5, 1913, Joseph Fielding again found himself in charge of an overflow session in the Assembly Hall. At the same time, Elder George F. Richards of the Twelve presided at a second overflow meeting held outside adjacent to the Bureau of Information. Joseph Fielding was the concluding speaker at the meeting in the Assembly Hall. During the course of his remarks, he mentioned two subjects that he frequently emphasized during the remainder of his ministry. The first related to the need for personal revelation to help the Saints find their way safely through life. "We are walking in the knowledge and the understanding of the gospel of the Lord Jesus Christ," said he, "and are entitled to that inspiration which will warn us of danger and guide us in the path of duty, and give us power to resist and overcome evil. We have the right to call upon the Lord in prayer and in faith for help, guidance, for assistance of his Holy Spirit and we will receive it." The second related to the need for personal integrity in our relationships with the Lord and with each other. "I pray," he continued, "that we may be true to our covenants, true to each other; that we will cast out of our hearts all that is evil, that we will not speak evil one of another, or be given to backbiting or contention or strife, for the spirit of wickedness destroys faith and tends to divide and separate instead of uniting and strengthening the people."

In these words, uttered only three years after his call to the Twelve, we already see the qualities of mind and character that were so evident in the man who would later become president of the Twelve and president of the Church. The man Joseph Fielding Smith ultimately became was anxious to be led constantly by the Spirit. And he was equally concerned about observing with exactness the covenants he had made with the Lord and maintaining a loving relationship with his brethren and sisters.

A month after the general conference, Elder Smith missed his first assignment since being called to the Twelve; he had to be excused from attending the Juab stake conference. "I was unable to fill my appointment," he wrote on November 8, 1913, "being confined to bed with a high fever and headache. A very severe sore throat also developed which distressed me." He had recovered sufficiently to attend the Jordan stake conference the following weekend, however. Four days later, he left on a trip to Arizona that would take him away from home for more than three weeks. With him were Horace H. Cummings, the superintendent of Church schools, and Hyrum G. Smith, Patriarch to the Church. The Patriarch, who was three years younger than Joseph Fielding, had succeeded his grandfather, John Smith, having been ordained by President Joseph F. Smith on May 12, 1912. This trio traveled by train through Colorado and New Mexico to the Santa Fe line and thence to Holbrook, Arizona. From this small railroad town on the Little Colorado River, they were driven "in an auto over muddy roads and in a rainstorm to St. Johns." Their route of travel took them through the heart of the Petrified Forest, the clay soil of which caused them "some delays." Arriving after dark on Friday, November 21, the three travelers were accommodated in the home of stake president David K. Udall.

Over the weekend, Joseph presided at the usual meetings of a stake conference, where he "imparted such instructions as we were led to give." He was even busier on Monday following the conference, when he wrote, "I accompanied Bro. Cummings to the Academy where I addressed the students in a devotional exercise and attended one of the classes. In the afternoon we were busy administering to the sick and afflicted; and I assisted Hyrum G. in the giving of blessings, writing for him." Leaving St. Johns the following day, the visitors traveled to nearby Concho, where they held meetings; the day after that, they went on to Snowflake, walking part of the way.

At Snowflake, the three brethren were met by a party from Salt Lake City led by President Joseph F. Smith. The party included the president's wife Edna and two daughters, President Anthon H. Lund, Elder George Albert Smith, and Bishop Charles W. Nibley and his wife. In addition to participating in a conference of the Snowflake Stake, this large party from Salt Lake City had come to this remote area for a special purpose explained by Joseph Fielding: "Services were held in the new Academy building," he wrote on November 27, "and the building was dedicated, President Smith offering the prayer. Three years ago the Snowflake Academy was destroyed on thanksgiving day, and the new building, which is much better, was dedicated on thanksgiving day." This building, like many other similar structures erected at the time, was used both for school and church purposes.

President Smith and his party traveled from Salt Lake City on a private railroad car that had been left on a siding at nearby Holbrook. Returning there Sunday afternoon, an evening meeting was held in the courthouse. And the next morning, the President's party, augmented by Joseph Fielding and his two companions, left on a journey that would take them ultimately to Arizona's southernmost communities. Along the way, they passed through small villages founded by Mormon colonists, such as Joseph City, Brigham City, and Sunset; and they enjoyed the beautiful pine forests surrounding the San Francisco Peaks and the spectacular vistas of the Grand Canyon, where they remained a day and a half. Later the journey assumed the aspect of a triumphal march as at Douglas Station, the train was met "by the Mayor and a number of leading citizens," and at Phoenix, the state capital, it was met "by Governor George W. P. Hunt and Col. Massie, his chief of staff, and the Mayor of Phoenix and others." Here the party left the train and were driven by automobile to nearby Mesa. The governor attended the dedicatory services for two new chapels in Mesa, speaking at one of them, and, according to Joseph Fielding, he praised the Latter-day Saints in Arizona "very highly."

The next day, Joseph Fielding accompanied his father and others on a trip to inspect the new Roosevelt Dam, which was a key element in the long-range plans to develop the water resources of the Salt River Basin. "The dam is a wonderful piece of engineering skill," Joseph Fielding wrote, "and will mean a great deal to the people of this part of Arizona."

The following weekend, the visitors attended various meetings connected with the Maricopa stake conference held in Mesa. One of these Joseph Fielding presided over separately when he was sent to nearby Chandler to organize a new ward. There he called and ordained Henry L. Peterson as the bishop.

Leaving Mesa, the visitors traveled to the Gila Valley in southeastern Arizona, where they held a series of meetings in Thatcher and Safford. The leading Latter-day Saint in this area was President Joseph F. Smith's brother-in-law, Andrew Kimball, the twin brother of his wife Alice. Included among Andrew Kimball's children was an eighteen-year-old son, Spencer W., who, a few months later, would receive a call from his uncle, President Smith, to serve as a missionary in the Swiss German Mission. And thirty years later, Spencer Kimball would be called to share the apostleship with his cousin by marriage, Joseph Fielding Smith. The Salt Lake visitors then traveled to Tucson, Arizona, where they were "entertained by a number of leading citizens, and visited places of interest in and near Tucson, including the San Xavier Mission . . . and had lunch at the Tucson Commercial Club."

Because of a special anxiety, Joseph Fielding left the other travelers at this point to return home. His concern was Ethel, who was in the last stages of pregnancy, and he wanted to be near when she gave birth to the baby. He arrived home on Friday, December 13; five days later, Ethel gave birth to her first son. "The baby was born at 2:10 P.M.," wrote the father on December 18, 1913, "and on account of [Ethel's] sickness, I did not attend the regular meeting of the Council in the temple today." Then, in a pensive mood, he reflected on the implications of the birth of his first son, who would be given his father's name, Joseph Fielding Smith Jr. "I feel thankful to the Lord for this blessing," wrote the father, "and hope and pray the boy may grow to be an honorable man in the service of the Lord. And I pray my Heavenly Father to help me to so teach him and all my children that they may be true to the Gospel and love to do the will of the Lord." Elder Smith lived to see this blessing fulfilled. Without exception, all of his eleven children grew to maturity, faithful and obedient to the teachings of their father. All five of the sons filled missions for the Church, as did the husbands of the six daughters. All the children were sealed in the temple to worthy companions, except Lewis, who was killed before he could marry. No achievement Joseph Fielding attained in life and no honor bestowed upon him could impart the sense of joy and achievement he experienced in seeing his children faithfully follow his teachings and emulate his life.

Chapter Eleven

The Shifting Tide

The first four years of Joseph Fielding Smith's apostolic service was a time of extraordinary personal growth. His reputation as an apostle, a historian, a scripture scholar, and a successful family man was firmly established during this period. No longer was he looked upon by some critics merely as the son of the president of the Church who owed his high position to an accident of birth. He was regarded rather as a man of intelligence and discipline, careful and precise in speech, and faithful and prompt in service. He was also seen to be a man of strong opinions who was forthright in speaking his mind and fearless in admonishing the Saints about what they should do. This quality of character, which became more evident as he grew older, is clearly reflected in the talk he delivered at the general conference in April 1914. After commenting on the past achievements of the Church and its members, he cautioned that there was much room for improvement. "There are many among us who are not living up to their duties," he warned. "There are many among us who fall short and fail in various ways in keeping the commandments of the Lord." Indicating that it was to this class his remarks would be directed, Elder Smith read as his text verses 26 through 29 of the 58th section of the Doctrine and Covenants. He emphasized that Latter-day Saints should not have to be commanded in all things, that men should be "anxiously engaged in a good cause" and should "do many things of their own free will." He said, "Let every man set his house in order and see that his family is taught the principles of the Gospel of Jesus Christ." Specifically, he admonished "that they keep the word of wisdom; that they abstain from the use of strong drink, from the use of tea, from the use of coffee, tobacco and other stimulants and narcotics which tend to destroy and to break down rather than to build up the system." He also urged parents to teach the principle of faith in their homes, to obtain knowledge and understanding, and to "walk uprightly and justly before the Lord and keep the commandments as they have been given to us." (*Conference Report,* April 1914, pp. 91, 92.) These themes would find their way into Joseph's sermons throughout his apostolic career. Invariably they would be buttressed with pertinent scriptures and reinforced with personal admonitions. His sermons were never anecdotal or trivial but were always solid and immovable like the man himself.

Four months after this sermon was delivered, a massive political upheaval occurred in Europe, underscoring the need for the kind of virtues taught by Elder Joseph Fielding Smith. His diary entry for July 31, 1914, sets the stage for this violent commotion, whose rippling effects would ultimately be felt in America. "For several days," he wrote, "there has been ill feeling manifest in Austria Hungary against Serbia because of the assassination of Archduke Francis Ferdinand which resulted in a declaration of war by Austria against Serbia. The papers this morning declare that Germany has declared war on Russia and has invaded France." Then, in a spirit of foreboding, he added, "There is great commotion in the world and at present it appears that other nations will be drawn into the conflict." Joseph's concerns proved well founded; four days later he wrote, "It is reported that Germany has also made war on Belgium and England is involved and has issued an ultimatum to Germany." The next day he noted that England had declared war on Germany, which had retaliated by sinking a British ship; that Europe was in an uproar; and that "all the nations [were] mobilizing their forces." Against this bleak background, Elder Smith speculated whether all this portended that the millennial reign was imminent. Wrote he, "It begins to look like the commencement of the great destruction and conflict preceding the end, which I hope is the case, preparatory to the coming of the reign of peace."

The comparative remoteness of the conflict and the imperative demands of Joseph's church and family responsibilities soon lowered the priority of the European war on his agenda of personal concerns. More immediate and pressing were the continual round of stake-conference assignments and the infinite variety of choices and challenges facing a family of six children ranging in age from twelve years to eight months. Joseph had four conference assignments during the month following the outbreak of the war in Europe — to the Boise, Nephi, Young, and Rigby stakes. The travel entailed in attending these conferences and the marathon schedule of meetings during the weekends represented the largest block of Elder Smith's available time. Next came the hours he spent at his office during mid-week. And Ethel and the children got what was left over. Ethel understood the reasons for this and fully approved of her husband's priorities. She knew of the constraints on his time dictated by the apostolic charge he had accepted. And when the children reached the age of understanding, they were taught this so they came to accept without question why their father had little time to spend with them. Indeed, when the full significance of his calling was brought home to them, his role in the Church and the restrictions it imposed on him and the family became a point of personal distinction if not of pride for them.

Joseph understood well the hazards to family unity and harmony that his preoccupation with church work entailed. He was careful, therefore, to squeeze in a family activity whenever possible. This entry illustrates a typical way he was able to do this: "In the evening," he wrote on August 28, 1914, "I took my family to see the 'wizard' parade and later left for Rigby to attend the Rigby stake conference." During the week following his return from this conference, he noted, "Took my family out for a short ride once or twice during the week." These rides were in the family's new Model T Ford, which Joseph had purchased the day before leaving for Rigby. Since this was the first car he had owned, the novelty of it undoubtedly accounted for the initial frequency with which he and the family used it for the mere recreation of riding around town. When the novelty of owning a car wore off, however, the frequency with which it was used merely for pleasure declined. Yet, this remained as an occasional source of diversion and recreation for Joseph's family; and for him personally, it was something he enjoyed for the rest of his life.

Notwithstanding Elder Smith's commitment to his Church assignments, occasional emergencies reversed these priorities. A case in point was the illness of two-year-old Lois. "Most of the day I was at home," he wrote on September 9, 1914, "Lois being sick." Two days later he stayed home from work again "on account of Lois' sickness." She had had a fever for several days. "I was excused from going to Rexburg to attend conference," he explained, "and remained home Saturday and Sunday, nursing my baby girl." He stayed home for two more days, hovering over the child. By Tuesday evening, he was able to report with obvious relief, "Lois was much improved." So it was that sickness or other emergencies at home always elevated the family to the top of his personal agenda, subordinating everything to that until the problem had been solved. Meanwhile, if a family incident or situation was not an emergency, he would merely sandwich it in with his church duties as best he could. So, three days after Lois' recovery, Joseph wrote: "Josephine's birthday anniversary—she is 12 years old. I left with Seymour B. Young for Elsinore to attend the Sevier Stake Conference."

This trip to Elsinore was Joseph's last out-of-town assignment before the 1914 October general conference. "All through the rest of the month," he recorded on October 1, "I was at the office and engaged in meetings, including the quarterly meeting of the Twelve." It was four days later, at the Monday morning general session of the conference, that Joseph Fielding Smith delivered the most significant sermon of his comparatively young apostolic career. In it he focused on the Savior, decried those Christian ministers who deny the divinity of Christ, affirmed that implicit faith in Christ is a characteristic of Latter-day Saints, explained that the scriptures abound with testimonies of the Savior's divinity and resurrection, and cited the experiences of Joseph Smith, Oliver Cowdery, and Sidney Rigdon, who had seen the Savior in vision in the latter days. Having laid that groundwork, he proceeded to the heart of his discourse, which had special relevance to his hearers. "We have an individual testimony," said he, "given through the Spirit of the Lord to all who have lived in accordance with the Gospel. . . . We are not dependent upon the testimony of anyone else for this knowledge for we know through the Spirit that Jesus is the Christ, the Redeemer of the world." (*Conference Report,* October 1914, p. 98.) Then, reading from the second chapter of 2 Nephi, he emphasized the limited scope of the redemption effected by the Savior's sacrifice as it applies to the individual transgressor. "Behold, He offered Himself a sacrifice for sin," quoted Joseph, "to answer the ends of the law, unto all those who have a broken heart and a contrite spirit; and unto none else can the ends of the law be answered." Finally, Elder Smith read verse 8 from that chapter, underscoring the vast envangelical responsibility resting upon the Church. "Wherefore," he read, "how great the importance to make these things known unto the inhabitants of the earth, that they may know that there is no flesh that can dwell in the presence of God, save it be through the merits, and mercy, and grace of the Holy Messiah, who layeth down His life, according to the flesh, and taketh it again by the power of the Spirit." This evangelical responsibility, resting upon the Church as a whole, is magnified many times over as it applies to the members of the Twelve, who comprise the general missionary committee of the Church. Joseph Fielding Smith served as a member of the Twelve for sixty years and as president of that quorum for nineteen years; thus, he bore principal responsibility for the proselyting activities of the Church longer than any other man of this dispensation. He was anxious that the message of the gospel, the message of salvation and exaltation, be given to all people. It was this responsibility that absorbed a disproportionate amount of his time during the years of his apostolic service. And the doctrines interwoven with this message and the responsibility to teach it would claim the attention and the speaking and literary skills of Elder Smith throughout his life. One need only review the titles of some of his many books to understand this preoccupation: *The Way to Perfection,* for instance, and his three-volume work *The Doctrines of Salvation,* not to mention the dozens of articles he wrote for the Church publications that elaborated on these concepts.

Several weeks after this conference, Joseph Fielding joined his father and other Church leaders on a historic two-and-a-half-week trip that would take them deep into the heart of the southern states. They left Salt Lake City on Thursday, November 19, 1914, comfortably accommodated in a private car provided by the Union Pacific Railroad. Special porters were assigned to the car to prepare meals and provide valet services. This would be the luxurious home on wheels of President Smith and his party throughout the trip.

Since their departure was late in the evening on the 19th, darkness overtook them before they reached Ogden, where their private car was hitched to the Union Pacific

Mainliner headed east. The night was spent twisting and rocking through the canyons of the Wasatch up to the high plateau of southern Wyoming, where daybreak found them. This was the same train Joseph had taken years before on his way to the mission field. His upgraded accommodations on this trip paralleled the sudden rise that had occurred in his ecclesiastical status during the interval. Passing through Rawlins and Laramie, Wyoming, the train headed south at Cheyenne, arriving in Denver, Colorado, on Friday evening. Switching to another railroad line, they spent the second night and day crossing the table-flat lands of eastern Colorado and Kansas, whose autumn brown and stubbled fields bore mute testimony of a bounteous harvest. Five days later, the Prophet and his party would join all Americans in expressing thanks for the bounties of the land when they enjoyed a Thanksgiving feast in the mission home in Chattanooga, Tennessee.

Saturday evening, November 21, the travelers were met at the Kansas City depot by local Church leaders, who drove them by automobile to nearby Independence, Missouri. There the Prophet and Julina stayed with Mission President Samuel O. Bennion, while Joseph Fielding was accommodated in the home of Joseph E. Cardon, the editor of the *Liahona, the Elders Journal.*

The event that had drawn the Prophet and his party to Independence was the dedication of a new chapel. For weeks, President Bennion and his missionaries had worked side by side with the local members and leaders to make certain that everything was in perfect order for the president of the Church. There was last-minute painting and touching up in the interior of the building and extensive work outside landscaping the grounds. Among the missionaries who had been diverted from their customary proselyting work to help spruce up the chapel was a future president of the Church, Elder Spencer W. Kimball, President Smith's nephew. Spencer, whose original call was to Europe, had been reassigned to the Central

States Mission because of the outbreak of World War I earlier in the year.

Three dedicatory sessions were held on Sunday, November 19, 1914. At each session there was a sprinkling of members of the Reorganized Church in attendance, most of whom, reported Joseph Fielding, "paid respectful attention" although "a few were heard to make abusive remarks." Because of the sensitivities involved, Independence being the headquarters of the Reorganized Church, Joseph Fielding also noted that "not one [of the speakers] mentioned by word or intimation the Reorganization."

In a further attempt to bridge differences and to lay at rest any lingering enmities between the two churches, President Smith, accompanied by Joseph Fielding and others, paid a courtesy call on Joseph Smith III, president of the Reorganized Church, following the morning session of the dedication. "We found him very feeble, blind and deaf," reported Joseph Fielding. The interchange between these two sons of the Martyrs was cordial and conciliatory at a personal level, but was restrained and distant from an institutional point of view. It was Joseph Fielding's appraisal that Joseph Smith III was a "disappointed man," a condition that could be traced in no small part to his serious physical disabilities.

Leaving Independence the next day, the travelers went to Memphis, Tennessee, where, after touring the city in automobiles, they held a meeting with the missionaries from the Tennessee and Mississippi conferences. A preaching service was held in the evening at a public hall, attended by both members and nonmembers. There, according to Joseph Fielding, "the speakers presented the principles of the Gospel in power and with the guidance of the Spirit of the Lord." Present at these meetings and at others held in the South was Mission President Charles A. Callis, who, in less than twenty years, would join Joseph Fielding as a member of the Twelve.

The party arrived in Chatttanooga, Tennessee, on Wednesday morning, November 25, having traveled overnight from Memphis in their private car. Here the local leaders took the visitors on an automobile tour of the area, which included a stop at Chickamauga Park, where, Joseph reported, "vicious and bloody battles were fought during the Civil War." An evening meeting was held at the Lyric Theatre, "which was filled mostly with strangers." The diarist also noted that at the close of President Smith's remarks, "many of the audience applauded" and later "came to the platform and shook hands cordially with the brethren."

Following their Thanksgiving dinner on Thursday in Chattanooga, the travelers entrained for Atlanta, where the following day they were given the customary automobile tour of the city, during which they made a courtesy call on the mayor, Mr. Woodward. An evening meeting was held in Taft Hall, where an audience of "between four and five hundred" had gathered to hear the visiting Mormon leaders.

Going south into Florida, the party stopped briefly in Jacksonville and then traveled on to St. Augustine, located on the Atlantic Coast, the oldest European settlement on the eastern coast of North America. Here Joseph Fielding's historic instincts were aroused as he inspected the antiquities of the 350-year-old city, founded by the Spaniards in 1565. Of special interest to the diarist were the old fort, the oldest school house, the oldest dwelling, and the open slave market, where not too many years before, human beings were sold to the highest bidder as if they were chattel. At the fort, the visitors "saw the dungeon . . . where many poor Spaniards were punished, some even to death, by the cruelest methods of torture." In contrast to these ancient reminders of death and degradation, Joseph Fielding found something at St. Augustine that was a refreshing reminder of the joys of human life. Here he met a distant relative named Dr. Simon Ewing Smith, who was "108 years of age and as straight as a young man and very active." Joseph also reported that Doctor Smith was

Joseph Fielding Smith

"still riding a bicycle and was just as spry as if he were but sixty."

Returning to Jacksonville the same day, the Brethren held an evening meeting in a new chapel the Church had constructed. Joseph Fielding was the concluding speaker. The following day, a Sunday, three meetings were held, two at the small chapel and one in mid-afternoon at a public hall where seven hundred were in attendance, most of them nonmembers. As had occurred at a previous meeting, Joseph Fielding reported that following President Smith's address, "many in the congregation applauded."

Since the meetings in Jacksonville were the last ones in the South before the party headed home, Joseph Fielding wrote a brief summary of the trip and of its significance to the work. "The trip through the South has resulted in much good," he wrote, "and the results will be felt by the Elders for a long time to come. We have been entertained by the leading spirits in these communities, Mayors, Magistrates, Potentates, and many prominent men of national renown have paid their respects to President Smith. The newspapers throughout have spoken favorably, showing the great change in sentiment that has come over the people in recent years. Our trip has been most successful and encouraging to the Elders and Saints."

Leaving Jacksonville, the travelers began their long trip home, stopping in New Orleans, San Antonio, and Houston only long enough to do a little sightseeing. They found many of Houston's streets covered with two feet of water, the result of a heavy rainstorm that had deposited six inches of water on the city the night before their arrival. At El Paso, Texas, the party left the train to hold a special meeting in the local Odd Fellows Hall. Assembled there were many of the Saints who had been driven from the Mexican Colonies during the revolution. "President Smith gave the Mexican refugees some good, timely instruction," wrote Joseph, "regarding their situation and their future prospects."

Traveling on to Los Angeles, the members of the party

remained there for four days, enjoying the warmth of California's winter sun and speaking at special services held on Sunday. They arrived in Salt Lake City on Wednesday, December 9.

Aside from the length of this trip, the numerous meetings held during it, and the great impetus given to the work because of it, something about the trip was very special to Joseph Fielding Smith. It was the last time he was privileged to make a lengthy train trip with his father. It was the last time he had the privilege of sharing the pulpit with him in small, informal meetings, held with the Saints and nonmembers, away from the highly structured and formalistic meetings at general conferences and in the organized states. And it was the last time he would enjoy the luxury of spending long, uninterrupted hours visiting and relaxing with him, or occasionally engaging in a spirited game of checkers as their train wound its way across the continent to the Atlantic Ocean and back to the Pacific.

The years from 1915 through 1917 saw Joseph Fielding Smith continue with his heavy schedule of stake conference assignments, headquarters duties, and family responsibilities. They also saw him venture into an area of activity that until then was entirely foreign to him. In September 1915, he was appointed as a member of the board of directors of the Beneficial Life Insurance Company, a major insurer in the intermountain area, to replace Lewis S Hills, who had died recently. "This favor," Joseph Fielding reported, "is due to the kindness and favor principally of Lorenzo N. Stohl." At about the same time, he was appointed to the board of the Zions Savings Bank and the Consolidated Salt Company. Two years later, he became a member of the board of the Inland Crystal Salt Company. These appointments were welcomed by Joseph as they broadened the scope of his knowledge, led him into contact with prominent business leaders, and provided him with extra income to help augment the slender living allowance he received from the Church. Another welcome source of supplemental income was created in January 1917: "I have been requested," he noted on the nineteenth, "by the Bureau of the Census to prepare for the government the church census of the Church of Jesus Christ of Latter-day Saints. My commission was signed January 8 and I will proceed as soon as supplies are received from Washington." This appointment occupied a good part of Joseph's time for six months, until July 17, 1917, when he "finished and mailed the final report to the government on the church census."

Although Elder Smith did most of his own home repairs, helped Ethel pick and bottle fruit in season, and was extremely frugal in his expenditures, there never seemed to be a surplus of money during this period. The fee for handling the Church census came at a most fortuitous time. Because his immediate family had grown to nine with the birth of Amelia in June 1916, it became necessary for Joseph Fielding to purchase a new automobile. So two months after her birth, he traded in the Model T Ford on a new Reo, a seven-passenger car whose seating capacity could be increased by two or three by putting a table board across the two jump seats. The purchase of this larger and more expensive car became affordable because, reported Elder Smith, "I have just had some Deseret Building Society stock mature." Joseph did not learn how much larger the new car was until he tried to park it in his garage. It wouldn't fit. This made it necessary to enlarge his "automobile house."

The Reo was a source of great enjoyment to the Smiths. Frequently the whole family would load into the car merely to take a ride around town or to drive up the canyons of the Wasatch for picnics, fishing, or sightseeing. The car had detachable celluloid windows that could be removed during the warm months to allow for plenty of fresh air. A few idiosyncracies that developed later only made the Reo more endearing to the family — its tendency to boil over when it was driven uphill, the difficulty of patching its big-rimmed tires, and its occasional mechanical failures. Of the latter, the most dramatic and potentially dangerous occurred when a tie rod broke in downtown Salt Lake City. Because the Reo couldn't generate much speed, no collision or roll-over occurred. Afterward, one of the passengers walked alongside the car to kick the wheels straight until Joseph could maneuver it to a safe spot from where it was towed to a public "automobile house" for repairs.

The increased use of the automobile by Joseph Fielding and the other brethren as a means of transportation was dramatized a year after he bought the Reo. In September 1917, President Joseph F. Smith organized the first-ever automobile caravan of General Authorities to make a preaching tour into Southern Utah. Joseph Fielding and Ethel were invited to go along. Apparently sensing something of historic significance about the trip, Joseph kept a detailed log about it.

Leaving Salt Lake at exactly 1:45 P.M. on Tuesday, September 1, 1917, the caravan arrived in Provo at 4:00, where the members "were refreshed by a drink of sodawater." Traveling on to Payson, the group was met by stake president Jonathon Paige Jr. "and the people of the town who requested President Smith to make a few remarks, which he did." Joseph Fielding reported that at Mona, "we were met by the stake presidency and many citizens of Nephi in autos who came out to welcome us and escort us in to Nephi, headquarters of the Juab stake." The travelers seemed to ignore the clouds of dust kicked up by the procession of automobiles and were caught up instead by the novelty of the occasion and the excitement of having averaged twenty miles an hour during the ninety-mile trip from Salt Lake City.

The visitors were accommodated in the homes of the Saints in Nephi, the Joseph Fielding Smiths staying with Ethel's relative Orson Cazier and his wife. That night a standing-room-only crowd attended a preaching service in the Tabernacle, where some, unable to get in the building, stood outside, hoping to catch the drift of the speakers through the open windows and doors. And the line-up of speakers was impressive. It included all nine of the General

Authorities who were part of the caravan — President Joseph F. Smith and his counselor Anthon H. Lund; Heber J. Grant, president of the Twelve; and Hyrum M. Smith, Joseph Fielding Smith, and Stephen L Richards, members of the Twelve; Joseph W. McMurrin of the Seventy; and Presiding Bishop Charles W. Nibley and his counselor David A. Smith. The second day's trip covered the distance from Nephi to Beaver, during which brief stops were made at Levan (where Presidents Smith and Lund greeted the children who lined the streets to welcome the caravan), Scipio, Holden, Fillmore, Meadow, Kanosh, and Cove Fort. The travelers were met by local leaders and members all along the way, and in most of these towns, impromptu meetings were held where various members of the caravan spoke. At Beaver, where Joseph Fielding and Ethel stayed with the Gerrit DeJong family, old friends from the Seventeenth Ward, a three-hour preaching service was held from 8:00 to 11:00 P.M. where all of the General Authorities again spoke.

On the third day, Thursday the 13th, the travelers went on to Parowan, where stake conference meetings were held through the day. Friday morning, Joseph Fielding accompanied his father and part of the caravan to Cedar City, where special meetings were held while the remainder of the group remained in Parowan to complete the conference. That afternoon, both segments of the caravan joined for the final leg of the trip to St. George, through Leeds and Washington. Joseph Fielding reported, "At Leeds, where we arrived at about 6 P.M., we were met by the people who loaded us down with fruit, some of the best peaches and grapes that could be grown." That evening, a reception for the visitors was held at the St. George Tabernacle, following which everyone attended the county fair. "There we saw exhibits of fruits, grains and other products in abundance," reported Joseph Fielding, "and of the very first quality which we were privileged to sample."

After spending the weekend in St. George attending

stake conference meetings, the travelers headed home. At Cedar City, they crossed over the mountain to Panguitch and then continued north, passing through Circleville, Junction, Marysvale, and Monroe to Richfield. "All along the way we were met by throngs of people," wrote Joseph, "and the children had the privilege of shaking hands with President Smith and President Lund." Later at Manti, Joseph noted, "The sight of the children marching on each side of the automobiles as we entered the city in the afternoon was one worthy of preservation, and we all regretted that we had no camera or moving picture machine that could permanently record the scene." While at Manti, Joseph Fielding was able to visit the temple, where he examined the records, which, he wrote "are being kept according to the plan which I prepared for the Temples three or four years ago."

Traveling on, the caravan passed through Mount Pleasant, Chester, Spring City, and Fairview, and then on to the Utah Valley via Thistle and Spanish Fork Canyon. The party arrived home on Thursday, September 20, having been on the road for nine days. In summing up the experience, Joseph Fielding wrote: "The trip was most successful and will result in much good." Perhaps one unintended benefit from the tour was the realization by Joseph Fielding and the other leaders that this relatively new means of transportation would soon be the means of simplifying and expediting their work and of binding the widespread Latter-day Saint communities ever closer together. This was indicated by President Joseph F. Smith during his keynote address at the October 1917 general conference. "We made a short visit not long ago to some of our southern settlements," he said. "It is something that we should do oftener. I am conscious of it now, more so than I have been in times past." He went on to say it was "necessary that the presidency of the church, the Twelve Apostles, the Patriarch, the Seven Presidents of Seventies, [and] the Presiding Bishopric . . . should visit as far as possible, and see the people, and be seen of them." (*Conference Report,* October 1917, pp. 4, 5.)

Little did Joseph Fielding realize at the time that he would never again be privileged to tour among the Latter-day Saints with his father and his brother Hyrum. The following year would see them both unexpectedly carried to their graves. As 1918 dawned, nothing even remotely hinted that such a revolution would occur in the Smith family. Although President Joseph F. Smith was seventy-nine years old, he was in excellent health. And Hyrum was a robust forty-five-year-old, just coming into the most productive years of his life.

The suddenness of Hyrum's death would produce a shock from which the father would never recover. As late as Friday, January 18, 1918, there appeared to be nothing to suggest that Hyrum's time was near. On that day, Joseph Fielding wrote in his diary: "I was at the Historian's Office most of the day. With Bro. Orson F. Whitney, I listened to Hyrum read comments on the sections of the Doctrine and Covenants and also attended the Genealogical Board Meeting." That evening, Hyrum became nauseous. By Saturday night, he was in great pain. The next day, he was hospitalized. "Early this morning," wrote Joseph Fielding on Sunday January 20, "I received a call from Aunt Edna, asking me to go to Hyrum M's, as he was ill and they were going to take him to the hospital. . . . I arrived at his home just in time to accompany him, other members of the family also being present." Examinations at the hospital revealed that the patient had severe appendicitis and that surgery was imperative. "The operation was performed by Dr. Ralph T. Richards," Joseph reported, "assisted by Drs. Stephen L. Richards and Clarence Snow." The operation revealed that the appendix had broken, which caused serious complications. Because of his brother's critical condition, Joseph Fielding remained at the hospital most of Sunday and returned with David A. early Monday morning. Learning that the patient had spent a good night, and assuming that Hyrum was on the mend,

Joseph spent all day at the office and then returned to the hospital Tuesday morning with his father, Aunt Edna, and his brother Alvin. Although they found Hyrum had spent a restless night, they were told that he "was progressing favorably" and therefore gave no cause for alarm. Wednesday, Joseph Fielding spoke at the funeral of Lorinda P. Weike, a daughter of Parley P. Pratt and longtime employee of the Church Historian's Office. Stopping briefly at the hospital after the funeral, he was informed that Hyrum "was not so well." However, since his condition was not reported as being critical, Joseph attended an MIA board meeting, following which, at his father's request, he and his cousin George Albert Smith went to the hospital to administer to Hyrum. "We found him in a critical condition," wrote Joseph, "and I concluded to stay at the hospital with him and Ida during the night." Up until Wednesday, Joseph Fielding believed that his brother would recover. "I have felt that he had a mission to perform," he wrote in his diary, "and surely would be spared." It was not to be. "We did all that we could do for him," Joseph explained, "and tried to exercise faith, but it appeared that all that we and all Israel could do in faith and prayer could not avail." The end came at about 10:00 P.M. Wednesday, January 23, 1918.

The suddenness of Hyrum's passing engulfed the whole family in a dull sense of shock and disbelief. Why did this happen to one so young who had so much to offer? "The whole family is cast under a cloud of sorrow and gloom," Joseph wrote disconsolately. But this melancholy mood was short lived. The Smith family was too deeply imbued with the Mormon concepts of immortality and eternal life to be distracted for too long by the death of a loved one. So, soon after Hyrum's death, the persistent optimism typical of the Latter-day Saint mentality surfaced. "And yet," mused Joseph Fielding in his diary, "with it all, our hearts are filled with joy because of the faithful, honorable, and worthy life of our brother." The one most severely tried by the apostle's death was his father, President Joseph F. Smith. "My Father, himself stricken in years," Joseph Fielding explained, "bears up wonderfully under the sorrow, for the blow which comes to him is a severe one, indeed."

The funeral services were held in the Salt Lake Tabernacle on Sunday, January 27, 1918. "The building was packed," Joseph Fielding reported, "and excellent remarks were made by the brethren who spoke." These included Charles W. Penrose, counselor in the first presidency; Heber J. Grant, president of the Twelve; three other members of the Twelve; and a family friend, Frank Y. Taylor.

Death would strike the Smith family four times during 1918. Only eight days after Hyrum's funeral, Joseph Fielding's brother-in-law, A. P. Kessler, the husband of his sister Donnette, died as the result of an accident. He was working on a scaffold from which he slipped and fell, breaking his back. He lived only a few hours after the fall. Joseph, having been called to the hospital after the accident, remained there comforting Donnette until her husband passed away. The funeral services were held in the 17th Ward chapel two days later.

When Hyrum Smith died in January 1918, his wife, Ida, was carrying a child. Eight months later, on September 18, Joseph Fielding recorded with obvious joy, "The wife of my brother, Hyrum M., gave birth this morning to a son. . . . We are all pleased that a son has come to bear his name." Yet a few days later, that joy turned to sorrow as this entry of September 24 indicates: "This morning after the temple meeting in the annex," wrote Elder Smith, "I was called to go down to Sister Ida B. Smith's as she was reported to be ill. I went immediately and found other brethren there. We administered to her. She was suffering an attack of heart failure and in a critical condition. I remained there a good part of the day, but in the afternoon returned to the Bee Hive House and went out with my folks. On our return, we received the report that Ida had just passed away, leaving her five children, the youngest only seven days of age. All was done that could be but without avail." The funeral was held on Friday, September 27, just a week before the commencement of the October general conference.

Unknown to all, this general conference would be the last one attended by President Joseph F. Smith. And his participation in it would be limited. He gave a brief but significant keynote address on Friday, October 4, 1918. "As most of you, I suppose, are aware," he began, "I have been undergoing a siege of very serious illness for the last five months." He explained that because of this, it would be impossible to say all he wanted to say, but he indicated there were a few things he must say. "Although somewhat weakened in body," he continued, "my mind is clear with reference to my duty, and with reference to the duties and responsibilities that rest upon the Latter-day Saints." He then made a veiled statement, the meaning of which would be made clear later: "I will not, I dare not, attempt to enter upon many things that are resting upon my mind this morning, and I shall postpone until some future time, the Lord being willing, my attempt to tell you some of the things that are in my mind, and, . . . that dwell in my heart." Having then aroused the interest and the curiosity of the audience, President Smith made this brief but far from satisfactory explanation of what had prompted his guarded comments. "I have not lived alone these five months," said he. "I have dwelt in the spirit of prayer, of supplication, of faith and of determination; and I have had my communication with the Spirit of the Lord continuously." It remained for the Prophet's son Joseph Fielding Smith to shed light on this mystery. "In the afternoon," Joseph recorded on Thursday, October 17, 1918, "I wrote, at my father's dictation, a revelation, or vision, he received on the 3rd." Two weeks later, on Thursday October 31, 1918, Joseph Fielding provided this further insight into the matter: "I was in council with the presidency and the twelve," he wrote that day. "My father was not present on account of his illness, but he presented to the brethren his *vision* in writing, which I read at the request of the brethren and which was fully endorsed by all the brethren." This extraordinary vision of President Joseph F. Smith now appears as section 138 of the Doctrine and Covenants.

The events of this time brought Joseph Fielding and his father closer together than ever before. With the death of his son, Hyrum M., the Prophet turned almost exclusively to Joseph Fielding in all his personal affairs and, as the circumstances surrounding his vision of the dead implies, as to many ecclesiastical matters. Joseph Fielding was with his father almost daily, helping with his private and official correspondence, representing him in contracts and negotiations affecting his personal estate, and acting as his intermediary in matters involving other General Authorities. During the last few months of his life, the only time President Smith ventured outside the Beehive House was when he went for a ride in his automobile with Joseph Fielding at the wheel. A typical entry in Joseph Fielding's diary during this period is the following one for Sunday, October 27, 1918: "In the forenoon I was at home and in the afternoon took my father out for a ride."

During the week preceding this entry, Joseph was with his father every day, apparently to prepare in final form the vision, which was read to the brethren on the 31st. During this same week, Joseph Fielding also commented on the flu epidemic, which, he wrote, was "spreading," noting that there had been "many deaths." On the day before President Smith's vision was read to the Brethren, Joseph also reported that he had filled out a "questionnaire for the government selective draft for the army or military classification." And only twelve days later, the diarist reported the public reaction to the end of the World War that rendered meaningless his draft registration. "We were awakened about one A.M." he wrote on Monday, November 11, 1918, "by the blowing of whistles, which are understood to mean the unconditional surrender of Germany to the Allied Nations. The reports in the paper state that the terms were signed early this morning in France." Joseph also reported that the "German Kaizer" had abdicated and fled to Holland and that anarchy reigned in many German cities. "My father prophesied many months ago," he added, "that peace would come to the nations after those who were responsible for the war were humiliated in the dust." He added, "All day long our city has been in an uproar and the streets filled with rejoicing people who have been wild with joy."

The day before the armistice, a Sunday, all of President Smith's family gathered at the Beehive House to pay their respects to the Prophet. The day marked the seventeenth anniversary of President Smith's sustaining as the head of the Church. Joseph Fielding reported that his father participated in the sacrament while "propped up in bed." Several of the sons spoke, and the Prophet "said a few words." The following Sunday, the First Presidency and the Twelve held a special prayer circle in the Salt Lake Temple. There, Joseph Fielding reported, they "prayed for President Joseph F. Smith who has gradually been failing since the general conference." He added that his father was "suffering extremely from pleurisy" and was "very weak."

The next day, Monday, November 18, his last full day on earth, was difficult for President Joseph F. Smith. "My father is in a critical condition," wrote Joseph Fielding. "With others of the family I was at his bed side a good part of the day." In the evening when presidents Heber J. Grant and Anthon H. Lund came to visit, the Prophet "begged . . . that he might be released." Joseph Fielding and other members of the family continued the vigil through the night. "He rested easier towards morning," wrote Joseph, "but grew weaker and about 10 minutes before five, peacefully passed away. Commenting that "all Israel and many not of our faith mourn," Joseph Fielding met later in the day with some of his brothers and the Council of the Twelve to discuss plans for the funeral. "It was decided," he noted, "that we could hold no public funeral because of the influenza."

211

On Thursday the 21st, the meeting of the Twelve in the temple was devoted to "testimony and eulogy" of the deceased Prophet, and the following day, brief graveside services were held, attended only by the members of his family and his close associates in the leadership of the Church.

Because of the precedent set following the death of President Wilford Woodruff, it was decided that the First Presidency should be reorganized without delay after the death of President Joseph F. Smith. So, on Saturday, November 23, the day following the funeral, the Quorum of the Twelve Apostles met in the upper room of the Salt Lake Temple for this purpose. At that time, Heber J. Grant was ordained and set apart as the seventh president of the Church. Anthon H. Lund was set apart as first counselor and as the president of the Twelve, while Rudger Clawson was set apart as the acting president of the quorum. Charles W. Penrose was set apart as the second counselor.

The death of his father brought about vast changes in the life of Joseph Fielding Smith. From the son's earliest remembrances, the father had played a dominant role in the Church, especially during his last seventeen years when he served as its president. His influence not only traced to the ecclesiastical authority he wielded but also to the power of his personality and to his persuasive eloquence. Many people who heard Joseph F. Smith speak declared him the finest speaker the Church had produced. He was absolutely fearless and forthright and was stubbornly loyal and partial to his family and friends — especially his family. Because he bore his father's name and shared the apostleship with him, Joseph Fielding was the chief recipient among the family of the advantages and opportunities that inherently derive from a close relationship to such a man of power and influence. Because of this, doors had been automatically opened to Joseph Fielding throughout his life that were closed to others. The usual deference shown to one as eminent as Joseph F. Smith was naturally transferred to the great man's son and namesake; and when Joseph Fielding became a member of the Twelve, as has already been noted, he played a more prominent role because of his relationship to the Prophet than would ordinarily be expected of a junior member of the Twelve.

All these advantages, of course, ended with the death of President Smith. And the previous death of his brother Hyrum M., his uncle John Smith, and his cousin John Henry Smith had further diluted the influence Joseph Fielding had in the leading councils of the Church. One can only speculate, of course, about the extent to which these changes affected Joseph Fielding Smith's feelings and self-perception. There can be little doubt, however, that they did have a negative impact on him and that the passing of his powerful father, perhaps for the first time in his life, produced a sense that he stood alone, unsupported by earthly influences, and was dependent entirely upon his own character and abilities and upon those spiritual influences that more and more dominated his life. A stressful incident that occurred the day before Christmas, 1918, illustrates one facet of the significant changes that occurred in the life of Joseph Fielding Smith. "On Tuesday Dec. 24," wrote Joseph, "I received a blow to my feelings from which it will take me a long time to recover." He explained that he had accidentally overheard a conversation between a man whom he had erroneously assumed was a good friend of the Smith family and President Heber J. Grant. This man had told President Grant he understood that "Aunt Julina," Joseph Fielding's mother, intended to request permission to remain in the Beehive House until her new home was built, which she did not "contemplate building until the following spring." The informant had characterized this as "supreme gall never before heard of," adding that asking for such privileges while the Grant family occupied the house was the "greatest piece of nerve" he had ever heard of. He wanted to "forewarn" President Grant so he would be prepared to respond when the request was made. Understandably hurt by this, es-

213

pecially since he had thought the man was his friend, Joseph explained: "My mother has never contemplated asking for such privileges. She is anxious to get out of the Bee Hive House. The home she expects to move into is now being plastered and in the course of a week or two will be ready for her to move into." Joseph went on to reflect about the frailties of human nature and the shock of discovering a false friend who, once the Prophet was dead, felt free to openly malign his widow. It would be difficult to conceive of a more painful way than this for Joseph Fielding and his family to have discovered the revolution in their family status caused by the death of President Joseph F. Smith.

Chapter Twelve

Continuing the Course

As Elder Joseph Fielding Smith continued with his ministry after the death of his father, he soon discovered that false friends like the man who had maligned his mother were a rare breed. He found instead a vast host of friends and supporters who honored the memory of his father and who respected the large Smith family. This was never more apparent than at the first general conference after President Smith's death. The conference was held the 1st, 2nd, and 3rd of June 1919, rather than in early April, because of the cancellation of public meetings during the flu epidemic. The first session of this conference, held in the Tabernacle on Sunday morning, June 1, was a Solemn Assembly in which President Heber J. Grant was sustained as seventh president of the Church. In his lengthy remarks following the sustaining of the General Authorities, President Grant not only eulogized President Joseph F. Smith in superlative terms but also gave instructions that the speakers at an overflow meeting in the Assembly Hall were to "devote the time and their remarks to the memory of President

Joseph Fielding Smith

President Heber J. Grant

Joseph F. Smith." In his own eulogy, President Grant read a letter he had written to the Smith family, which included this statement: "I have said many times that no man who ever lived, with whom I have been associated, had been beloved by me as much as your dear departed husband and father." He related how Joseph F. Smith had been a surrogate father to him, taking the place of his own natural father, whom he had never known. He also told how as a young man he would leave his own ward to attend other meetings where he had heard Joseph F. Smith was to speak. "I bear witness to you," he told the Tabernacle audience, "that from my early childhood days, when I could not thoroughly understand and comprehend the teachings of the gospel, that I have had my very being thrilled, and tears have rolled down my cheeks, under the inspiration of the living God, as I have listened to Joseph F. Smith when preaching the gospel." He then added this significant appraisal of the oratorical ability of President Joseph F. Smith and his deceased son, Hyrum: "I believe that Joseph F. Smith and his son, Hyrum M. Smith, more than any other men to whom I have listened, who were born in the Church of Christ in our day, were the greatest preachers of righteousness." (*Conference Report*, June 1919, p. 13.)

Many other speakers during the conference eulogized the deceased prophet. Most of them focused on his superb character, his family, or his preaching ability. Elder Melvin J. Ballard, who had been sustained as the newest member of the Twelve the first day of the conference, said this of President Smith: "How I want to live to go where he is! I do not care whether the streets are paved with gold, whether there are diamonds and jasper in the walls. I do not care what kind of place it is. If I can go where President Smith has gone and be with him and men like him, it will be heaven to me; I want to be there." (Ibid., p. 71.) Elder David O. McKay, as others had done, emphasized the strength of President Smith's family. Said he: "I know of no better example than the home of our late beloved President Joseph F. Smith. His sons, his daughters, his wives, are true to the gospel, true to the truth. They loved and honored President Smith, but through that, they love and honor that which is even greater—the truth, the gospel." (Ibid., p. 79.) And presiding bishop Charles W. Nibley lauded the deceased prophet's powerful speaking ability. Said he, "As President Grant said this morning in the Tabernacle, no two preachers of righteousness like him and his son, Hyrum, has this church ever produced. I endorse that sentiment." (Ibid., p. 63.)

Amidst this extraordinary outpouring of adulation for his father, Joseph Fielding Smith did not mention his father's name in the talk he delivered at the conference. He did, however, mention him impliedly. "I realize perfectly," he said, "that time is passing, that man's probation here, or his days upon the earth, are limited, and when his work is finished, in the natural course of things it is to be expected that he will be taken home." He then revealed the positive, forward-looking attitude he had toward the work when he added: "I accept the changes that come, rejoicing in the fact that the gospel which we have received is true. Changes of necessity must come, conditions vary from day to day, and new scenes are bound to present themselves as time rolls on." Then showing his unconditional support of the new leaders of the Church, he said: "I voted with full purpose of heart and with the determination, with the rest of you, to uphold and sustain the constituted authorities, to stand by them, because I realize that they hold the power and the priesthood which has descended from the day of the Prophet Joseph Smith." Finally, he bore his testimony: "I know just as well as it is possible for me, I believe, to know in this life, that Joseph Smith was a Prophet of God. There is no doubt in my mind in the least that Brigham Young was called and appointed to be his successor and that he presided over this people by the will of God and was filled with the spirit of inspiration and prophecy. So likewise it was with President John Taylor, President Wilford Woodruff, President Lorenzo Snow, and all others who have presided, and so it must be unto the end." Joseph Fielding then added this statement, which, at the time, he did not realize would have such special meaning to him: "The Lord will not permit any man to reach the presidency in this church who is not prepared, who is not worthy, and who he does not want." (Ibid., pp. 93, 94.)

With the death of his father, President Joseph F. Smith, and his brother, Hyrum M. Smith, Joseph Fielding acquired a new identity. Throughout his ministry before their deaths in 1918, Joseph Fielding had been overshadowed by these two powerful men. As the appraisals of President Heber J. Grant and Bishop Charles W. Nibley indicate, this pair had been generally regarded as the premier preachers of their day. They were eloquent, fiery, and possessed of a powerful pulpit presence. Through their speaking ability, they had the power to lift and motivate people as none of the other General Authorities could. His status as the Prophet, of course, added great weight to the words of President Joseph F. Smith. And the comparative youth of Hyrum M. and his seniority in the Twelve held out the reasonable prospect that he would one day be president of the Church, thereby increasing the attentiveness with which members of the Church listened to his words. At the time of his death, Hyrum was only forty-five; the only ones who outranked him in apostolic seniority were his father, President Anthon H. Lund, President Heber J. Grant, and Elders Rudger Clawson and Reed Smoot. Of these, Reed Smoot who was older by ten years, was nearest in age to Hyrum. In these circumstances, Hyrum was the one among President Smith's sons who drew most of the attention of the Church membership. It was Hyrum that the conventional speculation of the day surmised would one day become president of the Church, a speculation that had foundation, for had he lived, he would have been the senior apostle at the death of President Heber J. Grant.

The principal focus on President Smith and his son Hyrum inevitably diverted attention from Joseph Fielding who, in terms of public popularity, suffered by comparison with them. Joseph Fielding's speaking style was the opposite of his father and brother. While theirs was marked by a fiery, convincing eloquence, accompanied often by the use of telling anecdotes or parables, Joseph Fielding's sermons were characterized by a measured, deliberate, analytical quality, almost professorial in their tone and content. Such a style was not calculated to create excitement and enthusiasm in an audience, or to cause people to go out of their way to hear him speak. Aside from these considerations, Joseph Fielding had been somewhat in the shade from the beginning of his ministry because of the public furor at the time of his call to the Twelve. In the minds of many, therefore, his call was tainted by the charge of nepotism that had been so vigorously pressed by Frank J. Cannon and the *Salt Lake Tribune*.

But with the death of President Smith and Hyrum, a

transformation occurred in the life of Joseph Fielding Smith. Symbolically, that change was never more evident than at the general conference of June 1919. In this the first general conference since the death of his father, he was not introduced as Joseph F. Smith, Jr., as had been done previously, but as Joseph Fielding Smith, the official name by which he would be known during the remainder of his life. However, the change in his official name was, in a sense, merely cosmetic and did not signify or adequately express the fundamental changes that recent events had wrought in Joseph Fielding Smith. In a sense, he had stepped out of the shadow of his father and brother and become his own man. Moreover, he had suddenly become the head of the extended Smith family. Because he bore his father's name and occupied high position in the Church, all members of the family intuitively looked to him for leadership and counsel, even those who were older than he. And his leadership in the family was strengthened by his role as the executor of his father's will. For months prior to the Prophet's death, Joseph Fielding had counseled with his father about his personal affairs, and the father had instructed his son how he wanted his estate to be handled at his death. Added to this, of course, was Joseph's expanding role as a husband and father, the head of a family of eight children ranging in age from seventeen to the year-old toddler, Lewis Warren, who had been born March 10, 1918. Finally, the events of 1918 seem to have caused a marked change in attitude toward him by those detractors who had said nepotism was the reason for his call. Because four high-placed members of the Smith family had died since then, and because Joseph Fielding Smith had proven himself a man of character and ability, such critics had largely fallen silent and no longer trumpeted this baseless, humiliating charge.

While the events of 1918 made vast changes in the life and status of Joseph Fielding Smith, some things did not change and, indeed, would never change for him. Chief among these was the continual round of stake conference assignments. In the weeks following the general conference in June 1919, he attended conferences in the Cache Valley, Panguitch, South Davis, St. Johns, Snowflake, Emery, Portneuf, San Luis, Moapa, and Star Valley stakes. Nor was there any change in the basic message he delivered to the Saints at these conferences. "I have considered that it has been my mission," he told the audience at the October general conference in 1919, "having been so impressed, I think, by the spirit of the Lord in my travels in the stakes of Zion, to say unto the people that *now* is the day of repentance and to call upon the Latter-day Saints to remember their covenants, the promises they have made with the Lord to keep his commandments, and follow the teachings and the instructions of the Elders of Israel, the Prophets of God—as they have been recorded in the holy scriptures. In all things, we should walk humbly and circumspectly before the Lord that we might be blessed and guided by his Holy Spirit. I think this is the day of warning. . . . There is a constant need of warning, teaching and calling upon the people to remember the promises the Lord has made unto them; urging them to be true and faithful in all things, to his holy word, that none may go astray, nor falter, or be overcome and trodden down and be cast back again into the world, to partake of the sins of the world from whence they came. And so I feel it is my mission to cry repentance and to call upon the people to serve the Lord." (*Conference Report,* October 1918, pp. 88, 89.)

Here then, expressed in his own words, is the basic statement of purpose that would govern Elder Smith throughout all the days of his apostolic ministry. He never deviated from it. It was a theme to which he returned again and again and which will be found interwoven throughout his voluminous writings and sermons over the years. Often the words changed, as did the illustrations or citations of authority, but the basic message was always the same—repent, search and ponder the scriptures, keep the commandments, be true and faithful to your covenants. And if the message did not get through to the Saints by reason of the cumulative effect of his words, repeated thousands of times over the years, it did come across through the exemplary life of this Latter-day Saint. He never ceased his quest for a more complete understanding of the holy scriptures, nor his efforts to live a perfect life.

Between the never-ending stake conferences, Joseph continued to divide his time between family affairs and his headquarters assignments. His high position provided no immunity from the normal trials and traumas of life. "In the afternoon," he wrote on New Year's day, 1920, "Ethel and I called to see my mother, who fell on the 26th and broke her arm. Lewis is somewhat improved, but far from well yet." The baby was ill during most of the month. When he was home, the concerned father hovered over the baby and several times during January stayed home from the office all day to nurse him. By the 27th he was able to report: "Lewis somewhat better." Then it was Ethel's turn. "I left Ethel sick with acute gastritis," he recorded on the last day of January as he left to attend the Curlew stake conference in Snowville. He returned two days later to find her "somewhat improved." The conferences for the first two weeks in February were cancelled because of the flu epidemic, which, he wrote, was "again raging." He spent the extra time "visiting the sick."

Later in the month, Joseph himself was almost sick with annoyance as he tried to raise money to pay the large inheritance taxes on his father's estate. "This is indeed an outrage," he fumed, "and a most unjust and vicious law." As Joseph saw it, the inheritance tax law was "a fine against a man's family for permitting him to die!"

At his office, Elder Smith was busy conducting research for a one-volume history of the Church. During the course of this work, a major change occurred in the administration of the Historian's Office that affected him significantly. Following the death of President Anthon Lund on March 2, 1921, Elder Smith was appointed as the Church Historian replacing him. In this position, Joseph would outrank Elders Orson F. Whitney and Brigham H. Roberts in historical matters despite the fact that, at the time, they had a far wider reputation as historians than he. Elder Whitney, for instance, had written and published a four-volume *History of Utah*, while Elder Roberts had edited Joseph Smith's *History of the Church*, a multivolume work, and had written a six-volume *Comprehensive History of the Church*. But Joseph's overall experience in the Historian's Office had been of a far broader scope than theirs, which better qualified him to give administrative direction to the work of the office. While Elders Whitney and Roberts had been engaged chiefly in the research and writing of their major works, Joseph had been working diligently behind the scenes, acquiring a detailed, firsthand knowledge of the inner workings of the department. The charter that governs the work of the Church historian was given by revelation in November 1831, in which John Whitmer, who was then the historian, was admonished to travel throughout the Church, "writing, copying, selecting and obtaining all things which shall be for the good of the church, and for the rising generations that shall grow up on the land of Zion." (D&C 69:8.)

The core element of the Church's historical archives is the Journal History, which is an ongoing chronological record of the activities and progress of the Church. Shortly after his appointment as an assistant Church historian in April 1906, Joseph Fielding was given the responsibility to compile the Journal History for the twentieth century. This comprised his major activity during the years of his service in the Historian's Office, and it provided him with a more intimate knowledge of the Church during this period than any other person as he sifted through the voluminous materials to condense what he considered the most important information to be preserved in this basic record. In addition to this primary responsibility, Joseph was involved in classifying and indexing the historical archives and in preparing summaries of ward and stake histories. He also proofread most of Elder B. H. Roberts's manuscripts, suggesting editorial changes where he thought needful. And he also provided research assistance for Elder Roberts, preparing summaries on various subjects for his use.

With this background, Elder Smith was well qualified to serve as the Church historian. He undertook his new duties March 17, 1921, and discharged them for almost fifty years, being released on February 11, 1970, nineteen days after he was ordained as the tenth president of the Church. The one-volume history he had been working on before his appointment was completed and published in 1922. Titled *Essentials in Church History,* this useful work has gone through more than twenty editions and has been translated into several languages, including Spanish, German, and French. As its title implies, the book does not purport to be a detailed, definitive work but rather sketches the salient points of Church history. It is written in Joseph's usual taut, unadorned style, which aims for clarity and accuracy, objectives he attained without question. No one reading this book can honestly misunderstand the author's meaning. Nor can anyone reasonably question the accuracy of the facts it states. But like all histories, Elder Smith's book reveals the bias of the author, a bias he never sought to hide or deny. His analysis and interpretation of the facts, and his emphasis, or lack of it, given to certain facts have, therefore, been criticized by some whose own biases, perhaps, cause them to question Elder Smith's objectivity. This never troubled him, however. He was willing to let the book stand on its own merits. He patiently stood by, prepared to defend against any criticisms leveled against it.

Essentials of Church History was only the first of many books on historical themes that Elder Smith published during his tenure as Church historian. In addition to these, he also wrote numerous articles for the Church publications and carried on a voluminous correspondence with persons all over the world who wrote in for information or for answers to questions. Some of these questions and their answers were published as a regular feature of the

Improvement Era and were ultimately compiled in five separate volumes called *Answers to Gospel Questions.* These covered the whole field of gospel study and research, extending from the premortal life to the millennial reign and beyond. Like all of Joseph Fielding Smith's other writings, these were carefully crafted, lean, concise, and precise.

A month before Elder Smith was appointed Church historian, Ethel gave birth to her seventh child and third son, George Reynolds, who was born February 13, 1921. The arrival of this boy further adjusted the imbalance between males and females in the Smith family. When Reyn appeared on the scene, the score stood at six to three. Three years later, it would go to six to four. "Ethel gave birth to a fine baby boy today at 1:18 p.m.," the proud father recorded on May 5, 1924. After noting that his wife had endured "considerable suffering" in the birth, he added, "This is her fourth son and eighth child, making my tenth." An entry made a week later implies that the infant's name emerged from a family council: "My mother came down tonight," the father recorded a week later, "and I blessed the baby, giving him the name chosen by his mother and the children, that of Douglas Allan."

Joseph and Ethel were never able to bring the girl-boy ratio into complete balance, although they came close. In the end, it stood at six to five when the last child, a boy, was born prematurely on March 4, 1927. Eight days later, the mother and her baby were brought home from the hospital. "This afternoon," Elder Smith wrote on March 12, "I had Ethel brought home from the hospital in an ambulance and I brought the baby, Josephine helping me, in a closed automobile. In the evening I blessed and named the baby boy, giving him the name Milton Edmund."

Chapter Thirteen

A New Home and Old Routines

The home to which Elder Smith brought his new son was the family's new home located on the east bench of Salt Lake City at 998 Douglas Street. The decision to build this gracious two-story brick home was made only a few months after the birth of Douglas. Several circumstances drove the decision. First, the Smiths were crowded in the old home. They needed more room to comfortably accommodate the parents and their ten children. Second, the Salt Lake City business district had begun to encroach upon the residential neighborhoods to the west, robbing them of the quiet serenity that had once made them appealing. A third factor that doubtless influenced the decision was a desire to get away from the heavy pall of smoke that often blanketed the downtown area during the winter months, which was aggravated by the output from thousands of coal-burning stoves and by atmospheric inversions that sometimes locked in the polluted air mass for weeks at a time. The Douglas street home site was on the valley's east bench, which was usually above this pollution.

As it was designed, the new home was to have a tennis court and a horseshoe pit to provide recreation for the entire family, and especially for Elder Smith's troupe of growing boys. After the work got under way with a groundbreaking in 1925, the whole family watched the progress of the construction with avid interest. A ride in the evening became a favorite family activity, usually ending with a stop at 998 Douglas to see what new features had been added since the last inspection.

The new house was ideally located for the convenience of a growing family. Within a radius of five blocks were the ward chapel and the primary, junior high, and high school buildings, while the University of Utah Campus was within easy walking distance. The street-car line was only half a block away, and the downtown and neighborhood shopping areas could be reached within minutes. Except for Josephine and Julina, who were in their twenties when the Smiths moved into it, the Douglas Street house became the "family home" for the children. It was here that Joseph and Ethel performed their most important work of parenting, implanting in the minds of their children ideas, images, and remembrances that would help form their character and guide them through life.

The perceptions most people have of a prophet are based upon his written or spoken words, his demeanor in the pulpit, or things written about him. A few who are closely associated with him get a better view of the man, learning about his work habits on the job, his likes and dislikes, his reactions to stressful situations, his personal philosophy, and his general attitudes toward people and life in general. And a still smaller number see him in the intimate surroundings of the home where he lives from day to day, eating, playing, visiting, studying, working, or relaxing with his family. Occasionally a curtain is parted temporarily to enable us to get a glimpse of a prophet in that setting, where he is viewed strictly as a man—as a husband, or as a father. We have already seen the appraisal of Joseph Fielding Smith written by his wife, Ethel, which provides a revealing insight into his character and some of his behind-the-scenes activities. We are also indebted to Amelia Smith, the youngest daughter, who later married Elder Bruce R. McConkie, and to Douglas Smith, the next-to-youngest son, who kindly provided the author with written answers to a lengthy set of questions that throw further light on the human qualities and characteristics of Elder Smith from the perspective of his children. Amelia was about ten when the family moved into the Douglas Street home and Douglas was a toddler of two. How, then, was life with father? Amelia remembers that he "was kind yet firm," and that "he never resorted to physical punishment for any misbehavior on our part, but would put his hands on our shoulders and say in a very hurt tone, 'I wish my kiddies would be good.' That was the most effective punishment he could give us and was far worse than any spanking could have been, simply the thought that we had hurt him."

Douglas reported that discipline by his father ordinarily consisted of "a gentle lecture," although "on rare occasions he would give what was more of a pat than a kick with the side of his foot to the seat of your pants." Even such a mild punishment was usually followed by "a hug and an expression of love." When he was younger, Douglas's "main discipline was sitting on a chair until things quieted down," a penalty imposed for "running around the house and being too rough." This son, brimming with boyish energy, seems to have had a penchant for tripping over the carpets and running into things, leaving a train of havoc behind. Mindful of this failing, when the father went through the family "to kiss everyone good-bye as he headed for work in the morning," the kiss given to Douglas was usually accompanied by the admonition to "remember your failing."

As to the practice of kissing in the Smith family, Douglas said: "President Joseph F. Smith apparently kissed his children and my father followed his example. As a matter of fact, Dad kissed his brothers and sisters; and Uncle

Willard Smith would kiss everyone. A trip to the bank would bring a kiss which was a little embarrassing when you were in the lobby. Dad's children always greeted him with a kiss, even in public. This went on right up to his dying day."

Elder Smith was very much involved with his children and joined with them in their activities around the home. "He played games with us," wrote Amelia, and "he provided musical instruments . . . books, magazines and other opportunities for us to become cultured." In explaining that her father took a personal interest in her education, she noted, "More than once I had to retrieve my school books from him to do my studying."

As one might expect, Elder Smith was anxious to share his convictions with his children. "Probably the most important thing he did," wrote Amelia, "was to never miss an opportunity to bear his testimony to his family when we were together, to let us know what a great debt of gratitude we all owe to the Savior for what he did for us, and how much he loved him."

Douglas remembers how his father joined in games and competitions with the children. "I recall taking chairs and tipping them over," he wrote, "and covering them with blankets to make caves and tunnels out of the front room and he entered into the fun of crawling through them." As the children matured, the nature of the games Elder Smith enjoyed with them underwent a radical change. "We played checkers together," wrote Douglas, "and more frequently chess." In reflecting on the fact that in his maturity he often bested his father in chess, Douglas observed, "I have since thought it may have been just a little graciousness on the part of my father, which kept me interested."

The preparation of the tennis court and the horseshoe pit at the Douglas Street home clearly implies Elder Smith's avid interest in sports and his desire to involve his children in them. "In particular, he enjoyed playing baseball with the boys, or family," wrote Amelia, "and for many years played handball at the Deseret Gymn. He also enjoyed watching a basketball or football game, especially if his son was playing." Indicating the frame of mind with which her father approached competitive sports, Amelia noted: "I would not say that he was aggressive as an athlete. He enjoyed winning, but it was the sport and not the winning that was important to him."

Given his mild and loving nature, it may come as a surprise to some to learn that Elder Smith encouraged his sons to engage in boxing. "Our family had boxing gloves," wrote Douglas, "that from time to time were put to use by the boys. On occasion, Dad would put them on and act like he was boxing with us; but I remember I would not hit him out of respect, and he would not hit me out of love, so our fights were not like Paul suggested, but we did fight like one 'that beateth the air.' "

This atmosphere at home naturally influenced the boys toward competitive sports at school. Douglas, in mentioning this, tells in his own words the incident referred to in the preface when he was injured in a football game. "In an effort to make a tackle of a running back, I caught his heel under my chin and was knocked out. I lay on the sidelines until the game was over, and then in the locker room I was again instructed to lie down on some blankets. Dad came down to be with me and as happens in locker rooms, the language got to be a little rough. My father stood up on a bench and called everyone to attention and delivered a sermon on swearing that was very effective, but embarrassing to me, so I feigned that I had passed out again."

Life at 998 Douglas Street when all the children were home was never tame, especially when friends came calling. The Smith children were gregarious and outgoing, and their many friends felt very much at home when they visited the Smiths. Ordinarily there was a game of some kind going on there amid music practices, studying for tests, or sprucing up under Ethel's efficient, low-key direction.

A typical day in this household got under way early. Speaking of her father, Amelia noted that "he was an early riser, always up by 5 A.M. She remembered, during the days of coal furnaces, "hearing him cleaning out the furnace and getting the fire started to warm up the house for when we got up." And in the summer, she reported, "we would hear the sprinkling system running, and then usually by 7 A.M. we were assembled for family prayer and then breakfast." As Douglas reported it, breakfast in the Smith home was an adventure: "Our home on Douglas Street had a long kitchen with a long table," he wrote, "that would seat the whole family. Two long benches were on either side of the table with one of them being against the wall. . . . The younger kids had to sit on the bench against the wall, which meant crawling under the table to get to our place." Joseph Fielding always sat at the head of the table. "No one sat at the foot of the table," Douglas explained, "for it ran to the refrigerator." The meals were always commenced with prayer, which was usually offered by the father, although others prayed from time to time as invited. Doug had mixed feelings about his father's prayers when he was a growing boy, anxious to get on with the business of a meal. "When Dad prayed," he reported, "it was often long, it seemed to me, and the prayer would generally ask the Lord to keep the Saints 'true and faithful.' He would pray for the Lord to hasten His coming and I did not particularly join him in those feelings for I figured the Lord's coming was going to bring some unhappy events."

Like its predecessor, the Douglas Street home had a library whose walls were lined with shelves from floor to ceiling, crammed with books or magazines. It was here that Elder Smith worked early in the morning or late at night, researching, writing, and editing the numerous books, pamphlets, and articles he published over the years. To the extent it was feasible to do so, Elder Smith involved his children in these writing projects. "Some of us were given the opportunity to proofread some of his writings," wrote Amelia. And Douglas noted that sometimes his father provided a strong incentive for the children to delve into his writings by paying ten cents "for every error they could find by checking, either before or after him." Illustrating the meticulous care with which Elder Smith labored over his manuscripts, Douglas wrote, "He never let anything go without personally checking it himself."

Joseph Fielding was also precise with the spoken word and encouraged the children to follow his example. "He had two corrections he would make in our speech," wrote Douglas, "but he fought a losing cause. One, when people said 'each and every,' he would want to know which is the each and which is the every. He considered it a redundant phrase and would have preferred 'each and all.' . . . Two, he claimed that a person was truthful and the Book of Mormon or the Church was true." Because of the frequency with which these grammatical errors were and are repeated, Douglas lamented that his father was unable to "sell" the correct usage, either to certain members of his own family, or to the Church at large.

Only a few months after the Smiths moved into their new Douglas Street home, Ethel gave birth to her ninth and last child. It was by far her most difficult birth. Everything proceeded normally until Wednesday, March 2, 1927, when Elder Smith recorded in his diary: "In the evening while at the table eating, Ethel was taken with a hemorrhage." Joseph immediately got her to bed and sent for the family doctor, D. G. Edmunds, and a nurse, Lillian Jennings. They were able to stanch the bleeding so that by Thursday the doctor believed that the problem was under control and that Ethel would be able to carry the baby to term. But on Friday, Joseph reported, "It was evident that she would have to go to the hospital as her condition was worse." She was taken there in an ambulance early Friday morning, and Dr. Edmunds induced labor. "Everything went on successfully," Joseph noted, "and at 5:20 Friday March 4, she was delivered of a son, prematurely, weighing about 5 1/2 pounds. With skillful medical attention, both she and the baby were saved, the case being very critical for both of them." Eight days later, Ethel was returned home in an ambulance while Joseph, assisted by Josephine, took the baby home in the auto-mobile. "In the evening," Elder Smith wrote, "I blessed and named the baby boy, giving him the name of *Milton Edmund*." This helpless infant, whose middle name ho-nored the doctor whose skill had preserved his life, grew into the athletic young man whose name would be re-membered in the annals of University of Utah football, except there the Milton was shortened to "Mit."

So with the birth of this baby, the childbearing cycle of Joseph Fielding and Ethel's marriage ended; and two months later, another cycle began as this diary entry ex-plains: "I united in marriage at the Salt Lake Temple, Elder Henry Max Reinhardt and my daughter Josephine. I be-lieve this young man is a good, clean Latter-day Saint, and hope they will be happy forever." Within ten years, this new family cycle would see six more of the Smith children married in the temple to "good clean Latter-day Saints." It would end in March 1950 with the marriage of Milton. And the third Smith family cycle began in 1932: "Josephine gave birth to a daughter, 7 pounds 9 2/3 ounces," Elder Smith recorded on August 15 of that year. "This is my first grandchild. We are all very happy as it began to appear that she would have no children."

When the Smiths moved into their new home, it was within the boundaries of the Yale Ward of the Liberty Stake. Their chapel, a new brick structure, dignified by white two-story-high colonial pillars at its entrance, was only a block and a half east of Douglas Street. The building, although in use at the time, had not been dedicated because the ward members had not yet contributed their share of the cost of constructing and furnishing it. Soon after the Smiths moved in, the local bishopric levied a "building assessment" on the members of the ward to raise the money needed to pay their share of the cost. Elder Smith made a generous donation for this purpose; and when the fund-raising effort bogged down, he also donated the Reo to the bishop for resale. "There were feelings of nostalgia as the old automobile was driven away for the last time," reported Elder Smith's son, Joseph.

It was a time of celebration in the neighborhood when, at last, the chapel was paid for and ready to be dedicated. President Heber J. Grant accepted the invitation to dedicate the building. On the stand with the Prophet at the service, held March 18, 1928, were elders George Albert Smith and Joseph Fielding Smith of the Twelve, both of whom resided in the ward. The audience of five hundred and fifty filled every seat in the chapel, the cultural hall, and the connecting foyer of the new building.

In a sense, the dedication of the Yale Ward chapel marked a milestone in the style of Church buildings. Ward chapels were unknown in the Mormon settlements in Ohio, Missouri, and Illinois, and also in Utah and surrounding areas for several years after the exodus. When chapels were first built in the West, and for several decades thereafter, their entrances usually consisted of small vestibules, or cloak rooms, adjacent to the chapel. The change made by the Yale Ward chapel, and soon copied elsewhere, introduced a large foyer at the entrance that not only provided adequate space for people to remove coats and hats or winter wear but also served as a suitable place for small receptions or other social gatherings.

As Elder Smith continued with his apostolic ministry during this period, he noted other major changes in the structure and procedures of the Church. It had now grown to over 650,000 members, an increase of more than 60 percent since the time of his call in 1910, and the number of stakes had increased from 62 to 101 during the same period. Yet, the number of General Authorities had remained constant, thus greatly increasing the administrative burdens on Joseph and his brethren. Beginning in January 1928, meeting schedules were rearranged when priesthood quorums discontinued midweek meetings, holding instead gospel instruction classes during the Sunday School hours. This experimental change also included Sunday classes for all age groups, thereby reserving Tuesday evening as an activity night for young men and women. At the same time, the young men introduced another innovation, the Vanguard program for fifteen- and sixteen-year-old boys. Later when the Boy Scouts developed the Explorer program, patterned largely after the Vanguards, the Church adopted Explorer Scouting.

These and other changes were evidences of a vibrant church that altered its procedures and programs as necessary to serve the needs of a rapidly growing membership. But the basic doctrines and objectives of the Church remained unchanged, as did the role and the methods of Elder Smith and his brethren. They continued their customary round of stake conferences and other meetings at an accelerated pace. During the first few weeks of 1929, Joseph attended conferences in the Woodruff, Coalville, and Magna stakes in addition to special Sunday School meetings at Brigham City where the new class procedures were explained. He also participated in the annual Leadership Week at BYU, where he spoke at the general assembly as well as in a workshop where he discussed "Marriage according to the LDS View." While in Provo on this occasion, Elder Smith had a nice visit with Julina and Emily, both of whom were attending BYU. Their absence from home and Josephine's marriage had removed some of the pressures on the family home on Douglas Street, where Joseph Jr. and Lewis were kept very busy shoveling snow this winter season. There were frequent, heavy snow storms throughout January, accompanied by freezing temperatures. "Coldest night of the winter," Joseph recorded on January 23, "one degree below, officially in S. L. Colder everywhere else." Four days later, he noted that in returning from Brigham City, "snow drifts delayed the train about 2 hours." In Salt Lake City, frigid temperatures made life unpleasant, especially for those, like the Smiths, who lived on the east bench of Salt Lake City. At the time, there were only a few houses east of Douglas Street, so that the cold winds blowing out of the canyon to the east swept down there without impediment. "The past night has been the most disagreeable for us since moving to 998 Douglas," Elder Smith wrote on February 7. "The wind from the mountains was very strong. We could not warm the house above 55 degrees except in the basement, where we had to go to keep warm." The foul weather and drafts in the house gave Joseph a bad cold. "My eyes and nose are running," he reported on Saturday the 9th. Notwithstanding this, he had to leave early the next morning to drive to Garland in northern Utah with Milton H. Welling to attend the Bear River stake conference. "I was miserable all day and glad to get home," he wrote. Elder Smith spent most of the two following days in bed recuperating. He felt well enough on Wednesday, February 13, to do something that belied his illness and typified the interest he always took in his children. "Today I baptized my son, George Reynolds Smith, in the Tabernacle font," he recorded on that day. "Also confirmed him. He is 8 years old today." With the exception of Amelia, Lewis, and Douglas, all of Joseph Fielding's children were baptized and confirmed on their birthdays, which made it easy for them to remember this significant date. Had not unavoidable conflicts made it impossible, these other three children would doubtless have been baptized on their birthdays also. Such a practice reveals the orderly caste of Elder Smith's mind and his preoccupation with historical events.

Chapter Fourteen

Shepherding amid Challenges and Crises

Joseph Fielding continued to work regularly in the Historical Department as he had for many years in the past and as he would continue to do for more than four decades in the future. The detailed knowledge of Church history he had gleaned from this service and his thorough grasp of Church doctrine had prompted his appointment as a member of the reading committee of the Twelve, whose duty it was to scrutinize manuscripts prepared for publication by General Authorities of the Church to determine if they contained doctrinal or historical inaccuracies or questionable analyses. His diary contains several entries about a manuscript the reading committee was then reviewing, of which this one is typical: "We met with the committee reading B. H. Roberts M.S. at 8:15," he recorded on January 15, 1929. "We met with some difficulties in theories advanced by the author." The manuscript referred to was titled *The Truth, the Way, the Life*. And the "difficulties" related to the author's speculations about the possible existence of earthly beings resembling men whose lives on earth had predated Adam. Because

Joseph Fielding Smith

Joseph Fielding Smith
in midlife

of the absence of scriptural authority to support such a theory, the reading committee withheld approval of the manuscript unless Elder Roberts would edit it to remove the offending speculations. As he was unwilling to do this, the manuscript was never published.

When word of this incident leaked out, it generated lively and widespread discussion and debate, as there were some in the Church, a few occupying high position, who concurred in Elder Roberts's analysis. Apparently wanting his views to be understood by the public, Elder Smith gave a speech at a genealogy conference on April 5, 1930, in which he said in part: "Even in the church there are a scattered few who are now advocating and contending that this earth was peopled with a race — perhaps many races — long before the days of Adam. These men desire, of course, to square the teachings in the Bible with the teachings of modern science and philosophy in regard to the age of the earth and life on it. If you hear anyone talking this way,

238

you may answer them by saying that the doctrine of 'pre-adamites' is not a doctrine of the church, and is not advanced nor countenanced by the church. There is no warrant in the scriptures, not an authentic word, to sustain it." Elder Smith went on to reject the scientific inferences to be drawn from fossil evidences that life on earth predated the advent of Adam.

Stung by this speech, which he apparently interpreted as an attack upon him personally, Elder Roberts spoke out publicly in defense of his views. Moreover, he directed a letter to President Heber J. Grant in which he vigorously criticized the tone and substance of Elder Smith's speech and asked whether it represented the official views of the Church or merely his personal opinion. "In the latter event," wrote Elder Roberts, "I feel that that fact should have been expressed in the discourse." Because of the turmoil created by two General Authorities speaking out publicly in opposition to each other on such a sensitive issue, they were invited to present their views at a special meeting of the Council of the First Presidency and Quorum of the Twelve. The outcome of this hearing is indicated by the following journal entry of President Heber J. Grant on January 25, 1931: "After reading the articles by Brothers Roberts and Smith, I feel that sermons such as Brother Joseph preached and criticism such as Brother Roberts makes of the sermon are the finest kind of things to be left alone entirely. I think no good can be accomplished by dealing in mysteries, and that is what I feel in my heart of hearts these brethren are both doing." (Heber J. Grant Collection, Church Archives.)

These comments likely were prompted in part by an experience President Grant had had twenty years before. At the time, there was a controversy on the campus of the Brigham Young University over the issue of organic evolution. President Grant and four other members of the Twelve were assigned by President Joseph F. Smith to study the matter. The upshot was that three members of the BYU faculty were dismissed because of their insistence on teaching and advocating the theory. In the aftermath of this incident, President Joseph F. Smith wrote an article that was published in the *Juvenile Instructor* and that read in part: "In reaching the conclusion that evolution would be best left out of discussions in our church schools, we are deciding a question of propriety and are not undertaking to say how much of evolution is true, or how much is false. . . . The church itself has no philosophy about the *modus operandi* employed by the Lord in His creation of the world, and much of the talk therefore about the philosophy of Mormonism is altogether misleading. God has revealed to us a simple and effectual way of serving Him, and we should regret very much to see the simplicity of these revelations involved in all sorts of philosophical speculations." (*Juvenile Instructor,* April 1911, p. 209.)

As a result of the hearing before the Council of the First Presidency and Quorum of the Twelve, Elder Smith and Elder Roberts discontinued the open advocacy of their conflicting views upon this controversial subject. It is apparent from the decision of the Council and the statement of President Heber J. Grant that the Brethren considered that there were no authoritative scriptures that resolved the issue, that the conclusions either of them reached represented only their own thinking and analysis, and that until there was clear, unequivocal revelation to resolve the issue, it remained in the realm of speculation, or what President Grant chose to call the "mysteries."

But while Elder Smith and Elder Roberts discontinued the open advocacy of their contrary views, they continued to harbor them privately, and the freedom to do so was inherent in the decision of the Brethren and in the plan of the Gospel they all accepted. That this was true as to Elder Roberts is apparent from the fact that he refused to edit his manuscript, preferring to leave it unpublished rather than to change it. And that it was true as to Elder Smith is clear from the fact that more than twenty years later, long after the death of Elder Roberts and President Grant, he wrote and had published a book entitled *Man, His Origin and Destiny,* in which he repeated the basic arguments, with supporting analysis, that he had used years before during the controversy with B. H. Roberts.

A few months after *Man, His Origin and Destiny* was published, Elder Smith was invited to review his book at a conference of institute and seminary teachers held on the campus of the Brigham Young University. Before the conference, the book was made required reading for all the participants so they would be better prepared to understand Elder Smith's presentation. He spoke twice during the conference and afterward participated in questions-and-answer sessions. Because of Elder Smith's position in the Church at the time and the emphasis given to his book before the conference began, questions were raised whether his views represented the Church's official position on organic evolution and the age of the earth. Many attending the conference were, of course, acquainted with the contrary views of B. H. Roberts, deceased, and naturally wondered whether his views had been formally or impliedly rejected by the Church.

Later in the conference, President J. Reuben Clark, counselor in the First Presidency, was invited to address the assigned subject, "When are the Writings or Sermons of Church Leaders Entitled to the Claim of Scripture?" In his talk, President Clark began from the fundamental premise that only the president of the Church "has the right to receive revelation for the church, either new or amendatory, or to give authoritative interpretations of scriptures that shall be binding on the church, or change in any way the existing doctrines of the church." (*Church News,* July 31, 1954.) President Clark recognized that the words of a leader other than the president of the Church could be accorded scriptural status if, as stated in the Doctrine and Covenants, "they shall speak when moved upon by the Holy Ghost." (D&C 68:4.) Explaining how the Church would know when this had occurred, he said, "The church will know by the testimony of the Holy Ghost in the body of the members . . . and in due time that knowl-

241

edge will be made manifest." (Ibid.) He added, "When any man, except the President of the Church, undertakes to proclaim one unsettled doctrine, as among two or more doctrines in dispute, as the settled doctrine of the church, we may know that he is not 'moved upon by the Holy Ghost' unless he is acting under the direction and by the authority of the president." (Ibid.)

President David O. McKay, who was president of the Church at the time, never endorsed Elder Smith's views on this controversial subject. And after he became the head of the Church, President Smith never specifically affirmed them. Since those who have succeeded President Smith have not spoken out on the issue, it remains where President Grant and the Council of the First Presidency and Quorum of the Twelve left it in 1931 and as President Joseph F. Smith stated it in 1911.

Elder Smith never allowed differences of opinion of this kind to alter the kindly feelings he had toward those who disagreed with him. So, while he disagreed with Elder Roberts on these and other matters, he retained a high regard for him. And this was true of all the Brethren. "The general authorities were spoken of with respect," wrote his daughter, Amelia. "I never heard my father speak critically of any of the Brethren, and always sustained or spoke of them with great respect."

A few months after the questions involving B. H. Roberts's manuscript arose, a financial crisis struck Salt Lake City. "The Deseret Savings Bank was forced to close its doors today," Elder Smith wrote on February 15, 1932, "and the Deseret National was taken over by the First Securities National. This caused a great panic and a run on Zions Savings Bank by depositors who became panicky. The bank met all demands successfully, remaining open until 6 P.M. and inviting the foolish people to get their money." The run on the bank continued the following morning "but subsided by noon." Perhaps to explain his characterization of these people as "foolish," Elder Smith noted later, "Several who drew their money lost it to thieves."

The shock waves from this panic persisted for months, causing concern throughout the community and the country. It was one of the manifestations of the great depression that had descended upon the world. This economic crisis affected Joseph Fielding in several ways. It jeopardized his own financial stability because his meager savings were on deposit in the bank. Its failure would destroy a fragile facade of financial security that he had built up over the years. It also increased the pressure he was under, exerted by his role as a director of the bank. "This morning, with Arthur Winter, Asahel Woodruff, and the state examiner," Elder Smith recorded on Monday, May 9, 1932, "I was called to commence the examination of Zions Savings Bank." Throughout the entire week until the following Saturday at noon, Joseph was at the bank from early until late, poring over the records with his associates and the bank examiner. It was a most stressful and uncertain time. No one knew what the outcome would be. Steeped in the history of the Church, Joseph Fielding knew well of the financial debacle in Kirtland, Ohio, a century before that had swamped the early brethren who were involved in a banking enterprise and that had precipitated a massive apostasy. That, in turn, had brought about the exodus of the high leaders of the Church from Kirtland, including his grandfather Hyrum Smith and his great-uncle Joseph Smith. Knowing, therefore, how financial chaos can quickly dissolve ties of love and loyalty, Elder Smith was undoubtedly uneasy about this volatile situation. At the ecclesiastical level, Joseph shared with his brethren concern for the Saints who were pinched by the economic crisis. "Matters of importance concerning the distress of the people were considered," he wrote on June 9, 1932, "and ways of meeting our problems were considered." This entry foreshadowed the first struggling steps taken by Elder Smith and his brethren to help alleviate the heavy economic burdens the great depression had imposed on the people. These steps would ultimately lead to the creation of the Church welfare plan (originally called the security plan) in 1936.

Meanwhile, the shepherding duties of the Twelve remained unchanged. Stake conference and mission tour assignments continued to come with regularity, regardless of the economic problems created by the depression. So, the day after the temple meeting where the Brethren had discussed "the distress of the people," Joseph was on the road again. "At 10 P.M." he wrote on June 10, 1932, "Ethel and I left on the D&RG [Railway] for Wichita, Kansas, where I am to begin a tour of the Central States Mission which will occupy the time until the end of June." Now that her youngest child, Milton, was six years old, Ethel felt comfortable in leaving for such a long trip because the older girls, including Naomi, who was twenty-two at the time, were still at home to supervise him and his older brothers.

Ethel did not go along merely for the ride. As a member of the Relief Society General Board, she would hold training sessions for district and branch Relief Society sisters living in the areas where the mission president had scheduled meetings.

On arriving at Wichita, Kansas, the Smiths were met by mission president Samuel O. Bennion and his wife, their hosts and guides throughout the tour. President Bennion, who was two years older than Elder Smith, would be called as a member of the First Council of Seventy the following year to fill the vacancy caused by the death of Joseph W. McMurrin, who passed away in October 1932.

The routine followed at Wichita, where the Smiths arrived at 9:15 A.M. Sunday June 12, set the standard for the entire tour. "Meetings were held in our own church building at 10:00 A.M., 2 P.M. and 7:30 P.M.," Joseph wrote under that date. "Also, after the 2 P.M. meeting [a meeting was held] with the missionaries. Ethel and Sister Bennion also held a meeting with the Relief Society sisters. It was rather late when we retired." The combination of member and

missionary meetings was typical of mission tours conducted during this period. Since there were no stakes
within the mission, President Bennion had direct authority
as to all local units, branches, and districts, as well as the
responsibility to direct the work of the full-time missionaries.

Although they retired late Sunday night, the touring
party was up early Monday morning to be on their way
in the mission automobile. Driving for them was Elder
Player, one of the full-time missionaries. Arriving at Tulsa,
Oklahoma, about noon, after a journey of 200 miles in
"very warm weather," the party checked in at the Bliss
Hotel, freshened up, ate a light lunch, and went immediately to a meeting scheduled for 2:00 P.M. As there was
no chapel in Tulsa at the time, the meeting was held in an
assembly room at the City Hall. Gathered there were members of the church who lived within a wide radius of Tulsa,
some of them traveling as far as two hundred miles on a
weekday to see and hear an apostle. The congregation also
included some nonmembers, brought there by the missionaries or member friends. "In the evening we held another public meeting and also one with the missionaries,"
reported Elder Smith, "the sisters meeting with the Relief
Society."

Tuesday's journey took the travelers from Tulsa, Oklahoma, to Little Rock, Arkansas, with intermediate stops
in Muskogee, Oklahoma, for lunch and Fort Smith, Arkansas, for an afternoon meeting with the Saints. "Our
journey was pleasant," noted Joseph, "a rain storm preceding us all the way from Fort Smith — a long day's journey."

An early start Wednesday morning from Little Rock
enabled the travelers to arrive at El Dorado, Arkansas,
shortly before 1:00 P.M. "After lunch," noted Elder Smith,
"we held a meeting with the members of the church in
the meeting house." In the evening, the visitors were
treated to a fish fry. "Great pans of fish were cooked and

the people held a feast," he wrote. Thus fortified, they "commenced another meeting."

On Thursday, the party traveled from El Dorado to Memphis, Tennessee, via Greenville, Mississippi; and on Friday from Memphis to St. Louis, Missouri. During this last leg of their journey, the touring party traveled three hundred miles in four different states, passing through a long string of picturesque towns in America's heartland. Such was their schedule this day, complicated by a late start when a shackle bolt had to be replaced in their car at Memphis, that the travelers were unable to hold meetings along the way. However, they did take time to stop briefly in Fulton, Kentucky, "to see a family of Saints named Williams." And, after ferrying the Ohio River, they visited the lonely cemetery at Mound City, Illinois, where "Union soldiers are buried."

Using modern missionary terminology, Saturday was the travelers' "P" day. "We spent the day in St. Louis," wrote Joseph. "We visited the large park where the World's Fair was held in 1904, and the historical building, also the Catholic Cathedral." Making no effort to conceal his bias, the diarist commented as to the cathedral: "A most magnificent structure, devoted to error and superstition." Their day of relaxation ended at "the elaborate Fox theatre." The show playing there, perhaps a double feature with newsreel and a cartoon, customary theater fare for that day, made no apparent impression on Elder Smith, whose diary was totally silent about the program.

We get the impression that Elder Smith was not quite comfortable with Saturday's relaxed routine and that he came to life, as it were, on Sunday. "This morning at 10:00 A.M. we held a general meeting," he reported. "At 2:30 we held a meeting with the missionaries until 5 P.M. Ethel and Sister Bennion also met with the sisters and instructed them in Relief Society work. At 7:30 we held a public meeting." Interspersed with these meetings were private interviews, priesthood blessings, and the interminable handshaking with those present, some of whom, perhaps, had never before seen let alone shake the hand of an apostle, an event never to be forgotten by the individual and to be remembered forever in family lore. The travelers left St. Louis early Monday morning, June 20, crossing the Mississippi into Illinois. They were reminded that this fabled river had been the pathway for thousands of Mormon converts as they migrated from their homes in Great Britain and Continental Europe via New Orleans, upriver to Nauvoo. A light rain the night before and an overcast sky had cooled the air, making their trip to Springfield especially pleasant. As they approached the Illinois capital, a rock thrown up from the unpaved highway punctured their radiator. During the three hours it took to repair the leak, the Smiths and Bennions visited Lincoln's home and other places of historic interest in the city. Leaving Springfield in midafternoon, they drove on to Carthage, where they arrived shortly before 5:00. "We went to the old jail," wrote Joseph, "where I have a feeling of depression." The gloomy place aroused terrible thoughts of the brutal murder of his grandfather and granduncle that had occurred there eighty-eight years before. "Surely the curse of God is on the place to this day," he confided to his diary.

The travelers had to pick their way carefully out of Carthage. "A cyclone had passed over the town a day or two before," explained Joseph, "and trees were lying everywhere in the streets." The damage was localized in a small area so that once out of town, they made the short trip to nearby Nauvoo without difficulty.

Because of the delay in Springfield, the travelers were unable to spend as much time in historic Nauvoo as they would have liked to do. It was possible, however, to visit the temple site and some of the old homes, including the Mansion House, the Prophet's home, which were unkempt and falling into decay. Elder Smith was incensed on visiting the burial plot of Joseph and Hyrum to find that someone had attempted to remove the bodies. "A malicious act of desecration," he wrote. Joseph's impression of the city was succinctly summarized in this concluding sentence of his

247

diary entry for the day: "The curse of the Almighty is still on Nauvoo and shall remain until Zion is redeemed." Because of the sentiment this statement implies, Elder Smith could never generate much enthusiasm for the later restoration efforts made in Nauvoo.

Since Nauvoo had no suitable accommodations for overnight visitors, Joseph and his party drove on to Keokuk, where they spent the night of the 20th. The following day they drove to Jefferson City, Missouri's capital. En route they stopped to inspect the dam in the Mississippi River below Keokuk. "Joseph Smith, the Prophet, suggested that a dam be placed [at that point] months before his death," Elder Smith noted. They also stopped briefly in Hannibal, Missouri, the home of Mark Twain, whose novels of Tom Sawyer and Huckleberry Finn memorialized life on the river. They arrived in Jefferson City early enough to go to the capitol building, where they had hoped to be granted an interview with the governor. Unfortunately, he was not in his office. However, they did meet there a man named Juell Mayes, "a friend of Geo. Albert and our people." But, the edge of the friendly greeting extended by Mr. Mayes was taken off when Joseph Fielding saw portraits of former governors Daniel Dunklin, L. W. Boggs, and T. Reynolds, who, he wrote, "aided the enemies of our people in the 30's." Until the time of his death, President Smith was rankled by the maltreatment the Latter-day Saints had received at the hands of Missouri's officialdom. And these feelings were translated into a persistent negative attitude toward the state and its subsequent leaders that the passage of time could not erase.

Bending northwesterly from Jefferson City the next day, the travelers drove to Joplin, Missouri, near the borders of Kansas and Oklahoma. On the way, they saw the major dam on the Osage River, "where the water has been backed up many miles, creating several pleasure resorts." Noting that the area traversed during the day was known as the Ozarks, Elder Smith observed that "the people here call the country mountainous." One detects here an implied put-down of the size of the Ozark Mountains. This is understandable, coming from one who was born and reared in the shadows of the towering peaks of the Wasatch.

Meetings were held in and around Joplin Thursday afternoon and evening. The next morning, the travelers drove to Independence, where they arrived at 10:00 A.M. Because of the numerous meetings scheduled over the weekend and the need to recuperate from several days of arduous travel, the party held no meetings Friday afternoon or evening.

Instead of staying at the mission home with the Bennions, Joseph Fielding and Ethel drove to nearby Kansas City, where they stayed with their friends Alfred and Bertha Holmes. Here the travelers freshened up and read the cache of mail that awaited them. Elder Smith was not too impressed. "Received letters from the children," he wrote, "but they did not say much." At least they did not tell of any injuries or illnesses in the family, and that of itself was good news, given the penchant of his young sons to tear around the house.

During the early afternoon, Joseph did something that was typical of his visits in the homes of Latter-day Saints. "I spent a good portion of the time answering questions for Alfred and Bertha Holmes," he wrote. Elder Smith's reputation for gospel scholarship was so well known that members, given the chance, would ply him with doctrinal questions. He patiently responded, often at length, as he did with these trusted friends. Afterward, Elder Smith accepted Alfred's challenge for a game of handball at the Kansas City Athletic Club. Here the apostle worked off the tensions of travel while enjoying the spirit of friendly competition. Later, the Bennions drove to the Holmes's house, where the three couples spent a pleasant evening of dining and conversation.

Thus refreshed, they were ready for the weekend. "I met with the missionaries," Joseph noted on Saturday, June 25, "to hear their reports; and I answered questions."

During part of the day, Ethel and Sister Bennion were excused from the missionary meeting to instruct the Relief Society sisters. On Sunday, three general meetings were held. "I occupied the greater portion of the time," Joseph reported, "and we heard short talks from the missionaries. Ethel spoke at the evening meeting. Good attendance."

On Monday the Smiths and Bennions toured some of the historic sites north of Independence. The first was Richmond, Missouri, where they visited the graves of David Whitmer and Oliver Cowdery and the site of the jail where Joseph and Hyrum were imprisoned for a while. It was here that the Prophet Joseph Smith, incensed by their vulgarity, rebuked the soldiers who guarded the prisoners. The ramshackle building in Richmond that had served as a prison at the time no longer stood, so the visitors had to imagine what it had looked like. At nearby Liberty, however, the old jail where the Smith brothers were next imprisoned was still standing, leaving nothing to the imagination. The squalid little building, which measured only 22 1/2 by 22 feet on the outside, had walls of double construction. A four-foot space between the outer walls and the inner oak walls was filled with loose rock. Inside were two levels, each about fourteen feet square. The only ventilation came from two small windows with iron bars. The original beds consisted of hewn logs covered with straw. It was reported that the food served to the prisoners was so filthy that they could not eat it until they were driven to it by hunger. It was also reported that at mealtime, the Prophet Joseph Smith insisted that Hyrum sit at the head of the table, symbolizing his status as the elder brother. To see this dreary place, which he called a "dungeon," where his grandfather had been imprisoned, was an emotional experience for Joseph Fielding Smith, especially since the visit occurred on June 27, the 88th anniversary of the martyrdom of his grandfather and his greatuncle in the Carthage jail.

Other historic sites visited during the day were Gallatin; Adam-ondi-Ahman; Haun's Mill, where several

Saints were massacred; and Far West, where Joseph Fielding's father was born in 1838. There was no evidence of the small house where the birth occurred; it had stood across the street from the temple site. Nor was there evidence of any construction on the temple site other than the huge cornerstones. Joseph Fielding could not have failed to remember that it was on the southeastern cornerstone that his cousin George A. Smith and Wilford Woodruff were ordained to the apostleship and set apart as members of the Twelve prior to their missions to Great Britain.

Except for the Liberty Jail, no buildings standing in Missouri could be identified with the Latter-day Saints, even though the Church had had a presence there longer than in either Ohio or Illinois. The widespread pillaging, looting, and burning of Mormon buildings in Missouri, connected with Governor Lilburn Boggs's order to exterminate the Saints, had literally scoured the countryside of any evidence that they had been there. It was as if the state had wanted to erase all vestiges of Mormon influence. In return, Joseph Fielding Smith had ill feelings toward the state and blamed it for the indignities and woes heaped upon the Church and his family. He was reluctant to applaud the state for any positive accomplishments and was always ready to condemn it for its shortcomings. Joseph and Ethel were entertained by the Ellsworth family in Kansas City the evening of June 27 and spent the following day with the Bennions. "Ethel did some shopping," wrote Elder Smith. "We all visited the Longview Farm in the afternoon where some of the world's finest horses and cows are found. This farm is owned by a woman and is most wonderful in all particulars." Elder Smith also accompanied President Bennion to the hospital three times during the day and evening to visit one of the missionaries who had been operated on for appendicitis. The frequency of the visits implied concern about the elder's condition as did Joseph Fielding's final entry about him: "He was feeling as well as possible in the afternoon."

That night, the Smiths left for home on the Missouri Pacific, transferring to the D&RG Western at Denver. After two nights and a day en route, they arrived in Salt Lake City at 8:30 Thursday morning, June 30.

One might think that after twenty days away from home, Joseph would have taken the day off to unwind before resuming his headquarters duties. Instead, he took a taxi home from the depot, had a bath, changed his clothes, and went immediately to the temple, where the apostles were in session. In recording the events of the day, Joseph Fielding made one of the rare critical entries to be found in his diaries. "Several matters were discussed," he wrote, "including the writing of lessons on the D&C and ——— who has sought the honor, was granted the privilege." Elder Smith was offended by people who sought to aggrandize themselves. It had been his settled practice never to laud his own achievements or to push himself forward. He was content to let his actions speak for themselves, and if they merited commendation, that must come from others, not from his own mouth. Because of his innate modesty and his refusal to actively seek personal recognition or preferment, such a quality in others was irritating to him and occasionally prompted a response of the kind contained in this diary entry. And once in a while the conceited or arrogant conduct of another would bring a verbal response showing his displeasure. Such an incident, related to the author by a person who was present at the time, occurred one day on the elevator of the Church Administration Building. Among those present was the son of a prominent member of the Church who, by his demeanor and words, betrayed an exaggerated sense of self-importance. After the young man left the elevator, Elder Smith said quietly but with apparent feeling, "He makes my tired ache." This phrase eloquently expressed the apostle's disdain for those who are conceited or puffed up.

Another object of Elder Smith's disdain at this time was those members of the Church who, despite the strong admonitions of President Heber J. Grant and other Church leaders to the contrary, persisted in supporting the efforts to repeal the eighteenth amendment, which instituted the prohibition of alcoholic beverages. This issue was conceived in Utah as an effort by Church leaders to perpetuate a legal restriction based upon a religious principle. What concerned the Brethren was the negative social effects that would follow repeal. And so Joseph Fielding had joined President Grant and other Church leaders in speaking out on this issue. On Sunday, August 14, 1932, Elder Smith was invited to speak at the sacrament meeting in the 25th ward. The proposed repeal of the eighteenth amendment was the main topic of his discourse. "I advised the people to sustain the 18th amendment," he wrote of his talk, "which is now being attacked by politicians and many ignorant people." It was a source of sorrow to Elder Smith and his brethren when Utah later became the state whose vote was the last one necessary to adopt the amendment, which repealed prohibition.

As has already been noted, it was in 1932 that Joseph Fielding's career as a grandfather began. He was privileged to bless Josephine's baby, his first grandchild, whom he named Maxine Reinhardt. Thereafter as other grandchildren were added to the family, he blessed some of them, or stood in the circle as they were blessed by their own fathers. But, regardless of who was voice in bestowing the name and a blessing, each grandchild was looked upon with special affection as "belonging" to him. The reservoir of love Joseph Fielding Smith had for his family was inexhaustible. Each member, whether wife, child, or grandchild, felt of that love and sensed a special kinship to him. "He was always affectionate with his family, kissing boy and girl alike," wrote a grandson, Hoyt W. Brewster. "I recall being kissed in the lobby of the chapel one Sunday when I was just entering my teenage years—a time when many young men are embarrassed to kiss or be kissed. One of my friends, having observed this exchange of affection, later came up to me and said 'How was the big kiss, Hoyt?' I simply said, 'It was great. He's my grand-father.' I thought it a privilege to be kissed by my grand-father and my father." (Statement in possession of the author.)

This grandson has never forgotten another kissing in-cident involving President Smith that occurred under more unusual circumstances. Hoyt was serving as a missionary in the Netherlands in 1958 when the London Temple was dedicated. Having been invited to attend this service, along with all the other Dutch missionaries, he was filing into the assembly room with his companion when President Smith saw him. "Without a moment's hesitation," wrote Hoyt, "he jumped up from his chair and extended his arms, motioning me towards him. In that instance I did not see Joseph Fielding Smith, President of the Council of the Twelve Apostles . . . but a grandfather who saw one of his grandchildren for whom he had great love. I didn't hesitate to break ranks and rush to the stand where he embraced me and kissed me in front of that entire solemn assembly. That to me was one of the most sacred and memorable moments of my life." (Ibid.)

Through the eyes of this grandson, we get other re-vealing glimpses of President Smith: "He was a happy, fun loving grandfather," he wrote. "Until his physical lim-itations would no longer allow it, he regularly joined in the baseball games that were played at the annual family picnic in July. I recall his once hitting a line drive down the third base line right into the lens of my Uncle Ren's camera who was filming the event." Hoyt also dispels the unfounded rumor that his grandfather was a vegetarian. "While he may have cut down on the eating of meat in later life, the claim that he was a vegetarian is not accurate for he ate meat in our home." As to his preferences in food, Hoyt writes, "He really enjoyed a bowl of bread and milk as a light supper." And a key personality trait he observed in his grandfather was a genuine sense of hu-mility, a reticence to push himself forward, to boast, or in other ways to draw attention to himself.

This grandson finds it significant that the same humility and reticence existed in his mother Naomi. "She was so shy about their relationship that when we attended the solemn assembly where he was sustained as the Prophet, she identified herself as a sister-in-law of Elder Bruce R. McConkie when questioned by the usher about being a family member." This daughter, like the other children of Joseph Fielding Smith, seemed to feel perfectly secure in the mere knowledge of their special family relationship, and the publication of that fact was not necessary to give her a feeling of self-worth or importance. The manner in which this unusual sense of family integrity, cohesion, and self-confidence was created has already been mentioned. Additional insight into this process is provided by the grandson, Hoyt W. Brewster Jr.: "When grand-daddy set me apart as a missionary, he reminded me that my fore-fathers had given much to the work and much was expected of me. I have always understood that to mean that I was expected to live worthily and to be an example to others so that none could fault the church or my family because of some misdeed on my part. I do not claim perfection, but my life is significantly better because I have acted on the desire to keep my family free from shame." (Ibid.)

To fully understand the character and motivations of Joseph Fielding Smith, one must grasp the overriding influence of his family upon him. His name alone was a constant reminder of his identity and of the duties owed to those who had preceded him. One of these was to implant in his children and their descendants the principles and ideals of the Smith clan. The constant watch-care he maintained over his family is evident from his diaries, which abound with references to its various members. The frequency and variety of these references are illustrated by a few of the entries made during the first few weeks of 1932. On January 3, for instance, he noted that he and Ethel "visited at the home of Bro. and Sister Farr, where Joseph Jr. is paying attention to one of the Farr daughters."

Apparently Elder Smith wanted to gauge the qualities of the Farr family. The fact that Joseph Jr. was sealed to the Farr's beautiful daughter, Zella, the following year implies that Elder Smith was satisfied. A few days after visiting the Farr family, Joseph Fielding called on his cousin Patriarch Hyrum G. Smith, who was in "poor health." He visited the Patriarch often until his death on February 4, 1932, and then worked with David A. and George Albert Smith to make the funeral arrangements. He was one of the speakers at the memorial services.

During the period of the patriarch's last illness, Joseph was excused from attending a conference in the Summit Stake in order to speak at the funeral of Ruby Brewster. "Her son Hoyt W.," he explained, "is in the Netherlands Mission. He is engaged to my daughter Naomi." Two years later, Elder Smith performed the temple marriage for this couple. Ten days after speaking at the funeral of Hoyt Brewster's mother, Joseph Fielding wrote, "My sister Jeannette, who has been ill for several days, passed away today shortly before noon." He explained that his sister's later years had not been "the most happy" because of illness and because "her husband Blanchard Ashton lost his life a few years [before] attempting to rescue his sister from drowning." After the funeral, he dedicated his sister's grave. Finally, on February 8, Joseph Fielding wrote: "Ethel returned from the (Patriarch's) funeral and went to bed ill from an attack of influenza. She has been in bed all day. . . . Douglas also ill." A few days later he was able to report: "Ethel feeling better. Douglas also."

These are typical of thousands of Elder Smith's diary entries about members or potential members of his family that amply demonstrate the paramount position they occupied in his thoughts and that reflect the ebb and flow of life among a large and active Latter-day Saint family. Except for Josephine and Emily, who were married; Naomi, who was working and who in September would marry; and Milton, who was too young, all the Smith children were now attending school. Julina and Lois were at

Brigham Young University, where Lois was an undergraduate and Julina was working on a master's degree. "Went to Provo in the afternoon," Joseph noted on March 18, "and took the two babies, Douglas and Milton, and Ethel; we brought Julina and Lois home." That night, the apostle "went with Lois to see the basketball games," which were part of the annual high-school tournament. Only two nights before, Elder Smith had attended other tournament games with his fourteen-year-old son, Lewis. Douglas, who would have been insulted had he known he was then classified as a baby, was baptized in the Tabernacle font by his father on May 5, his eighth birthday. Only two days before this event, Joseph Fielding had reported with ill-concealed pride, "Julina successfully passed all requirements at the BYU for a masters degree. She has written a thesis on inter-relations of the Latter-day Saints and the American Indians." Julina received her degree the following month at the commencement exercises in Provo, which her parents attended with their friend Susa Y. Gates.

Meanwhile, Elder Smith never missed an opportunity to spend time with his growing sons. On the Sunday prior to Julina's graduation, he took his son Joseph with him to Logan to attend the conference of the Cache Stake. Eighteen-year-old Joseph Jr. was at the wheel of the family car. The eighty-mile drive to this northern Utah city enabled the pair to engage in unhurried conversation. Young Joseph, who sought to emulate his father, was an avid student of the gospel and never missed the opportunity to ply his father with doctrinal questions. Indeed, he later wrote a book, *Religious Truths Defined,* which was based in large part on the answers to questions he had put to his father. We may safely assume, therefore, that much of their conversation focused on doctrinal and spiritual themes as they traveled to Logan and back on this Sunday.

Elder Smith was patient and practical in responding to the questions of his children about the doctrines of the Church. And, if time permitted, he answered in great detail. So, a few months after this trip to Logan, young Joseph, who was then a missionary in England, received a letter from his father that answered questions about the role of Jesus Christ as the Creator. Among the many things contained in the father's lengthy answer was this wise advice: "It is sufficient for us, until we are prepared by faith to believe and understand greater things, to confine our study to the salvation of men and the dealings of the Lord with us here and now. Until we can comprehend the simple things of the gospel and put them into practice, we better not try to get off on some other world. If we do we may get lost in transit." Since his son's question was prompted by an inquiry made by someone he was teaching, Elder Smith added this: "If any investigator or member of the church desires to know these things, tell them that they better learn the simple truths and how to live them first. It is foolish to attempt to teach children of the primary grade higher mathematics. We must first master each rung of the ladder, we cannot reach the top in one jump from the bottom. Let your attitude be for the present the same as the Psalmist: 'Such knowledge is too wonderful for me; it is too high, I cannot attain to it.' (Ps. 139:6)."

A few months after the trip to Logan, Elder Smith took eleven-year-old Reynolds with him to the Tintic stake conference. They drove there early Sunday morning and returned that evening following the second general session in the afternoon. Because of Reyn's youth at the time and his avid interest in sports of all kinds, whether as a participant or a spectator, we can safely assume that the father's conversation with this son did not dwell exclusively on doctrinal themes. It is also safe to assume that the father derived as much enjoyment from his conversation with this eleven-year-old sports enthusiast as he did the conversation with Reyn's more mature brother. And that enjoyment would not have been feigned, for, in fact, the father was as much a sports fan as any of his sons. "In the afternoon attended a 'football' game between the U. of U. and BYU," he wrote two weeks after the Tintic conference. Then, tongue-in-cheek, he added: "They call the game 'football' altho only *one* man on each side kicks the ball. The others run with it or throw it."

When they became old enough, Elder Smith also enjoyed competing with his sons in handball and horseshoes, as well as other sports. And hiking was an enjoyable sporting activity in which all could join regardless of age or sex. "Today with all the children who were with me," Elder Smith wrote on July 27, 1932, "I climbed to 'Sunset Peak' and other peaks, and to several of the lakes. It was quite a long journey before we returned." The occasion was a four-day holiday the family spent at Brighton in Big Cottonwood Canyon east of Salt Lake City at the cabin of their friend George A. Holt. On the last day, the doting father "took the boys, including the two little fellows, on a 'kyke' up the canyon." The "little fellows," of course, were eight-year-old Douglas and five-year-old Milton. On another occasion, Elder Smith took all of his sons on a long hike up Mill Creek Canyon, where they had to force their way through thick underbrush to reach their destination. As much as he liked to hike, the father vowed he would never again take a hike of *that* kind. And as far as is known, he never did.

Chapter Fifteen

Another Shadow Falls

A s 1932 drew to a close, the Smith family was secure, healthy and happy, looking forward with optimism to the future. While the depression had created great want and had alarmingly increased unemployment across the nation, Elder and Sister Smith, who had been reared during a period of economic stress, were accustomed to living frugally. They therefore made the adjustments necessary to conserve their modest resources. which they used wisely in caring for their own family while reaching out to others less fortunate. Meanwhile, they counted their blessings, the most important of which were their children. Josephine, Emily, and Naomi were now happily married to husbands who were faithful and active in the Church and with whom they were wholly compatible. Julina had excelled academically and had received her master's degree. Lois and Amelia were busy discovering boys while pursuing their educational goals. And Joseph Jr. was preparing to leave for England on his mission. Lewis, now a teacher in the Aaronic Priesthood; Reyn, who was looking forward to becoming a deacon soon; and Douglas, a newly baptized member, were developing in a way that filled their parents with Latter-day Saintly pride. Meanwhile, Milton, the baby and pet of the family, lived in that insular, remote world of young childhood where he probably sensed that everybody thought he was pretty special and that he had the unusual power to bring joy to the whole family merely by doing the most ordinary things like expressing thanks for the privilege of going on "kykes" with his father and brothers.

Of all the family, perhaps Ethel was the one most optimistic about the prospects for the future. She was now only forty-three years old, just approaching the prime of her life. For twenty-one years, she had served as a member of the General Board of the Relief Society, the most prestigious and influential group of women in the Church. Not only that, she had stood out as one of the most able and articulate members of this board. "Sister Smith was one of the most brilliant women I ever knew," said Amy Brown Lyman, president of the Relief Society General Board. "I considered her the finest writer and speaker I had on my board." (Stewart and Smith, *Life of Joseph Fielding Smith,* p. 243.) As during the tour of the Central States Mission earlier in 1932 when Ethel accompanied her husband on his Church assignments, she would ordinarily hold training meetings with local Relief Society sisters and would often share the pulpit with her husband at the general sessions. Occasionally Ethel attended stake conferences with members of other general boards, independent of her husband, as she did on Friday, August 26, 1932. "This evening," wrote Elder Smith on that date, "Ethel left with representatives of the MIA for Zions Park Stake." She was gone all weekend and did not return until the following Monday morning. "Met Ethel at 11:40 A.M.," Joseph Fielding noted on August 29, "and took her home."

For the first time in her married life, Ethel was able to get away from home several days at a time because there were older children at home who could take care of the

Ethel Georgina Reynolds Smith later in life

younger ones. This gave the mother a sense of freedom and independence she had not known before. And with the younger children growing rapidly, there was the expectation that within a few short years, all the children would be out of the home, leaving Ethel free to travel more extensively with Joseph, to continue her work on the Relief Society board, to pursue her interests in history and writing, and to savor the grandmother's role. Moreover, she continued to enjoy the reflected recognition emanating from her husband, whose extensive writings and steady rise in the hierarchy of the Church shed a special light of distinction upon him and the entire family.

In these favorable circumstances, life was rich and rewarding for Ethel Smith. And prospects for the future were abundant and promising. Yet, within a few months, this rosy picture started to fade. The change began with vague feelings of apprehension that Ethel was unable to explain or mitigate. These down moods were cyclical, coming and going at irregular intervals and varying in their strength and duration. In time they came with greater frequency and intensity, causing deep feelings of depression and fear that so disturbed Ethel that she was unable to perform her daily tasks. Then sometimes, when these dark shadows lifted temporarily, she would be driven to sudden spurts of hyperactivity as if to compensate for any time lost during her periods of disability.

Doctors of today, looking back on Ethel's symptoms, would see in them indications of a chemical imbalance that can now be treated effectively with drugs. At the time, however, her only relief came from the struggling prayers offered regularly in her behalf, the priesthood blessings given by her husband and others, and some professional help. "After the meeting," Joseph wrote on January 30, 1934, "Bro. McKay (David O.) gave Ethel a blessing at her request. She has been ill for several weeks." These blessings always brought peace and comfort. But they were only temporary in their effect and in time wore away, exposing her again to the terrors of her illness.

Every avenue of potential aid for Ethel's relief was explored. "Ethel, who has not been well for some time, is staying with Dr. Pearl U. Nelson for a few days," Joseph wrote shortly after Elder McKay's blessing. Dr. Nelson, a naturalist and chiropractor, was Elder Smith's sister-in-law, the wife of Joseph Nelson, who was first married to Joseph Fielding's deceased sister, Leonora.

Like other professional treatments Ethel received, Dr. Nelson's ministrations brought no lasting relief. "Ethel not well," her concerned husband wrote later. "She has been for several months greatly concerned over supposed physical ailments, and worried."

Frequent rides in the family car always brought some relief, and occasionally Ethel accompanied Joseph on his conference assignments to nearby stakes, which offered a welcome diversion. "I attended the North Davis stake conference," Elder Smith wrote on February 11, 1934. "Ethel went with me at her request. . . . I fear the day was too strenuous for her."

After the April general conference, the family decided that a trip to California might help. "I left with Ethel for Los Angeles for a few days on the coast," Elder Smith wrote on April 16, "the object being to give Ethel a change, as she has been ill for several months due to nervousness and shock (worry). We were on the coast from the 17th of April when we arrived until the 29th." During this time, they toured with the mission president, holding meetings in Whittier, Santa Ana, San Bernardino, San Fernando, Santa Barbara, and Baldwin Park. Then, on the weekend of April 28 and 29, they attended conference in the Hollywood Stake. But, the change of scene and routine failed to bring relief to his beloved wife. "I regret to say," he wrote, "that her condition is little improved and she will have to have special care for her ailment."

A few days after returning from California, Elder Smith made arrangements for this "special care" for Ethel, providing her with the best diagnostic treatment available at the time. Unfortunately, the state of medical knowledge in this field was still in its infancy so that no permanent improvement was made in her condition. In these circumstances, the entire family rallied around to support the beloved mother and each other. Out of this came a greater sense of love and unity and a greater appreciation for the simple joys of family life. Within the limits of Ethel's illness, the flow of events in the Smith household continued unabated. There were school, sports, and social activities for the children, and for Joseph Fielding there was the constant round of his apostolic duties. With help, Ethel was able, intermittently, to carry on her domestic responsibilities. And the Smiths continued to enjoy the periodic outings that had been so much a part of the family's routine.

A notable vacation was planned for the summer of 1935, two years after Ethel first began to suffer. Elder Smith was able to block out twelve days from his church duties during the last part of July for a trip to California. With six of their children (Julina, Amelia, Lewis, Reynolds, Douglas, and Milton), Joseph and Ethel left Salt Lake City early Monday morning, July 15. Because of the large number who went along, it was necessary to take two cars. The driving chores were divided among Elder Smith, the two girls, and newly licensed Lewis, who was most willing to shoulder more than his share of the driving load.

The first day's travel took the vacationers through scenic Bryce and Zion's canyons and colorful St. George to Mesquite, Nevada, where they arrived at 11:00 P.M., hot, tired, and dusty. "The weather was very warm," Joseph reported, "and in our crowded condition, we did not sleep much." So they were up and on their way by 4:00 A.M. the next morning in order to beat the desert sun. Fifteen hours later, they arrived at Long Beach, California, where they were "fortunate in securing two tent cabins," which they rented for a week. "Hardly had we located ourselves," wrote the father, "before the boys were in bathing suits and on the beach." Thus began one of the most relaxing and enjoyable vacations the Smith family had ever spent together. They lived by the sun and mostly in the sun. All the children were big enough that they did not require constant surveillance. They were allowed to swim at will, to inspect the nearby pier, or to sunbathe on the beach as the whim of the moment dictated. This left the parents free to do as they wished, whether to take a dip, visit in an unhurried way, or merely sit and gaze at the ocean, lulled by the rhythmic pounding of the surf. Such an unstructured routine, free of pressures and deadlines, was especially soothing and calming to Ethel. It was also an idyllic interlude for the entire family.

Joseph and Ethel were able to tear the children away from the beach long enough to visit the planetarium and the museum. And on Sunday the family attended Sunday School in the morning and sacrament meeting in the evening at Long Beach. It requires little imagination to guess who the main speaker was at the evening service. It was a busman's holiday for Joseph, who, even during his vacation, found himself in the pulpit.

Monday evening, the 22nd, the Smiths were guests in the home of Dr. J. Douglas Barnes, where they spent "a very delightful evening." The next morning, they drove south to San Diego, where, after finding "comfortable lodgings at an auto park," they drove on to Tijuana "just to satisfy the children in crossing the U. S. line."

The family celebrated Pioneer Day by spending the entire day at the San Diego Fair, which was then in progress. "The Tabernacle Choir was there," reported Elder Smith, "and gave concerts in the Ford Bowl near Henry Ford's exhibit. We attended the concert that afternoon and also visited the L. D. S. building." At day's end, they "were tired."

On Thursday morning, the Smiths packed and started for home. During the day they paused briefly in San Bernardino and at the San Luis Rey Mission, stopping for the night at Las Vegas, Nevada, "by request of the children." And the next day they made the last leg of their return trip to Salt Lake City, "glad to be back again."

To be home meant the resumption of the daily routines that made life alternately enjoyable and tedious. Joseph was pleased to find that his daughter, Josephine, and her husband, who had stayed at the Douglas Street home during the family's absence, had kept the lawns and flower beds well watered. One of Joseph's main means of relaxation was to tend his flowers and plants. Less enjoyable was the "donkey" work around the house, which he performed willingly but with far less enthusiasm. "Cleaned auto and did other odd jobs," he reported the day after returning from California. As for Ethel, she too was glad to be home amid her treasured things, surrounded by a loving family and thoughtful, caring neighbors. But the respite in California, while temporarily relieving her of the trauma of her illness, had not cured it. So, she lived from day to day, struggling against the emotional pressures exerted upon her while trying valiantly to fulfill her wifely and motherly duties. It was not easy, either for her or for her husband and children. Yet it was a burden they could not lay down. So, they accepted it stoically as a natural legacy of the human condition in which all humanity must share.

Notwithstanding this, it was sometimes difficult for the Smiths to be entirely philosophical and objective about their plight. It must have seemed at times that the fates had served up an overdose of misfortune for them. Such a time occurred during the first few months of 1936. In early January, Mary Reynolds died; she was a polygamous wife of Ethel's father, George C. Reynolds. Five days after the funeral of Ethel's Auntie Mary, Joseph Fielding's mother passed away. Her death was preceded by several weeks of intense pain caused by a fall that fractured several of her ribs. A few months later, the whole Smith family was devastated by the death of Lois's seven-month-old daughter, Dorothy. The passing of this sweet child was undoubtedly of special poignancy to Ethel as the little girl had been born on October 23, 1935, Ethel's forty-sixth birthday. While death of itself seems not to have held any special terrors for the family, yet the circumstances surrounding the death and the resulting loneliness and yearning for the departed one brought great sadness and mourning.

Overshadowing all these stressful events, of course, was Ethel's illness, which seemed to defy diagnosis. The oscillating swing of her moods was unpredictable. The effect was not unlike a roller-coaster ride. There were periods of relative calm when everything was in gear and life moved on at a deliberate, measured pace. Then suddenly, at the summit of this slow upward trend, would come a precipitous, sometimes frightening descent into the depths of despair. "This is a sad day for me and my children because of the condition of my wife," Joseph Fielding wrote on February 19, 1936. It was difficult for them to grasp how such a radical change could have occurred in the condition of their beloved wife and mother in such a short time. And, given the failure of divine or professional help to provide permanent relief, they were baffled and balked, not knowing what more to do.

Yet, the family coped with their problems, continuing an orderly course in their lives. For Elder Smith, there were the constant demands made by his calling. Through all the upset and uncertainty at home, he continued to handle his share of stake conference and mission tour assignments. In early September 1936, he left Salt Lake City by train to tour the Eastern States Mission. He was met at Pittsburgh, Pennsylvania, by the mission president, Don B. Colton, on Sunday morning, September 5. With the mission secretary, Wayne F. Richards, they went directly to the chapel, where the first meeting of the two-week tour was held. Leaving Pittsburgh the next morning by automobile, the touring party made a side trip to Kirtland, Ohio, as Elder Smith wanted to visit the temple. "There we were *lectured*," he wrote, "and the LDS roundly abused." During the tour, Joseph was aroused by certain erroneous statements made by the guide, which he disputed and corrected. This "won the friendship of a Mr. Green," wrote Elder Smith "who handed me a dollar bill 'for the cause.' " After leaving Kirtland, the party drove on to Erie, Pennsylvania, where they held an evening meeting. The next morning, the apostle met with the full-time missionaries laboring in that area. This set a pattern he would follow during the next two weeks, alternately holding meetings with members and missionaries. From Erie, the touring party traveled to Jamestown; and the next day, en route to Scranton, they saw some of the most famous sites connected with the early history of the Church— Harmony, the home of Isaac Hale, the father of Emma Hale Smith, the Prophet Joseph Smith's wife; and the Susquehanna River, on whose banks John the Baptist and later Peter, James, and John appeared to the Prophet Joseph Smith and Oliver Cowdery and in whose waters Joseph and Oliver were baptized. Next came Altoona, Pennsylvania, followed by Fairview and Hagerstown, where arrangements were made for Elder Smith to speak over the radio.

On the way to Washington, D.C., after leaving Hagerstown, the travelers paused briefly at Gettysburg, where they inspected the famous Civil War battlefield, tracing in their mind's eye how the soldiers of the blue and the gray had fought savagely over the rolling countryside, drenching the field with their blood. Endowed as he was with a sense of history, we may be assured that Elder Smith reflected too, as he gazed on the scene, about how the clipped eloquence of Abraham Lincoln had later fixed forever in the American mind the significance of that critical battle.

At Washington, Elder Smith and President Colton were the guests of Edgar B. Brossard and his gracious wife, who, Joseph noted, were very kind to them. The Brossards accompanied the visitors to Baltimore, Maryland, on Sunday morning, September 13. There a meeting was held, and then they went to the "beautiful" meeting house in the nation's capital for an evening sacrament service. The next morning, the Brossards also took the visitors on a tour of the city before they left for Philadelphia. A tight schedule did not permit any sight-seeing of Philadelphia's historic sites, there barely being time for a missionary-member meeting before the travelers left for New York, where they arrived at 1:30 A.M. Tuesday morning.

New York City was the headquarters of the Eastern States Mission. Joseph Fielding spent the morning of Tuesday, September 15, inspecting the mission office at 155 Riverside Drive and visiting with the members of the office staff. And in the afternoon, he and President Colton were driven northward, up the Hudson River, by Elder Richards to Newburgh, where they held a meeting, On the way, they passed through West Point, the site of the United States Military Academy. Here also were seen the restored remains of large fortifications built to enable Colonial America to control traffic up the Hudson. During the revolutionary period, that control was aided by a heavy iron chain, stretched from the west bank to Constitution Island, that prevented British ships from ascending the river. No doubt Joseph Fielding's historic sense was excited by recalling that General Benedict Arnold's treason arose from his abortive attempt to betray this key military post to the enemy.

From New York City, Elder Smith was driven to New Haven, Connecticut, where more meetings were held and where the apostle was shown around part of the sprawling campus of Yale University. That afternoon, the party drove to Boston, Massachusetts, where an evening meeting was held. Afterward, the apostle was taken to nearby Lexington, where he was a guest in the home of a brother and sister Knecht. "Sister K," Joseph explained, "is the daughter of S. Norman Lee of Brigham City."

It sometimes happens that a backward glance will invest a certain day or incident with an importance not understood at the time. Friday, September 18, was such a day in the life of Joseph Fielding Smith. Early that morning, his party left Lexington destined for Fort Henry, New York. Their route of travel took them through Sharon, Windsor County, Vermont, the birthplace of the Prophet Joseph Smith. Here they paused to view the impressive granite monument that honors the Prophet and to visit Elder Angus J. Cannon and his wife, who were in charge of the visitors' center there. Traveling on, they arrived at Fort Henry in time to hold a meeting at 8:00 P.M. In recapping the events of the day in his diary, Elder Smith wrote in conclusion: "Met Elder Bruce R. McConkie, a most excellent Elder." Over the years of his apostolic ministry, Joseph Fielding Smith met literally thousands of missionaries. Many of their names found their way into his personal record by way of acknowledgment and thanks for services rendered to him. In only one instance, however, did the diarist both mention an elder's name and extol his virtues. The single instance involved this "most excellent Elder," Bruce R. McConkie, who would later become Joseph Fielding's son-in-law, the husband of his youngest daughter, Amelia. Moreover, this young elder would later emulate his father-in-law's example of strict reliance on the scriptures in speaking and writing, in his prolific literary output, and in his stern, unbending pulpit presence. As fate would have it, Bruce McConkie would fill the vacancy in the Twelve resulting from Joseph Fielding Smith's death; it would be in Elder McConkie's home that the Prophet would spend his last days; and he would die there.

Bruce McConkie and Amelia Smith had been acquainted before he entered the mission field. And that acquaintance was rekindled soon after his release. "In the evening," wrote Elder Smith on February 7, 1937, only five months after he met Bruce McConkie in Fort Henry, "with Julina, Amelia and Bruce, attended the joint meeting of the Yale, Yalecrest and 33rd Wards in the Bonneville Stake (split) conference." And within thirteen months after Joseph Fielding Smith and Bruce R. McConkie met at Fort Henry, "the most excellent elder" and the apostle's baby daughter were sealed as man and wife in the temple.

But before that happy event would take place, another mournful experience awaited Elder Smith and his family. After months of illness, Joseph's beloved Ethel passed away. "Intended to be present and take part at the funeral of my mother's sister, Melissa J. L. Davis," he wrote on August 26, 1937, "but was called suddenly to the bedside of my wife, who was suddenly stricken. She has been ailing for many months, and in spite of all aid passed away at 3:15 today. A better woman could not be found, or truer wife and mother."

Economical with words, especially when writing, Joseph usually masked his feelings, as he did in this brief entry. We can only guess, therefore, about the full impact of Ethel's death upon him. During the twenty-nine years of their marriage, she had given birth to and nurtured nine of his children, had reared Louie's two, had made a haven and a heaven of their home, and had been his most ardent admirer and supporter. She was always there to encourage, to counsel, and to assist him, to accompany him to social and church gatherings, and to share with him in the joys

271

and trials of rearing their family. She was his lover, his friend, his partner and counselor wrapped into one. Therefore, it was undoubtedly a trying and traumatic thing to have that relationship severed, even though temporarily. "The funeral services for my beloved wife, Ethel, were held today," he recorded on Monday, August 30, 1937. "The Deseret News contained an excellent report. The speakers were Bishop T. Fred Hardy, Nettie D. Bradford, Samuel O. Bennion and President David O. McKay. Music by John Longden, Harry Clark and Jessie Evans. Organ, Sister Darrell Ensign."

Chapter Sixteen

Another Dawn

E thel's death came in the midst of a rush of important activities for the Smith family. Amelia was planning her nuptials. Lewis was getting ready to enter the mission field. And the three younger boys were preparing to return to school. Sixteen-year-old Reyn was beginning to earn his athletic spurs at East High School, while thirteen-year-old Doug was in junior high and ten-year-old Milton was in elementary school. Since Amelia was preoccupied with her own affairs, Joseph supervised the preparations for his missionary and his student sons. "Went with Lewis," he wrote four days after Ethel's funeral, "to make purchases preparatory to his mission, also to obtain a passport." Several days later, the father accompanied Amelia and Lewis through the temple when they obtained their endowments. Present also were Julina and Amelia's fiancée, Bruce R. McConkie.

Meanwhile, Joseph's church responsibilities continued unabated. At the office he was preoccupied in preparing a manuscript that would contain some of the key writings and sayings of the Prophet Joseph Smith. This entailed a thorough canvass of the early historical records and the extraction and arrangement by date and subject matter of choice excerpts from these. While Elder Smith had able research assistance for this project, he bore the ultimate responsibility for checking the accuracy of the quotations and for proofreading the completed manuscript. This was detailed and sometimes tedious work that demanded Joseph Fielding's most concentrated efforts. However, because of the admiration and respect he had for the Prophet, it was obviously a labor of love from which he seemed to derive great personal satisfaction. His satisfaction became complete the following year when the manuscript was published under the title *Teachings of the Prophet Joseph Smith.*

The apostle's activities outside his office continued as usual with stake conference visits, board meetings, funerals, weddings, and, of course, family responsibilities. It was the latter which, at the moment, gave Elder Smith the greatest concern. He still had the three young sons at home who were already in or who were fast approaching a critical stage of their development. While his married daughters rallied around to help, they had their own family responsibilities that made it difficult for them to give their young brothers the kind of attention and supervision they urgently required. These were the circumstances that prompted Elder Smith to begin seriously thinking about remarriage two months after Ethel's death. As he did so, his thoughts focused on Jessie Evans, Salt Lake County Recorder and well-known contralto soloist with the Salt Lake Tabernacle Choir. Curiously enough, Joseph hardly knew Jessie Evans. She had sung at Ethel's funeral, but this was done to fulfill Ethel's specific request, for she had known Jessie and admired her singing. The request for her to sing at the funeral was made through Joseph Fielding's brother-in-law, William C. Patrick, who was well acquainted with Miss Evans and who had been invited to help arrange for the funeral. Following the services, Elder Smith wrote a note of appreciation to the singer in which he not only thanked her for participating but also expressed admiration for her talent, going so far as to say that he enjoyed her singing as much as any he had heard. This letter brought an appreciative response from Jessie. And later, because Joseph had worked for a while in the recorder's office when he was a young man, there were telephone calls and some correspondence back and forth about Jessie's work. With a letter dated October 9, 1937, Elder Smith forwarded material from the Church Archives that he felt would be helpful to Miss Evans in establishing the real date of the creation of Salt Lake County. He added that if in the future he could be of assistance, he would consider it a pleasure, not a duty, to respond. Because of the personal allusions in this letter, Joseph suggested that it not be filed in the recorder's office.

Between October 9 and October 23, Elder Smith made a decision to radically alter the nature of his relationship with Jessie Evans. *"Wrote an important letter,"* he noted on the 23rd, "but held it for several days." In this letter he told Jessie that he would like to develop a relationship with her on a personal level. He obviously had matrimony in mind. But it was a delicate step for him to take, given his position in the Church and the relatively short time that had elapsed since Ethel's death. Clearly, however, his family situation caused him to act with greater speed than he otherwise would have done. He held this "important letter" for four days, mulling over the pros and cons of entering into a courtship. Finally, on October 27, he decided to take the plunge. "Went to *County Recorder's* office," he wrote on that date, "and signed specially prepared document of historical nature, etc. *Had interview with recorder, very important,* and left her the letter I wrote on the 23rd." Thus began one of the most sedate, proper, albeit interesting courtships on record. It extended more than two months before Joseph popped the question. The manner in which he conducted it is a model of judgment and prudence, interspersed with a restrained ardor.

The weekend after he delivered the letter, Elder Smith was in Oakland, California, for a stake conference. Reflecting a practice that had then become fixed, he was joined by a representative of the "Security Committee," the forerunner of today's Welfare Committee. During the conference, Joseph accompanied stake president Eugene Hilton to inspect possible sites for "Security Quarters." There seemed to be a sense of urgency about moving the Security Plan forward, and much of the instruction given over the weekend focused on the theory and the practical application of the plan.

Between meetings on Saturday, President Hilton and his counselors drove the apostle to San Francisco across the newly completed Bay Bridge. Excited by the experience, Joseph pronounced the bridge "one of the wonders of the world."

Back in Salt Lake City, Elder Smith resumed his unorthodox courtship. "5:10 met Miss *Jessie Evans*," he wrote on November 2, "and had *important* interview with her." By now, after only two brief "interviews," both of which were held in public places, the couple had apparently reached an understanding. So, three days later, Joseph "spent the evening out with J. E. and met her mother." The following Sunday, Elder Smith attended services in the Tabernacle, where Jessie sang a solo; and that night, after a meeting in the Burton Ward where Joseph was the speaker, the couple had another "interview." On Armistice Day, after the weekly rehearsal of the Tabernacle Choir, Elder Smith "brought Jessie Evans to the house and had her meet Amelia and Bruce." And Sunday evening, November 21, after returning from a conference in the Wasatch Stake, Joseph called on Jessie again when he "left her a ring which she was willing to accept."

During the remainder of the year, there were frequent visits back and forth in the Smith and Evans homes, where different members of the families gathered to become better acquainted. Typical of these was one held two days after Christmas. Joseph wrote of the occasion, "Josephine, Julina, Amelia, Bruce and I spent the evening at the home of Jessie Evans who entertained us with songs. A very pleasant and enjoyable evening." And on the 28th, he added, "Jessie E. and her mother spent the evening at the home with music, etc., children happy." Having achieved his purpose in winning the consent of Jessie Evans to be his wife, while obtaining the approval of both families, he noted with obvious satisfaction on the following day: "Spent the evening with Jessie Evans, this day being her birthday, and because she has consented to become my *wife*, for which fact the children are happy as well as I. The Lord bless her."

The person who consented to become Joseph Fielding Smith's third wife was an attractive, vivacious woman of thirty-five who, through her talent and charm, had carved out a successful career in both music and politics. Endowed with a rich contralto voice, she had, through years of training, become a professional singer of note. However, she gave up a promising operatic career because of the responsibility to care for her widowed mother and the lack of opportunity for professional employment in Salt Lake City where the family lived. The reputation she had gained as a singer had given Jessie Evans widespread recognition in Utah, and this, coupled with her jovial, outgoing personality, made her a natural for politics. So, she had been elected to the office of Salt Lake County Recorder without difficulty. And her musical talent had earned her the role as a soloist with the Salt Lake Tabernacle Choir, whose performances were broadcast weekly over a national radio network. As a result, at the time of her marriage, she was better known among the general public than was Joseph Fielding. Due to the circumstances of her age, talent, and reputation, Jessie Evans's prospects for marriage had almost dwindled to the point of extinction. She was simply overqualified as a potential wife. Most suitors would have been intimidated to approach her with matrimony in mind. Only someone with the stature and reputation of a Joseph Fielding Smith would have had any reasonable prospect of winning her as a bride.

Elder Smith considered himself fortunate to have found

someone with the qualities of Jessie Evans to become his wife and the mother to his children. He later told his son Douglas, "Your Aunt Jessie always belonged to me. I know that the Lord intended it. And the Lord sent her to me when I needed a wife and needed help and somebody in the family to help us and take care of us, and the Lord had raised her up and sent her to me. And oh, how grateful I am, for she has been just as true and faithful as anybody could possibly be, and we all love her."

Elder Smith and Jessie continued their courtship until April 12, when they were sealed in the Salt Lake Temple by President Heber J. Grant. Previously, Joseph had received an assignment to conduct a stake conference in Honolulu and to tour the Hawaiian and Japanese missions in the Hawaiian Islands. Accompanied by members of their families, they went directly from the temple to the depot, where they boarded a train for San Francisco. Remaining there two days, they then boarded the luxury liner *Lurline* on Friday morning the 15th for the short voyage to Los Angeles, where the ship was to pick up the rest of its passengers destined for Hawaii. Since the Smiths had several hours before the ship's departure from Los Angeles, they visited with Jessie's adopted sister, Lily, and her husband, Heber Simpson, at nearby Santa Monica before reboarding the *Lurline*.

The five-day voyage to the islands was picture perfect, with "a very smooth sea all the way." The long, languid days afforded the newlyweds the opportunity to reflect on the marvel of their marriage and to contemplate their future as man and wife. Despite a difference of twenty-six years in their ages and differences in temperament, background, and training, Joseph Fielding and Jessie Evans Smith were remarkably compatible. She was an irrepressible extrovert, full of fun and good humor, who enjoyed the limelight of public attention. Joseph, on the other hand, was a quiet, retiring introvert, dignified and detached, who always seemed somewhat uncomfortable in a public setting and who never sought to call attention to himself. The thing that bridged the wide gulf between these two disparate personalities was the genuine love and respect they had for each other. During their courtship, Joseph had written of Jessie that she had "the most lovely voice — to me — that I ever listened to, whose music and song have charmed thousands, but more especially me. Always willing and ready to bless others, never refusing to sing at funerals and entertainments, if it is possible to accommodate all who make requests. I love her for her goodness, virtue and loveliness; her consideration and care for her mother, and because she loves me. May the Lord bless her always, I humbly pray." Jessie reciprocated these feelings in full measure. She frequently expressed her love for Joseph and was heard to say, "He is the kindest man I have ever known. I have never heard him speak an unkind word."

The lazy days aboard ship, in addition to providing uninterrupted hours for visiting and reading, were punctuated with turns around the deck for exercise, interludes at the rail to admire the fish that surfaced occasionally, or the gliding albatross that followed their ship most of the way, and with entertainments that were staged each afternoon for the enjoyment of the passengers. The director of activities aboard ship, having learned of Jessie's musical talents, approached her hesitantly to ask whether she would be willing to favor the passengers with a song. Her pleased and proud husband reported the result: "Jessie added to the entertainment on the vessel by singing at the afternoon concerts Tuesday and Wednesday, receiving encores and singing by request of many who were aboard." And when Joseph's identity as a high leader of the Mormon Church leaked out and it was learned that he and this charming, effervescent songstress were on their honeymoon, they acquired immediate celebrity status.

That reputation was hardly diminished by the scene that unfolded as the *Lurline* docked at Pearl Harbor. Waiting on the pier to greet the Smiths was a large group of Saints, led by Oahu stake president Ralph Woolley and presidents Bailey of the Hawaiian Mission and Robertson of the Japanese Mission, who joined with enthusiasm to sing the traditional Polynesian songs of welcome. And when the Salt Lake visitors disembarked, they were almost smothered with fresh and fragrant leis; "fifty in all," wrote Joseph. So overwhelming was this demonstration of love and respect that Elder Smith cast aside his customary reticence and wrote with unabashed pride, "We were met by the largest, best and most worthy group of any who got off the ship."

The travelers were taken directly to the stake president's home, where Sister Woolley, whom the brethren called "the queen of hostesses," had prepared an elaborate dinner for them. The entertainment that followed capped a memorable day for the newlyweds. "We were royally entertained by two groups of Hawaiian women," explained Joseph, "who came with their ukuleles, guitars and a bass viol and sang for us." The first group of singers was comprised of eight women. Later in the evening, four other women, with two male accompanists, came to perform. "Their singing of Hawaiian songs was a delightful thing," he wrote. Predictably, Jessie joined in the singing and, to the satisfaction of all, especially her husband, learned one of the Hawaiian songs. "They were delighted with her singing," noted Joseph, "and have made arrangements for her to sing with them at the conference on Sunday."

The following day, Friday, was spent quietly and lazily at the Woolley residence, where the Smiths divided their time between writing letters, visiting with their gracious hosts, and inspecting the lavish and beautiful grounds surrounding the home.

On Saturday, President Robertson of the Japanese mission took Joseph for a ride to see the sights of the city, ending up at the "Punch Bowl," which afforded them a spectacular view of Honolulu.

Time off with no church assignments was an oddity for Joseph Fielding Smith. Usually during the annual summer break, he changed his normal routine, but ordinarily he would sandwich in speaking assignments or interviews that robbed the interlude of any semblance of a vacation. Now, however, during this April of 1938, he had spent ten full days entirely free from official duties while enjoying the companionship of his new bride. But, we get the sense that the end of this period of leisure was not unwelcome to him. "At 7:00 P.M." he wrote on Saturday April 23, "the priesthood session of the Oahu stake conference was held and reports were made which were equal to that I have seen and heard in any other stake of Zion." And the following day he seemed elated by the crowded schedule of meetings arranged by President Woolley. The first general session was held at 10:00 A.M., followed by a "musical meeting" at 1:30 P.M. where Jessie and her new friends sang for the entertainment of the conference. The afternoon general session "was all in Hawaiian" except for Elder Smith's remarks. Immediately following this meeting, the apostle attended a special session for the Samoans, only to return at 7:00 P.M. for a gathering of the youth. "The MIA meeting was equal to any session in any stake," he wrote appreciatively. "The young people did splendid work. Jessie sang two numbers and thrilled the congregation."

Jessie's participation in these meetings set a pattern for the rest of their married life. Whenever Joseph Fielding presided, he wanted her to perform if for no other reason than that he never tired of hearing her sing. Beyond that, however, her well-trained contralto voice, singing sacred hymns, added a special touch of spirituality to the meetings, inspiring the listeners and elevating his own capabilities in delivering the spoken word. Later, through the persistent and playful urging of his wife, Joseph would occasionally join Jessie in a duet, blending his own fine baritone voice with hers. On these occasions, they would usually sit together on the piano bench while Jessie played the accompaniment, moderating her usual, full-throated voice so as not to drown out the singing of her husband. In time, Elder Smith began to refer to these performances as "do its" rather than duets, implying that he joined in them with reluctance only to humor Jessie. The fact is that he really enjoyed them as he enjoyed other aspects of his relationship with this puckish, irrepressible woman who had become his wife. Her zest for life, her almost perpetual gaiety, her love of music, and her comedic tendencies added a certain carefree quality to Joseph Fielding Smith's life that he had not had before. And in his own modest, restrained way, he joined in, or at least approved of Jessie's frequent high jinks. So, he never complained about the cast-iron plaque that hung on Jessie's kitchen wall proclaiming, "Opinions expressed by the husband in this household are not necessarily those of the management." Nor did he question or reprimand her for insisting that she had a special dispensation from the Utah Highway Patrol to speed in their little white car. And there is no indication he objected to her carrying on conversations with passersby from the second-floor balcony of their Eagle Gate apartment on State Street. During one such conversation of which the author is aware, she playfully threw down an orange to a friend who was walking by and with whom she had been carrying on a conversation.

This apartment was in view of the office her husband occupied while he was the president of the Church. Jessie had a spy glass that one day she trained on the window of President Smith's office. Seeing there a bust of his grandmother, Mary Fielding Smith, she called on the phone to demand, "Who is that woman in your office?" Confirming the playful banter that sometimes passed between them, he said to her when she came once to help in his office during an emergency, "Remember, Mama Dear, over here you are not the speaker of the house." And again in the same vein, once when they drove away from a chapel where he had spoken, he rolled down the window and said with mock anxiety, "Look out! Woman driver." Such was the charming relationship between Joseph Fielding and Jessie Evans Smith, a relationship solidified during their honeymoon in Hawaii.

As already noted, however, this honeymoon was arranged around ecclesiastical responsibilities that were the principal reason for Elder Smith's presence in the islands. So, on the Tuesday following the Oahu stake conference, the apostle held meetings in Honolulu with the missionaries from both the Japanese and the Hawaiian missions. Later in the week, he inspected and attended a session in the temple at Laie. He spoke twice at Laie, at a service that preceded the temple session and at a chapel near the temple. Jessie sang on both occasions. Returning to Honolulu, the following Saturday the visitors enjoyed an elaborate luau that featured pig, poi, fish, and sweet potatoes. Joseph was fascinated to learn how the food for the luau was cooked with hot rocks in the ground.

Elder Smith spoke and Jessie sang at morning services the day after the luau; and in the afternoon, they flew to Maui, where, in the evening, a public meeting was held. There the Smiths teamed up again to speak and to sing. At their request, Joseph and Jessie were awakened early Tuesday morning, May 3. By 4:00 A.M. they were on their way toward the summit of Haleakala, reputed to be the largest extinct volcano in the world. Winding upward, their automobile was driven through the clouds that hovered around the mountain like a halo. Emerging from the cloud cover, they arrived at the summit just in time to witness the extraordinary sight of the sun seemingly rising out of the Pacific Ocean to the east. "It was a beautiful sight above the clouds," wrote Joseph. "We could see the mountains of Mauna Kea and Mauna Loa on the island of Hawaii." Turning around, they could also look into the black depths of the great crater from whose mouth had flowed the molten lava that had given birth to the island.

The Smiths flew from Maui to North Kohala in the afternoon. There they were met by the customary greeting party, were laden with fragrant leis, and were driven to a chapel at Waimea. "I spoke and Jessie sang," wrote Joseph. The following day, they were driven to Kona. "Our reception at Kona was very warm and friendly," he noted, "a gathering awaiting us when we arrived with music and song." The meeting held that night followed the usual routine with Jessie singing and Elder Smith speaking from the scriptures. Leaving Kona, the visitors were driven to Hilo, passing through vast lava beds produced by the volcano Kilauea they passed on the way. The meeting held that night at Hilo was a disappointment. "The attendance here was not as large and responsive as in other places," he noted. If that was the low point of the tour, the high point came two days later on the island of Molokai. On Saturday, May 7, the apostle and President W. W. Bailey were driven by an elder to the leper colony over a narrow, treacherous road that descends over two thousand feet down the Pali. There Elder Smith held a meeting with the members of the Church who were mourning out their lives in that dreary, isolated place. "The poor people were praying that I would come and visit them for no other brother has visited them of the authorities for many, many years," he wrote. As Elder Smith assessed the impact of this experience, seeing people whose only hopes seemed to lay in the atonement of the Savior and in the promised rewards hereafter, he wrote, "My visit here was one of the most important things in my visit to the islands." Back at the main city on Molokai, Joseph and President Bailey attended a luau whose elaborate menu and accompanying music and joviality seemed to accentuate the cheerless condition of the lepers he had just left.

After the luau, Elder Smith attended "a very excellent MIA meeting," and then, to gain insight into the strength and maturity of the local native leadership, he participated as an observer in a district council meeting. The following day, a Sunday, was filled with the usual worship services.

Back in Honolulu, Joseph yielded to Jessie's playful pressure and took her shopping to buy gifts for those at home. And that night, they were the guests of Brother and Sister Henry Oki, who treated them to a sumptuous meal of Chinese food. In typical oriental fashion, the meal was served slowly, almost ritualistically, in many courses, allowing ample time for leisurely conversation.

After several days of travel, interspersed with numerous meetings and interviews, the visitors decided to take off for two days. The first day, Tuesday, May 10, was spent quietly at the comfortable home of President and Sister Ralph Woolley, where the Smiths rested, wrote letters, and roamed around their hosts' beautiful gardens. The next day, the visitors intended to experience the pleasures of deep-sea fishing, but the trip proved to be a colossal bust. The Smiths left the Woolleys early in the morning and were driven across the Pali to the beach, where they joined a jubilant party that boarded Mr. Elkington's yacht. The jubilation was short lived. In the open sea, the yacht was battered by waves so heavy that probably not a single line was cast. The decision to turn back seems to have been unanimous, although it is questionable whether some members of the party had the desire, or even the ability to vote. Back on shore, they compensated for the lost fishing opportunity by taking "a sea bath instead."

The next morning, the Smiths were flown to Kauai, "The Golden Island." Here they were driven to see the "Grand Canyon of Waimea," which bears some resemblance to the Grand Canyon of the Colorado on the mainland. After visiting other places of interest on the island, the Smiths participated in a missionary meeting that was followed by a general meeting where Joseph spoke and Jessie sang.

This was to be the last formal meeting for the honeymooners during their twenty-three day stay in the Hawaiian Islands. They flew back to Honolulu the morning of Friday, May 13, and spent the day packing for their return voyage to the mainland. That night they dined at the home of President and Sister Robertson, where the Baileys were also present. During the course of the evening, the Robertsons and their guests were treated to the unusual sight of a total eclipse of the moon.

It would have been hard to distinguish the scene at

the Pearl Harbor pier Saturday morning, May 14, from the one there on April 21 when Elder and Sister Smith arrived. The pier was thronged with scores of singing, joyous Saints who loaded the departing dignitaries with colorful, fragrant leis. Now, however, the warm alohas, spoken or sung by all, meant "Good-bye, come again" instead of "Hello, welcome to Hawaii." "Everywhere we went we were royally treated by the Hawaiians," wrote the apostle after their ship, the S.S. *Matsonia,* had cleared the harbor. "We received 283 leis and attended five or six luaus. We have held numerous meetings, met many hundreds of members and I hope were able to do some good. Jessie's singing won the hearts of the people and we have made many friends."

There was unaccustomed excitement on the S.S. *Matsonia* shortly after it left Pearl Harbor with the Smiths aboard. A member of the crew, who apparently was intoxicated, fell or jumped overboard. Once the alarm was sounded, the ship began to circle in an attempt to locate and rescue the man. Although it did so for an hour while both crew and passengers anxiously scanned the sea for any sign of the lost crewman, the search was in vain. This unfortunate incident seemed to cast a pall over the entire return voyage.

Waiting to greet the Smiths at the Wilmington pier in California was President W. Aird MacDonald, whom Elder Smith had cabled while the *Matsonia* was at sea. After spending two days in the Los Angeles area, the travelers left by train Friday evening, May 20, and arrived in Salt Lake City the following day. They were greeted at the Salt Lake depot by Jessie's mother and two brothers and by Julina, Amelia, Bruce, Reyn, and Douglas. "We all went home where the girls had prepared dinner, with the help of Sister Evans," Joseph wrote.

Chapter Seventeen

Readjustments

At home, some readjustments were necessary to merge two families into one. While Jessie had never been married and therefore had no children, she had been supporting her mother, Jeanette Buchanan Evans, who lived with her. It was decided, therefore, that "Mother Evans" would move with her daughter to 998 Douglas to take up residence with the Smiths. There she would remain until her death in 1957. It was a happy arrangement. Since it was intended that Jessie would accompany Joseph Fielding whenever possible on his church assignments and since Jessie had many outside commitments because of her singing, it was fortunate that Mother Evans was available to provide continuity and stability in the home for the three sons during times when the father and Aunt Jessie were both away.

The news at home was good and bad. The good news was that the three boys were in good health and the house was intact, having suffered no observable damage. The bad news was that Julina had recently undergone a tonsillectomy and Emily's husband, L. Garrett Myers, had

287

had major surgery for the removal of a goitre. Moreover, the day after Joseph and Jessie returned, Julina was hospitalized for the removal of her appendix; Cousin Silas Smith performed the surgery. Three days later, Garrett was released from the hospital and four days after that Julina followed suit.

Thus Aunt Jessie was speedily introduced to life in a large, active, and growing family. And that indoctrination accelerated when on June 8 she accompanied her husband to the Salt Lake Temple to watch him perform Julina's sealing to Eldon Charles Hart, then accompanied him and the newlyweds to Provo, where they watched the new groom graduate from Brigham Young University. The next day, it was to East High School to see son Reynolds graduate. And three days after that, word was received from Chicago that daughter Lois had given birth to a son. In the midst of all this, Jessie thought it was a good idea to host a dinner for the neighbors on Douglas Street as a means of getting acquainted. And, of course, there were the customary festivities to honor Julina and Eldon.

Meanwhile, Jessie soon gained insight into her duties as the wife of a busy General Authority. The weekend following the return from Hawaii, she accompanied Elder Smith to Ogden for the conference of the Mount Ogden Stake. The following weekend found them in Springville for the Kolob stake conference. And the weekend after that, they attended meetings of June conference together. Before the Sunday general session, Jessie sang with the choir during its weekly national broadcast. Notwithstanding their hectic schedule, this was undoubtedly a time of excitement and exhilaration for both Joseph Fielding and Jessie Evans Smith as they began their married life together.

Soon after returning from Hawaii, Elder Smith commenced working in earnest on the biography of his father, a project he had had in mind for many years. He had intermittently done some work on it, gathering materials and poring over his father's numerous diaries and other personal papers. Now, however, he focused on it almost to the exclusion of all other noncurricular activities. He worked steadily on the manuscript during the summer break in 1938. And afterward, when he had a few spare hours, usually early in the morning or late at night, he continued with the project. It was a labor of love that ended six days before Christmas, 1938. "Received the first copies of the biography of my father from the News Press," he wrote on December 19. "The Deseret News gave me a very fine announcement Saturday."

The months during which Elder Smith was preoccupied writing this biography typified the oscillating nature of his life as it alternated between events of joy and sorrow. The joy came chiefly from the elements of order and excitement that were introduced into the Smith household with Joseph's marriage to Jessie. While Jessie had many commitments outside the home, she arranged them so that she could devote sufficient time to the care and training of the three boys who were still living there. And on the occasions when she was unable to be present for special events or needs, her mother was available to fill in. Also, Jessie's effervescent personality and musical ability added a certain tone of carefree gaiety to the family. She soon became involved in attending sporting and other events with Joseph and his sons, and in helping the boys with their personal affairs. "Jessie and I went shopping with Reynolds," Joseph noted on September 16, "in order to fit the boys out for school." Then expressing a point of view with which most parents can relate, the father added, "Rather expensive." Earlier the parents had accompanied Reyn to a softball tournament.

Jessie was an enthusiastic traveler and added a genuine zest to family trips. So during July, Joseph and Jessie and the three boys enjoyed an outing at Yellowstone Park, where they visited Old Faithful and other attractions. And on the way home, they camped overnight at Bear Lake, taking a swim in its frigid waters. The weekend following their return from Yellowstone, the extended Smith family joined to honor Joseph's brother David and his wife, who had been called to preside over a mission in Canada. Earlier in the year, at the April general conference, David A. had been released as a member of the Presiding Bishopric, where he had served for thirty-one years. The extended Smith family joined together for another happy occasion later in the year to celebrate the marriage of Hyrum Mack Smith. Joseph Fielding, who performed the ceremony in the Salt Lake Temple on December 21, noted in his diary on that day: "Hyrum will leave for the British mission in January. He was born after his father's death, and his mother passed when he was about 2 weeks old."

Aside from these major social events involving the extended Smith family and the smaller ones involving only Joseph and Jessie and the boys, we find during this initial period following the marriage that Elder Smith was becoming more involved in entertainment events, doubtless reflecting Jessie's influence. Some he seemed to enjoy, as when on October 6 he accompanied Jessie and Lois to the oratorio *Elijah*. "It was an excellent performance," Joseph wrote approvingly. No doubt his enjoyment was enhanced by the fact that Jessie took a leading part. Later, Joseph went with Jessie, Lois, and Amelia "to hear the great Italian tenor Gigli in the Tabernacle." On this occasion, he offered no comments about the performance. However, he was quite outspoken about some of the movies Jessie inveigled him into attending. "Did not enjoy it," he wrote of the movie *Marie Antionette* which he and Jessie saw in early September. And of the movie *Kentucky*, which they saw during the Christmas holidays, he noted analytically, "It was good and clean, but I think I could have improved on it."

The day after the Smiths saw this movie, President Heber J. Grant and his wife, Augusta, called at their home to visit. While there, the Prophet prevailed on Joseph and Jessie to sing a duet. In reporting the incident, Elder Smith was self-deprecating, as usual, about his singing ability, but he was obviously pleased about the response of their guests. And when, the next day, he received a congratulatory letter from President Grant, Joseph Fielding was so touched that he copied it in his diary, something he had never done before. Because he obviously attached special significance to the letter, it deserves to be quoted verbatim here: "My Dear Joseph," it began. "I was delighted last night to listen to you and your good wife sing. I am thankful to think that you are going to take a little bit of time to sing and to visit with your loved ones, instead of working, working, working. I am sure that the singing will prolong your life. I don't want to flatter you, Joseph, but I want you to know that I consider you the best posted man on the scriptures of the General Authorities of the church that we have. I want you to prolong your life. I want you to make a business of trying to take care of yourself. Now I am not overworking so long as I can get my quota of good sleep. I am not the least bit alarmed if I go on singing and travelling around, releasing myself from the steady grind of work. I want you to do the same to the best of your ability. Your father worked altogether too hard. If he had taken a little more exercise, moving around, travelling away from home, and getting away from the cares and troubles of other people, it would have been better for him. He took a greater interest in the welfare of other people than almost any man who ever lived. He was my ideal of all the brethren from my childhood up to the day of his death. I am very grateful indeed for the fine letters I have from him, my dear cousin. May the blessings of the Lord be and abide with you perpetually, and may you be enabled to work less and accomplish more, is the prayer of my heart. I am, your affectionate relative, Heber J. Grant." After quoting the letter verbatim, Elder Smith added, "I certainly appreciate the letter very much."

Near this time, Elder Smith was warned by his doctor friend that his life would be endangered were he to continue to play handball. Given Joseph's faithful nature and the Prophet's direct admonition to prolong his life and to "make a business" of trying to take care of himself, it is reasonable to assume that President Heber J. Grant's letter was an important factor in Elder Smith's seemingly precipitate decision to give up the game he had enjoyed so much for so long. Nor is it far-fetched to infer that an assignment President Grant gave him a few months after writing the letter was in part an effort to encourage Joseph to pace himself more and to moderate his tendency toward overwork.

Chapter Eighteen

The Hectic Honeymoon

The assignment came as a distinct surprise. Shortly after the 1939 April conference, President Heber J. Grant advised Elder Smith that he would be going to Europe, where he was to tour the missions. He was also told that Jessie was to accompany him. The apostle was given wide latitude in arranging his itinerary, which would take him and Jessie to England and throughout Europe. Since it was intended that the assignment would occupy several months, there would be ample time between meetings with missionaries and members to visit places of historic interest or of special beauty and charm. It was this last aspect of the assignment that gave it the romance of a second honeymoon. It was undoubtedly intended as such by President Grant, who seems to have taken this means to provide Joseph with an enjoyable break in his strenuous routine while giving him enough official duties to salve a conscience seemingly obsessed with the need to be constantly at work.

Elder Smith was especially surprised to receive the assignment to tour the missions in Britain and Europe because it had been only a year since his marriage to Jessie and since, on assignment, he had toured the missions in Hawaii with her. To receive this assignment only a year later, affording the opportunity for a second honeymoon while performing his apostolic duties was wholly unexpected, although greatly appreciated.

Aside from the prospect of visiting ancient Britain and Europe with his new bride and mingling with the missionaries and members there, two other circumstances endowed this assignment with special significance. The first was the nostalgic prospect of returning to the mission field of his youth, which he had not visited since his release forty years before. So much had transpired in those four decades: The death of Louie; his marriage to Ethel and her subsequent death; the birth of his eleven children; his call to the Twelve followed by almost three decades of apostolic service; his establishment as a noted historian and as the premier scripture scholar in the Church; his marriage to Jessie; and all the challenging, joyous, or traumatic happenings connected with these significant events. All these seem to have aroused in Elder Smith feelings of reflective enjoyment as he and Jessie prepared for their departure. The other thing that made the coming tour special for Elder Smith was the fact that his son Lewis was then serving as a missionary in the Swiss-German mission. The prospect of seeing this much-loved son in the mission field and, perhaps, of sharing a pulpit with him was pleasing.

Joseph advised Lewis of his assignment in a somewhat jocular letter written on April 11, 1939. "If Mr. Hitler and Mr. Mus— whatever his name is, and he is a muss—will just keep cool for a few more weeks and not cause another war, I will be with you in June." A week later, the father wrote a second letter to his son advising that he and "Aunt Jessie" would leave Salt Lake City on April 21. "We will go from here to New York . . . [and] will sail on the 29th." Commenting on the planned visit to England, he added, "It is now 40 years, or will be on the 12th of May, since I left home for my mission to England. There have been many changes, no doubt, in that land since that time, and also in all of Europe."

Not the least of the changes during this interval was that in the status of Joseph Fielding Smith. Forty years before, almost the only distinctive thing about him was his distinguished name. Until that time he had done nothing to set him apart from the missionaries who accompanied him into the field or from those who awaited him there. And during his stay in England, he accomplished nothing of significance that hinted of future distinction.

While the influence of his powerful father had weighed heavily in his employment at the Historical Department and in his call to the Twelve, it was his own industry and superior qualities of mind and character that had enabled him to carve out a place of eminence among the leaders of the Church. The mark of distinction Joseph Fielding had richly earned during these forty years was particularly evident throughout the seven months he and Jessie were abroad. Everywhere they went, Elder Smith was treated with honor and respect. This began with their departure from the Salt Lake depot on Friday, April 21, 1939. Present to bid them good-bye were many members of the family, friends, neighbors, and associates from Church headquarters. Similar crowds would welcome them or bid them farewell at cities all along the route of their tour.

On the way to New York City, from where they were to embark for England, the travelers made a side trip to Palmyra. Here, at the cradle of the Church, Joseph was privileged to again visit places of historic importance to the Latter-day Saints and to explain their significance to Jessie. Of particular interest were the old Smith home where Joseph's grandfather Hyrum had lived as a boy; the sacred grove where his great-uncle, the Prophet Joseph Smith, had received the vision of the Father and the Son; and the Hill Cumorah, where the Prophet had obtained the golden plates from which the Book of Mormon had been translated. This visit could not have failed to arouse deep reflections about the miraculous origins of the Church and to underscore the significance of the tour that lay ahead.

The voyage from New York to England was quite unlike the previous year's journey to Hawaii. The turbulence of the Atlantic robbed this trip of the relaxed enjoyment that had marked the days en route to Honolulu. And, unlike that trip, there was now an undercurrent of tension and foreboding. This foreboding had been hinted at in Elder Smith's letter to Lewis in which he had made lighthearted remarks about Hitler and Mussolini. The fact is that as their ship carried the Smiths toward England, there was widespread speculation about the possibility of another war erupting in Europe. A month before, Hitler's troops had entered Prague, thereby annexing Czechoslovakia to the Third Reich and dashing the false hopes raised by the Munich Conference the previous September. A month before the Smiths' ship eased out of the harbor for England, Neville Chamberlain, Britain's prime minister, had announced that if Poland's independence were threatened, His Majesty's Government would be obligated to lend Poland all support in its power. And a week after that, Mussolini invaded Albania. It was under the pressure and uncertainty of these events, stirred by the wild speculations they produced, that Elder Smith and Jessie arrived in England to begin their tour.

Here they were met by Hugh B. Brown, the president of the British Mission who, with his missionaries, helped them gather their baggage and then took them to the mission home at 9 Gordon Mansion in London. This would be the Smiths' headquarters during their stay in Great Britain.

Elder Smith was well acquainted with Hugh B. Brown, who had been the president of the Lethbridge Canada stake in the 1920s and who was later the president of the Granite Stake in Salt Lake City. Moreover, the future held in store an even closer relationship between this pair. In 1953 President Brown would be called as an assistant to the Twelve; and in 1958 his call to the Twelve would place him in the quorum over which Joseph Fielding Smith then presided. Still later, they would jointly serve as counselors to President David O. McKay.

Before beginning their tour of the British Mission, which would take them into many cities in England and Scotland, Joseph and Jessie were shown around historic London by President Brown and his charming wife, Zina Card Brown. For Joseph, the occasion aroused nostalgic memories of his visits to London four decades before. The same nostalgic remembrances occurred when the touring party visited Nottingham and Derby. While many things had changed, the parks and old buildings still remained, arousing memories of his struggling efforts to succeed as a missionary and his periodic bouts with homesickness.

A highlight of the tour was a mission-wide MIA convention held at Sheffield. In attendance were members and investigators from England, Scotland, Wales, and Ireland. The convention featured sports, dances, and talent shows, in addition to a Sunday evening worship service where Elder Smith and President Brown shared the speaking time. Also, an instruction and testimony meeting for the missionaries was held in conjunction with this convention.

After completing the tour of the British Mission, Elder Smith and Jessie crossed the channel, holding meetings in Holland, Belgium, and France.

By early June, they were at Lucerne, Switzerland, where Elder Smith presided at a conference of all the mission presidents serving in Europe and Great Britain. In addition to President Hugh B. Brown of the British Mission, there were in attendance Thomas E. McKay of the Swiss and East German Mission, Mark B. Garff of the Danish Mission, Franklin J. Murdock of the Netherlands Mission, Joseph E. Evans of the French Mission, M. Douglas Wood of the Swedish and West German Mission, John A. Israelson of the Norwegian Mission, and Wallace F. Toronto of the Czechoslovakia Mission. Here each president gave a stewardship report of the past work in his mission and a projection about his goals and activities during the coming months.

A somber theme interwoven with all these reports was the spectre of another general war in Europe that would embroil all of the countries in which these mission presidents were laboring. An ominous development had occurred on May 20 when V. M. Molotov, the new foreign commissar in the Soviet Union, announced, following a meeting with the German ambassador, that mutually profitable economic agreements might be reached between the two countries, provided that a suitable "political basis" could be established. Because of the uncertainties this and other crucial events had created, one of the chief items on the agenda of the conference was contingency planning for a possible war.

Leaving Switzerland, Elder Smith and Jessie traveled into Italy. Here they would spend several weeks. There were no organized branches in Italy at the time, nor was missionary work being done there. Freed from holding church meetings, the Smiths became typical tourists, enjoying the rich store of cultural treasures in this ancient land.

They arrived in Milano on June 22, spending several days browsing in the city's museums and galleries, visiting its quaint shops, admiring its classical architecture, and sampling its tasty cuisine. After visiting the ancient cathedral where Leonardo da Vinci's original painting of the Last Supper is found, Joseph pronounced it "wonderful." Later they visited a gallery that displayed an extensive collection of da Vinci's works, both artistic and inventive. After visiting Milano's famed cathedral, Elder Smith wrote that it "looks like lace from the outside."

At Vatican City a few days later, Joseph was particularly impressed by the Church of the Capuchin Friars. "Seven rooms are decorated with the bones of dead Friars," he wrote with astonishment. "You see thousands of them." The next day in Rome, the tourists visited the usual points of interest, including the Coliseum and the tomb of Caesar

Augustus. Also, they visited and were impressed by the Mussolini Forum, an academy devoted to the training of Italy's future leaders. Here youths ages fifteen to twenty-one were schooled in history, science, and other academic disciplines with emphasis on the martial arts. "The grounds and buildings are magnificent," Joseph wrote approvingly, remaining silent about the man after whom the academy was named.

Traveling on to Naples, the honeymooners took a launch to the Island of Capri, famed for its mild climate, beautiful scenery, and its Blue Grotto, a large cavern whose walls bristle with stalactites that reflect a brilliant blue light when touched by the sun's rays. Here amid groves of citrus and olive trees and grape orchards were found the remnants of magnificent villas built by the Roman emperors, Augustus and Tiberius. Joseph and Jessie's night on Capri must have seemed almost magical as the couple watched the moon rise over Monte Salaro, the tallest mountain on the island, which rises to a height of almost two thousand feet. The moon's reflected light glimmering on the sea and the sweet aroma of orange blossoms created a romantic mood the Smiths likely never forgot.

That mood was shattered a few days later in Florence. The Smiths had spent July 3 browsing in the city's quaint shops; visiting its magnificent cathedrals, chiefly the Santa Maria del Fiore with its exterior facing of red, white, and green marble; and admiring the prolific collection of Renaissance art in its museums and galleries. Here were classic specimens of the works of Michelangelo, Leonardo da Vinci, Giotto, and other noted Renaissance artists. As the Smiths relaxed on the veranda of their hotel room that evening, with the wide and meandering Arno River in clear view, they seem to have been imbued with an unusual sense of peace and contentment. But that changed early the next morning, America's Independence Day, when the Smiths were awakened by the rhythmic sound of jack boots pounding the cobbled streets below as some of Mussolini's brown shirts strutted by. It gave the visitors a "terrible feeling" as they were brought back to the harsh realization that the peace and contentment they had experienced in pleasant Italy could be changed overnight with the onset of war.

Joseph and Jessie completed their Italian tour with a visit to fabled Venice, called by some the Queen of the Adriatic. Here the visitors from Utah, accustomed to the arid deserts of the western United States, were astonished to find a magnificent city built on pilings buried beneath a lagoon of the Adriatic Sea.

From Venice, the Smiths traveled northward through Austria to Czechoslovakia, where they were joined by mission president Wallace F. Toronto and his wife. A pall of uncertainty and discontent hung over this beleaguered country, which, at the time of the apostle's visit, had been under Hitler's domination for four months. Holding meetings with members and missionaries in various cities, the visitors attempted to lift the spirits of the Saints and to prepare them for the uncertainties that lay ahead. Talk of another war was everywhere, so that the contingency planning considered in Lucerne had special relevance for the local leaders. It was understood that if war broke out, the foreign missionaries would be withdrawn, leaving the governance of local Church units in the hands of local leaders. This, of course, was a fearful prospect for the Czech Saints, which made Elder Smith's visit even more meaningful.

Joseph and Jessie ended their visit to Czechoslovakia on July 24 with a series of meetings in Prague. The presence of Hitler's storm troopers on the streets bore ominous witness of the country's subjugation to dictatorial rule, which doubtless overrode any feelings of elation the visitors may have had in remembering that it was also Utah's pioneer day.

Leaving Prague, the Smiths traveled to Berlin, the heart of Nazi power. Because they were Americans, whom Hitler considered to be future enemies, their movements were kept under close surveillance by the Gestapo, although they were free to travel about the city at will. Indeed, the travelers received wider publicity here than in any other city during their European tour because Jessie was invited, for a fee, to sing over Germany's largest radio station. This, of course, publicized Elder Smith, who was identified as the singer's husband. Notwithstanding this, Joseph and Jessie had uneasy feelings during their stay in Berlin.

However, the tensions there could not compare with what the travelers found in Danzig on July 27. Danzig was then the subject of intense international speculation and concern. The media focus on it arose from demands Hitler had made that it be given to Germany, together with a strip of land across the Polish corridor. The series of previous "demands" made on European neighbors by the Nazi leader, followed by German occupation, had instilled a sense of foreboding in the citizens of Danzig that their city was next. And that foreboding was intensified because Britain and France had drawn a line on Poland, which threatened that this ancient Baltic city might become an actual battleground.

Despite this, Danzig had not allowed the uncertainties it faced to interfere with the normal flow of its civic and cultural life. So, government officials hosted Elder Smith and Jessie at a special luncheon upon their arrival. And that night, the visitors were honored at an open-air presentation of Richard Wagner's opera *Siegfried*. As much as she might have wanted to do so, Jessie restrained herself from joining in the chorus.

Returning to Berlin, the travelers attended services in the LDS chapel on Sunday, July 30. As Elder Smith entered the building, the members spontaneously began to sing "We Thank Thee, O God, for a Prophet." Later in the day, this surprising and, to Joseph, somewhat embarrassing incident was repeated at services held at nearby Chemnitz. While Elder Smith had been regularly sustained as a prophet at general conferences during the previous twenty-nine years, he knew well that he was not *the* prophet. Ordinarily this song refers to the president, who is empowered to guide the Church "in these latter days."

To have it sung under these circumstances seems to have been a source of embarrassment to this sensitive, reticent man. But, there was nothing Elder Smith could have done gracefully to correct the misconception, so he let it pass without comment. At each of these Sunday meetings, the usual procedure was followed, with Elder Smith giving the concluding address and with Jessie speaking briefly and singing.

The mood in Berlin was tense, as it was in other German cities, as the visitors toured in West Germany with President M. Douglas Wood and in East Germany with President Thomas E. McKay. Nazi troops were everywhere. The nation was clearly gearing up for war. And the delicacy of Elder Smith's position imposed limitations on what he could say in public. So his sermons focused only on the principles of the gospel and were devoid of any reference to political or military matters. He shared with Lewis the restraints under which he had to act while in Germany. "From here," he wrote from Copenhagen on August 16, "we will go to other parts of Denmark, and then we have to go back into the West German Mission to finish our labors. As far as Germany is concerned, we would just as soon go to Holland and France. If we had the same freedom in Germany, it would be better. However, we got along well when we were there, but we had to be more guarded in our remarks and were watched by secret agents. These things do not add to your peace of mind."

Prior to writing this letter, Elder Smith and Jessie had spent two weeks touring the missions in Denmark, Norway, and Sweden. In these countries, the visitors did not detect the tension they had felt in Czechoslovakia, Poland, and Germany. "It is very quiet and peaceful here," Elder Smith wrote to Lewis from Denmark on August 18. Everywhere he and Jessie went in that country and in Scandinavia, the same placid conditions prevailed. This was surprising in a way, given the proximity of these countries to Germany and considering the belligerent attitudes Hitler had shown toward other European neighbors. So, it was an enjoyable and peaceful interlude as the Smiths traveled alternately with Mission Presidents Mark B. Garff, M. Douglas Wood, and John A. Israelson and their wives, meeting with missionaries and the Saints in various parts of Scandinavia. The royal treatment the travelers received is hinted at in the already mentioned letter of August 16 that Elder Smith wrote to Lewis: "In Germany we got much synthetic food, but in Sweden we had a good supply of the very best. Good butter and cream were furnished us in Sweden in abundance and also good bread. Then again they give you a square meal before they serve you the meal you order. You have the privilege of going to the table and helping yourselves as often as you like, and it is all good too. In Norway they give you good things to eat, but they are not so elaborate with it."

Within a week after writing this letter, Elder and Sister Smith were back in Germany. Writing to Lewis from Hanover on August 24, he noted: "We are hoping now that nothing will arise to interfere with the program as it has been arranged for us." This was written without knowledge of the feverish negotiations that had gone on behind the scenes between Germany and Russia as a prelude to Hitler's invasion of Poland. The foreign ministers had been in regular contact during the period to clarify certain "territorial questions in Eastern Europe." By August 20, the terms had been agreed upon, and, three days later, the day before Elder Smith wrote his letter to Lewis, Molotov and Ribbentrop signed a nonaggression pact in Moscow.

From that point on, the descent into the maelstrom of war was swift and sure. The Brethren in Salt Lake City had been carefully monitoring the course of negotiations between Germany and the Soviet Union. And when it became clear that the nonaggression pact would be signed, they acted promptly. Later in the day on August 24, after he had written the letter to Lewis, Elder Smith received a cablegram from the First Presidency instructing that all missionaries in Germany be transferred to neutral countries. At the same time, similar cablegrams were sent directly from Salt Lake City to M. Douglas Wood and Thomas E. McKay, presidents of the West German and East German missions. These instructions required the cancellation of all meetings Elder Smith had scheduled to be held in Germany. However, he decided to go forward with the one scheduled in Hanover the night of August 24. "It was quite exciting," Jessie wrote of that meeting. "We . . . had a very splendid service, but everyone was still wondering about conditions." The next morning, Elder Smith received word from President Thomas E. McKay that pursuant to the direction from Salt Lake City, all of the missionaries in the East German mission were being sent to Denmark. Later in the day, the Smiths traveled by train to Frankfurt, the headquarters of the West German mission. President and Sister Wood had preceded them there, having gone by plane. According to Jessie, "things were surely popping" when they arrived at the mission office in Frankfurt with "phone calls, telegrams and cablegrams, and everyone busy packing."

One of the cablegrams was from the First Presidency, directing Elder Smith to go to Holland or Denmark, where he was to coordinate the work of shepherding and reassigning the missionaries being withdrawn from Germany. This instruction required a change in his plans as Joseph had previously made arrangements to go to Basel, Switzerland. Despite the urgent demands for transportation out of Germany, the Smiths were able at the last minute to book passage on a train that left Frankfurt for Holland shortly after midnight on Saturday, August 26, 1939. Four hours later, their train arrived at Cologne, where they were scheduled to make only a brief stop. Instead, they were kept waiting an hour and a half. "That wasn't a very pleasant feeling," wrote Jessie of this unscheduled delay. "We could see many people running and making a lot of noise." Between Cologne and the Dutch border, the Smiths saw other things that made them uneasy. "We could see through the train windows soldiers out in the fields putting up guns," reported Jessie, "and soldiers lined up along the way. It was a terrible feeling." At the border, the German authorities first questioned the right of the Smiths to enter Holland. However, when Elder Smith produced tickets he had previously obtained for a liner from Holland to the United States, he and Jessie were allowed to pass. "We were the last to cross the border," wrote Jessie, "because one hour after, we received a phone call that they wouldn't let any of the elders [who had been serving in West Germany] across, so we were surely in a fix." A chief problem faced by the elders in satisfying the immigration officials at the border was the lack of sufficient money. This deficiency was cured, however, when Elder Smith directed both President Wood of the West German Mission and President Murdock of the Netherlands Mission to send representatives to the border with money. It was later decided to send these West German missionaries to Denmark, where the East German missionaries had already been sent. On this account, Elder Smith decided that he too should go on to Denmark, where he could better coordinate the work of reassigning the missionaries who had been working in Germany. So, he and Jessie flew from Holland to Copenhagen. Here they were met by mission president Mark B. Garff, who took them to the mission home, where they would remain for two months. President Garff also turned over the mission office to Elder Smith for use in his work.

By Monday morning, August 28, Elder Smith was at his desk in the mission office in Copenhagen. Following the departure of the missionaries from Frankfurt, Salt Lake had ordered the evacuation of the missionaries from Czechoslovakia, instructing them also to go to Denmark. In a letter to Lewis, the apostle described the scene at his headquarters in Copenhagen, where frantic efforts were being made to accommodate the missionaries who were arriving there from the south: "Since arriving here, we have been kept extremely busy," he wrote, "trying to reach the different missions and with communications from and to the First Presidency. From the reports we received, conditions

are getting more grave and communications more difficult. . . . We are both well but kept constantly near the
telephone and typewriter. We still have one worry, in addition to the many others, as President Toronto and his
missionaries have not arrived [from Czechoslovakia]. We
hope they will be here tonight."

Meanwhile, the political situation was deteriorating
rapidly. The day before the Smiths departed from Frankfurt, France had warned Hitler it would stand by Poland;
and on the same day, Neville Chamberlain announced the
signing of an Anglo-Polish Alliance. These actions served
as a temporary brake on the dictator's plans to invade
Poland. He pleaded for "understanding" in his attempts
to negotiate a settlement of German claims in Danzig and
the connecting corridor. Grasping at straws to prevent
war, the British and French pressured Poland to negotiate.
Yielding, Warsaw sent envoys to Berlin for discussions.
There Hitler refused to negotiate unless Poland's ambassador had full power to cut a deal. When Warsaw insisted
that the final approval of any plan must be made there,
Hitler claimed the Poles were stalling and didn't want to
negotiate.

And when on August 30 Warsaw ordered a general
mobilization, Germany's media trumpeted that Poland was
planning to attack. To lend credence to this false charge,
the next day the Feuhrer rigged an attack on a German
radio station near the border, claiming it was made by
Poles, who were actually Germans dressed in Polish uni-
forms. It was on this pretext that Hitler sent his Panzer
divisions into Poland at dawn, September 1. In an impas-
sioned radio speech in which he attempted to justify the
invasion, the dictator cynically claimed that he had had to
meet force with force. Later he rejected allied demands to
withdraw. Left with no alternative, Great Britain and
France formally notified Hitler on September 3 that a state
of war existed.

These shocking events radically altered Elder Smith's
task. It was no longer a matter of shifting missionaries to

different parts of Europe. Now the aim was to evacuate them entirely. This presented the apostle and the mission presidents with an enormous logistical problem that was aggravated by bureaucratic red tape and the paralyzing fear and anxiety the war had produced. Added to these complexities were the hurried and harried steps that had to be taken to transfer the direction of the European districts and branches to local leaders and to respond to the many anxious inquiries received from home as to the whereabouts and condition of the missionaries.

There were 697 who had to be evacuated, including 611 elders, 63 young women missionaries, and 23 others comprising mission presidents and their families. They returned to the United States on twenty-three different ships, most of them freighters. Writing to Lewis on September 8 from Copenhagen, Elder Smith said that a hundred missionaries had left that day on two freighters, sixty on the *Scanyork* and forty on the *Mormachawk*. "They were furnished cots in the hold instead of freight in the space they occupy," he explained. "They were all happy and seemed to be very comfortable." While the remaining missionaries were waiting for passage home, they were kept as busy as possible under the circumstances. "Each morning we have had the missionaries together in meeting, and I have given them one hour to one hour and a half in which they have asked questions. . . . I hope, at least, that we are able to clear up some of the funny notions some of them had."

Elder Smith and Jessie had originally booked passage home on the *Manhattan*, which sailed from Southampton on September 8. However, when Joseph saw that his duties could not be completed by then, he turned their tickets over to a missionary couple who had been serving in West Germany. Within a month, however, nothing remained for him to do, and he was ready to go home. "I am willing to remain here indefinitely," he wrote to Lewis on October 7, "but cannot see anything more that I can do. I am no help to you in Switzerland, and cannot assist you or the missionaries in France or Holland to get away." Since there were no open berths on ships leaving Denmark, the Smiths traveled to Holland, where, after a two-week delay, they were able to book passage on the freighter *Zaandam*. The apostle did not enjoy the delay. "We have found the past two weeks very trying," he wrote to Lewis on October 18, "because there has not been anything to be done. I have held my hands or spent [my time] walking the streets or reading while Aunt Jessie has knitted."

The return voyage on the *Zaandam* introduced the Smiths to spartan life aboard a freighter. It was hardly the kind of luxurious fare they had enjoyed on their previous voyages together. Yet, there was a special congeniality among the passengers, an unusual sense of camaraderie, coming from a shared perception that they had just escaped from a great scourge that had descended upon Europe. That sense of escape was moderated by the knowledge that German U-boats prowled the Atlantic so that they could not feel absolutely safe until they reached the shores of America. Once there, Joseph and Jessie traveled across the United States by train, arriving home on November 12, 1939, almost seven months after they had left on their so-called second honeymoon.

It would take some time for them to sort out the meaning of the things they had seen and heard. For Elder Smith, two perceptions stood out above all others. The first was his conviction that the war stemmed from a general rejection of Christ's message delivered by the Latter-day Saint missionaries. "They have not appreciated the message which we sent to them," he wrote in a letter to Lewis. "They did not want us and are glad to see us go. . . . We have been crying repentance among the nations for all these years as the Lord commanded us to do, but steadily and persistently the nations have been growing more corrupt and more ungodly year by year." The second was his sorrow for the faithful, god-fearing people among these nations who would innocently suffer from the war. "My heart was sick," wrote Elder Smith, "every time we held a meeting and shook hands with the people at its close. They all greeted us warmly, and their [friendship] meant more to me than they perhaps realized. Some of them shed tears and said they were looking for grave trouble, and we would never meet again in this life. I feel sorry for them now, and pray each day that the Lord will protect them through this dreadful time."

Chapter Nineteen

The War Reaches Home

The Smiths' Christmas in 1939 was, at the same time, joyous and sad. Jessie, with her artistic and dramatic flair, her irrepressible good humor, and her music brought gaiety and excitement into the Douglas Street home. Two of the children still lived there, fifteen-year-old Douglas and twelve-year-old Milton, while Reynolds, a freshman at Brigham Young University, came up from Provo for the holidays. Yet, beneath the surface of joy as the family gathered to sing and to laugh, to exchange gifts and to reflect on the deeper meaning of their celebration, ran a deep current of foreboding. The war in Europe had escalated dramatically. Following the German invasion of Poland, the Soviets had attacked from the east, and in short order all of Poland had been subjugated and carved up between the two aggressors. Meanwhile, Soviet troops had invaded Finland, where bitter fighting was then taking place. And there was much talk about a German invasion of the Scandinavian countries. All the while, of course, Great Britain and France were feverishly gearing up for the major armed conflict everyone knew was com-

Joseph Fielding Smith at the typewriter

ing. Aside from their general concern for the Europeans they had so recently visited, the Smiths had a personal apprehension about the war in Europe because Lewis was still there. He was serving as an assistant to Thomas E. McKay, president of the Swiss and East German Mission. It would be two more months before he would return. So, the holiday celebrations of the Smiths were necessarily alloyed with gnawing concern about the future.

Meanwhile, life in Salt Lake City went on unabated. Following Joseph's return from Europe, he had resumed his normal routine of stake conferences, mission tours, and work in the Historian's Office. He was also busy making editorial changes for another printing of *The Way to Perfection,* a little volume that had been well received by the public. His other writings at the time consisted mostly of answering the questions that were put to him in ever-increasing numbers. By now, his reputation as the leading scripture scholar of the Church had been well established so that most doctrinal questions gravitated to him for handling. He usually banged out the answers on his old typewriter, using the hunt-and-peck method. Over the years, he had become adept in using the typewriter, zipping along at a speed almost equal to that of the secretaries in the office.

During this period, Joseph's writings and sermons took on a more somber tone as he reflected on the causes and implications of the war. "I have been crying repentance among the stakes of Zion for thirty years," he told a Tabernacle audience, "calling upon the people to turn to the Lord, keep His commandments, observe the Sabbath Day, pay their honest tithing, do everything the Lord has commanded them to do, to live by every word that proceedeth forth from the mouth of God." (*Conference Report,* October 1940, p. 117.) Elder Smith saw the European war as the direct result of disobedience to the laws of the gospel. He also believed that the same fate awaited America unless its people repented. Said he, "I am going to repeat what I have said before, for which I have been severely criticized from certain quarters, that even in this country, we have no grounds by which we may escape, no sure foundation upon which we can stand, and by which we may escape from the calamities and destruction and the plagues and pestilences, and even the devouring fire by sword and by war, unless we repent and keep the commandments of the Lord, for it is written here in these revelations." (Ibid.)

Some of the criticism directed at Elder Smith for his outspoken calls to repentance came from within the hierarchy of the Church. One of the Brethren went to him on January 19, 1940, to read a letter containing "severe criticism" of Elder Smith because he persisted in telling the people to repent and that if they failed to do so, the "judgments of the Lord [would] overtake them." This brother endorsed the criticism and urged Elder Smith to speak only that which was "good and commendatory." Joseph's answer was predictable, "I informed him I would [continue] to cry repentance in all the stakes of Zion for

312

our people need to repent." A few days later, Joseph Fielding wrote a long letter to this brother, which he hoped
would "do him some good." It was troubling that he not
only refused to preach repentance but also criticized Joseph
for doing so. Elder Joseph Fielding saw it as his duty to
raise a warning voice when the people began to drift away
from the path marked by the scriptures. And he had no
intention to abandon that duty, regardless of what anyone
said. That speaking out made him unpopular in some circles seems not to have had any deterring effect upon him;
his purpose was not to become popular or famous in the
eyes of the people. Instead, he saw his role as that of a
watchman on the tower whose duty it was to sound the
warning call to those below who could not see the approaching danger.

The stream of bad news that flowed from Europe was
a constant reminder of the calamity that had befallen the
nations there. Joseph continued to receive reports from
Europe and from those who had been evacuated. But these
reports were sporadic and incomplete and furnished only
a vague picture of the conditions of the Church and its
members. In order to obtain a clearer and more focused
understanding, the First Presidency and Quorum of the
Twelve assigned the mission presidents who were in the
field when war broke out to maintain regular contact with
the local leaders in these countries. At the same time, Elder
Smith was assigned to direct and coordinate these efforts.
"These brethren," he wrote on February 6, 1940, "will
counsel and advise the local presiding officers; receive reports from them, and then consult with me."

In this capacity, Elder Smith made a trip East later in
February. His ultimate purpose was to meet the last of the
missionaries to be evacuated from Europe. Meanwhile, he
would preside at two stake conferences along the way. He
left the Salt Lake City Union Pacific depot Thursday evening, February 22, Washington's birthday. Jessie, who
would stay home this time, drove him there. The next day,
as his train streaked across Wyoming and Nebraska, Joseph

was caught up in a reverie. "Spent the day on the train, reflecting on the journeyings of the pioneers over these plains, and how my father, when a boy, drove his ox team all the way from the Missouri to the Salt Lake Valley. And now we cross in comfort in two days on the train and can in a few hours by airplane. It is wonderful."

The first stake conference was held in cold and windy Chicago, where Elder Smith arrived on the 24th to find the heaviest snowfall the city had had all winter. There to greet him were Julina and Eldon, who then lived in nearby Urbana, and Chicago stake president William A. Matheson. Over the weekend, the apostle presided at the usual meetings of a stake conference, in between which he "had a good visit with Julina and Eldon," who, with Elder Smith, were guests in the Matheson home.

The following weekend found Joseph in New York City, where the second stake conference was held. Here he found a situation he had not encountered before during thirty years of service in the Twelve—local leaders who were more or less indifferent toward him and his instructions. The reasons for this attitude are unclear. Perhaps their advanced education, their wealth, and a condescending attitude toward Elder Smith's call to repentance lay at the root. He was troubled by their attitude and commented on it at some length. "I left the stake," he wrote on March 3, 1940, "feeling some restriction existing or barrier, between me and the stake officers, who are PhD's and scientific mechanical professors, who lack some of the human qualities found in those of less scholastic and scientific training. At the close of the meeting, not one of the presidency of the stake as much as noticed that I was present and although I spent some time talking with members of the congregation, I was not approached and wished a pleasant farewell and journey, but without any farewell greeting was permitted to leave the building in company with my niece, Donnette McAllister."

The cold reception Elder Smith received at the stake conference was matched by a heavy winter storm that struck the New York area the next day. It was reported to be one of the worst and most destructive storms to hit New York in many years. "The falling rain froze on whatever it touched," Joseph wrote. "The ice then formed made the trees look like the limbs and branches were made of rock candy." The ship carrying the last of the returning European missionaries, the S.S. *Washington,* was delayed in arriving because of the ferocity of the storm. So Elder Smith and members of the staff of the mission headquarters at 155 Riverside Drive had to make two trips to the pier of the United States Lines over the treacherously slick Manhattan streets.

They arrived at the pier for the second time about 9:30 A.M., just in time to see the big ship ease into the dock. Among the passengers were President Thomas E. McKay, his wife and daughter, and four elders, including Elder Smith's son Lewis. The father's joy at seeing this son again was heightened by relief that Lewis was at last out of the war zone and safely home on American soil. "We were all happy . . . and glad to have the group home," wrote Elder Smith, "the last of the missionaries out of Europe. The foreign nations requested the missionaries to leave; and our own country requested all Americans to leave Europe; and now we are all home." The relief this entry implies would be shattered in less than two years when the United States would be drawn into the conflict. And not long after that, the tragedy of war would directly strike the Smith family when this beloved son, Lewis, would be killed in military service.

Later in the afternoon, Elder Smith and mission president Frank Evans made still another trip to the docks. This time, they met a ship arriving from Brazil with a missionary, Elder Quasley, who had been sent home because of illness. "The father and mother were also there to meet him," wrote Joseph, "so we felt relieved."

While Elder Smith was busy winding up his affairs in New York City, Lewis spent the time profitably, doing missionary work with the elders who labored in the mission office. Two days later, father and son traveled by train to Washington, D.C. Establishing their headquarters in the Hamilton Hotel, the Smiths spent two days in the capital, visiting places of historic interest. Their guides were Sterling Wheelwright and his wife and Elder Smith's nephews Edward and Elmer Smith, sons of his brother, David A. The talented Sterling Wheelwright gave organ recitals at the Washington, D.C., chapel and the two nephews were furthering their education. These hosts alternated in showing the visitors around. They inspected the Washington and Lincoln memorials, the White House, Arlington National Cemetery, and the capitol building, among other places. At the Capitol, they sat for a while in the gallery of the Senate to watch the proceedings. Elder Smith was not impressed. Vice-president John Nance Garner left the chambers immediately after the roll call, as did Utah senator Elbert Thomas. Utah's other senator, William King, was not present. The visitors remained for an hour, listening to Senator George W. Norris of Nebraska. Elder Smith pulled no punches in his appraisal of the speaker. "He is one senator who has a good opinion of himself," he wrote, "but is over estimated by his state and many people who can be fooled much of the time." From the Senate, the visitors went to the supreme court. Here the diarist was more impressed by the building ("one of the finest in Washington") than by its occupants. He bluntly expressed the appraisal of the court that was then held by most persons of conservative views. "The court now contains a majority of men," Joseph Fielding reported, "who are under some control by the U. S. President and who are reversing decisions previously made. Some of these men were noted for radical views on government."

Reared in a community where initiative, independence, and rugged enterprise were among the most admired qualities, and by parents who, without government subsidy, had helped tame a wilderness, Elder Smith never endorsed the social legislation enacted during the administration of Franklin D. Roosevelt. He thought that subsidies, or what he derisively called "hand-outs," destroyed individual initiative and created a dangerous and deadening dependency on government. While he recognized that the poor among us who are sick, aged, or incompetent required special help, he looked to the family, the Church, and local governments to fill these needs. At the same time, he abhorred those who glutted themselves on the public wealth through large and unconscionable subsidies to businesses. These views reflect the basic conservative political philosophy Joseph Fielding Smith embraced throughout his life. His philosophy coincided with that of his brethren in the Church hierarchy and helped to shape the Church welfare program.

Leaving the nation's capital, Elder Smith and Lewis traveled by train to Chicago, where they arrived the morning of March 8. Transferring to a bus, they went on to Champaign, Illinois, where Julina and her husband lived. "We arrived there about noon," noted Elder Smith, "and spent the day visiting the University of Illinois, and especially the library. It was a happy visit as Julina had not seen Lewis for two and a half years." The travelers returned to Chicago the following day, where they were to catch the train to Salt Lake City. As they left the elevated municipal train at Chicago's northwestern station, Elder Smith was jostled by a woman and two men in a narrow passageway. "When I felt in my pocket," he wrote, "I found that I had been relieved of one purse which contained five dollars." Fortunately, most of the money Elder Smith had with him was in another pocket; and the lost wallet did not contain valuable personal documents.

The travelers boarded their train for home late Saturday night, March 9. The following day was a special one for both father and son. It was Lewis's twenty-second birthday and provided their first opportunity for a long, easy visit since the son arrived in New York six days before. And, as it turned out, it was the last time they would have such an opportunity, for within two years Lewis would be in the army and their crowded schedules during the interval would not allow them the luxury of such a long time alone together. So, as their train sped westward during the entire day, they were able to visit quietly and companionably about many things of mutual interest. Elder Smith had good reason to be proud of this son who had distinguished himself in the mission field, serving at the end of it as the assistant to the mission president. And the son admired and sought to emulate his distinguished father. Aside from the filial relationship between them, they were bound by their shared convictions about the Church and its mission.

At home there was a repetition of what had occurred at Champaign, as Lewis became reacquainted with the other members of his family whom he had not seen for two and a half years. "We had a celebration," wrote the father, "and gave thanks that he was home from troubled Europe."

During the following year, the scope and the intensity of the war in troubled Europe increased explosively. Like a spectator at a horror movie played on a gigantic screen, Elder Smith traced the progress of the war in his diary. In April 1940, the month after he and Lewis returned home, he reported Germany's lightning-quick invasion of Denmark and Norway. On May 9, he reported the German invasion of Holland and Belgium, made, as he put it, "without any warning and on the flimsy and lying excuses similar to those which were made at the sudden and wicked invasion of Denmark and Norway." The next day Joseph had much to say about Germany's fanatical leader and about the biblical implications of the war. "The career of the German Madman," he wrote of Hitler, "will continue as far as the Lord permits and then he will come to his end. The prophets have warned the world of these destructions, but the world, and many, very many, members of the church have not heeded the warning." When in June Italy joined Germany in the war, Elder Smith also had harsh comments to make about its leader. "Yesterday, Benito Mussolini, the dictator of Italy, forced the Italian nation into the war against France and England. This act is that of a sniveling coward who, like the jackal, strikes from behind at a wounded and helpless foe." Then scorning the objectives of Hitler and Mussolini, he added, "It appears that Satan's plan, dictation and compulsion, is prevailing; but it cannot triumph in the end."

While this prediction ultimately proved correct, the events that followed soon after created serious doubt. Within days after Italy's entry into the war, the French government declared Paris an open city, moving its headquarters first to Tours, then to Bordeaux. On the heels of that, a new French government, under World War I hero Marshal Philippe Petain, asked for an armistice; and by June 25, France lay prostrate, defeated in only forty-two days.

As Great Britain stood alone following its shattering defeat at Dunkirk in June, and as Germany's air attacks on England were accelerated, a growing perception in America was that the United States would ultimately be drawn into the war. That perception became clearer when in January 1941, American and British officers met in Washington, D.C., where it was agreed that the two nations would maintain joint planning staffs. Two months later, the Lend-Lease Act was passed, authorizing the United States to provide war materials for nations under attack by the Axis powers. Reacting to this, Elder Smith noted in his diary on March 27, "The war abroad is increasing in intensity and the attitude of our own government is ominous."

Meanwhile, life in the Smith family went on despite the gloomy prospect that the United States would be drawn into the war. Elder Smith had continued to fulfill his apostolic responsibilities by attending stake conferences and touring missions. Following the October general conference in 1940, he and Jessie toured the Central States Mission in company with mission president John F. Bowman and his wife. All along the way in meetings with members and missionaries, Elder Smith bore down strongly on the theme that the war in Europe was the result of disobedience

319

to God's laws and that unless the people of the United States repented, they would suffer a similar fate. A diary entry made on October 24, following a meeting in Oklahoma City, reveals the intensity of Elder Smith's preaching on this subject and the reaction of some people towards it. "While I was speaking and mentioned the fact that the world needs repentance, and as I referred to the filthy practice of drunkenness and tobacco, two men got up and left in disgust or contempt; but nevertheless, we preached repentance and bore witness of the restored gospel and warned the people, as we have done consistently, of the calamities, bloodshed etc., if they do not repent." In token of Elder Smith's unswerving belief in the rightness and timeliness of his views, he added, "We had a very good meeting."

Amid the troubling news of the war in Europe and Elder Smith's fiery denunciation of evil and threats of dire consequences to follow, family life among the Smiths went on as usual. In May of 1940, Reynolds was ordained an elder, and his bishop approached him about filling a mission. In less than a month, Reyn's papers were processed, and on June 11 he received a call to serve in Argentina. "He seems very pleased," his father wrote of the call. The son entered the mission home July 1, and by mid-July he had been set apart by his father and sent on his way.

During the period of Reynolds's preparation to go on his mission, Jessie underwent an appendectomy and later became gravely ill when peritonitis set in. Joseph learned of the emergency surgery while he was attending a stake conference in Safford, Arizona, where Spencer W. Kimball presided. Canceling plans to go on to the Mexican colonies for a series of meetings, the apostle returned home immediately. He was driven to Phoenix, Arizona, by President Kimball and there took a bus to Salt Lake City. "After riding all night and most of all day Monday, [I arrived] in Salt Lake City at 4 P.M. As soon as I could, I went to the LDS Hospital where I found Jessie in considerable distress but cheerful. . . . She was very glad to see me, as I was to see her, and I left her feeling encouraged." Because of her perilous condition caused by the infection after the appendectomy, it was necessary for nurses to attend Jessie for many weeks at home following her release from the hospital. She recovered gradually and, after months of convalescence, regained her full health.

Meanwhile, at a purely personal level, Elder Smith continued to enjoy the role of father and grandfather. The traditional celebration of Elder Smith's birthday was delayed this year because of complications in getting Reynolds into the mission field. But this neglect was rectified the following week when the family gathered at Liberty Park to commemorate Joseph's sixty-fourth birthday. "During the week from the 21st to the 27th [of July], I was at the office and at home. Played ball with my boys two or three times which amused them." Had the sons been consulted, there is little doubt that their reaction would have been one of admiration, not amusement, that their sixty-four-year-old father was vigorous enough physically and young enough at heart to enjoy a game of ball with them.

The following week, Elder Smith took Douglas and Milton with him to the Alpine Summer School, where he spoke to the students and teachers. While they were there, Professor Carl F. Eyring permitted them to look at the heavens through a telescope. Even though it was daytime, they were able to see some of the stars and planets because of the high altitude and the clearness of the atmosphere. And Venus could even be seen with the naked eye. The next day back in Salt Lake City, Joseph was pleased to be able to share his new-found knowledge: "Venus was visible to the eye here in Salt Lake City," he wrote on July 31, "and I pointed it out to my children." And the proud patriarch reached another milestone on August 15, when he baptized his oldest grandchild, Maxine Reinhardt, Josephine's daughter.

During this period, when the General Authorities were in recess, Elder Smith was able to do something that he

seldom did during all the years of his apostolic service—
he prepared and gave a Sunday School lesson to an adult
class in the Garden Park Ward. The following week, he
was off on his never-ending round of stake conference
visits when he traveled to Malad, Idaho, with Roscoe W.
Eardley of the Welfare Committee. And the following
week, Elder Smith was in Oakley, Idaho, with another
welfare worker, Harold B. Lee, who within a few months
would be called to the Twelve and who later still would
serve as Joseph Fielding Smith's first counselor in the First
Presidency. "Bro. Lee and I did all we could to encourage
and help the stake to better their condition in Priesthood
activities," reported Elder Smith of a welfare meeting they
held. The apostle's instruction at the general session "emphasized the need of repentance, loyalty and obedience."

These themes were interwoven in practically all of the
sermons Elder Smith delivered during the period leading
up to the entrance of the United States into World War II.
He sensed a deterioration in loyalty and obedience, even
among the Latter-day Saints, and therefore called upon
them to repent and to prepare for the terrible days he saw
ahead for them. Although the United States was not then
at war, he saw it draw ever closer as in July 1941, when
American troops replaced British troops in Iceland; and
later that summer when the United States began to construct naval and air bases, presumably for the use of the
British. These and other circumstances had created a general perception that the direct involvement of the United
States in the war was inevitable. The only uncertainty was
when and under what circumstances it would occur. All
became clear on December 7, 1941, when the Japanese
attacked Pearl Harbor. At the time, Elder Smith was presiding at the conference of the Uvada stake in Caliente,
Nevada. "Sunday afternoon," he noted in his diary, "the
report came over the radio that the Japanese had made a
sudden dastardly, cowardly attack on Honolulu, without
any warning, creating a considerable destruction and loss
of life." When the next day the United States declared war

on Japan and three days later Germany and Italy declared war on the United States, Elder Smith and the entire nation knew that the terrible event they had sensed would come, but had fervently hoped could be avoided, had become a reality.

Like all other parents, Joseph's first and immediate concern was for his sons who were of military age. At the time, three of them were in that category, Joseph, who was twenty-seven; Lewis, twenty-three; and Reynolds, who was almost twenty-one. And Douglas would reach draftable age the following May. Moreover, all of the apostle's sons-in-law were of an age that made them vulnerable to the draft. The prospect that these sons and sons-in-law might be sacrificed filled him with revulsion. While he was convinced that the challenges facing the American nation came from a general rejection of God's laws, he held the country's leaders to a higher and more specific standard of accountability. Thus, while he participated in the government's call for a day of national prayer on January 1, 1942, he was critical of what he perceived as a lack of humility among its leaders. Elder Smith's diary entry for that day tells the story best: "This morning at 10:30, I was in the Winder Ward where the people had assembled in a prayer meeting in keeping with a proclamation from the President of the United States because of the trouble and difficulties in the world. I addressed the meeting at some length. My own feelings are that it would have been better if the President had called on the people—including himself—to *repent*, as well as to pray. Prayer without humility and the spirit of repentance avails nothing. I take it that in most instances it will be like this in the prayers: 'O Lord, we need thy help, come to our aid, but we do not intend to keep thy commandments.' "

A personal tragedy in the Smith family during this period added to the somber feelings created by America's entry into the war. Elder Smith was awakened at 3:00 A.M. December 17 by a telephone call from his daughter, Lois, who tearfully explained that his little grandson and namesake, Joseph Fife, had just passed away in a San Francisco hospital. "It is a very severe blow," wrote the grandfather, "as this is the second child Lois and her husband have lost. Jessie and I will leave tonight for Stockton." Snarled rail traffic caused by the new war emergency prevented the Smiths from leaving until the next morning. This put them in Stockton at 3:00 A.M. on Friday the 19th. "We learned that funeral arrangements for our precious baby were for 1:30 P.M. Saturday," Joseph noted on that day. "Jessie and I spent the time all day Friday with Lois and Dr. Fife and helped to comfort them in their sore affliction. Beautiful services were held Saturday. Jessie sang and the speaking by the Bishop and others was comforting." The Smiths left at midnight following the services. Because of complications in their train schedule, they did not arrive home until almost twenty-four hours later.

As Elder Smith monitored the news daily, he became more convinced that the war was the direct result of personal and collective sin. And it seemed to nettle him that others did not understand this and that they failed to speak out about it in their public addresses. So when in early January he attended a meeting where Arthur Gaeth, a well-known Mormon news commentator, was the speaker, Joseph deplored the fact that in discussing the war and its causes, Mr. Gaeth "failed to give the principal reason — violation of the Lords commandments and wickedness." This lack in others was compensated for to an extent by Elder Smith's persistent focus on this theme. His recorded sermons during this period uniformly dwell on it. His diary is filled with entries about it. So we can safely assume that his unrecorded talks featured some discussion about it. And as had been true from the beginning of his apostolic ministry, Elder Smith had many opportunities to speak. Indeed, during this period such opportunities were multiplied because of special instructional meetings for priesthood leaders that the General Authorities had begun to conduct. In early January, Elder Smith, accompanied by Marion G. Romney, newly called assistant to the Twelve, went to northern Utah to conduct such meetings with priesthood leaders in the Cache and Logan stakes. "We were able to discuss matters of priesthood much better than in a stake conference," Joseph Fielding wrote of them, "and search the hearts of the people who had the responsibility." The following weekend, Elder Smith, accompanied by another new assistant to the Twelve, Thomas E. McKay, traveled to Idaho, where similar priesthood training meetings were held in the Rexburg and Yellowstone stakes.

The meetings Joseph Fielding held with Elders Romney and McKay actually had two main purposes. The first, of course, was to instruct the local leaders in their duties. The second, equally if not more important, was to train his companions in their duties as General Authorities. As already indicated, they had been recently called as assistants to the Twelve. At the same time, April 6, 1941, three other men had been called to the same position, Clifford E. Young, Alma Sonne, and Nicholas G. Smith. Initially, Joseph Fielding had had misgivings about their calls. His concern did not relate to these brethren's ability or qualifications, nor to the need for help at the general level. It related instead to the absence in the scriptures of any reference to the office of "assistant to the Twelve." He understood that scripturally the Seventy were intended to be those whom the Twelve would call on for assistance. Yet, because of restrictions then imposed on the Seventy, they were incapable of providing the measure of help the Twelve urgently needed. The Seventy then lacked the authority to ordain high priests, authority that was essential in reorganizing stakes. Nor could they ordain bishops or call and set apart high councilors. Laboring under these restrictions, members of the First Council of Seventy could not be sent alone to reorganize stakes, nor could they relieve members of the Twelve of much of the load in reorganizations when they went out as companions. This was a crucial problem as the Church continued to grow worldwide, thereby increasing the workload of the Twelve.

The solution lay in the broad authority vested in the prophetic office to take the action necessary to carry on the work. Therefore, when President Heber J. Grant decided to call assistants to the Twelve who could function without the restrictions imposed on the Seventy, Elder Smith and the other apostles approved.

The men selected as assistants to the Twelve were experienced in Church matters but not at the general level. So, for a time, they were sent out with members of the Twelve to learn their new duties. Because Elder Smith was by now one of the senior members of the Twelve, he had a major responsibility in training these new brethren. He knew them all well. At the time of his call, Elder Romney was the president of the Bonneville Stake where Elder Smith resided. Joseph had known Thomas E. McKay for many years through their related Church assignments and through association with Elder McKay's brother, President David O. McKay. And he still had another official relationship with Thomas E. McKay because of the continuing responsibilities they shared to shepherd the Saints in Europe through correspondence. Elder Smith was also well acquainted with Alma Sonne and Clifford E. Young, both of whom had served as stake presidents. Both were also prominent bankers, Elder Sonne from Logan, Utah, and Elder Young from American Fork, Utah. Moreover, Elder Young, because of his status as a son-in-law of President Heber J. Grant, had long been a member of the unofficial and loosely structured "Church family" comprised of General Authorities and their kin. Finally, Joseph and Nicholas G. Smith were cousins—Nicholas, a former mission president and acting Church patriarch, being a brother of George Albert Smith of the Twelve and a descendant of "Uncle John," who was a brother of Joseph Smith Sr., the Prophet's father.

In turn, then, with other members of the Twelve, Joseph Fielding accompanied these assistants to the Twelve on visits to stake conferences and other Church meetings where the new men learned by observation what was ex-

pected of them in their callings. But more important, perhaps, they absorbed the learning and lore of the Church
at the general level as they traveled with members of the
Twelve. Over time, these assistants and others who would
follow them were by this means thoroughly indoctrinated
into the Church hierarchy. And within a few years, when
he became president of the Quorum of the Twelve
Apostles, Joseph Fielding Smith would not only have training duties with the assistants but would also have authority
and responsibility to direct them in their work.

On the same day in April 1941 when the first five
assistants to the Twelve were called, Elder Harold B. Lee
was sustained as the junior member of the Twelve. This
initiated a twenty-nine year association between Elder
Smith and Elder Lee as members of the Twelve. Despite
a difference of twenty-three years in their ages, the pair
had a special affinity that far transcended their apostolic
association. Joseph Fielding had visited the Pioneer Stake
in Salt Lake City on assignment during the 1930s when
Elder Lee served there as the stake president. With the
other General Authorities, Elder Smith had watched this
young leader struggle, with his associates, to alleviate the
economic want among their members brought on by the
Great Depression. The creative welfare initiatives developed by Harold B. Lee in the Pioneer Stake caught the eye
of the First Presidency, resulting in his eventual call as the
managing director of the Church welfare program. In this
capacity, Elder Lee had accompanied Joseph Fielding and
other members of the Twelve on stake conference assignments over several years as they teamed up to teach welfare
principles to local priesthood leaders. A particularly memorable assignment they shared was in August 1937 when
they traveled to Canada to attend conferences in the Cards-
ton and Lethbridge stakes. Elder Lee and his wife, Fern,
had gone to Canada by automobile with their friends
Charles and Lenora Hyde, while Elder Smith had traveled
there by train. After the conferences ended, it was discovered that Elder Smith could save a day by traveling

home with the Lees and Hydes. So, he canceled his train reservations, and the five of them piled into the car for the trip home. Joseph was particularly anxious to get home early because Ethel's condition had worsened, preventing her from accompanying him. The two-day trip, with a stopover in West Yellowstone, afforded the travelers with a rare opportunity for long, uninterrupted visiting. In less than a week after the travelers arrived in Salt Lake City, Ethel passed away, thus setting off the chain of events already described. And more than twenty years later, Elder Lee's dear wife, Fern, would pass away, thereby creating another strong affinity between him and Elder Smith. Over the years of their apostolic ministry, many other shared events strengthened the bonds of understanding and mutual confidence between this pair. Thus, when Elder Smith selected counselors upon being ordained as the tenth president of the Church, he turned first to this trusted friend and associate, Harold B. Lee, who acted as the voice for the members of the Twelve in the ordination of President Smith. Thereafter during the period of his prophetic ministry, Joseph Fielding Smith's friend Harold B. Lee served ably at his side, faithfully carrying out the many tasks delegated to him. And when President Smith passed on, his successor would be Harold B. Lee, who was then the senior living apostle, notwithstanding that when Elder Lee was called to the Twelve in 1941 there were eight other living apostles between him and Joseph Fielding Smith who outranked him in apostolic seniority.

All this, of course, was in the distant future when on Monday, January 26, 1942, Joseph Fielding Smith and Harold B. Lee of the Twelve joined to conduct another of the special priesthood training meetings then being held throughout the Church. This one was in the Bonneville Stake of Salt Lake City, where Joseph Fielding resided. "It was a very successful meeting." he noted.

The first week of February 1942 found Elder Smith and Jessie in Los Angeles, California, where they had gone to attend the quarterly conference of the Inglewood Stake.

Traveling on the *Challenger,* one of the new diesel stream-
liners, they were met at the depot by Jessie's nephew,
Robert L. Simpson, who, nineteen years later, would be
called as the first counselor in the Presiding Bishopric of
the Church. Later, Bishop Simpson would be called as an
assistant to the Twelve and, on October 1, 1976, when the
First Quorum of Seventy was reconstituted, he was inducted into that quorum.

Although Elder Smith was the official visitor at the
Inglewood Stake Conference on the weekend of February
7 and 8, 1942, he found on arriving at the stake center
Sunday morning that President Heber J. Grant was also
present. The Prophet had traveled to California to seek
relief from the cold and dismal weather in Salt Lake City.
And he had also come to the lower elevation of California
for relief from a stroke he had suffered two years before.
It is an unusual coincidence that President Grant experienced the first episode of the stroke that had debilitated
him on Sunday, February 4, 1940, as he attended a session
of the Inglewood Stake Conference. Four days before, the
eighty-three-year-old Prophet had played a vigorous round
of golf in San Diego with a foursome that included Joseph
Anderson, his secretary and dear friend. "The best game
for a long time I have played," President Grant had confided to his journal. It was also to be his last game of golf.
Perhaps the fact he had shot well was explained in part
by a session before the round when he had practiced "fifty
cents worth of balls." Apparently the vigorous exercise in
San Diego four days before was the main cause of what
happened on Sunday February 4, 1940. At 9:30 A.M. that
day, California Mission President W. Aird MacDonald
drove President Grant and Joseph Anderson to the Inglewood Stake Center for the morning session of the conference. As the car pulled into the parking lot, the prophet
became dizzy. When he stepped from the car, the vertigo
caused him to lose his balance and stumble to the ground.
Despite the urging of Joseph Anderson and President
MacDonald that he return to the mission home, President

Grant insisted on attending the morning session. Because his tongue was thick he did not speak, although after a nap during the noon hour, he felt better and spoke for about forty minutes at the afternoon session. The next morning as President Grant attempted to get out of bed, he suffered another attack of dizziness and fell. On being helped back into bed, he discovered that his left side was paralyzed. This and his slurred speech were the infallible signs he had suffered a stroke. During the two intervening years, the Prophet had struggled with his disability, attempting to regain the strength and stamina he had enjoyed so abundantly before. But the attempt had failed. He was still unable to get around without assistance. And his speech was quite slurred and indistinct. However, he continued to work at it, carrying around a hard rubber ball in his left hand and squeezing it to strengthen his muscles. He shared the pulpit with Elder Smith at the Inglewood Stake Conference on Sunday, February 8, 1942, speaking briefly and extemporaneously. It was the last talk President Grant ever gave in a stake setting. And two months later, he delivered his last public address when he spoke for a few minutes at the April general conference. He then withdrew into silence until his death three years later.

There was another unscheduled speaker at the Inglewood Stake Conference on this Sunday in February 1942. It was Hugh B. Brown, the former president of the British Mission, with whom Joseph Fielding had been working to encourage the British Saints through correspondence. But Elder Brown participated at this conference in another capacity. After his return from England, he had been appointed as the coordinator for LDS servicemen. At the time he was visiting military camps in southern California to encourage and strengthen the Latter-day Saints in military service. Learning of the conference, he had come to worship with the Saints and was called on to speak. While it was the last time Hugh B. Brown would share a pulpit with President Grant, it was not so as to Elder Smith. On many occasions in the future Joseph Fielding Smith and

Hugh B. Brown would share speaking assignments following Elder Brown's call as a General Authority. What happened later to this pair provides an interesting commentary on the shifting roles of Mormon priesthood leaders. After Elder Brown's call as an assistant to the Twelve, and still later after his call as a member of the Twelve, his file leader was Joseph Fielding Smith, who was president of the Twelve. Then when Elder Brown was called as a member of the First Presidency, he became one of President Smith's file leaders, a condition that continued to exist even after Elder Smith was called as one of President McKay's counselors. Then when Elder Smith became the president of the Church and Elder Brown was returned to his position in the Twelve, the roles were reversed again.

The day after the Inglewood Stake Conference, Elder Smith and Jessie spent the day at the Simpson home, relaxing and visiting. In the afternoon they went to the beach. While the apostle had no great yen for swimming in the surf, he enjoyed watching the waves and walking on the sandy shore. And later when he became the Prophet, a favorite diversion was to spend a few secluded days at the Laguna Beach cottage owned by the Church. There with Jessie he enjoyed many quiet hours, gazing at the sea and watching the changing patterns of light as the sun glimmered through the early morning fog or blazed at midday, then, like a glowing red ball, dipped into the ocean at sunset. Now, however, as he and Jessie visited the beach with Jelaire Simpson, Robert's wife, Joseph was distracted by the events that brought the war ever closer to his own family. "By government edict," he wrote on that day, "the nation went on advanced time called 'war time'. The clocks were set ahead an hour." Then after questioning the need for such a change, whose effect, he felt, was 'to disrupt nature,' he added pensively, "The whole world is in turmoil and war, and many of our young men are being drafted into service."

What Elder Smith had stated as a general proposition in this entry became very personal and pointed a month later. "My son Lewis W. reported to the U. S. draft board and was inducted into the U. S. Army," Joseph recorded on March 4, 1942. "This condition brought sadness to us all. It is a shame that the clean and the righteous are forced into a conflict of world proportions, because of the wickedness of men." After repeating his conviction that the war not only resulted from disobedience to God's laws but also fulfilled ancient prophecies, the concerned father added this benediction: "May the Lord guide and protect the sons of the Latter-day Saints and all others who will live righteously." At this time, Elder Smith seems to have had no inkling that this noble son would be sacrificed. He seemed confident that the boy would be spared. At least, he fervently hoped and prayed it would be so, realizing that the righteous are not immune to the death and devastation caused by war.

Two days after Lewis was inducted into the army, Elder Smith and Jessie left for California, where stake conferences were held at Gridley and Sacramento. Sandwiched between the meetings of these two conferences was a nice visit with daughter Lois and her husband, Dr. William J. Fife, at Stockton. While there, the Fifes arranged two social gatherings where Jessie sang and Elder Smith responded to questions. In such an intimate setting, people came to know the apostle better, to observe the loving and relaxed relationship he enjoyed with his family, and to find that he had a wry and charming sense of humor. These qualities usually came as a surprise to many who had only seen Elder Smith from afar as he spoke from the pulpit, where his message, especially during these days of war and turmoil, was usually one of warning and a call to repentance.

Everywhere he went now, Elder Smith found the same conditions that existed at the meetings in Sacramento. "Many young men in uniform were present," he wrote of the general session held on Sunday, March 15. On arriving home the following evening, he found a postcard from his own serviceman. It was written from Shepard Field, Texas, where Lewis had arrived the previous Saturday night. Betraying a sense of uncertainty and helplessness, Joseph wrote complainingly, "The government will not tell parents when their sons are leaving or where they are going."

The new conditions imposed by the entry of the United States into the war were most evident at the April General Conference, 1942. Because of restrictions placed on travel, only stake presidencies and other designated priesthood leaders were invited to attend. "The church has restricted the excessive travel of the people," Joseph explained. "Moreover, the precaution was taken against any act by enemies or cranks which might occur." The meetings on Sunday were held in the upper room of the temple. Following the morning session, the brethren took a half-hour break and returned at 12:30 for a three-and-a-half-hour testimony meeting to which they had come fasting. "The sacrament was administered by the apostles," reported Elder Smith. "It was a very inspirational and glorious occasion. The spirit of the Lord was present and every heart was touched."

While the exigencies of the war imposed restrictions on the General Conference of the Church, they had no such impact on the stake conferences. These meetings continued unabated with the same frequency as when Joseph Fielding was called to the Twelve thirty-two years before. During that entire period, he had been on the road most of the time, visiting the stakes or touring missions. Now at age sixty-six, at a time when most men have either retired or are looking toward retirement, he was still in the harness, pulling his share of the load, a load that grew with each passing year as Church membership continued to increase rapidly. So, during the two months following the April General Conference, Elder Smith presided at the stake conferences in Denver, Colorado; the West Jordan, Panguitch, and Beaver stakes in Utah; the Teton Stake in Wyoming; the Pasadena Stake in California; and the Montpelier Stake in Idaho. Meanwhile, he spoke at sacrament meetings in the Bonneville and North Twentieth wards, installed a new bishopric in the Yalecrest Ward, and ad-

*Joseph Fielding
Smith expounding
the scriptures*

dressed the students at the Brigham Young University. Also, during the three or four days each week when he was at home, he was heavily involved in "board and committee meetings," in directing the usual work in the Historical Department and in handling a mountain of paperwork that changes caused by the war had imposed upon him. "It appears that nearly everyone desires to get government employment in some plant or office," he noted in his diary, "and all have to have certificates of birth. We have issued about 9,000 in this office. I have to sign all certificates in duplicate which keeps me busy. I have signed some 18,000 times, and they still come."

On the day Elder Smith made this entry, he encountered still another annoyance that had been spawned by the war — rationing. He and Jessie went to the federal building to register for their ration of sugar. Joseph was irritated

334

by the glacial speed with which the clerks performed their duty, taking as long as a half hour for an applicant. "It struck me," he wrote with characteristic candor, "that the method was one more evidence of incompetent methods of which we have seen so many manifestations." Then revealing the wry sense of humor that surfaced at times and under circumstances that were wholly unpredictable, he added: "The ration of sugar is 1/2 lb. per person per week, with time and sugar *out* if you have sugar on hand."

The rationing of sugar was, of course, merely the camel's head under the tent. It was followed by a large and rapidly growing bulk of foodstuffs and commodities that were in short supply. The main priority was to provide military personnel with an abundance of everything. Nothing was too good for the GIs. The circumstance under which the country had been plunged into war had raised patriotism in the United States to torrid levels. And such was the hoopla and ballyhoo connected with it that entry into the armed services was made to appear glamorous and exciting. But a peek behind the curtain was sobering and shocking to a man like Lewis Smith, who had been reared in the sheltered environment of a prophet's home and who, only weeks before his induction, had been preaching the gospel of love and peace. Lewis had been unable to spell out what he was faced with in the terse postcards and letters he sent home periodically. However, he had that chance on June 10, 1942, three months after his induction, when he spent several hours visiting with his father and Aunt Jessie in Bellville, Illinois. At the time, Lewis was stationed at Camp Scott. On their way to tour the Canadian Mission, Elder and Sister Smith had stopped in St. Louis and, having a nine-hour layover before their train left for Chicago, had taken a bus to Belleville, to which Lewis had also traveled by bus from his base. It was an emotional reunion and a bittersweet experience for the father, sweet merely because he was in Lewis's presence and bitter because of the insight he gained into what his son faced in the service. "We found him looking well," wrote Joseph, "but not too well pleased with army life, where he sees so much evil and rottenness among the men in the service. . . . We spent about four hours with him and found it difficult to leave. We returned to St. Louis and he went back to Scott Field."

The Smiths left St. Louis at midnight, changed trains at both Chicago and Detroit, and, after an unscheduled two-hour delay, arrived at their first destination, Windsor, Canada. There they were met by Joseph's brother, David A. Smith, former member of the Presiding Bishopric, who was then presiding over the Canadian Mission. With David was his wife, Emily, and a son, Edward. Soon after their arrival in Windsor, Joseph and Jessie found themselves in the first of the missionary meetings they would attend during the mission tour. Teaming up the next day at a meeting in Chatham, Joseph and David "taught the straight gospel," something they did unsparingly during the next two weeks.

The schedule David A. had arranged was hectic. It included meetings with members and missionaries all along the way. After leaving Chatham, the touring party visited London, Kitchner, Hamilton, Toronto, St. Catherine, Montreal, and Ottawa. At both Hamilton and Montreal, Joseph Fielding dedicated LDS chapels, both of which were renovated and refurbished private homes.

A highlight of the tour for Joseph was a visit to the Russell Farm near Toronto. It was here that his grandmother, Mary Fielding Smith, was baptized in 1836 as a result of the preaching of Parley P. Pratt. Baptized at the same time were Mary's brother, Joseph Fielding, and her sister, Mercy Rachel Fielding. Another convert of Elder Pratt's preaching was John Taylor. Those events, obscure at the time, profoundly influenced the history of the Church. Mary later married Hyrum Smith and bore his son, Joseph F., the father of Joseph Fielding, both of whom would become presidents of the Church. Mercy later married Robert B. Thompson, who once served as one of the Prophet Joseph Smith's private secretaries. John Taylor became the third president of the Church and was with Joseph and Hyrum when they were murdered in the Carthage jail, himself being severely wounded. And Joseph Fielding, Mary and Mercy's brother, was with the first group of missionaries sent to England in 1837. This group, led by Heber C. Kimball, opened their proselyting efforts in England at Preston by preaching in the protestant church of James Fielding, Joseph Fielding's brother.

The extraordinary results of Parley P. Pratt's mission to Toronto was a powerful object lesson to the missionaries in the Canadian Mission as Elder Smith conducted this tour, illustrating the far-reaching results that can flow from a single proselyting effort.

Joseph and Jessie left Canada on July 2, arriving in St. Louis the following evening. There they met Lewis, who had obtained a weekend pass. With Lewis were four returned missionaries who were also stationed at Scott Field. One of these was Lewis's cousin, Joseph Peterson, the son of Elder Smith's sister. On Saturday, July 4, Joseph and Jessie celebrated Independence Day with the five young men at a special dinner in the Jefferson Hotel, where they were staying. "We had a pleasant visit," Elder Smith reported. "It was hard to leave our boy to return home."

Arriving in Salt Lake City on July 6, Joseph Fielding found the so-called General Authority recess in full swing. So, on the following weekend, he and Robert Judd of the Welfare Committee traveled to Richmond, Utah, for a conference of the Benson Stake! He took this glitch in his schedule in full stride. And the day after returning from this conference, his annual period of relaxation commenced in earnest: "Monday 13th [of July] to Saturday 18th, I spent the time quietly, part of the time at the office and part at home, working around the lot, etc. I purchased some furniture and a carpet to replace some that is worn out." During this week, Joseph and Jessie joined the members of the board of directors of the Beneficial Life Insurance Company at a dinner hosted by President Heber J. Grant at his summer cottage up Emigration Canyon, east of Salt Lake City.

This week began a month of relaxation for Elder Smith, during which he was able to get a reprieve from the steady grind of stake conferences and mission tours. And his headquarters work was reduced to a minimum, consisting only of attending a few essential meetings and responding to correspondence that required immediate attention. He did accept two invitations to speak at ward sacrament meetings during the period, but these did not require travel or extensive preparation. His loosely structured schedule during this period provides an interesting insight into how an apostle unwinds: On his birthday, Sunday, July 19, he accompanied Jessie to the weekly Tabernacle Choir broadcast; and in the afternoon his family assembled to wish him a happy birthday. Following his talk at the 24th Ward sacrament meeting a week later, Joseph "met with the members of my brother Hyrum's family and instructed them." The next day, he and Jessie drove up Millcreek Canyon to look at a cabin Taylor Merrill had advertised for sale. Within two weeks, the Smiths had purchased the cabin and, before the recess was over, they had refurnished it and were enjoying spending time there. The day after looking at the cabin for the first time, Joseph assisted Jessie with housework in the morning, and in the afternoon they went with their neighbors, Richard L. and Alice Evans, to see the movie "The Pride of the Yankees." The Smiths and Evans ended the day with dinner at a Chinese restaurant. Although they were separated in age by the wide gulf of thirty years, there was a remarkable compatibility between Joseph Fielding and his young colleague, Richard Evans. Of course, their shared status as General Authorities and residents of Douglas Street provided strong ligaments of bonding. But, there was much more that bound them together. Both enjoyed the written word and were careful and precise in the use of language. Both were published authors. Both were former missionaries to England. In temperament, both were quiet and thoughtful with a wry

sense of humor. And, finally, their relationship was enhanced because of the long artistic relationship between
Elder Evans and Jessie Evans Smith. From 1930, when
Elder Evans became the narrator of the weekly Tabernacle
Choir broadcasts, he and Jessie had been closely associated
through Jessie's role as a choir soloist. And because Jessie's
maiden name was Evans, there was a playful pretense
between her and Richard that they were cousins. Moreover, the two couples were drawn even closer together
socially because only four years separated Jessie and Richard in age. So the Smiths and the Evans genuinely enjoyed
each other. As a result, they developed a good-natured
camaraderie unlike any other Joseph Fielding Smith seems
to have formed. This is best illustrated by letters that passed
between Joseph Fielding and Richard in 1941 while plans
were being made for a tour of the Tabernacle Choir to
California. Wrote Joseph: "You are hereby authorized, appointed, chosen, designated, named, commanded, assigned, advised and otherwise notified, informed, advised
and instructed . . . to see that the said Mrs. Jessie Evans
Smith, is permitted to travel in safety, comfort, ease, without molestation and that she is to be returned again to her
happy home and loving husband and family." Richard's
good-natured response was in the same vein: "Your mas-
terful document of August 15 has cost me a good deal of
brow-wrinkling and excruciating concentration. I think
without question it will go down in history with the Bill
of Rights and the Magna Charta. The remarkable thing
about it is, as my legal staff and I have studied it over,
that it conveys to me no privilege that I did not already
feel free to take and imposes on me no responsibilities that
it was not already my pleasure and intention to assume.
However, it is a good idea, as many men can testify, to
have the consent of a husband before traveling two thousand miles with his wife." Against such a background, it
is not difficult to imagine that the Chinese supper the
Smiths and Evans shared on July 28 was marked by gaiety
and good humor.

The supper the Smiths had the following night at the home of Elder and Sister Harold B. Lee was doubtless as enjoyable but in a different way. Assembled at the Lees' home were several General Authorities and their wives, along with key leaders from the Welfare Department and their wives. While this was a relaxed social event, it also served an institutional purpose by bringing together and solidifying those involved in a common enterprise. Many of the social events Joseph Fielding and his companions had attended over the years were of a similar institutional character, helping those involved to focus even more devotedly on the immediate and distant goals they all shared. Those having only a superficial knowledge of the forces that drive the Latter-day Saints will never grasp the depth and intensity of the motivations these objectives generate. These become the dominant force in their lives, taking precedence over all else. What is of overriding importance to them is the filial relationship all bear to Deity and the duty of obedience this entails, the indebtedness owed by all to the Savior, the key role of his restored church in leading the world back to God's presence, and the special responsibility given to the Latter-day Saints to direct the earthly affairs of the Church. The pervasive effect of that responsibility filters into every aspect of life, influencing if not controlling the way the Mormons work, play, and socialize. What is said here of Latter-day Saints generally applied with particular force to Joseph Fielding Smith, who was a special witness of Jesus Christ and his mission and doctrine in all the world.

The events of the day following the supper hosted by Elder and Sister Lee demonstrate this. After spending part of the day bottling fruit, Joseph and Jessie drove to Brighton to visit Mother Evans, who was on vacation there. "Then we came part way in the canyon," Joseph reported, "and met in a social with the Priesthood of the Cottonwood Stake." It requires little imagination to guess who capped the program, or what he talked about. It was understood by all when Elder Smith accepted the invitation to the social that he would be expected to speak for his supper. And everyone would have been disappointed had he not focused on some aspect of the work that bound them together.

During the final two weeks of the recess, Elder Smith and Jessie spent several days picking chokecherries and service berries and making them into jelly. Meanwhile, there were other opportunities to socialize in a pleasant setting and to relax. One Sunday after Joseph had spoken and Jessie had sung at the sacrament meeting in their own ward, they joined Presiding Bishop LeGrand Richards and his wife and other guests at the home of Wesley Smith, Joseph's brother, for conversation and refreshments. And a few days later, the Smiths were driven by Richard and Alice Evans to Salt Air on the Great Salt Lake, where they joined the members of the Tabernacle Choir and their partners for a banquet and outing. And for pure, uninterrupted relaxation, they spent several days and nights at their new cabin up Millcreek Canyon.

By mid August, Elder Smith was prepared to again take up his arduous duties. During the week prior to the October General Conference, he presided at six stake conferences, beginning with the conference in Richfield, Utah. In turn, there followed conferences at the Bear River, Franklin, Smithfield, Star Valley and Big Cottonwood stakes. At each of these, Elder Smith was accompanied by a representative of the Welfare Department who helped him teach priesthood leaders the principles and procedures governing the Church Welfare Program, which by now had become a vital part of the program of the Church.

Meanwhile, Joseph's headquarters assignments continued apace. Much of the load of the Historical Department was now on the shoulders of his assistants. However, the ultimate responsibility was still his, which required regular, consistent supervision and follow-through. There were, of course, the regular meetings with the members of his quorum and with the First Presidency where the final decisions were made for the governance of the

Church. And there were regular meetings of various committees on which he served, including the Missionary Assignment Committee.

A critical issue facing the Brethren as the October General Conference approached was the desire of President Heber J. Grant to fill the office of Patriarch to the Church, which had stood vacant since the death of Hyrum Gibbs Smith in February 1932. In the meantime, both Nicholas G. Smith and George F. Richards had served successively as the acting Patriarch. Traditionally, the office of Patriarch to the Church had passed lineally to the eldest son descending from Joseph Smith Sr. But it was the intention of President Grant to call Joseph F. Smith, the nephew of Joseph Fielding Smith, to that office, even though he descended through the line of President Joseph F. Smith, who was not the oldest son of the martyr Hyrum Smith. Following the death of Hyrum Gibbs Smith in 1932, members of the Twelve had recommended that his eldest son, Eldred G. Smith, be called to the patriarchal office, but President Grant had declined to make the call. As the 1942 October General Conference approached, President Grant went to Joseph Fielding's office to discuss the matter privately with him. "He said he could not feel right about accepting the recommendation of the apostles," Joseph wrote of the interview, "that the office be given to Eldred Smith and for ten years he had only had a 'stupor of thought' in the consideration of this appointment. Now he felt clear regarding his duty and his mind was at rest that Joseph F., son of my brother Hyrum M., should receive this office. I said, so far as I am concerned, when the President of the Church says the Lord has manifested to him or inspired him to do anything, I would support him fully in that action. . . . If the president is inspired to change the order of descent the Lord has indicated, I will be with him with my support."

Few other instances in his life demonstrate more clearly than this one Joseph Fielding Smith's unqualified support of the one who occupies the prophetic office. Although

342

when asked about it earlier, Joseph had expressed a contrary view, he yielded that view immediately upon learning that the Prophet was inspired to do otherwise. And in giving that support, Elder Smith powerfully endorsed the idea that the Church is directed by revelation and that the Lord inspires and directs the living oracles according to the needs of the moment.

Three days after President Grant's surprise visit to Joseph's office, the Prophet presented the name of Joseph F. Smith to the Council of the First Presidency and Quorum of the Twelve as the Patriarch to the Church. "The Brethren accepted the nomination unanimously," he reported. And at the first session of the conference on October 3, 1942, Joseph F. Smith was unanimously sustained as the Patriarch to the Church.

The attendance at this conference was by invitation only and was restricted to designated priesthood leaders — general officers of the Church, general superintendencies of Sunday School and YMMIA, and selected stake and ward leaders. The new Patriarch was called to speak at the first session of the conference. In introducing him, President David O. McKay, who was conducting, after tracing his lineage to the martyr Hyrum Smith, said, "Elder Smith's right to the office therefore is not only by lineage, but by direct inspiration to the President who holds the keys of this high priesthood." The Patriarch's words were brief, consisting of a testimony, an expression of support for the Prophet, and a prayer for strength and commitment. He was followed by Elder Joseph Fielding Smith, who delivered a short but significant sermon. After reminding the brethren of their heavy responsibilities as holders of the priesthood, he explained the rewards that lay ahead for those who were faithful and diligent. Said he: "I wonder if we realize the greatness of our callings — yes all the elders in this church — do they realize that they hold the Melchizedek Priesthood? Do they know that through their faithfulness and their obedience, according to the revelations of the Lord, they are entitled to receive all that the Father has, to become the sons of God, joint heirs with our Elder Brother, Jesus Christ, entitled to the exaltation in the Celestial Kingdom?" (*Conference Report*, October 1942, p. 18.)

Here, in his own words, stated as clearly as he ever stated it, is the essence of all that Joseph Fielding Smith hoped and strived and struggled and prayed for. He wanted nothing less than to share with the Savior all that the Father has. (See D&C 84:38.) And he wanted everyone to receive the same blessings. To accomplish this, of course, required obedience to all of the commandments, ordinances, and covenants of the gospel. In this is found the reason and justification for the undeviating message Elder Smith delivered throughout his apostolic ministry. He wanted people to repent and to keep the commandments because he knew that this is the only way they can become exalted.

The reason Joseph Fielding and the other speakers at this first session spoke so briefly was because of the long time taken by President McKay to present the officers for sustaining vote and for President J. Reuben Clark to read a special message of the First Presidency. This wide-ranging message, whose obvious purpose was to strengthen the moral fiber of the Saints during the war, touched on many subjects of vital concern — chastity, the Word of Wisdom, parenthood, and unity. In addition, it contained pointed comments about the war and its causes and gave pertinent instructions to Latter-day Saints in the armed services and their families. "We pray . . . that you will live righteously," it read, "that you will be preserved, that God will hasten the working out of His purposes among the nations, so that peace may come and you be restored to your loved ones, as clean as the day on which you left them." (*Conference Report*, October 1942, p. 14.) The families of servicemen were urged to write regularly as were their friends and local priesthood leaders. As to the war, the message affirmed that it was the responsibility of the Church to renounce war and proclaim peace. "As those chosen and ordained to stand at the head of the

Savior's church," it continued, "we must call upon the leaders of nations to abandon the fiendishly inspired slaughter of the manhood of the world now carrying on and further planned." (Ibid., p. 15.)

Sharing the concerns expressed by the First Presidency, Joseph Fielding prepared a series of lectures following the October General Conference that he titled "The Signs of the Times." In them he traced the awful happenings in the world against the background of the scriptures which had predicted that wars, desolations, and destructions would precede the second coming of the Savior. "At 8 P.M." he wrote on Wednesday, October 14, 1942, "I gave the first of six talks on 'The Signs of the Times' in the Lion House. The attendance was so large that they concluded to go next time to Barrett Hall." Several hundred people crowded into the Barrett Hall for each of the succeeding lectures to hear the apostle expound on subjects that the war had brought so prominently to the thinking of all. Intense publicity given to the lectures, both in the press and by word of mouth, generated a wide interest in them so that at the urging of those who had sponsored the lectures, Joseph reviewed and prepared them for publication. "The first copies of *The Signs of the Times,* with paper covers, were off the press today," he wrote on December 19. "I was promised cloth bound copies by Monday." These lectures were planned as a means of raising money for the renovation of the Lion House, all of the proceeds going for this purpose.

The doleful nature of these lectures, treating, as they did, the terrible winding-up scenes that will precede the millennial reign, were not calculated to lift Elder Smith's spirits. And news from abroad and events at home may have reduced his comfort level about Lewis. On Sunday, November 1, Elder Smith attended memorial services in his own ward in honor of Lt. Donald Poulton, who had been killed in the line of duty when his plane crashed in the Pacific. As he mourned with the family of this young man, little did the apostle know that in not too long a time, he would receive the same loving ministrations as neighbors and friends would join to share his grief at the death of Lewis, who also died in a plane crash.

Curiously, only a few days after he attended the memorial services for Lt. Poulton, Elder Smith made a diary entry about allied landings in North Africa, the area where Lewis would be based at the time of his death. Wrote he on November 12, 1942: "The papers report the last few days the landing of American and British on the coasts of Morocco and Algiers in Africa, and the utter rout of General Rommel and the Nazi forces in Egypt. The American troops have had to fight some of the French, but many have welcomed them. The terrific struggle is going on all over the world."

The following month, another of Elder Smith's sons would be enlisted in that struggle when, on December 21, eighteen-year-old Douglas was sworn into the United States Army. In reading his journal entry of that day, some of the frustrations, and even anger, Elder Smith had on seeing this obedient, exemplary son taken into military service at such a young age are evident. "This morning at 6:40, I left home taking my son Douglas and some of his companions down to be inducted into the army of the United States. It is a shame that boys 18 and 19 have to be called in to this service." Then followed pointed remarks about the ineptitude of some leaders and their wrong-headed decisions, about the satanic forces he saw at work in the world, and about the prophetic patterns found in the scriptures that he traced into the events of the day. "I have looked for years for this dreadful day which I knew would come," he wrote. "May the members of the church turn to the Lord in humility and faith and forsake all evil ways. This is our only protection."

Joseph Fielding was not only troubled that Douglas had been inducted into the army, but he was also annoyed that he and his companions had been taken only four days before Christmas and had been loaded into a truck like animals, packed together so tightly that they all had to stand up as they were driven to Fort Douglas, located on the east bench of Salt Lake City. This fort, and the street on which the Smith family lived, were named after Stephen A. Douglas, the United States senator whose debates with the Springfield, Illinois, lawyer had catapulted Abraham Lincoln into national prominence, which he then used as a springboard to the presidency. Unknown to his father, Douglas had received a pass to spend Christmas with his family. Instead of asking to be picked up, he decided to walk the several miles from the fort to his home. It was late when he arrived, and the entire family was in bed. Trying the front door of the darkened house, he found it locked. At the side of the house, he also found the kitchen door locked. Without keys and not wanting to awaken the family, Douglas decided to break in. He was able to jimmy a small window next to the kitchen door, inching it up high enough to reach in an arm to unlock the door from the inside. The operation was not as noiseless as the son had thought. Elder Smith, awakened by the racket, arose to investigate. He switched on the kitchen lights about the time Douglas surreptitiously closed the outside door. As the father saw this son dressed in uniform, the irrepressible son who as a small boy he had had to caution about tearing around the house, he was overwhelmed with emotion. With tears filling his eyes, the father strode across the kitchen to take the beloved son in his arms. To be embraced by his father was nothing new to Douglas; it was an almost daily occurrence. But the unusual circumstances on this occasion, the spontaneity of the father's action, and his unusual show of emotion demonstrated to the son as never before the depth of the father's love for him. It was a never-to-be-forgotten experience, to be cherished in memory and relived over and over throughout life.

The day after Christmas, Douglas was ordained an elder by his father. And that evening, at the sacrament service in the Garden Park Ward, he and eight other young servicemen were honored before leaving for their training bases.

The following afternoon, Elder Smith drove Douglas to the Fort to report in following his Christmas leave. "Jessie was with me," wrote Joseph, "and we turned our boy over to the forces of the U. S." Then, the concerned father repeated the lament he had made when his son was first inducted: "It seems a shame that boys 18 and 19 have to go to war." Although this son was involved in military action in Europe, he escaped from the war unscathed. The same was true of Reynolds, who was inducted into the Navy after his release from the Argentine Mission. Only Lewis was to pay the ultimate price.

Chapter Twenty

The War Wears On—
Death of Lewis

With such a personal stake in its outcome, Joseph Fielding Smith avidly followed the progress of the war, regularly listening to newscasts and scanning the daily newspapers. The month following Doug's induction into the army, the Combined Chiefs of Staff of the allied forces met at Casablanca to plot strategy. This occurred amid a flush of optimism for ultimate victory. Rommel and his Panzers had been crushed in North Africa; the Soviets had turned back Hitler's hordes at Stalingrad and were now on the offensive; and the Japanese were stalled in the Pacific. Out of this and later councils came the overall strategy to secure the Mediterranean first, thereby eliminating Mussolini, while preparing the enormous buildup necessary to defeat Germany and Japan. These plans matured apace with the conquest of Sicily during July and August 1943, the fall of Mussolini on July 25, and the unconditional surrender of Italy as announced on September 8. Then in December 1943, Dwight D. Eisenhower was appointed as supreme commander of the Allied Expeditionary Force with overall responsibility for the projected cross-channel invasion of the European mainland.

Notwithstanding the methodical way in which the allies had executed their strategy and the bright prospects for ultimate success, all informed persons knew that the price of victory would be exceedingly high, with hundreds of thousands of young men slaughtered or savagely wounded, tens of thousands of civilians indiscriminately killed or maimed, and ancient cities, rich in cultural treasures, pounded to dust by the relentless power of modern warfare. Joseph Fielding Smith was among those who foresaw what lay ahead and who winced at the consequences. On January 1, 1944, as he looked back on 1943 and contemplated the future, his mood was subdued and melancholy. "The year which has just closed has not been a happy one," he wrote on that date. "The words of our Lord and his prophets are being fulfilled. Peace has been taken from the earth. Fifty years have passed since President Wilford Woodruff declared that the angels who were waiting to reap the earth had been loosed and sent on their mission. He declared that calamity, trouble and distress would increase in the earth; and this is to precede the coming of the Lord. Today war is raging in nearly all parts of the earth and the countries where open conflict is not found, the people are partakers of the effects of the war and are suffering. We have three of our boys out, Lewis far away, perhaps in Egypt at this writing; George Reynolds, in South America and Douglas in the army service in New York at present. We are praying that the Lord will protect our boys and all others who are serving him."

The terrors and dislocations of war did not, of course, suspend the routines and rhythms of Elder Smith's official and private lives. So, the weekend of January 9 and 10, 1944, found him in Spanish Fork, Utah, where he had been assigned to reorganize the stake presidency. His companion was Joseph L. Wirthlin, a counselor in the Presiding Bishopric. They followed the customary procedure, interviewing the local leaders to get their recommendations

about men whom they considered to be qualified to serve
as the stake president. This was neither a popularity contest nor an election since as often as not the one finally
selected was either not heavily recommended or was not
recommended at all. It was rather an essential part of the
process of selection through analysis and spiritual confirmation in cases where the new president had not previously been designated by direct revelation. Later as Elder
Smith and Bishop Wirthlin reflected and prayed, they were
impressed to call William J. O'Bryant as the new stake
president. They invited the candidate to the home of the
outgoing stake president, Henry Gardner, where they
were staying, and interviewed him at length about his
worthiness and other qualifications. By midnight on Saturday, Joseph Fielding and the bishop were satisfied they
had their man—but a problem remained: Brother O'Bryant
was employed by the Utah Idaho Sugar Company, and he
was "fearful he would be in trouble with his employer."
This fear was based on possible intrusion on his working
hours caused by his duties as the stake president. This
issue was easily resolved when Elder Smith called President J. Reuben Clark, who was on the board of the sugar
company, "who said go ahead." President O'Bryant's
counselors and new members of the high council were
interviewed and called between midnight Saturday and
the 2:00 P.M. Sunday afternoon session of the conference
when all were presented and sustained. Afterward, they
were set apart and blessed by the visitors.

"Most of these men are comparatively young," noted
Elder Smith. "We expect them to take hold and labor faithfully." With that, the visitors returned home, leaving the
new leaders in charge, responsible for the spiritual and
temporal welfare of several thousand Latter-day Saints.
No detailed instructions were given to the new leaders,
whom the visitors barely knew, if at all. Their understanding of what to do was based solely on what they had
observed their predecessors do, upon the scriptures, upon
written instructions in handbooks, and upon the inspira-

351

Joseph Fielding Smith

Joseph Fielding Smith

tion that would come to them as they struggled prayerfully to fulfill the mandate of the apostle.

Perhaps none of his contemporaries understood this procedure better than Joseph Fielding Smith. The son of a former president of the Church, grandson of the martyr Hyrum Smith, and great-grandson of the first Patriarch to the Church, Joseph had been raised from infancy with an understanding of the spiritual power that could be used in the management of his personal affairs, or, as at Spanish Fork in January 1944, in the management and direction of the Church.

While Joseph Fielding was fully conscious of his authority, he was always meek and mild mannered in exercising it. His character was devoid of arrogance, posturing, or self-importance. He never put on airs, never flaunted the prerogatives of his office, and never insisted on a strict observance of protocol. When, for instance, his bishop asked him to teach an MIA class, he responded

352

willingly: "At 7:45 I met with the MIA class in Garden Park Ward," he wrote on Tuesday, January 4, 1944, "where we had an interesting time in the study of the revelations in the Doctrine and Covenants. The class was well attended, altho there had been a recess over the holidays." This assignment from the leader of his ward continued for many months, even though it was a large ward with many able people who could have easily and effectively taught the class. Yet this senior apostle, who was heavily burdened with duties of worldwide scope, was humbly willing to accept an assignment from a subordinate Church official to teach a ward MIA class. And this was not an isolated case. Many times he acceded to requests to teach classes at the local level or to speak to small groups in a home setting. Such an instance occurred only two days before he taught the MIA class on January 4, 1944. "After the meeting [ward sacrament meeting]," he wrote that day, "I went to the home of Bro. Ted C. Jacobsen and met with a group of young people in a fireside chat, and answered their questions."

Some leaders are assiduous in teaching the families of others while neglecting their own. Joseph Fielding Smith could never be charged with that neglect. He seldom missed an opportunity to instruct and counsel members of his family, either individually or in a group setting. And after his children were married and out of the family home, he continued to call them together periodically to instruct and encourage them. "At night the members of my family assembled at my home in a study class," he recorded on Wednesday, January 12, 1944. "This we attempt to do each month, when other duties do not interfere. We cannot get them all together as some members are scattered." In this practice, Elder Smith emulated the example of his father, who followed a similar pattern.

While the continual round of church and family responsibilities were absorbing and enjoyable, Joseph could never quite elude the nagging worries generated by the war. And incidents of the kind reported on January 30,

1944, which occurred with ever greater frequency, removed the war from the realm of abstraction for Joseph
Fielding and invested it with a very personal and terrifying
aspect. "The morning papers," he recorded on that day,
"reported that word had been received that Heber J., son
of my brother Willard R., had been killed in action in
Germany, November 26th. The report that he was missing
was received shortly after the 26th of November and we
had hoped that he was a prisoner. This is one of the sad
things coming out of the war." As more relatives and
friends became fatalities of the conflict, young men of virtue and faith who were cut off in the prime of life, Elder
Smith seems to have reached an accommodation with the
idea that war, like the God he worshipped, was no respect-
er of persons. Once set upon its murderous course, war
was wholly indiscriminate, cutting down the righteous
with the unrighteous. While he did not articulate the idea,
his journal hints that for the first time he began to face the
reality that his sons were at great personal risk and might
not survive the war. Thus, it was with a sense of trepidation
that Joseph Fielding saw a third son, Reynolds, taken into
the armed services. "This morning at 6:45," he wrote on
May 15, 1944, "we took our son, George Reynolds, to the
Federal Building where he was taken into the navy. This
brought back memories of our other boys being taken from
us into the army. The world is in a frightful condition with
war and bloodshed because mankind is uncivilized and
cannot live in peace because of unrighteousness." The
morning after he had put Reynolds on the train to the
Naval Training Station in San Diego, the father wrote de-
jectedly: "I returned to the office filled with thoughts and
memories of departing boys." A few years later, after the
war had ended, Elder Smith elaborated on the feelings he
had had about his sons' service in the armed forces. "It is
a joy to be in the service of the Lord," he wrote to Milton
following his departure for the mission field in April 1947,
"but not in the service of his adversary, or be called upon
to contend by force of arms against the Lord's adversary.

354

We were very blue when we turned our boys in each instance over to Uncle Samuel, not knowing what the end would be, or whether they would return or not." Despite the uncertainties that faced his sons, Elder Smith retained a hope that they would be protected, which he nurtured up to the very day of Lewis's death.

Meanwhile, significant changes were being made in the organizations of the Church and in Elder Smith's responsibilities. At the April General Conference in 1944, Mark E. Petersen was called to fill the vacancy in the Twelve caused by the excommunication of Richard R. Lyman. The circumstances surrounding Elder Lyman's fall were most painful to all the members of the Twelve, but especially to Elder Smith and Elder Harold B. Lee, who had the unpleasant task of corroborating the facts that led to the excommunication. Elder Petersen was well known to Joseph Fielding and was a good friend who for many years had worked for the Deseret News. These two had much in common, sharing an interest in writing, a taut literary style, a conservative approach to interpreting the scriptures, and an outspoken opposition to transgression in all its forms. Neither ever pulled any punches in the pulpit. When either of them finished a sermon, no one who understood English should have had any doubt about the meaning of what was said. Still another link that bound them together was their wives, both of whom were fine musicians, Sister Emma Marr Petersen being a skillful organist and pianist.

Soon after Elder Petersen's call to the Twelve, Joseph Fielding received two special assignments that in the months to follow would occupy much of his time. The first was to give a series of Sunday evening sermons over the radio. Beginning in June, Elder Smith gave these sermons each week during the remainder of 1944. Because of the time required to prepare these talks and the need for him to be in Salt Lake City each Sunday evening, Joseph was excused from attending stake conferences during this period. He titled the series "The Restoration of All Things." The first sermon, "The Dispensation of the Fulness of

Times," was given on Sunday, June 4. Jessie and her brother, Thaddeus, sang. Richard Evans introduced the speaker and the music. The scope of the series gave Elder Smith wide latitude in selecting the weekly topics to be discussed. And the powerful transmitter of radio station KSL over which the talks were given gave the apostle a large audience to whom he expounded his views on subjects he considered of vital importance. Included among these were "The Testimony of Martyrdom," "Is the Canon of Scripture Full?" "The Restored Church," "A Voice from the Dead," "A Marvelous Work and a Wonder," "The Witnesses of the Book of Mormon," "A Witness against the World," "A Parallel Evidence" (dealing with Dr. William Paley's "Evidence of Christianity"), "The Redemption of Judah," "The Times of the Gentiles," "The Coming of Elijah," "Faith, the Foundation of All Righteousness," "Pedobaptism," "Salvation for the Dead," "The Eternal Marriage Covenant," and "The Resurrection." On his final broadcast given the last day of the year, Elder Smith's sermon was titled "A Closing Testimony." In conclusion, Jessie sang "The Lord's Prayer." The wide variety of these and other subjects suggests the gospel scholarship that was necessary to prepare them in such a short time. It was an extraordinary achievement, admired and appreciated by many who either wrote or called Elder Smith to express their thanks. The only comment he made about these was this terse entry: "I have received some favorable comments regarding my talks."

The other special assignment Elder Smith received during this period was to serve as chairman of the Committee on Publications. The other members of the committee were elders John A. Widtsoe and Harold B. Lee of the Twelve and Elder Marion G. Romney, assistant to the Twelve. At the same time, a "Reading Committee" was appointed which included Christian Jensen, chairman; A. Hamer Reiser, secretary; and these members: Daryl Chase, ElRey L. Christiansen, H. Aldous Dixon, Frank Evans, and George Q. Morris. Elder Smith explained that "these committees were appointed to pass on all literature of a religious nature to be used in texts for our schools, seminaries and auxiliaries." These were some of the forerunners of the present-day correlation and curriculum departments of the Church that branched off from the Department of Internal Communications in the 1970s. While the Reading Committee did most of the detailed work of reading and analyzing the various texts and manuals, still Elder Smith's Committee on Publications did some of this work in addition to setting the course and giving overall supervision. "At one P.M., I was with the Committee on Publications," he wrote on September 27, 1944, "reviewing manuscripts until 4:45 P.M. and at 8 P.M. addressed the teachers and ward officers of the 27th ward. In the meantime, I was examining manuscripts."

Three days later, Salt Lake City received its first good storm of the summer when it rained steadily all day. This was also the day of the first football game of the season for the University of Utah. Mit was a starter. It would have taken more than a steady rain to have kept sixty-eight-year-old Joseph Fielding Smith away from a game where one of his sons was playing. So he and Jessie took their umbrellas and other rain gear and sat in the open stadium for two and a half hours to watch Mit play. Even though he mildly berated himself for doing this, Elder Smith was obviously pleased to be there. He wrote, "Jessie and I (foolishly) went to the University of Utah Stadium to see a football game in which Milton played as quarterback. His team won." The final score and the identity of the opponent apparently were thought to be irrelevant as they did not rate a bare mention in the diary. Nor would it have seemed to make any difference to the father had the son's team lost. What was important was the boy and his self-perception, which doubtless was enhanced because his parents were willing to sit in the rain all afternoon merely to watch him play.

What applied to Milton applied equally to all of Elder Smith's children. He cherished them and held out high hopes for each of them. It was his unqualified love for them and his expectations for the future that made the events of December 29, 1944, so difficult to accept. Under that date Elder Smith made this sad entry: "My son Lewis W. was killed today in the service of his country. He was returning from an appointment which took him to India. He spent Christmas day in Bethlehem and from all we know was on his way back to his base somewhere in Western Africa when the plane crashed. We received word from the government January 2 at 5 P.M." Having recorded the bare facts of his son's death, the grieving father then offered this appraisal of him: "If Lewis ever did or said a mean thing, I never heard of it. His thoughts were pure as were his actions. He labored as a missionary in Switzerland from October 1937 to February 1940, returning to the United States March 4, 1940 with the last group of missionaries, accompanying Prest. Thomas E. McKay out of Europe because of the war. He was taken into the service of the army March 4, 1942. While the published article states that he was a staff-Sgt., he was actually serving and had been [serving] in the army intelligence."

The suddenness and finality of Lewis's death was shocking to Elder Smith. While he had reluctantly recognized that war tragically touches both the guilty and the innocent, he seems about to have persuaded himself that an exception would be made in his case. "This word came to us as a most severe shock," wrote the distraught father, "as we had high hopes that soon he would be back in the United States. We had felt that he would be protected as he has escaped several times before from danger. It was hard for us to realize that such a thing could happen."

Once the reality of what had happened was fully absorbed, Elder Smith quickly regained his composure and began to make a rational appraisal of the situation. "As severe as the blow is," he wrote philosophically, "we have the peace and happiness of knowing that he was clean and free from the vices so prevalent in the world and found in the army. He was true to his faith and is worthy of a glorious resurrection, when we shall be reunited again." These feelings about Lewis were confirmed by correspondence the father later received from some of his son's associates in the army. "We got further word about Lewis from one of his companions, Gene F. Walburn," Elder Smith wrote in a letter to Lois and her husband. "He gave us the information regarding the accident to the plane and said the bodies were taken to Maiduguri, Nigeria, and buried in a 'beautiful military cemetery' there. One thing that helps us is the fact that each of the men who has written to us has testified to Lewis' clean life, his high principles and his integrity to his principles. When each writes this way without any consultation, it is a great tribute to our boy, son and brother. . . . Such words as these are comforting, and each has testified in the same manner about him. The beautiful thing about it all is that it is so true. A better boy could not be found. A more worthy one could not be taken. We are sure that he was called to some other work on the other side."

Five years after Lewis was buried in Nigeria, his body was exhumed and sent to Salt Lake City, where it was interred in the family burial plot. Elder Smith explained what happened in a letter to Milton, who was then serving in the Argentine Mission: "Friday morning, December 2 [1949] the body arrived with an escort, a sergeant named Strange, [who] remained until the services were over. The same day we met in the Larkin Mortuary, the family and some friends, and had a prayer, Elder Richard L. Evans offering the prayer, and then we went to the cemetery. It was a beautiful day just like spring, and for this we were grateful. At the grave, Bishop Joseph W. Bambrough made a few remarks, also Richard Gunn who was with Lewis in India and the last member of the church to see him. Then Bruce [McConkie] made a very fine talk which was impressive. We had no singing. Uncle Roy Taylor dedicated the grave. Then the military honors were paid him according to the custom in the army, and we laid his body away. Now we feel much better knowing that it is here and we are happy because we know he was clean and was worthy in every respect and entitled to every blessing that can be obtained."

When Lewis was killed, Reynolds and Douglas were still in the armed forces, and their safety continued to be a matter of anxious concern to Elder Smith, who eagerly searched their censored letters for clues as to their whereabouts. He also traced with avid interest the progress of the war in both the European and Pacific theaters. In Europe, the German legions were slowly being crushed by the giant pincers of the allied and Soviet armies; and in the Pacific, the island-hopping campaign of the United States had been inexorably pushing the Japanese back toward their home islands. By April 1945, the Allied cause seemed invincible. The U.S. invasion of Okinawa, presumed to be the springboard for the final assault on Japan, appeared to be a success; and a feeler from Germany's Heinrich Himmler on April 23 for a negotiated surrender clearly presaged the end of Hitler's mad adventure. Two weeks later, at Reims, the German high command signed a formal document of surrender with American and British generals; it was confirmed two days later at a second ceremony attended by Russian commanders. These events touched off jubilant celebrations in Europe and the United States. And they infused the allies with great enthusiasm and urgency to bring the conflict in the Pacific to an end.

Meanwhile, on May 14, 1945, exactly a week after the ceremony of surrender at Reims, eighty-eight-year-old President Heber J. Grant quietly passed away. Thus ended the ministry of the Mormon prophet who had presided over the Church for twenty-six and a half years, longer than any other president except Brigham Young. At the time, George Albert Smith, president of the Quorum of the Twelve Apostles, was on a train traveling east toward New York City. In the early hours of May 15, a porter awakened President Smith to advise him that President Grant was dead. Leaving the train at the next stop, Buffalo, New York, George Albert Smith promptly arranged to return to Salt Lake City by train, there being no flight accommodations available.

Among the group that met President Smith's train upon its arrival in Salt Lake City were George F. Richards and Joseph Fielding Smith of the Twelve. Elder Richards, who, after President Grant's death, was second to George Albert Smith in apostolic seniority, would become the president of the Quorum of the Twelve Apostles in the new administration. And Joseph Fielding Smith would then become the second senior member of the Twelve, although he would be the fourth in apostolic seniority, being outranked not only by President George Albert Smith and George F. Richards but also by President David O. McKay, who would continue to serve in the First Presidency as second counselor. The special meeting of the Twelve Apostles where the reorganization took place was held in the upper room of the Salt Lake Temple on May 21, a week after President Grant's death. In addition to the changes already mentioned, at that meeting J. Reuben Clark was sustained and set apart as first counselor to President George Albert Smith in the First Presidency.

This reorganization had little effect on the duties and status of Elder Joseph Fielding Smith. It did, of course, bring him closer to the president of his quorum, so that on the occasions when Elder George F. Richards was out of town or indisposed, Elder Smith would preside. And there would be a greater inclination for the president of the Twelve to seek counsel from Elder Smith as the two of them sat side by side at quorum meetings.

The end of the war came with surprising speed. Less than three months after the death of President Heber J. Grant, the atomic bomb was dropped on Hiroshima. Three days later, a second atomic bomb was dropped, this one on Nagasaki; and suddenly the war was over. The night after Japan formally signed the papers of unconditional surrender, Joseph Fielding and Jessie hosted a dinner in their home. The guest of honor was President George Albert Smith. Other guests were elders Ezra Taft Benson and

President George Albert Smith

Mark E. Petersen of the Twelve and their wives. "A very pleasant evening," President George Albert Smith wrote of the occasion. There was good food, good conversation, and good entertainment. The latter, of course, was provided by Jessie, who sang, and Emma Marr Petersen, who played the piano. And everyone joined in the conversation. The end of the war and what that portended for the Church and for the world at large was undoubtedly the topic most frequently discussed. This could not have failed to remind Joseph Fielding and Jessie of their trying experiences in Europe at the outbreak of the war six years before. And the discussions about what lay in the future most assuredly did not include the key role Elder Benson would play in the revitalization of the Church and its members in Europe after the war. A few months after this dinner, President George Albert Smith appointed Elder Benson to spearhead the Church's efforts to help rehabilitate the Latter-day Saints in the war-torn countries there. Because the parents of Elder Mark E. Petersen were both born in Denmark, Elder Benson's experience in that country in the aftermath of the war sheds an interesting light on the composition of Joseph Fielding and Jessie's guest list at their dinner: "The welcome for the Apostle [Ezra Taft Benson] in Copenhagen was enthusiastic," wrote Elder Benson's biographer, Sheri L. Dew. "The people of Denmark had survived the war perhaps better than those of any other European nation. The Danish saints had even sent welfare packages to distressed Latter-day Saints in Holland and Norway. Membership had steadily increased and tithing receipts in the Danish Mission had more than doubled. Ezra was astounded at the faithfulness under the conditions. The Danish Saints considered their circumstances a direct fulfillment of a prophecy that Elder Joseph Fielding Smith had made at the outbreak of the war—that because Denmark had allowed missionaries being evacuated from Germany and Czechoslovakia to enter, its people would not suffer for lack of food during the war." (*Ezra Taft Benson*, p. 204.) With the end of the war, Elder Smith and his brethren were anxious to turn their attention and energies to the work of the Church in its various phases.

Chapter Twenty-one

Acting President
of the Twelve

In June 1945, the month after the death of President Heber J. Grant, Elder Joseph Fielding Smith was called as president of the Salt Lake Temple. He would serve in that position for four years. This call was the culmination of many years of activity directly or indirectly related to the temple and the sacred work performed in it. Indeed, it would not be too much of an exaggeration to say that his involvement with the temple commenced many years before it was completed and dedicated. At least, he played the role of a sidewalk superintendent during the later years of its construction. When Elder Smith was born in 1876, the walls of the temple were only about half completed. The huge granite blocks used in constructing the walls were taken from a quarry near the mouth of Little Cottonwood Canyon some twenty miles from the temple site. It was once planned to construct a canal connecting the quarry to the temple site with the idea of floating the granite blocks down on barges. This canal was partially completed when it was decided instead to construct a spur track to the quarry, after which the stone was transported to the temple site on flatcars. As a little boy, Joseph Fielding had watched this process, both at the quarry and on Temple Square. At the quarry, when it was cold, the stone blocks were split by drilling holes, pouring in water, and waiting for the expanding ice to do its job. In warm weather, explosives were used. At the temple site, the rough blocks were fashioned into shape by the stonemasons and then hoisted into place with winches. Judging from the frequency with which Elder Smith mentioned it in later years, watching this process had a profound impact upon him and kindled in his mind keen anticipation as to how the temple would appear when it was completed and as to the nature and significance of the sacred ordinances to be performed there. His curiosity about the appearance of the structure was satisfied in 1893 when it was completed and prepared for dedication. Although he had not received his own endowments at the time, he was allowed to inspect the interior of the temple before its dedication and to attend the dedication services during the first week of April 1893. There, as an interested and serious seventeen-year-old, he watched and listened as the president of the Church, Wilford Woodruff, read the dedicatory prayer. The incident was all the more impressive to him because seated at the left of the Prophet on the top level of the east stand of the temple's assembly room was his father, President Joseph F. Smith, Wilford Woodruff's second counselor. Also seated in the assembly room were twenty-five hundred other Latter-day Saints who showed their appreciation for the temple and their joy at its completion by joining in the Hosannah Shout and by singing "The Spirit of God Like a Fire Is Burning" at the end of the service. This song, which was composed especially for the dedication of the Kirtland Temple, had been sung as the climax of all temple dedication services held afterward. The song's lyrics and its stirring, almost militant, music, sung in the holy house under such circumstances, produced an emotional response seldom equalled in any other setting.

Joseph Fielding Smith would have to wait for several years after the dedication before being initiated into the sacred ordinances of the temple. Then he would make solemn covenants that would define and influence his conduct for the remainder of his days. The impact of the temple experience upon Elder Smith is suggested by his consistent practice, followed until the time of his death, of imploring God in prayer for help in keeping his covenants.

But while the symbolism of the holy endowment would be withheld from him for several years after the temple dedication, the visual symbols shown in the building itself were intriguing and significant to Joseph from the beginning. The representations of the heavenly bodies on the outer walls, the sun, the moon, and the stars, taught symbolically that there are gradations hereafter as there are here and implied that one's status in the future is governed by one's earthly conduct. Etched there, too, on the outer walls were the all-seeing eye, suggesting God's omniscience, and the clasped hands, suggesting the filial relationship between God and his children. Inside the building were other symbolic representations, paintings of the creation, of the Garden of Eden, and of the world of mortality. On the knobs of the doors were representations of the beehive, symbolizing industry. So much about this temple stirred the imagination and aroused the desire for improvement and achievement. Indeed, the thoughts and aspirations planted there intimated that human potential is nothing less than to become like God. Such is the exalted nature of the things taught in the temple that it is not uncommonly referred to as the University of the Lord.

Five years after his call to the Twelve, Elder Smith was appointed as a counselor to President Anthon H. Lund in the presidency of the Salt Lake Temple. He served in this position for twenty years, during the last part of which he was a counselor to President George F. Richards. There he learned all the procedures involved in the administration of temple work. When, therefore, he was called as the president of the temple in 1945, Joseph Fielding Smith was prepared for that service in every way. He was sixty-nine years old at the time and had served as a member of the Twelve for thirty-five years. He had about him a benign, patriarchal quality that was accentuated by his white hair and his placid, kindly disposition. Moreover, Elder Smith's profound understanding of the doctrines of the Church and the significance of the temple ordinances lent an unusual air of authority and conviction to the instruction he gave to the temple workers and patrons.

The successful supervision of a temple requires the combination of a variety of skills. There is the facility itself, an expensive, complex building whose equipment and fixtures must be constantly maintained and repaired. Then the furnishings, the carpets, the draperies, and the woodwork must be regularly cleaned. Also, there is the preparation and serving of meals to the workers and patrons, the laundering of the clothing needed for the temple ordinances, and the purchase of food and materials. While these physical elements connected with the operation of the temple are important, its most vital aspect is the sacred ordinances performed there. To administer them correctly and efficiently entails elaborate training and supervision. Hundreds of temple workers must be called and trained in their duties. Supervisors are appointed to oversee various aspects of the work. This includes not only the administration of the ordinances themselves but also the checking, recording, and summation of the work performed, whether for the living or the dead.

While many qualified people assisted Elder Smith in carrying on the work of the temple, the final responsibility for every aspect of it rested with him. He took the responsibility seriously and performed it with his customary thoroughness. He was constantly aware of every aspect of the work and was anxious to see that it was done in the right way. He was especially concerned that the ordinances were performed accurately, clearly, and with the reverence their sanctity required.

For these reasons, during the four years Joseph Fielding

Smith served as the president of the Salt Lake Temple, he was probably as busy as he was at any other time of his life. In addition to his work in the temple, he continued to serve in many other capacities connected with his apostolic calling. Among these was his work as president of the Genealogical Society, Church historian, chairman of the General Church Melchizedek Priesthood Committee, member of the Church Board of Education, member of the BYU Board of Trustees and Chairman of the Executive Committees of both of these, and also chairman of the Church Committee on Publications. And, of course, he continued to fulfill his responsibilities as a member of the Twelve, although because of his numerous other duties his assignments for stake conferences and mission tours were reduced.

During Elder Smith's tenure as the president of the Salt Lake Temple, he developed a closer relationship with the Genealogical Society, chiefly because he was the president of both. That relationship smoothed and expedited the processing of names for vicarious work in the temple. Joseph Fielding's connection with the Genealogical Society of Utah began in 1922 when he was named as the secretary and a director. Twelve years later, he became the president of the society, a position in which he served for thirty years. Ten years after Elder Smith became president of the Society, it was reincorporated as the Genealogical Society of The Church of Jesus Christ of Latter-day Saints. Also during Elder Smith's tenure as president, the society began its aggressive efforts to microfilm records throughout the world. When they were microfilmed, these records were catalogued and stored in Salt Lake City, where they were available to researchers who compiled the data necessary to have the vicarious work performed in the temple. L. Garrett Myers, one of President Smith's sons-in-law and a longtime superintendent in the Genealogical Society, described how the Society first became involved in microfilming records. (The superintendent gave a series of interviews conducted in 1976 by Bruce Blumell as part of the

James Moyle Oral History Program.) "When we first started microfilming," said Garrett Myers, "I took some of these samples to President Smith and he told me at that time that he thought that it was in our interest to continue with the microfilming and to find out all that we could about the possibilities of using the records in our library that had been photographed. He felt that we would have to wait until we could acquire some equipment that would enable us to read the small print on the microfilm without using a magnifying glass. He said, 'Keep abreast of everything that's going on in the world in that field. The Spirit of Elijah has rested down on record keepers to such an extent that I feel that we should take an advantage of their interest in the field and their willingness to cooperate with us and help us in acquiring records. I feel very earnestly that we should not neglect any avenue that could be followed to enhance our acquisition of these records that can be obtained through microfilming. If you want to you can write this in your little black book and you'll find that it will be true.' I said, 'I will never need to record that because I will never forget it.' I thought that it might be well to put it down somewhere." (Myers Interview, p. 60.)

The first large-scale microfilming project was undertaken in early court records in Tennessee. The procedure followed there was, with some variations, followed elsewhere. For the privilege of microfilming the records, the Church gave the government agency, free of charge, a copy of the microfilms the Church made. From Tennessee, the microfilming was extended into other southern states and into the eastern and New England states as well. After World War II ended, these operations were also extended to Great Britain, Holland, Switzerland, Italy, Germany, Finland, and the Scandinavian countries. Later still, the work was extended to many other foreign countries and other parts of the United States. While numerous microfilmers in the field did the actual work, the motivating force behind it, as Garrett Myers indicated, was Joseph Fielding Smith. "He was a man of great vision," said

George H. Fudge in his James Moyle oral interview. "When we were contemplating getting into microfilming back in 1938 . . . he could see the benefit of this microfilming and collecting records way back at that time. So it was men like Brother Joseph Fielding [who] have had a lot of vision." (Fudge Interview, p. 28.) George Fudge also reported how Elder Smith gave monetary support to this work in addition to the motivating impetus he provided: "President Smith . . . gave all of the royalties from the book, The Way to Perfection, to the Genealogical Society. That automatically came, and still does even now [as of January 1976]. I'm sure there are other books where he's done the same thing that I'm not aware of, but I do know that The Way to Perfection was one of those and we still get checks on a regular basis. He contributed some books originally to the Society, to the library. So he's been a great mover." Aside from the insight these statements give us into the behind-the-scenes impact of Elder Smith's leadership, they also throw light on his modesty. His diaries will be searched in vain for any reference to his philanthropies. He gave in silence with no expectation of receiving praise for his charity. It apparently was sufficient for him that he, the recipient, and the Lord knew. It is only from the reports of others that we learn about it.

These oral interviews by those who were most closely associated with him in the work of the Genealogical Society also reveal facets of Elder Smith's leadership style. Garrett Myers, for instance, reported on how Joseph Fielding first introduced him to his new associates as their superior. "He took me and introduced me to the members of the research department first and said, 'This is Garrett Myers. He'll be a sort of a straw boss in this institution.' And that's about all he said." (Myers Interview, p. 7.) Later, the superintendent was given the responsibility to take care of the records and finances of the society and described the way in which this delegation was made. "One day he [Elder Smith] came into my office," said Garrett Myers, "and he had his arms full of journals and check books and ledgers. He threw them down on my desk and said, 'I don't want to see these again' and walked out. He didn't say any more to me, I assumed from that he wanted me to take care of them which I did. I took care of them for four or five years." (Ibid., p. 39.) Elder Smith had the means to know whether the work was being done as he intended. Knowing the superintendent as he did, it was unnecessary to spend time in needless explanations.

This incident suggests another facet of Elder Smith's personality. "He was very closed mouthed," said Garrett Myers, "and never talked unless it was absolutely necessary. I've seen him in groups where . . . he'd wait for hours without saying a word unless it was specifically asked. If it was just a friendly gathering . . . he sat there and listened and never spoke." The apostle always lost this reticence when subjects of doctrine or the scriptures came into the conversation. Then he spoke out forcefully and, if need be, he would argue the point. "I know once or twice that President McKay questioned him. . . . Brother Smith said, 'No, President McKay, this is the way that it is.' " On one such occasion, Harold B. Lee, who was present, in confirming Elder Smith's statement is reported to have said, "Oh, that is a direct quote from the Doctrine and Covenants."

In giving his appraisal of Elder Smith's mentality, Garrett Myers said: "There wasn't a member of the General Authorities, in my opinion, that was his equal in knowledge and alertness. I would say that in front of any of the brethren. He had a mind as sharp as a razor." (Ibid., p. 41.) It was this aspect of his personality that, according to Garrett Myers, sometimes caused him to show irritation or impatience. "He was somewhat hasty and a little irritated when he had to listen to something he already knew well and it was clear to him." (Ibid.) He also commented about his father-in-law's punctuality and his penchant for hard work. "Brother Smith was punctual in every way," said he. "The Historian's Office was opened exactly at eight o'clock and it was closed at five — not one to thirty seconds

371

after five, but at five." And to illustrate the apostle's work habits, he told of an instance when he and a companion had an early morning appointment with him: "Just before eight o'clock we were ready to go into his office and he came out the door. We said, 'We came to fill our appointment with you. We've been waiting outside.' He said, 'Well, why didn't you come in when you first got here?' We said, 'We didn't know you were here. We didn't see you go in while we were here.' He said, 'I've been here since five o'clock. You could have come in any time after five and it would have been alright with me.'" (Ibid., p. 42.)

Elder Smith's heavy work schedule made long hours on the job an absolute necessity. Mention has already been made of the other duties he had during his tenure as the president of the Salt Lake Temple, including membership on the Board of Trustees of Brigham Young University and chairman of its Executive Committee. Joseph's first official connection with this board occurred when he was called to fill a vacancy caused by the death of his cousin John Henry Smith, who was a counselor in the First Presidency at the time of his death in October 1911. This began a sixty-year affiliation with this board that ended only with President Smith's death in July 1972. Following a major restructuring of the educational arm of the Church, Elder Smith became chairman of the Executive Committee of the BYU Board of Trustees on April 18, 1939. The other members of the Executive Committee were Elders Stephen L Richards, John A. Widtsoe, Joseph F. Merrill, Charles A. Callis, and Albert E. Bowen of the Twelve. Three of these, Stephen L Richards, Charles A. Callis, and Albert E. Bowen, were lawyers; the other two were professional educators, Elder Widtsoe having once served as the president of both Utah State University and the University of Utah, and Elder Merrill, one of the first Latter-day Saints to receive a Ph.D., once having served on the faculty of the University of Utah. Both Elder Widtsoe and Elder Merrill had once served as Church Commissioner of Education.

Despite the limited nature of his formal education, Elder Smith felt no sense of inferiority in directing the work of this key component of a major university. It was this committee that had the most direct and continuing contact with the president of the university and his staff and therefore was in the best position to exert a positive influence on the course the university would follow.

Through all the years of his affiliation with Brigham Young University, Joseph Fielding Smith took his responsibilities most seriously and discharged them with uncommon diligence. His participation in the meetings of the full board and the executive committee and the meetings of the BYU Board of Trustees and its executive committee was not perfunctory. He carefully studied the issues facing these bodies and brought to their meetings his best thinking, which he shared in his usual deliberate style. While he was impressed with the growth in size and reputation the institution had experienced since its beginnings, he foresaw a greatly expanded role for it in the future. And while he looked upon the temple as "the University of the Lord," he regarded Brigham Young University as "The Lord's University." Therefore, BYU was, in his view, entitled to the best of everything so it could take its place as one of the great universities of the world. His vision of its future was expressed in a letter he wrote to President Ernest L. Wilkinson on December 4, 1951. In it he expressed the expectation "to see Brigham Young University grow and become very great, with an expansion that will cover all fields that are of value to the members of the church, including, of course, the teaching of faith in God and in the mission of our Redeemer and also that of the Prophet Joseph Smith. I can see where this school can become a great power for good, not only to the members of the church but to all good people throughout the world." (Wilkinson papers.)

Elder Smith's role as a leader in the development of Brigham Young University casts him in a new light. From a strictly ecclesiastical point of view, he was perhaps more conservative than any of his brethren. His sermons were invariably grounded in the scriptures, whose precision and certainty, as he interpreted them, did not allow for any latitude in meaning. He was scornful of those who argued for a more liberal construction of the scriptures or who advocated policies or practices that deviated from the pattern of conduct established in the past. The notable exception to this attitude, of course, occurred in the case of the Patriarch, when President Grant made a change in established procedure through inspiration. In all other cases, however, Elder Smith insisted on a strict compliance with established procedure and norms. Yet, alongside that strict, conservative attitude in ecclesiastical matters was a creative, somewhat daring point of view in others. This side of Joseph Fielding Smith's personality was revealed repeatedly during the years he served as a leader of the Brigham Young University. A notable example was the construction of the physical science center on campus. Designed to house the departments of chemistry, physics, and geology, this 214-room building was to have more floor space than the total of the five largest academic buildings on campus at the time. It was intended to be a world-class science facility, incorporating the best of what Dean Carl F. Eyring (for whom the building was named), found in other similar facilities on campuses throughout the country. At the time this building was first proposed, it had a projected price tag of $250,000 to $300,000. By June 1946, when it came before the board for final vote, that had ballooned to $950,000. The actual cost turned out to be almost two million dollars. The enormous size and the cost of this building generated strong opposition from influential members of the board, who threatened the project. "But," it is reported, "Elder Joseph Fielding Smith, then chairman of the Executive Committee of the Board of Trustees, made a strong appeal on behalf of McDonald's proposal for the building." (*History of BYU*, 2:439.) Elder Smith's influence was a key factor in obtaining final approval for the project. The differences of opinion among members of the Board of Trustees of BYU over the construction of the physical science center reflected a basic difference in philosophy over the role of the university. One view, persistently advocated by Elder Joseph F. Merrill and others, was that the chief role of BYU was as a teachers' college to prepare students with bachelor's and master's degrees to teach in primary and secondary public schools and in Church seminaries and institutes. This group conceded that BYU might offer a doctorate in religious education but not in any other field. As already indicated, Joseph Fielding Smith and others held a different view, foreseeing that BYU would ultimately take its place as a major university, providing graduate training in many fields. So, those who advocated the first view saw no need for the kind of sophisticated, expensive physical science center that was finally approved.

Elder Smith was not always successful in winning support for his views and projects involving Church education. A notable example of a lost cause involved the proposal to establish a network of junior colleges that would become branches of Brigham Young University. This proposal was presented to the General Church Board of Education in the latter part of 1957. Spearheaded by Joseph Fielding Smith, chairman of the Executive Committee, with strong support from Presidents Stephen L Richards and J. Reuben Clark, counselors in the First Presidency, this proposal was approved by the board on December 6, 1957. At the same time, it was agreed that the enrollment at the university would be limited to a maximum of 15,000 students. The rationale supporting the proposal was that all students would receive religious instruction, that the teachers would not be restricted in teaching religious principles as they related to secular subjects, and that the distinctive qualities of Latter-day Saint culture could best be taught and preserved on the junior-college campuses. On the authority of that decision, the Church purchased about 1,650 acres of land in five states for a total of more than $8 million dollars as a preliminary to establishing a junior college

375

network. This included purchases in Salt Lake City, Utah; Idaho Falls, Idaho; the San Fernando Valley north of Los Angeles, California; Anaheim, California; Portland, Oregon; Fremont City, California, south of San Francisco; and Phoenix, Arizona. Meanwhile, there were discussions about purchasing other junior-college sites in the eastern and southern parts of the United States, in Mexico, and even in Europe. However, none of these was consummated.

It was the original intention that the junior colleges in the network would each have a maximum enrollment of 5,000 students. As the number of site purchases multiplied and as the costs mounted merely for the purchase of raw land, serious second thoughts began to assail some of the Brethren. Could the Church really afford to do this, notwithstanding the acknowledged advantages? The Church would not only become obligated to construct and continuously maintain costly facilities on these sites, but there would also be the even greater cost, in the long run, of paying the salaries of the administrative staff and the faculty required to operate them. Pointed to as a precedent was the decision in the 1930s, driven by financial considerations, to dispose of the Church academies, whose construction had been originally advocated by Karl G. Maeser of BYU. With this came a reemphasis of the idea that the seminary and institute program could provide many of the advantages of the junior colleges at far less cost. Moreover, those who opposed the plan for a network of junior colleges pointed to the rapid growth of the Church in outlying areas, particularly in the Latin American countries, and the impossibility of providing secular education for members in those areas and in other areas of potential growth. Taken together, these arguments became compelling as a matter of practical necessity. Under these circumstances, and with the intervening deaths of Presidents Stephen L Richards and J. Reuben Clark and the planned resignation of Ernest L. Wilkinson to run for the United States Senate (three of the strongest advocates of the junior college concept), Elder Smith joined with the other members of the General Church Board of Education Executive Committee in recommending abandonment of it. (Minutes of March 5, 1963.) The minutes spell out the rationale of the committee: "The cost would be prohibitive to furnish college work to all of the church . . . thinking of the thousands of our people in foreign countries who need the opportunity for education, and where our money for education could be more profitably spent in furthering the kingdom." The decision, therefore, was based on economics, not on any inferiority of the plan originally supported by Elder Smith. He was realist enough to know that sometimes there are good things we want but, at the moment, simply cannot afford.

Nevertheless, Elder Smith held firmly to the idea that BYU was designed to become one of the greatest institutions of higher learning in the world. (See Alumni Meeting Addendum, April 8, 1950, BYU Archives.) And he was prepared, therefore, to do all within his power and within reason to bring that about. So, in 1952, Elder Smith and the other members of the BYU Executive Committee recommended the immediate allocation of $500,000 for the acquisition of land around the university, notwithstanding the opposition of many who strongly opposed the expansion of the campus. Elder Smith sided with Elder Harold B. Lee, who was a member of his committee, who told Elder Smith at the time: "There are those who feel if we buy these properties, we'll never use them but are land grabbers. Others say that if we don't, we're short sighted. When the history of this school is written, I would rather go down as a land grabber." (*History of BYU,* 2:680.)

Elder Smith was a strong advocate of increasing opportunities for continuing education by adult Latter-day Saints. One way he did this was through sponsorship of off-campus centers directed by Brigham Young University. With the strong backing of the Executive Committee of the Church Board of Education, of which Elder Smith was chairman, Brigham Young University created four off-campus centers: the BYU–Ricks Center, the BYU–Ogden Center, the BYU–Salt Lake Center, and the BYU–California Center. The opening of these centers was usually announced to local priesthood leaders, stake presidents and bishops, in a letter from Elder Joseph Fielding Smith, acting as chairman of the Executive Committee of the General Church Board of Education. "This new service center," read the letter from Elder Smith about the opening of the BYU–Ogden Center, "is a forerunner of the type of adult education center which it is contemplated the Church Unified School System will organize in various places where there is a substantial church membership." (Ibid., 3:717.) When they were originally established in the 1950s, these BYU off-campus centers were intended to provide "audio-visual and other teaching aids, special lectures related to the fundamentals of the Gospel and other leadership training courses." (Ibid.) However, in 1969, Brigham Young University began a graduate program at the California center leading to a doctor's degree in education. Most of the credit leading to this degree could be obtained in local classes. Only limited residence work was required on the BYU Provo campus, which could be met by attending summer sessions.

Elder Joseph Fielding Smith was, of course, a strong advocate for higher education for the young as well as for older members of the Church. He demonstrated this not only by his long history of support as a member of the boards and as chairman of the executive committees of the Church Board of Education and the Board of Trustees of Brigham Young University but also by the example of his own family. He strongly encouraged his children to obtain higher education within the limits of their time and resources. And he was always very proud and supportive of his children in their quest for university training. In this we see not only a wise recognition of the worldly advantages of higher education but also an affirmance of his basic beliefs that the glory of God is intelligence and that

*Joseph Fielding Smith
at the office*

knowledge acquired during earth life will be useful in the hereafter.

Insofar as his schedule allowed, Elder Smith participated in the activities on campus, attending sporting and cultural events and joining in various ceremonials. He regularly attended graduation exercises and the related open houses sponsored by the president of the university. It was Joseph Fielding Smith who, in May 1950, turned the first shovelful of dirt for the construction of the George Albert Smith Fieldhouse. And it was he who dedicated the Harris Fine Arts Center and the Wilkinson Center on campus.

When BYU President Howard S. McDonald decided to accept the presidency of a college in Southern California, Elder Smith was appointed as the chairman of the search committee to find a successor. The result of that search was the recommendation that Ernest L. Wilkinson be appointed as the new president of Brigham Young University. While there were vast differences in the training, personality, and style of these two men, they were one in their vision of the potential of Brigham Young University, and they worked in tandem throughout the administration of President Wilkinson to help bring that about. They formed an interesting partnership. President Wilkinson was an aggressive, creative, and resourceful executive who had fixed ideas about what he wanted to do and boundless energy in pursuing them. But, as the president of BYU, he was working within a strict framework that he had never before had to deal with. As a highly successful attorney, it was unnecessary for him to consult with anyone other than himself to decide what to do or how to do it. At BYU, however, any major plan or proposal had to clear the Board of Trustees of the university, which was comprised of the First Presidency, designated members of the Twelve, and certain others. But, at the door to the board room stood the Executive Committee, whose chairman was Joseph Fielding Smith. It was this man, with forty years of experience as a member of the Twelve, who understood the ways, the wisdom, and the wariness of the hierarchy of the Church, who held the key to success of anything Ernest Wilkinson hoped to do as the president of Brigham Young University. Had not these two men shared the same vision, the history of BYU during Ernest Wilkinson's term as president would have been far different.

At the outset, President Wilkinson and Elder Smith had three main goals: to significantly increase the size of the student body; to expand the physical plant of the university to accommodate the increased enrollment; and to improve the status and qualifications of the faculty. The aggressive recruitment of potential students for BYU began in May 1951. This was the month following Elder Smith's designation as the president of the Quorum of the Twelve Apostles. In this capacity, he made the assignments to other General Authorities to attend stake conferences. Beginning in mid-May, he began assigning faculty members from BYU to accompany General Authorities to their conference assignments. This arrangement was continued from May to mid August, during which BYU faculty members participated in 179 conferences in stakes west of Denver, Colorado. At these conferences, the faculty members described the advantages of a BYU education and reviewed with prospective students the academic and cultural menu available there. This effort resulted in a 14-percent increase in enrollment, notwithstanding that most universities were then experiencing a decline in enrollment because of the Korean War. The following year, this recruitment program was discontinued because of complaints from other schools in Utah that its result was to reduce their own enrollment. However, with the unification of Church schools in 1953, the recruitment program was resumed but with a different format. At this time, faculty members from the eighteen institutes of the Church, Ricks College, and Brigham Young University accompanied General Authorities to stake conferences where Church members were made acquainted with the Unified Church School System and were encouraged to attend not only BYU but also Ricks College, LDS Business College, and LDS institutes and seminaries. This and other recruitment efforts produced remarkable results at Brigham Young University. Between 1951 and 1957, enrollment increased from 5,300 to 10,500.

The crush of the increased enrollment placed heavy pressure on housing accommodations, which resulted, during the following years, in the construction of Heritage Halls to house women students and Helaman Halls to house men students. Later, housing was provided for married students.

In 1953, a master plan for the physical development of the campus was cleared by Elder Smith's Executive Committee and approved by the Board of Trustees. In addition to the housing facilities already mentioned, this plan contemplated the construction of major academic buildings, which, in time, were completed. These included the Harvey Fletcher Engineering Building, the Student Service Center, the David O. McKay Building, the Benjamin Cluff

Jr. Botanical Laboratory Building, the Howard S. McDonald Student Health Center, and the Joseph F. Smith Family Living Center.

Four years later, a second master plan for buildings on the campus was cleared by Elder Smith's Executive Committee and approved by the Board of Trustees. Then followed another massive building program that created the BYU Motion Picture Studio, the J. Reuben Clark Library, the Jesse Knight Building, the William H. Snell Industrial Education Building, the Abraham O. Smoot Administration Building, the Alumni House, the Ernest L. Wilkinson Center, the Physical Plant Building, the Franklin S. Harris Fine Arts Center, Cougar Stadium, the Dairy Products Laboratory Building, and the Stephen L Richards Physical Education Building. Along with the construction of these and the other new buildings, a major landscaping project was undertaken to beautify the campus and to tie all its structures together into a unified whole. As the plant expanded, the student body grew apace, so that by the time Elder Smith completed his tenure as the chairman of the Executive Committee, it had expanded to more than 20,000; and one of his first acts after becoming president of the Church was to set a cap of 25,000 on BYU enrollment.

The two key figures in the phenomenal growth of the physical plant and the size of the student body of BYU, moving it toward the status of a major university, were Ernest L. Wilkinson and Joseph Fielding Smith. It was the university president who provided the essential executive drive to keep up the momentum, while Elder Smith, the wise and experienced apostle, skillfully navigated critical matters over the potential shoals of institutional opposition or inertia.

The third goal focused on at the beginning of the Wilkinson administration was to improve the status and qualifications of the faculty. An important preliminary step was the restructuring of the colleges at the university. At the beginning of the Wilkinson tenure, there were five colleges and the division of religion. At the end, there were thirteen undergraduate colleges and the graduate school. In the early years, Elder John A. Widtsoe played a key role on the Executive Committee in this restructuring, bringing into play his vast experience as a president of two universities. More important than this restructuring to the status and effectiveness of the university, however, was the recruitment and retention of qualified members of the faculty. Here, Elder Smith played a more active role. A root problem in recruitment and retention was the low salaries paid to faculty members. With the support of Elder Smith and the executive committee, significant increases in faculty salaries were obtained. Through 1960, for instance, overall salary increases totalled 62.4 percent, while the cost of living increased only 16.5 percent. Meanwhile, with an improved academic structure, increased salaries, and an expanding campus and student body, faculty recruitment picked up rapidly. Creative means were used to achieve it. A list of Latter-day Saint educators on university faculties around the country was prepared. From this, prospective new faculty members for BYU were identified, and aggressive efforts were made to recruit them. Even members of the Quorum of the Twelve became involved in this effort; they were asked to be alert to potential prospects as they attended stake conferences. Meanwhile, existing members of the faculty were encouraged to seek graduate degrees at prestigious universities and were given sabbatical leaves to accomplish this. As a result of these efforts, during the rapid growth of the university from 1951 to 1971, the full-time faculty grew from 244 to 932; and the number of faculty members with doctoral degrees increased from fifty to more than five hundred. The improvement in the university's academic and professional standing during this period is also suggested by the increase in the number of scholarly articles published by members of the faculty. In the academic year 1956–57, 72 were published compared to 292 in 1970–71.

When Elder Smith became president of the Church in 1970, he also became president of the Board of Trustees of

383

the Brigham Young University. While he had more authority over BYU as the Church president, he did not have the close relationship with it he had had while he was the chairman of the Executive Committee. Still, he retained a vital interest in the university and continued to participate in activities on the campus. On April 18, 1971, for instance, ninety-five-year-old President Smith addressed the first student-body devotional ever held in the Marriott Center. Over twelve thousand students gathered on that occasion to hear him speak. The occasion may have brought him nostalgic memories of the time, almost sixty years before, when he first became a member of the Board of Trustees. Then, BYU was only a small, obscure school housed in a few buildings below the crest of Temple Hill. Now on the hill was a sprawling campus with the largest full-time student body of any private university in the United States and a distinguished faculty to match. In this could be seen a partial fulfillment of the vision President Smith and many others had held of the future of the Brigham Young University, "The Lord's University."

On September 30, 1950, only nineteen days after Ernest Wilkinson accepted the presidency of BYU, Joseph Fielding Smith passed another milestone. On that date, he was formally sustained as acting president of the Quorum of the Twelve Apostles. Actually, he had been performing the duties of that office since the death of Elder George F. Richards on August 8, 1950. After Elder Richards's death, President David O. McKay ranked second in apostolic seniority. Ordinarily, he would then have become the active president of the Twelve. However, at the time, he was also the second counselor to President George Albert Smith. Therefore, President McKay assumed only a titular role as president of the Twelve, while the actual responsibility to perform the duties of that office was given to Elder Joseph Fielding Smith.

At the time, Elder Smith was seventy-four-years old. Behind him lay forty years of service as a member of the quorum he was now to direct. The duties of the office were

The Quorum of the Twelve Apostles, with Joseph Fielding Smith as president (seated, far left)

well defined, based upon revelations contained in the Doctrine and Covenants and upon experience gained since the first members of the Twelve were called in 1835. Actually, the revelation announcing the call of the Twelve was received in June 1829, about a year before the Church was formally organized. In it, the Twelve were identified as those "who shall desire to take upon them my name with full purpose of heart." (D&C 18:27.) Oliver Cowdery and David Whitmer were then designated to "search out the Twelve" who would have the requisite desire. (Ibid., verse 37.) Their main duty would be "to go into all the world to preach [the] gospel unto every creature." (Ibid., v. 28.) They were also empowered to ordain "evangelical ministers" or patriarchs, and to ordain all other officers of the Church (D&C 107:39, 58), "to open up the authority of [the Church] upon the four corners of the earth, and after that to send [the gospel] to every creature." (D&C 124:128.) Finally, the Twelve were designated as "special witnesses of the name of Christ in all the world," forming a "quorum equal in authority and power" to the First Presidency. (D&C 107:23–24.) Around these core responsibilities had gathered a host of other duties pertaining to the growth of the Church through missionary work and the direction of the Church and its members. On becoming the executive officer of the quorum, Elder Smith had, therefore, acquired vast authority to influence the Church and its members at all levels.

Those who were most directly affected by President Smith's leadership, the members of his quorum, were an unusual group of men. Next to him in seniority was Stephen L Richards, a distinguished lawyer who would later become President David O. McKay's first counselor in the First Presidency. Then came John A. Widtsoe, who, as already mentioned, had served as president of Utah State University and the University of Utah before his call to the Twelve. Joseph F. Merrill, as previously noted, was an educator. Albert E. Bowen, who sat next to Elder Merrill, was a brilliant lawyer, noted for his classic eloquence. Then followed a group of younger men who, in the years ahead, would exert a powerful influence on the growth and stability of the Church: Harold B. Lee, an educator and government leader who had played a key role in the development of the welfare program; Spencer W. Kimball, whose forte was his work and influence with those of Lamanite ancestry; Ezra Taft Benson, a nationally known agricultural executive; Mark E. Petersen, a newspaper editor and publisher; Matthew Cowley, a lawyer and electrifying speaker; Henry D. Moyle, another lawyer who had also become a wealthy businessman; and Delbert L. Stapley, the scion of a distinguished Arizona Mormon family who was called to the Twelve at the same time Joseph Fielding Smith became its acting president. It will be seen that among those whose work President Smith was to direct were three future presidents of the Church.

President Smith undertook his labors as presiding officer of the Twelve in the same spirit he had undertaken all other assignments he had received in the past. He approached it with a combination of faith, humility, and self-confidence. These qualities are embodied in this poem he composed, which was published in an article that announced his call as the acting president of the Twelve:

> By faith I walk on earth's broad plain,
> With hope forever in my breast;
> If valiant to the end I'll gain
> A glorious mansion with the blest.
>
> O Father, lead me by the hand,
> Protect me from the wicked here,
> And give me power that I may stand
> Entrenched in truth, to me made clear.
>
> The best is not too good for me
> That Heaven holds within its hand
> O may I falter not but see
> Thy kingdom come o'er all the land.
> (*Improvement Era*, April 1950, p. 317.)

Later, the other members of the Twelve lauded Elder Smith in a tribute that focused on the main qualities of his leadership and the guiding principles of his administration. They wrote: "We who labor in the Council of the Twelve under his leadership have occasion to glimpse the true solidity of his character. Daily we see continuing evidence of his understanding and thoughtful consideration of his fellow workers in making our assignments and in coordinating our efforts to the end that the work of the Lord might move forward. We only wish that the entire church could feel the tenderness of his soul and his great concern over the welfare of the unfortunate and those in distress. He loves all the saints and never ceases to pray for the sinner. With remarkable discernment, he seems to have but two measures in arriving at final decisions. What are the wishes of the First Presidency? Which is best for the kingdom of God? In his profound gospel writings and his theological dissertations, he has given to his associates and to the church a rich legacy which will immortalize his name among the faithful." (Ibid., July 1956, p. 495.)

Chapter Twenty-two

President of the Twelve

E lder Smith's tenure as acting president of the Twelve was short lived, lasting only six months. President George Albert Smith passed away on April 4, 1951, his eighty-first birthday. Five days later, David O. McKay was ordained as the ninth president of The Church of Jesus Christ of Latter-day Saints. In the upper room of the Salt Lake Temple, where the ordination took place, it was Joseph Fielding Smith who nominated Elder McKay to become the new president; and it was he who acted as voice in the ordination. During the same meeting, Elder Smith was sustained as the new president of the Twelve. Reciprocating the service he had rendered, President McKay then set Elder Smith apart.

The historic dimensions of this meeting were enlarged when President McKay selected J. Reuben Clark as his second counselor. Some were upset by this action, regarding it as a "demotion" since President Clark had served as first counselor to both Heber J. Grant and George Albert Smith for nearly two decades. During that time, David O. McKay had served as the second counselor. Typ-

Joseph Fielding Smith

*President David O.
McKay*

ically, Joseph Fielding Smith had nothing to say about the
incident. It seemingly was a matter of indifference to him.
His reaction would probably have been the same, even if
Elder Clark had been given no place at all in the new First
Presidency. The crucial thing was the desire of the new
Prophet. If, therefore, President David O. McKay wanted
J. Reuben Clark to serve as his second counselor, or not
to serve at all in the First Presidency, so be it.

It was during this period that the rich legacy of Elder
Smith's profound gospel writings and theological dissertations began to dawn on the general membership of the
Church. Over the years, Joseph Fielding Smith had built
up a vast body of doctrinal literature on almost every aspect
of the gospel. In his sermons, correspondence, books, and
column "Your Question," published for years in the *Im-*

provement Era, few if any gospel subjects had escaped his attention and his concise analysis and comment. However, these were so diffused over a period of forty years, in various places and at different times, that few really understood the significance of Elder Smith's achievement until they were gathered and arranged in a logical, meaningful pattern. This laborious project was undertaken by Elder Smith's son-in-law, Bruce R. McConkie, who was then a member of the First Council of the Seventy. Working early and late (during what his wife, Amelia, half jokingly calls "her" time) and in intervals between when he could squeeze out a few minutes for the task from his duties as a General Authority, Elder McConkie painstakingly knitted together a three-volume set of the sermons and writings of Joseph Fielding Smith entitled *Doctrines of Salvation.* The first volume, published in 1954, focused on the plan of salvation, including the Godhead, the premortal existence, the creation, the fall, the atonement, covenants, gospel dispensations, Joseph Smith and the Restoration, and the Church and kingdom of God on the earth. The second volume, published in 1955, was organized around the theme of salvation — "What it is; how to gain it; and the laws which pertain to it." Here are chapters about the three degrees of glory, exaltation, celestial marriage, salvation for the dead, and the resurrection. The third volume, published in 1956, treats a variety of subjects including priesthood organization, the scriptures, apostasy, the covenant race, the signs of the times, and the exodus of modern Israel. All these subjects are liberally documented with scriptural citations. And Elder Smith's treatment is phrased in his customary clear and concise style. Prepared with the object of clarity, not literary adornment, they represent a significant contribution to the doctrinal literature of the Church and doubtless will be one of the main things for which Elder Smith will be remembered by future generations.

During the compilation of these volumes a significant change was made in the organization of missionary work.

The modern revelations clearly designate the Twelve as the agency to direct the work of proselyting throughout the world. However, in 1951 when Elder Smith became the President of the Twelve, that responsibility had been divided among many different groups, in addition to the Twelve. These included the Radio, Publicity and Mission Literature Committee, the Mission Home Committee, the stake missionary programs under the direction of the First Council of the Seventy, the missionary appointment committee, and the Indian Relations Committee. To avoid overlapping duties and to streamline the work, in 1954 all authority and responsibility for missionary work throughout the world was placed under the Missionary Committee, comprised of the members of the Twelve, with Joseph Fielding Smith as chairman.

In this capacity Elder Smith embarked on an international tour during the following year. With him were Jessie, Herald Grant Heaton with his wife and baby, and eighteen missionaries. As the travelers sailed from the California coast in the fore part of July 1955, their ultimate destination was Tokyo, Japan. Their ship, the *President Wilson,* made its customary stop at Pearl Harbor, where stores were taken aboard and where some passengers left the ship and others boarded. This busy Hawaiian port, with its conglomeration of seagoing vessels — men of war, passenger ships like the *President Wilson,* tankers, and bulky cargo ships — reminded Joseph Fielding and Jessie of their honeymoon visit seventeen years before, which was three years prior to the Japanese attack on December 7, 1941. Mute evidence of that attack still remained in the harbor as a grim reminder of the shocking event that had thrust the United States into World War II and had instantly transformed Japan into a much-maligned enemy. In the meantime, however, the shifting tides of war and peace had worked another astonishing change, converting Japan into a friendly trading partner in the burgeoning world economy. With this change had also come a relaxed Japanese attitude toward occidental religions, with the result that the Church had begun an aggressive proselyting effort there with spectacular success. Thousands of native Japanese had joined the Church within just a few years as Mormon missionaries had traveled among the islands of Japan to preach the message of the restoration. Indeed, the growth had been so rapid that one of the chief purposes of President Smith's visit was to divide the Japanese Mission and reorganize proselyting work in the Far East. The apostle's traveling companion, Herald Grant Heaton, was to become the president of the new mission.

A few days after leaving Pearl Harbor, the passengers aboard the *President Wilson* joined in an impromptu celebration whose object was the Mormon apostle. The occasion was President Smith's seventy-ninth birthday on July 19, 1955. As the diners waited for their dessert that evening, an announcement came over the ship's intercom that it was the birthday of the distinguished passenger, Joseph Fielding Smith, president of the Quorum of the Twelve Apostles of The Church of Jesus Christ of Latter-day Saints. With a flourish and amid enthusiastic applause, waiters, dressed in Italian attire to carry out the Neapolitan theme of the evening, brought in a beautiful birthday cake and placed it on Elder Smith's table. Atop the cake was a single candle, which Joseph ceremoniously lit and then blew out as all the diners joined in singing the traditional "Happy Birthday."

Fortunately, the voyage from Oahu to Tokyo was on a placid sea that allowed outside activities — turns around the deck for exercise, shuffleboard or skeet shooting for diversion, and lounging in the deck chairs to read, visit, snooze, or meditate. Such a routine was calculated to ease away anxiety and produce a languid feeling of repose and well being. This interlude was a welcome change to Elder Smith, whose agenda was usually crammed with an unending series of meetings, interviews, and telephone calls, interspersed with study, research, and writing.

However, even here the apostle could not escape the mandate of his calling, even were he disposed to try to do so. Aboard was a new mission president and a corps of missionaries who would be looking to him for signals about how they should conduct themselves. Therefore, he was not off stage and never could be as long as the apostolic mantle rested on him. So, consistent with his customary habits of moderation and restraint, Elder Smith took his recreation in small doses. There was correspondence to handle, plans to formulate, diary entries to make, and talks to prepare. Moreover, there was counsel to give to the new mission president and questions to be answered for the eighteen missionaries, who likely felt a vicarious sense of self-importance at sharing a sea voyage with the president of the Quorum of the Twelve Apostles. And the diaries of most of them likely were lined with entries about the great man and the wisdom he imparted, entries that, in the years ahead, would provide many moments of quiet reflection and remembrance.

The *President Wilson* eased into Tokyo Bay on July 25, 1955. Waiting at the pier were Hilton A. Robertson, president of the Japanese Mission; his wife; elders from the mission office; and several members, including some U.S. military personnel stationed in Japan. After greetings all around and clearing customs, President and Sister Smith were driven to the mission home. When the travelers had regained their land legs and freshened up, they were feted at a reception where a group of Japanese singers provided the entertainment. As Jessie's reputation as a singer and entertainer had preceded her, she was invited to sing. The Japanese natives were surprised and pleased that one of her numbers was sung in their own language.

The apostle spent two days in the Tokyo area, visiting various army groups stationed there. The United States had maintained a significant military presence in Japan during the intervening decade since the war ended. Among these troops were many devoted Latter-day Saints who, imbued with missionary zeal, had played a key role in the growth of the Church in Japan. President Smith's purpose was to counsel and encourage these people. In the process, he was introduced to many nonmember army officials who received him cordially.

On the last day of his stay in Tokyo, Joseph was flown back to mission headquarters by helicopter after visiting an outlying military installation. This gave him an unusual view of Japan's sprawling capital city and its environs. From that vantage point, he saw how the Sumida River bisected Tokyo and how some of the numerous canals within the city formed concentric courses, enclosing small islands. On the innermost of these stood the imperial palace, enclosed by a high wall. Off to the southeast, seventy miles away, Mount Fuji, Japan's tallest mountain, could easily be seen.

Two days after arriving in Tokyo, Elder Smith traveled to Karuizawa for a conference attended by missionaries, service personnel, and other members. There, for three days, the visiting apostle directed a series of meetings to instruct and motivate those in attendance. During one of these, the congregation formally approved the division of the Japanese Mission to create the Northern Far East Mission, comprised of Japan, Korea, and Okinawa, and the Southern Far East Mission, comprised of Formosa, Hong Kong, the Philippine Islands, and Guam. Herald Grant Heaton was sustained as president of the Southern Mission, and Hilton A. Robertson was sustained as the president of the Northern Mission. Since all the members living in what was formerly the Japanese Mission were affected by this action, the division was presented for approval at all the other meetings held by Elder Smith during his tour of the area.

On Monday, August 1, the apostle and the two mission presidents, accompanied by Lt. Colonel Robert H. Slover and Captain Hildebrand, flew to Seoul, Korea. The next day, following a meeting with missionaries, service personnel, and Korean Saints, Elder Smith and a small group went to the top of a hill overlooking Seoul, the ancient capital of the kingdom of Chosen, where he dedicated the land of Korea for the preaching of the gospel. Jessie was unable to accompany her husband there. Nevertheless, she participated in this historic event vicariously. Unknown to President Smith, the American Army Officers had brought one of her recordings with them. Attaching a speaker to a nearby pole, they played her rendition of "The Heavens Were Opened" following the dedicatory prayer. "It was a thrill to hear her voice," wrote the apostle, "although she wasn't there."

By this symbolic act, the president of the Quorum of the Twelve Apostles formally introduced the restored gospel into a nation that for centuries had been dominated by beliefs in Buddhism and Confucianism. In not so long a time, the seed then planted would flourish in an extraordinary way among a people whose ancestral devotions produced a warm congeniality toward a religion that stressed the eternal significance of families. Within three decades, that seed would grow into a vigorous, thriving Latter-day Saint community comprised of many stakes and missions and with a beautiful temple in Seoul, where the Korean Saints could be linked to their ancestors in an eternal, binding chain.

Near the spot where President Smith offered the dedicatory prayer stood a monument erected in memory of those who had been killed in combat. Among these dead were many Americans, including some Mormon boys, whose blood had been spilled on foreign soil so far from home. It was a source of amazement to President Smith and his brethren that out of such tragic circumstances emerged a result wholly inconsistent with the carnage and destructions of war. For in Korea, as in Japan, the first baptisms of Korean Saints after World War II were performed because of proselyting carried on by Latter-day Saints in the armed forces of the United States. In Korea, that process began shortly after the end of the war in August 1945 when the U. S. Army's Seventy-seventh Division landed at Inchon, Korea, the port nearest Seoul. Latter-day Saint members of that division, and those who replaced them later as part of the army of occupation, lost little time in planting the seeds of the gospel among the Koreans. Several years later, the number of Latter-day Saint soldier-missionaries was greatly increased with the surprise landing of General Douglas MacArthur's army at that same port of Inchon during the Korean War. The landing was a surprise because there is a greater tidal fluctuation at Inchon than at any other major port in the world, creating large areas of mud flats during ebb tide. Therefore, seagoing ships must time their arrival and departure so as to avoid being left stranded on the mud flats that are exposed when the tide recedes.

These forces of occupation included many returned missionaries and other dedicated members of the Church, who missed few opportunities to share their religious convictions. The efforts of these industrious Saints created a primary base of Church members that was strengthened and built on when the Japanese Mission was created and full-time missionaries were sent to Korea. As Elder Smith divided that mission and formally dedicated Korea for the preaching of the gospel, he marveled at the phenomenal growth that had taken place and at the inscrutable ways of the Lord that had brought proselyting opportunity and success out of the chaos of war.

Leaving Seoul, President Smith and his party traveled to Munsani-ni, near the line of demarcation between South Korea and North Korea, where a special meeting was held. Then, going to Pusan via Seoul, he held a combined meeting with Korean members, service people, and missionaries. At both Seoul and Pusan, the apostle ordained priests and deacons so they could hold their meetings and administer the sacrament; and he set apart Dr. Kim Ho Jik, an elder, as the president of the Korean District, with Frederick Shumway, an American serviceman, and Houk Yung Gil, a native Korean, as counselors.

Returning to Japan, the apostle held additional meetings at Tokyo and Osaka, following which he flew to Okinawa. There, on Sunday, August 14, in the presence of a large group of members, Elder Smith dedicated this island for the preaching of the gospel. It was here that the last great battle of World War II was fought, a battle that involved many Latter-day Saints who were members of the armed forces, including five men who were unknown to each other at the time but who would later become General Authorities: Elders Neal A. Maxwell and Paul H. Dunn of the Seventy-seventh Division of the army, Elder H. Burke Peterson of the Corps of Engineers, and Elder Durrel A. Woolsey and the author, who were members of the amphibious forces. And involved directly or indirectly in that final battle were some Japanese or Okinawans who were not then members of the Church but who later joined. President Smith's dedication of this island for the preaching of the gospel took place ten years to the day after the surrender of Japan, and it served, in a sense, as a belated benediction to the bloody hostilities that had agitated much of the world for many years.

President Smith would perform two other dedications of "isles of the sea" during this tour. The first was the dedication of the Philippine Islands, which took place on Sunday, August 21, at a beautiful grove near Clark Field outside Manila. At the time, there were no known members of the Church in the Philippines other than the Americans who were there because of military obligations. The final dedication took place at the island of Guam on August 25 as President and Sister Smith were returning to the United States.

In reporting on this tour during the October General Conference, President Smith expressed his love for the new members of the Church whom he had met. And he paid a special tribute to the missionaries and to the Latter-day Saint service people who were stationed abroad. Of the latter, Elder Smith, quoting a nonmember chaplain, said, "I keep two of these young men of your faith with me all the time. If I lose one of them, if he is called away, I get another. . . . I keep them with me all the time because they are dependable." (*Improvement Era*, December 1955, p. 918.)

Elder Smith spent Monday, January 2, 1956, in a way sports fans around the world would applaud. "I remained home most of the day," he wrote, "and saw football games played in Miami, Florida; Dallas, Texas; and Los Angeles, California; also the parade at Pasadena. A very marvelous thing wherein we saw the plays of the teams clearly. "While intermittently sampling the contents of Jessie's refrigerator, the apostle also "entertained visitors during the day." Soon to be eighty years old and still in robust health, he enjoyed life to the fullest. His advancing age did not diminish in the least his interest in all that went on about him. Indeed, it was during this period that he developed an avid interest in flying—and not flying in commercial aircraft, which he had been doing for many years. He became interested in flying in the fastest, most modern military jets. His favorites were the Thunderbird and Sabre Jets. Typically, he referred to Thunderbirds as "T-Birds." Elder Smith was introduced to this unusual recreation by Colonel, later General, Alma G. Winn of the Utah National Guard, whom he had met through Jessie. When Elder Smith showed an interest in his work, Colonel Winn invited the apostle to take a spin with him. Joseph accepted with alacrity. His maiden flight was on June 9, 1954. "Colonel Alma Winn invited me to take a ride with him in a jet plane," he wrote on that day. "It was a wonderful experience to travel in such a plane at about 500 miles per hour." This was the beginning of a novel recreation that would continue until Joseph was almost ninety. Only two weeks after this first flight, Elder Smith went up again with Colonel Winn. "We could see in all directions," he wrote excitedly, "into Idaho, Wyoming, Nevada and as far south as lower Utah or beyond. It was a wonderful sight." Through Colonel Winn, Joseph Fielding also met General Maxwell E. Rich and Colonel Roland R. Wright of the Utah National Guard. These four men forged a fast friendship that centered around their shared interest in jet aircraft. On November 13, 1954, five months after his first flight in a T-bird, Elder Smith enjoyed an experience with these

Joseph Fielding Smith in the cockpit with Col. Alma G. Winn and Major Gen. Maxwell E. Rich

three that he recorded in language tinged with ecstasy: "This is my father's birthday," he wrote on that date. "I went up in a jet plane with Colonel Alma Winn; and General Maxwell Rich of the Utah National Guard [went] with Colonel Roland R. Wright in another plane. We pierced the dark heavy clouds up into the clear sunshine. It was the most beautiful scene I can remember, as the tops of the highest peaks penetrated the clouds like islands. The clouds on top were perfectly white [and those] below extremely dark, with some rain falling later."

The news of Elder Smith's avid interest in jets circulated around Church headquarters with lightning speed. Everyone was surprised; most seemed delighted; a few were probably envious; and at least one was appalled. That one was President J. Reuben Clark, who was obstinately opposed to flying and who used his considerable influence and authority to keep all his brethren out of the air. On

400

one notable occasion, following a meeting where it was decided that one of the brethren would fly to Washington, D.C., President Clark sought out the brother, who was one of his protégés, and said "Look, kid, you go by train." (As related to the author.) President Clark had flown in a plane only once, which was apparently enough to convince him that it was dangerous and not an acceptable way for him or anyone else to travel. So, when the president of the Twelve took up flying in jets, President Clark launched a campaign to get him to stop. While he was reluctant to order his apostolic senior, President Smith, to cease and desist as he had done with his protégé, President Clark hinted that he ought to give it up. It was then that Elder Smith sought to turn the tables and convince President Clark of the safety and the joys of jetting. How he did it remains a mystery, but two years after President Smith began to fly in jets, he persuaded President Clark to accompany him to the airport to at least check the plane out. He reported the results on June 15, 1956: "At the close of the board meeting [board of education]," wrote Elder Smith on that day, "Jessie and I took President J. Reuben Clark to the airport, where he was shown the workings of a jet plane; and then Col. Alma Winn took us for a ride . . . over the city. [It was] the 2nd time Prest. Clark was in a plane." A week later, Colonel Winn came to President Smith's office "with pictures of President Clark sitting in a saber-jet" which the two of them took to the president's office. He remained unconvinced. As far as is known, President Clark never again went up in a plane, carrying his aversion to flying to his grave. President Smith, on the other hand, continued to enjoy his hobby as often as he could find time to do so. On his eightieth birthday, July 19, 1956, for instance, the month after his abortive attempt to win over President Clark, he went for a long spin with Colonel Winn. With President Smith at the controls part of the time, the two friends flew south to Fish Lake, then north to the Utah-Idaho border and back again to the Salt Lake City airport. A week later, in a show of appreciation and friendship, Elder Smith invited his flying buddies to the Millcreek cabin. "In the canyon," he wrote on July 27. "We invited General Maxwell E. Rich, Colonel Alma G. Winn and Col. Roland Wright and their wives to come and have supper and spend the evening. They came at 6 P.M. and we had a very pleasant evening together. This is the last day we can spend in the canyon this summer." And on Labor Day, September 3, Elder Smith and Jessie accompanied General Rich and Colonel Winn to inspect the Utah National Guard base at Camp Williams, south of Salt Lake City. Six years later, August 17, 1962, at a special program held at Camp Williams, President Joseph Fielding Smith received the honorary rank of brigadier general in the Utah National Guard and was given a general's uniform as a surprise. And in 1964, the eighty-eight-year-old apostle was given the Minuteman Award in recognition of his support of the National Guard. Over the years, he had intermittently delivered sermons at their Sunday worship services.

While Elder Smith's enthusiasm for flying never diminished, he unaccountably took a dim view of space travel. During a stake conference held in Tulsa, Oklahoma, on May 1 and 2, 1962, a reporter questioned him about the plans of the United States to put a man on the moon. "I answered that they might, but evidently if so he might have difficulty to get back again." This comment was picked up and reported by the national wire services, producing a wholly unexpected reaction. "I am flooded by letters in relation to it," wrote the apostle, "with some editorial criticism." Although he never answered publicly, he confided this response to his diary: "The fact is . . . mortal man has no business trying to get on the moon, for earth is a probationary state and in mortality we are expected [to stay on] this earth." Elder Smith never attempted to reconcile the inconsistency of that view with his carefree enjoyment in flying at 30,000 feet above the planet in a sabre jet. Undoubtedly, President J. Reuben

Clark would have immensely enjoyed his attempts to do so.

Elder Smith's periodic flights with his military friends provided an important diversion from the grinding schedule he maintained as the president of the Twelve. Despite his advancing age and the prerogatives he enjoyed in directing the work of his quorum, he insisted on fulfilling his share of stake conference assignments. So, during the first half of 1956, the year when he celebrated his eightieth birthday, he presided at conferences in the Denver, Colorado; Long Beach, California; Ogden, Utah; North Rexburg, Idaho; North Sacramento, California; Hurricane, Utah; Mount Pleasant, Utah; Burley, Idaho; Seattle, Washington; Santa Barbara, California; Palmyra, Utah; and St. George, Utah. On average, this octogenarian was on the road every other week during this period. And, some of the trips were long and tiring as was the trip to Seattle, Washington, on the weekend of May 19 and 20. It was necessary for him to leave Friday evening, May 18, to accommodate a tight travel schedule. He arrived in Seattle at 1:00 P.M. Saturday in time to commence a series of meetings that afternoon and evening, including meetings with stake missionaries, the stake presidency, welfare workers, and priesthood leaders. This last meeting ended at 9:30 P.M., although he was not in bed until almost 11:00. Early the next morning, he held a special meeting with the stake presidency, high council, and bishoprics. He "talked to them on several matters, including moral conditions." Then followed general sessions at 10:00 A.M. and 2:00 P.M., after which he ordained and set apart three bishops, set apart eleven counselors in bishoprics, set apart new counselors in the stake mission presidency, and ordained six seventies. He was on the train all day Monday, arriving home at 10:25 P.M. Then at 7:30 the following morning, Tuesday, May 22, he attended a missionary committee meeting. Considering that Elder Smith was then fifteen years beyond the normal retirement age and that this was but one thread in a complicated fabric of activity, one sen-

ses the enormous reservoir of self-discipline and drive necessary to propel him forward from day to day. What he
did, of course, was typical of other General Authorities,
whose schedules were equally overcrowded. The wife of
one of the Brethren, seeing this for the first time at close
range, said half in jest and half seriously, "If the job description of a general authority were published in the help
wanted section of the classified ads, there would be no
applicants."

But, there were many compensations that made Elder
Smith's life and ministry full and satisfying. Not the least
of these was the joy he experienced in regularly meeting
with his Brethren in the upper room of the Salt Lake
Temple. Here on most Thursdays he could be found with
the First Presidency and the Twelve, counseling together
about worldwide interests of the Church, bearing testimony, and renewing their covenants of apostolic responsibility. And twice each year, he joined with his Brethren
and with leaders and members from around the world in
the general conferences. Here he was not only involved
in speaking in the general sessions but also in giving instructions to special leaders in attendance; to mission,
stake, and temple presidents; and to patriarchs. President
Smith had special responsibility as to the patriarchs since
they reported directly to him. He was painstakingly careful
about preparing for the general conferences, devoting special attention to the talks he delivered, knowing that unlike
stake conference talks, they would be recorded and preserved as a permanent record, available for review into the
indefinite future, perhaps for all time. He especially
wanted his testimony to be preserved for future generations so that they would know that he knew that the gospel
is, indeed, true. Of all the testimonies he bore during the
sixty years of his apostolic ministry, none was more complete and moving than the one he bore during the April
1956 general conference, five years after he became president of the Twelve. "This afternoon I wish to bear testimony to the restoration of the gospel," he said on Saturday

afternoon, April 7, "to the mission of our Redeemer, to the call of the Prophet Joseph Smith and the establishment of this work in the dispensation in which we live, known as the Dispensation of the Fulness of Times. I know absolutely that Jesus Christ is the only Begotten Son of God, the Redeemer of the world, the Savior of men insofar as they will repent of their sins and accept the gospel. Through his death he redeemed all men and took upon him that sacrifice which would relieve us of our sins that we may not answer for them if we will accept him and be true and faithful to his teachings. I am just as fully satisfied, because I know, that the Father and the Son appeared to Joseph Smith and revealed to him the great truth which had been lost because of the wickedness of the world; that they are separate distinct personages; that the Father and the Son, together with the Holy Ghost, constitute the Godhead, the great ruling power of the universe; that Jesus Christ volunteered to come into this world to redeem it; that John the Baptist came to the Prophet, as did Moroni before him, and Peter, James and John later, to give authority and to usher in the Kingdom of God anew in this dispensation in which we live, because men had turned away from the truth. . . . I am grateful for my membership in the Church, for the opportunity that has been mine to serve. My desire is to prove true and faithful to the end." (*Conference Report,* April 1956, pp. 58–59.) The expressions of gratitude and desire with which he ended this testimony are keystones in understanding the character of President Joseph Fielding Smith. To him, Church membership signified that he had taken upon himself the name of Jesus Christ, his King and Redeemer. And the "opportunity" to serve others was simply a means of demonstrating love and appreciation for his Savior. The desire "to prove true and faithful" was undoubtedly a chief force in motivating him to stay at his task from day to day. So frequently did President Smith express this desire, in his sermons, prayers, and daily conversation, that it became almost a motto for him. Indeed, his grandson Joseph F. McConkie used

Joseph Fielding Smith at the pulpit

it as the title for the biographical sketch he wrote of his grandfather. One need only look at his life in its totality to see how this prophet lived up to the demanding standard he had set for himself.

The last six months of 1956 were a repetition of the first six. They consisted of an unbroken chain of meetings, trips, and family duties, interspersed with some recreation. During the summer break, he and members of the family were able to use to good advantage the two spectator chairs he had received as a Father's Day gift. "Accompanied Milton to the softball park," he noted on August 21. "I was supposed to throw out the first ball, but meetings interfered and I was late." The night before, Elder Smith had attended a banquet for all the ball players where he "received a trophy for past interest in the encouragement in sports by the youth of the Church." Earlier in the summer, the apostle had dedicated the all-Church softball park on Second West and Twentieth South in Salt Lake City. Also during the break, he and Jessie had accompanied Richard and Alice Evans to the Lagoon amusement park for the annual outing of the members of the Tabernacle Choir and their partners. And, he and Jessie had been the guests of President David O. McKay in attending the premier showing of Cecil B. DeMille's *The Ten Commandments*. He called it "the most wonderful, magnificent performance I have ever seen."

President Smith ended the summer break by attending conference in Duchesne, Utah. "Conditions financially are poor, but people happy," he wrote. "Some of them, however, need repentance. I preached the Gospel to them, and stressed their duties." President Smith was never reluctant to speak his mind and to call people to repentance, if he felt they needed it. This caused some to bridle at his preaching. Soon after Joseph Fielding Smith became president of the Twelve, Elder Spencer W. Kimball wrote to his wife from Canada to say a bishop in Lethbridge had complained that "he talks like Joseph Fielding Smith and I don't like it." Elder Kimball than commented about those who have "itching ears," adding that he was proud to be thought "a sitter at the feet of President Joseph Fielding Smith." (Edward L. Kimball and Andrew E. Kimball, Jr., *Spencer W. Kimball*, p. 279.)

In the waning months of 1956, members of the Church in the Montpelier, Highland, Yellowstone, Fillmore, and West Jordan stakes had the opportunity to hear the straightforward, unadorned preaching of the eighty-year-old president of the Twelve. And in between these conferences, he participated in another general conference where he was equally forthright in instructing the general membership in their duties and about the consequences of their failure to perform them.

While President Smith enjoyed every aspect of his work, attending stake conferences, mission tours, general conferences, and fulfilling his headquarters assignments, his work in the temple seemed to be the most satisfying of all. The quiet dignity of the building in which were performed the most sacred and solemn ordinances seemed most congenial to his personality and character. Because of this, he and Sister Smith were especially pleased to be invited to attend the dedication of the Los Angeles Temple in March 1956. They left Salt Lake City by train Thursday night, March 8, with other General Authorities and their wives. Arriving in Los Angeles Friday morning, they barely had time to check into the hotel before attending a luncheon with President and Sister McKay hosted by leaders of the Los Angeles Chamber of Commerce. At the same time, other of the Brethren and their wives attended a luncheon hosted by the Los Angeles Rotary Club. By this means the city leaders expressed appreciation for the magnificent building that had been constructed on Santa Monica Boulevard on the former estate of movie star Harold Lloyd. The site had been purchased in 1937 during the administration of President Heber J. Grant. Work on the building was delayed until 1951, when, in September, five months after he became the president of the Church, President David O. McKay broke ground for the building and dedicated the site. As the construction proceeded during the ensuing five years, all Los Angeles had watched with interest as the distinctive building took shape atop a hill near Westwood Village, two miles west of Beverly Hills. When the main tower topped out at over two hundred and fifty feet, the temple was visible for miles around to residents of the most exclusive areas of the sprawling city. And the thousands of motorists who daily streamed by on Santa Monica Boulevard had come to assume a somewhat proprietary attitude toward the sacred building, which ultimately covered almost four and a half acres of the thirteen-acre site. When at last a fifteen-and-a-half-foot gold-leaf–covered statue of the Angel Moroni was put in place on the pinnacle of the main tower and graceful palm trees were planted on top of the lower levels of the building, the temple, with its carefully manicured grounds, indeed became an object of civic pride. In token of this, over 700,000 visitors were ushered through the building during a two-month period preceding the dedication. And the already mentioned luncheons, hosted by the city's leaders, demonstrated dramatically that the Latter-day Saints and their beautiful temple were welcome.

As the second-ranking apostle in attendance, and having served for many years as a counselor or as president of the Salt Lake Temple, President Smith played a key role in the dedication proceedings. He and Sister Smith attended all eight of the dedicatory sessions held over a period of four days, March 11 to 14. And he spoke at the Sunday and Tuesday afternoon sessions, dwelling on the eternal impact of the sacred ordinances to be performed in the temple. Because of his superior scriptural knowledge and his extensive experience in temple administration, President Smith, perhaps more than anyone else present, grasped the deeper significance and importance of the building and of the occasion that had drawn him there.

These services could not have failed to remind President Smith of the circumstances surrounding the death of his fellow apostle Matthew Cowley. In December 1953, the First Presidency and the Twelve and their companions had traveled to Los Angeles to attend the cornerstone-laying ceremonies of the temple. On Saturday, December 12, the day after the ceremony, President Smith had said goodbye to Elder Cowley, who intended to remain in California for a few days. The next morning, Sunday, December 13, 1953, Elder Cowley died peacefully in his sleep at about 4:45 A.M. He was only fifty-six years old, twenty-one years younger than the president of his quorum. The following April, the vacancy in the Twelve caused by Elder Cowley's death was filled by eighty-year-old George Q. Morris, who was two years older than President Smith. The combined apostolic service of these two brethren totaled only sixteen years, compared to the sixty years served by President Smith, all of which emphasizes the irregular patterns seen in the times of call and terms of service of members of the quorum over which Joseph Fielding Smith now presided.

Two years after the temple dedication in Los Angeles, President and Sister Smith traveled to England to participate in the dedication of the London Temple. They left

409

Salt Lake City by plane on Tuesday, September 2, 1958. To break up the long trip and to minimize the jet lag, they decided to stay overnight in New York City. Waiting to meet them at New York's La Guardia Airport were Eastern States Mission president Theodore Jacobsen and his wife, Florence, who was President Smith's niece, a daughter of Willard Smith, President Smith's brother. The travelers were driven to the Plaza Hotel by President and Sister Jacobsen; there they spent the night. The following afternoon, the Jacobsens again chauffeured President and Sister Smith, driving them to La Guardia, where they caught a transcontinental flight destined for London. There was an intermediate stop in Shannon, Ireland, where they had breakfast, before flying on to Heathrow Airport in London. From Heathrow, they were driven to the Grosvenor Hotel, which would be their headquarters for the next six days.

Also staying at the Grosvenor were President and Sister David O. McKay. Other members of the official party included elders Henry D. Moyle, Richard L. Evans, and Hugh B. Brown of the Twelve; Elder Gordon B. Hinckley, assistant to the Twelve; and Bishop Thorpe B. Isaacson of the Presiding Bishopric. Elder Hinckley, who had been sustained as an assistant to the Twelve at the previous April General Conference, had arrived in London earlier in order to coordinate the final arrangements for the dedication.

Unlike the Los Angeles Temple, which is located in the midst of a bustling urban neighborhood, the London Temple is located on the outskirts of the city in a rural setting. On Friday afternoon, September 5, President and Sister Smith accompanied some of the other visitors to the temple for a final inspection tour before the dedication, which was scheduled to commence the following Sunday. There they visited the various rooms of the temple, which were receiving a final cleanup following the open house, which had ended only two days before and during which more than 75,000 guests were shown through the building.

Being only one-sixth its size, the London Temple was

dwarfed by the one at Los Angeles. However, the picturesque setting of this building, on a thirty-two-acre site amid
ancient English farming lands, gave it a special rural charm
that the Los Angeles Temple could not match. Inside the
building, the visitors found the same quiet peace and dignity that typify all temples, along with the symbolic trap-
pings that distinctively set them apart from all other earthly
buildings.

The dedicatory services, presided over by President
David O. McKay, commenced on Sunday, September 7,
1958, and continued through Tuesday, September 9, with
two sessions each day. President Smith was again specially
recognized, speaking at sessions on both Sunday and Monday. As always, the conclusion of each session produced
an extraordinary emotional response as those in attendance
joined with the choir in singing "The Spirit of God Like a
Fire Is Burning."

The morning after the last dedicatory session, Brother
and Sister Smith flew out of London, destined for Zurich,
Switzerland. The President left with a heavy heart. In meetings with the European mission presidents held before the
temple dedication, it was reported that several missionaries
in the French Mission were in apostasy. President Smith,
as chairman of the missionary committee, assigned Elder
Henry D. Moyle to look into the matter and to give direction
to the mission president. As a result, several missionaries
were excommunicated. The anguish this brought to the
missionaries and their families and the setback to the work
in France were matters of grave concern to President Smith.
The cause of the difficulty—the failure to stay close to the
mandates of the scriptures and to follow priesthood direction—confirmed the validity of the counsel the president of the Twelve had repeatedly given throughout his
ministry. But this could not allay the dreary feelings the
incident aroused.

Elder Smith's spirits began to revive on reaching Switzerland. He and Jessie were met at the Zurich Airport by
mission president Jesse R. Curtis and were driven directly

411

to Bern. That evening, Wednesday, September 10, a meeting was held in Bern with missionaries of the Swiss-Austrian mission. A principal reason for President Smith's revived spirits can be inferred from this diary entry for that day: "Here we had the privilege of seeing our grandson, Douglas Myers, who is a very successful missionary, at present laboring in Vienna."

The following day, the apostle spent several hours in the temple at Bern, giving counsel to the temple presidency, who, after three years since the temple dedication in 1955, were now well schooled in temple administration but who still had many questions to ask President Smith. He answered all of them patiently and at length, making sure the temple presidency fully understood. There was no work in the Church more fraught with eternal significance than the work in the temple, and President Smith and all his brethren were doubly anxious that it be performed in the right way and with the right spirit.

At Jessie's persistent and good-natured urging, President Smith agreed the following day to accompany a group to a resort high in the mountains, where they had a pleasant lunch while admiring the rugged landscape, punctuated by the towering, jagged peaks of the Alps. His reluctance to go stemmed from a concern that any missionaries who might learn of the outing would take license from it to use their time sightseeing instead of proselyting. Of course, he was acutely conscious of the occasion during his mission to England when he and a group of missionaries had toured on the continent while visiting the World Fair in Paris. Yet, he knew also that many of the philosophies of missionary work had changed during the intervening half century and that now such activities were frowned upon. But, the apostle's concerns were overridden by a desire to accommodate the legitimate wishes of his wife. So, he went along, although it is safe to assume that he did not do so with any great enthusiasm.

The following day, the Smiths accompanied President and Sister Curtis to Basil, where the mission home was located. Visiting this place evoked a flood of memories, for it was here, nineteen years earlier, before the war broke out, that they had visited with their son Lewis and President and Sister Thomas E. McKay. Now, both President McKay and Lewis were gone, the former having passed away only nine months before.

The travelers spent two days in Basil, during which Elder Smith counseled with the mission president and held meetings with the missionaries and local members and leaders. They were driven to Zurich on Tuesday, September 16, and caught a plane to London. There, on the same day, President Smith formally dedicated the London Mission Home. Present, in addition to the mission president, his wife, and the mission staff, was Elder Henry D. Moyle, who had just returned from Paris.

On Tuesday, September 18, Elder and Sister Smith traveled from London to Southampton by train and boarded the *Queen Elizabeth* for the return voyage to the United States. This floating hotel, which was almost as long as two of Salt Lake City's blocks, was the largest and most luxurious of the superliners of the Cunard-White Star Line. It had been completed in 1940 as a troop ship but after the war had been fitted out as a cruiser, capable of accommodating almost twenty-three hundred passengers in complete comfort.

The five-day voyage to New York City was typical for the Atlantic. "Stormy day," the apostle noted on Sunday the 21st, three days out of Southampton. Earlier that day, he had held a worship service with several missionaries and other members who were aboard. The next day, he followed up with another meeting, attended only by the missionaries. "Many questions asked," Elder Smith reported. Aside from these meetings, "reading and watching the ocean" were the main activities of the Smiths during the voyage. "We took no part in the sports and other entertainments," the apostle explained. "Horse racing with dice and other games of chance are the chief amusements." After watching these a time or two as he passed by, Elder Smith noted suspiciously, "In these games, I noticed that the ship's officers always won."

The *Queen Elizabeth* berthed majestically at the New York waterfront on Tuesday afternoon, September 23, amid the customary confusion. On the pier to greet the travelers were President and Sister Jacobsen. Spotting them there and waving, the Smiths expected to join them promptly since their luggage consisted only of two suitcases, which they carried with them. But, it took more than an hour to clear customs. President Smith was obviously irked. "I never before saw so much confusion and lack of order at any port in Europe or elsewhere than we had here in New York," he wrote with complete candor. "After our cases were checked and I passed through the gate, I was called back and made to try it over the second time." The eighty-two-year-old traveler would likely have let the incident pass without comment were it not that after going through the procedure twice, he was stopped again. The watch he was wearing had set off the metal detection device at the final check point.

Once the hassle with customs was over, things took on a rosier hue. The Jacobsens drove their guests to the mission home, where a warm meal and relaxed conversation awaited them. President Smith was obviously proud of this niece and her husband. Three years after this visit in New York, Florence Smith Jacobsen would be called as the general president of the Young Women's Mutual Improvement Association and would serve in that position until November 1972, four months after President Joseph Fielding Smith's death. Thus, during the entire period of his presidency, his brother Willard's daughter would lead all of the young women of the Church.

Back in Salt Lake City, President Smith resumed his headquarters duties, but not for long. After participating in the October 1958 General Conference, he began preparing for a trip into the Pacific. By mid November, everything was ready. On Saturday evening, the 15th, he and Jessie were driven to the Salt Lake City Airport over streets

414

filled with slush from a mid-autumn storm that had deposited several inches of snow on the valley during the day. The conditions at the airport were good, however, with the runways cleared of the slush and with sufficient visibility to enable their plane to San Francisco to land and take off. They were met at the San Francisco International Airport by J. Leonard Love, president of the Northern California Mission, who drove them to the mission home. Here they spent the night. "We had a very pleasant visit at the home," noted the apostle. The Loves were friends of long standing. Trading on that friendship, Leonard Love had persuaded Elder Smith in the mid thirties to dedicate the Yalecrest Ward chapel in the Bonneville Stake, where he then served as bishop. A memento of that occasion, a large Bible autographed by Joseph Fielding Smith, had graced the Yalecrest Ward pulpit ever since then. This and other shared experiences had bound these couples together, providing grist for a long, enjoyable conversation — perhaps too long for the eighty-two-year-old apostle, who was scheduled to leave early the next morning for a flight to Honolulu. However, this flight was delayed and rescheduled for a midafternoon departure, which made it possible for the Smiths to attend Sunday School in San Francisco with President and Sister Love. After a light lunch at the mission home, Elder and Sister Smith were driven to the San Francisco Airport, where they boarded their plane for Hawaii.

Waiting for them at Honolulu was Elder Smith's nephew Joseph F. Smith, the son of Hyrum M. Smith, who had served briefly during the 1940s as Patriarch to the Church. Illness had necessitated his release. Afterward, he had moved to Hawaii, where he had regained his health. At the time of his uncle's visit in November 1958, he was on the faculty at the University of Hawaii. Following the unexpected death of his brother Hyrum in 1918, Joseph Fielding Smith had assumed a role of surrogate father to Hyrum's children, including this son, Joseph F. For this reason, the apostle enjoyed spending the night at his nephew's home and accompanying him to the temple at Laie on Monday. This afforded a welcome opportunity to visit and to catch up on family news.

Elder Smith and Jessie were taken to the Honolulu Airport Monday evening to catch their plane to Auckland, New Zealand. Since Brother Jensen of the Genealogical Society was to accompany them, the others in the party left the travelers at the departure gate, assuming they would leave on time. But, because of unforeseen delays, they waited in the airport for several hours, finally leaving Honolulu at 3:30 the next morning. They arrived in Auckland, New Zealand, November 19 at 8:45 P.M. and were met by the mission president, Heber Simpson, and his wife, Lily.

What followed that night signaled the kind of schedule the Smiths could expect during the three months they would remain in New Zealand and Australia. President Simpson stopped long enough at the mission home to leave the visitors' bags and to let them freshen up before driving them to the chapel. There, according to President Smith, "the Maori Saints met us with their usual Maori welcome." Although he had heard reports about the outgoing exuberance of these saints, they had scarcely prepared him for what he found here in Auckland. The vigor and enthusiasm of their response was like a tonic to the apostle, who should have been exhausted after the long trip with its unscheduled delays. But he spoke to them at some length, and Jessie delighted them with a song. It was after midnight when they retired.

The travelers remained in New Zealand a week, holding a series of meetings with the missionaries and members, before flying to Sydney, Australia. They would spend a month in "the land down under," following the typical pattern of a mission tour. After holding the customary meetings in Sydney, interspersed with courtesy visits to local dignitaries and stops at places of historic or cultural interest, the Smiths traveled in turn to Brisbane, Canberra, Melbourne, and Adelaide. All along the way, the President of the Twelve was greeted with awe by the members, who, in the isolation of this vast land, seldom saw a General Authority of the Church, let alone one of such high rank. And President Smith gained a new appreciation of Australia's vastness when, after leaving Adelaide, his party headed west toward faraway Perth. Along the way, they crossed the famous Nullarbor Plain, whose descriptive Latin name meaning "no tree" suggests the barren nature of the terrain.

President and Sister Smith returned to Auckland in late December and took a breather for several days, during which they celebrated Christmas and New Year's Day at the mission home and laid their plans for an extensive tour of New Zealand that would occupy them for the next five weeks. It was no picnic, especially for a man who was pushing eighty-three. Traveling by automobile and by air, the president of the Twelve and his wife were taken into most communities in New Zealand where there were members or missionaries. Often they stayed in the homes of the Saints, where the facilities were usually not what they were accustomed to. With a different bed almost every night, a diet that was often inadequate, and a schedule that would have been considered hectic by a man half his age, Joseph Fielding Smith went willingly to every place the mission president had scheduled a meeting—or rather, meetings. "District meetings all day," he wrote on Sunday, January 11, while in Hastings. "Auxiliary, genealogical, public. I spoke at each. Jessie sang. We have colds contracted several days ago." The next day they drove to Nuhaka, holding a general meeting at night. "We (all four) stayed at the home of Sister Solomon, whose husband has not been baptized," explained the diarist. "I was presented with a small clock in a shell—very beautiful." On Tuesday the 13th, they "drove over winding mountain roads to Gisbourne." There they stayed at the home of an Elder M. Poulson, a former missionary, who had married a Maori wife. "Meeting at night," reported Elder Smith, "entertainment followed until midnight. Our nights are usually

417

*Joseph Fielding and
Jessie Evans Smith*

very late following meetings." The next day, the travelers
flew to Wellington, where they spent a day at the mission
home writing letters and regrouping before traveling by
automobile during the following several days to Palmerton,
Wangari, Moksu, Waitangi, Kaikohe, and Waimaku. At
this last place, a late meeting was held after supper. "No
conveniences," noted the apostle. This was not said by
way of complaint or criticism, as Elder Smith was always
grateful for the "wonderful kindness of the people." And
he was amazed by their generosity, for almost everywhere
he and Jessie stayed, their hosts showered them with gifts.
"Had a wonderful reception at night," he wrote on January
27 while at Tauranga, "and received gifts, or tokens of
remembrance." One of these was a carved cane, which
President Smith prized. The last meeting of the mission
tour was held at Otorahanga on Friday, January 30. "Left
in rain; got bogged; had difficulty in getting out," the
apostle recorded succinctly. With that, the party returned

to Auckland, where a stake conference was held on Saturday, January 31, and Sunday, February 1.

After this conference, only one week of the South Pacific tour remained. Except for a meeting with the mission office staff and a trip to Hamilton, where President Smith spoke to the student body of the college, it was a period of relaxed, low-key activity, devoid of meetings and pressure. Monday was devoted to letter writing, and that night the Smiths attended the movie *South Pacific* with their hosts, President and Sister Simpson. "Did some pressing and laundry work," the apostle recorded on Tuesday. "The trips through New Zealand have been very hard on our clothes."

On Thursday, Elder Smith and Jessie went to the airport to meet Belle S. Spafford and a traveling companion who were visiting New Zealand and other South Pacific areas in the interests of the Relief Society. Most of Friday was spent trying to straighten out a kink in their travel plans. With that problem solved, the travelers boarded their ship, the S.S. *Monterey,* on Saturday afternoon, February 7, 1959. "Reception by Maori members on ship and greetings," Joseph noted appreciatively. "Wonderful reception."

With intervening stops at Suva and Pago Pago, it was a nine-day voyage to Honolulu. At both ports, President Smith went ashore, where he spoke to the missionaries and Saints. And at Pago Pago, he gave blessings to twelve people who pleaded for them. He never refused those who came for blessings of comfort and healing.

The *Monterey* was buffeted by tropical storms the first six days of the voyage. The weather was so foul at Pago Pago that the ship's captain refused to take her out at noon Wednesday, the scheduled time of departure. Instead, she sailed early Thursday morning, February 12. "Rough sea all day," wrote Elder Smith on that day. "Rain. Spent most of the day quietly." In the evening, Jessie responded to a request to conduct the community singing aboard ship. She also sang a solo, "Such Beautiful Things." When the one in charge said that it was the best performance they had ever had, Jessie's wholly objective husband reported, "I think it was!" For her efforts, Jessie was rewarded with an eight-day desk clock.

There can be little doubt that President Smith's life was prolonged and made happy by the energy and the enthusiasm of Jessie Evans Smith. Her attitude was perpetually optimistic and sunny. She had a bright, genuine smile and an infectious, deep-throated laugh that had a musical quality to it. She undoubtedly had her share of disappointments and setbacks and experienced times of sadness. But her music was like a talisman that could dispel gloom or despondency. A song sung in her deep contralto voice, or a number played on the piano, or an exuberant leading of others in song could lift her and those around her into a new mood of happy thought and reflection. And, as President Smith's entry aboard the *Monterey* implies, no one was more appreciative of Jessie's talent than was he. Repeatedly over the years, the apostle expressed the feeling that the Lord had "led" him to this unusual woman and that it was "intended" that she should be his wife.

With the Smiths aboard the *Monterey* was a neighbor from Salt Lake City, Elder Robert Evans, who had completed his mission and was returning home. On their first Sunday after leaving Auckland, the three of them met alone for prayer and worship. The second Sunday, they joined in the nondenominational service held on board, where, on request, Jessie sang "If Christ Should Come Tomorrow." Joseph noted ruefully that the implications of the song "evidently had no effect on the congregation." This remark reflected his annoyance at a condition he found on the ship. "Most of the women smoking cigarettes, and most of the men cigars or cigarettes," he wrote disapprovingly. "All of them with few exceptions, drinking in the liquor room between time. Both men and women running around with no more clothes on than nature demands. Gambling on dice, horse racing or bingo is the only sport—and the ship always wins." Because of his outspoken tendencies, there can be little doubt that if the eighty-two-year-old apostle had been invited to speak at the service, the audience would have heard a never-to-be-forgotten sermon on repentance.

Waiting to greet the travelers at the pier in Pearl Harbor was a group of members, bearing leis and singing the customary Hawaiian greeting song. Among the well-wishers were President Harry S. Brooks and President Jay Quealy. That evening, the Smiths were guests at a dinner hosted by President and Sister Quealy and attended by a group of the stalwarts in the local Mormon community, including the Clissolds, the Brooks, and the Woolleys. The next morning, Wednesday, February 18, the visitors attended a devotional at the Church College in Laie, where Elder Smith spoke and Jessie sang. And that afternoon, having had their fill of shipboard travel, the couple flew home to Salt Lake City, where they were met by members of their family.

Soon after returning from this extended tour, President Smith began to plot a trip into South and Central America, an area he had never visited. A few years before, in 1954, President David O. McKay had stopped briefly in Latin America in returning from a trip to South Africa. He had met with members and missionaries in Brazil, Uruguay, and Argentina; had flown across the Andes to Santiago, Chile, where there were no missionaries and only two known members of the Church; and had touched down in Peru, Panama, and Guatemala before returning to Salt Lake City. He told reporters on arriving home: "There is one definite observation I would like to make, and that is the need of more cordial relations between the United States and South American Republics. The North American attitude of superiority engenders ill will throughout these southern republics and should be changed if we are to bring about a better and more cordial spirit of cooperation." (*Church News,* February 1954.) Toward this end, it was decided in 1960 that the president of the Twelve would make an extended tour of Latin America, visiting the six

421

missions that then existed there — the Brazil North and South, Uruguay, Argentine, Andes, and Central America missions. This historic trip was to take three months. And the vast area to be covered, the inadequate transportation in some remote areas, and the danger of disease or infection in a strange environment made it clear that it would be strenuous.

However, these and other negative factors had no deterring effect on President Smith. The eighty-four-year-old apostle planned his itinerary with the enthusiasm of a young man.

The trip was historic because no General Authority had ever covered as large an area in Latin America over such a long period of time as was now projected for President Smith. In the 1850s, Elder Parley P. Pratt of the Twelve had traveled to Valparaiso, Chile, where he spent several months. Then, in 1925, Elder Melvin J. Ballard of the Twelve visited Argentina with Elders Rulon S. Wells and Rey L. Pratt of the First Council of the Seventy, dedicating South America for the preaching of the gospel in December of that year. And we have already noted the brief visit President David O. McKay made in 1954. Now, however, the president of the Twelve, who was the chairman of the missionary committee of the Church, was to travel extensively in many countries of Latin America, visiting and instructing the missionaries and preaching the gospel to members and nonmembers alike as the opportunity arose. It was an auspicious occasion, therefore, when, on October 13, 1960, members of his family and associates from Church headquarters gathered at the Salt Lake City Airport to wish President Smith bon voyage. Jessie and Elder A. Theodore Tuttle of the First Council of the Seventy were his traveling companions. At New York City, they boarded a ship for Rio de Janeiro, Brazil. Unlike many voyages on the Atlantic, often noted for its turbulence, the ten-day cruise to Rio was, according to Jessie, "as smooth as if we were riding in the air." Indeed, she said it was necessary to go on deck to see if the ship was moving. At Rio, the travelers were met by W. Grant Bangerter, president of the Brazil mission, which was headquartered inland at São Paulo. Fluent in Portuguese, the language of Brazil, President Bangerter, who would later become a General Authority of the Church, was a Church veteran in Brazil, having served there as a young missionary twenty years before. In those early days, many missionaries from the United States went to Brazil to work among the German-speaking people who had migrated there and had settled in communities in the south like Joinville, which had the appearance of a German village transplanted from the fatherland. Later, missionaries began to proselyte among those who spoke Portuguese so that in São Paulo, President Smith found strong branches, led mostly by Brazilians, where only Portuguese was spoken. A few years before the apostle arrived in Brazil, an aggressive proselyting effort had reaped a good harvest of strong, dedicated converts who would form the nucleus of the stake that would be organized in São Paulo in 1966, the first stake in all of South America. Chief among these converts were Helio da Rocha Camargo, Walter Queroz, and Saul Messias, who were studying for the protestant ministry at the time of their conversion, and all of whom would later become stake presidents and mission presidents. Helio Camargo, of course, later became the first native Brazilian to serve as a General Authority of the Church.

With President Bangerter and his wife, Geraldine, the three visitors held many meetings in the Brazil mission, which included the vast area north of São Paulo. The pattern established there would be followed in all of the other missions to be visited during the tour. President Smith, Elder Tuttle, and the mission president and his wife did all the preaching, while Jessie sang. Occasionally she would sing a song in the native language, which was always appreciated by the Saints. Since President Smith and Elder Tuttle spoke only English, they had to rely on translators in the general meetings, which significantly limited the scope of their teaching. However, the core of President

Smith's teachings throughout the tour were the same as the ones he had emphasized from the beginning of his ministry. He admonished his listeners to learn their duties as Church members by studying the scriptures and to obey the principles they contained. He also urged them to become perfect through persistent effort, day by day.

Interspersed with the public meetings were meetings with the missionaries. Here the brethren were not limited in their ability to communicate since the missionaries spoke English. In these meetings, President Smith usually focused on the spiritual and mental preparation for effective missionary work through prayer and diligent study, while Elder Tuttle stressed the "how to" aspects of the work. Teaching in tandem in this way, they made an effective team.

Leaving the Bangerters, the visitors traveled to Curitiba, Brazil, where they joined Asael T. Sorensen, president of the Brazil South mission, and his wife. Here the pattern set in São Paulo was repeated. On the coast, they visited the twin cities of Santos and São Vicente, the latter, which was settled in 1532, being the second oldest European settlement in Brazil. The oldest is Olinda in the north, settled by the Portuguese in 1530. Large and modern cities such as these two and São Paulo and Rio de Janeiro brought home to the visitors the fact that the European influence here predated that in New England by seventy-five years, a fact not understood by most North Americans. It was an understanding of this fact, as much as anything else, that radically altered the perceptions of LDS leaders about the growth potential for the Church in Brazil.

From Southern Brazil, the party traveled to Montevideo, Uruguay, where Arthur M. Jensen presided over the Uruguay-Paraguay Mission. Here the shift in language to Spanish made little difference to the brethren from Salt Lake City because they didn't speak or understand it, either. From this point to the end of the tour, the native language would be Spanish. Crossing the La Plata River, which at its mouth is so wide as to make it look almost like part of the ocean, the party traveled to Buenos Aires, Argentina. There Lorin N. Pace presided over the Argentine Mission. As already indicated, it was here in Buenos Aires, thirty-five years before, that Elder Melvin J. Ballard had dedicated all of South America for the preaching of the gospel. The seeds planted then had taken root, so that at the time of President Smith's visit in 1960, there were flourishing branches in Buenos Aires and other Argentine cities, many of which President Smith and his party visited.

Crossing the towering Andes by air, the travelers flew to Santiago, Chile, where they were met by J. Vernon Sharp, the president of the Andes Mission, which included Chile and South American countries to the north. In this long, stringlike country, which nestles against the bony spine of the Andes, the visitors found ten small but growing branches with a total membership of about seven hundred. Considering that six years earlier President David O. McKay had found only two members there, Billy Fotheringham and his wife, the growth, while small in numbers, was phenomenal in terms of percentages. And even the numerical growth in the succeeding twenty-six years would be phenomenal, increasing to 169,000 by the end of 1986. The visitors anticipated that growth as they continued their tour. "Elder Tuttle told the Elders assembled for the missionary conference," noted the *Church News* in its issue of January 7, 1961, "that the church is now in a new period of growth." Referring to Elder Smith's participation in this conference, the article continued: "President Smith told the missionaries that the qualities needed for success in their work includes greater faith, hope, charity, love and temperance. He admonished them to strive to perfect themselves and seek after godliness by being diligent in all of their days."

Before participating in this missionary conference, which was held in Santiago, President Smith and his party had visited the various branches in Chile. This had taken them to Valparaiso, on the Atlantic coast, not far from Santiago. It was here on November 8, 1851, that Elder

Parley P. Pratt had arrived with his wife, Phoebe, and Elder Rufus Allen. Elder Pratt, who was the first apostle of this dispensation to set foot on South American soil, remained in Chile only four months. He left because of a lack of funds and the inability to speak Spanish, which, in turn, made it impossible to obtain employment. However, while there he collected various works of history and literature in Spanish, which he expected to use in preparing for the translation of the Book of Mormon and other Church literature. His tragic assassination in 1857 prevented him from bringing that projected work to fruition. Also while there, Elder Pratt's wife gave birth to a child who lived only a short while and who was buried near Viña del Mar, thought by some to be the site of the landing of the Lehi group. President Smith and his party were unable to locate the gravesite of the Pratt infant, who was the first child of Latter-day Saints to be buried in South America.

From Santiago, President Smith's party traveled north to Lima, Peru, the headquarters of the Andes Mission. Here they were shepherded around by President Sharp as they visited the several branches and held instruction meetings with the missionaries. While in Peru, the visitors also traveled into Ecuador, where the Church was just gaining a foothold.

The last stop on the tour was in Guatemala. There the Smiths were met by Victor C. Hancock, president of the Central America Mission. There followed the usual round of meetings with members and missionaries before enplaning for home.

Gathered at the Salt Lake City Airport to meet the travelers were five members of the Twelve and other General Authorities, as well as members of President Smith's family. The president of the Twelve, who would be eighty-five-years old within a few months, was as alert and vigorous as his young companion, Elder Tuttle, who was only about half his age. Elder Tuttle "praised President Smith as a 'great traveler' who had energy to spare when other members of the party were tired." (*Church News,* January 14, 1961.)

President Smith and Jessie were driven to their apartment in the Eagle Gate, where they had lived for almost ten years. Not long after Joseph Fielding became president of the Twelve, he and Jessie decided that their lives would be greatly simplified were they to sell the Douglas Street home and move to an apartment. This would free them from the responsibility of caring for the yard, arranging for snow removal in the winter, and negotiating for the seemingly endless repairs that living in a home entailed. The Eagle Gate was only a half block from President Smith's office and a block and a half from the Tabernacle, which Jessie visited frequently for rehearsals and performances of the Salt Lake Tabernacle Choir. Their apartment was a spacious unit on the main floor of the Eagle Gate, looking out on Brigham Young's Beehive House and, beyond, on the Church Administration Building and the Salt Lake Temple. This location also put them within easy walking distance of the downtown shopping district, which was especially attractive to Jessie, who enjoyed nothing more than a shopping spree. And she often succeeded in persuading her husband to join her in these outings. Their apartment was filled with choice mementoes of the many trips they had taken together, family pictures and portraits, and many specimens of Aunt Jessie's skill as a quilter and crocheter. It was a comfortable, homey, and happy place that included a large living room, dining room, kitchen, bedroom, and a study for President Smith. There was ample room for Jessie's baby-grand piano in the living room and space for some of the president's choice books and his private papers. And in an upstairs attic were stored some of the priceless artifacts that had belonged to his ancestors, including some personal effects of his grandfather, the Patriarch Hyrum Smith.

The Eagle Gate had good security so that the Smiths could leave for a weekend — or for three months, as when they made their tour of South America — confident that their apartment and its irreplaceable contents would be adequately protected. Aside from the conventional means of security provided by the owner, which was one of the commercial arms of the Church, the multi-storied building was occupied mostly by members of the Church, who were very solicitous and protective of the Eagle Gate's most famous and beloved tenants — Joseph Fielding and Jessie Evans Smith.

Here in the very heart of Salt Lake City, the Smiths lived a very full life. Although President Smith turned eighty-five the July following his return from South America, he was in excellent health and was able to enjoy to the fullest the many attractions the city had to offer. He and Jessie ate out frequently, usually in company with friends or members of their family. During a period of five weeks in the summer of 1962 when President Smith turned eighty-six, he and Jessie sampled the cuisine of restaurants that specialized in Mexican food, Greek food, and seafood. They frequently attended the movies as well as the cultural events staged in the Tabernacle or elsewhere — the symphony and an occasional opera. And President Smith immensely enjoyed television, especially the sporting events. So, on January 1, 1962, he and Jessie "invited Bishop Simpson and Bishop Brown of the Presiding Bishopric to come and watch the football games, principally the Rose Bowl." The apostle added, "While watching the game we also conversed on various subjects. Things were so interesting that the day soon passed and it was evening before the brethren left." It must be remembered, too, that it was during this period that President Smith was very much into flying. This man, now pushing ninety, was as interested in and alert to everything going on about him as a man in his fifties. And yet, the beginning of the most distinctive period of his life still lay eight years in the future. There can be no doubt that his intense enjoyment of every facet of life at such an advanced age traces in large part to the influence of his charming and effervescent wife, Jessie

Evans Smith. Life around her was nothing less than fun. And they both enjoyed it to the fullest.

On returning from South America, President Smith's official duties continued at their usual hectic pace. Having gained the reputation of being the Church's supreme gospel scholar, much of his time at headquarters was now occupied in responding to questions put to him. "I answered correspondence which comes in on all questions and from all parts of the earth," he noted on February 15, 1962. Many of these were repetitious and could be answered merely by copying what had been written to previous questioners. Others involved complicated issues that required careful research and draftsmanship. And a few were obviously designed to lead the apostle into a doctrinal trap or a contradictory position with other answers he had given. These were usually handled either by referring the correspondent to the scriptures, or, in extreme cases, by ignoring them. In answering questions on Church history, he often relied on research by members of his staff in the Historical Department. But, in matters of doctrine and scriptural interpretation, he usually relied only on his own knowledge or personal research.

While this activity was time consuming, it constituted only a part of his headquarters duties. His main occupation was to give direction to the brethren of the Twelve, as well as the Seventy and the Presiding Bishopric, insofar as their work involved ecclesiastical assignments. As the Church expanded internationally, President Smith was hard put to provide General Authority coverage for stake conferences. "The First Presidency have engaged so many of the Brethren in foreign duties," he noted on May 5, 1962, "that it is very difficult to meet all conferences and many stakes have to go without visitors." The problem was solved in a few instances by combining the Saturday priesthood leadership meetings of two adjoining stakes and allowing the General Authority to alternate in attending separate general sessions on Sunday.

There were aspects of the international development

of the Church that troubled President Smith. A chief one was financial. "Attended the expenditures committee," he noted on June 12, 1962. "We are spending great sums, buying prospective sites for meeting places in foreign lands as well as at home. I wonder where all the money will come from." Later, when expressing the same concern, he concluded that the *expenditures* committee . . . is well named." At the same time, he expressed mild concern about the de-emphasis on the concept of gathering to the land of America the thrust for international growth had produced. In the years that followed, his thinking on this subject underwent a gradual change toward the idea that the concept also entailed a gathering to spiritual Zion, which could be anyplace in the world where stakes of Zion had been established. Thus, it was during his prophetic tenure that the first international area conference was held in Manchester, England, whose main focus was to emphasize that the members of the Church in the British Isles should remain in their own lands, gathering to the stakes that had been or would be created there.

It was during this year that the Smiths decided to dispose of their Millcreek cabin, which had become an onerous burden, not a joy as in the past. It had been vandalized several times, and the Forest Service, which owned the underlying land, had imposed more restrictions. Also, the municipal government had increased its service fees. Moreover, the Smiths were able to use the facility no more than two weeks of the year. So, they sold it, but not without feelings of ambivalence due to the enjoyment it had given them over the years. So, during the recess this year, instead of going up Mill Creek Canyon for diversion, they twice traveled out of state. In early July, with Jessie at the wheel of their new Rambler, they drove to Jacob Lake, located on the Kaibab Forest in northern Arizona. "This is a very peaceful, restful place," the apostle noted on July 9. The four days they spent there amid the pines were wholly unstructured. They read quietly, wrote in their journals, visited, and took occasional walks. They also befriended the young Latter-day Saint students who worked at the lodge to earn money for the coming school year. "At night," Elder Smith noted the day after their arrival, "we met with the young people in their MIA session, and I occupied most of the time instructing them." The visitors were touched when, at their departure, the young people presented them with "a very excellent cake" they had baked specially for them.

Later in the month, the Smiths traveled alone to Idaho, where they spent four days near Mack's Inn at a cabin owned by their son-in-law Hoyt Brewster. Here their daily regimen was much the same as at Jacob Lake, except that no one else was nearby as the cabin was in a secluded area.

Such interludes of peace and quiet reflection, free from the demands of their tightly organized schedules, provided a much-needed break in their routine. Back in Salt Lake City, the Smiths attended the finals of the Church-wide softball tournament, where Joseph distributed awards to the finalists and the key players.

Judged by any standard, President Smith qualifies as one of the most extraordinary travelers of his time. Aside from his extensive international travels, he made thousand of trips over the years in the United States by plane, train, automobile, and, in the early days, by horse-drawn vehicles. Consider a four-day trip he made in late September 1962 to attend a stake conference in Snowflake, Arizona, a remote Mormon colony almost seven hundred miles from Salt Lake City. Traveling by automobile, he and Jessie arrived shortly after noon the second day. Pausing only long enough to deposit their bags and to freshen up, the eighty-six-year-old apostle immediately commenced a series of meetings that occupied all Saturday afternoon. Late in the evening, the Smiths were driven in "heavy rain and darkness" to Clay Springs, where the president dedicated a new chapel. "We returned to Snowflake in rain and mud," he reported, ending his terse entry with "all well." The following day, Sunday, after two long general sessions where he was the main speaker in both, he set apart several officers from the Snowflake Stake, then did the same for officers from the Flagstaff Stake who had driven to Snowflake for this purpose. Finally, in late afternoon, they left for home, driving until dark overtook them at an Indian trading post on the Navajo Reservation, where they spent the night. They covered the last five hundred miles on Monday. On Tuesday morning, President Smith was in his office shortly after 6:00 A.M. to clean his desk before a series of meetings that started at 7:00 A.M.

Shortly after returning from Snowflake, he and Jessie had what was for them a novel experience, which he described in this diary entry of September 27, 1962. "I returned home to prepare with Jessie for a television broadcast over channel 7, our subject dealing with the writings and philosophy of Ralph Waldo Emerson and Henry David Thoreau. The broadcast commenced with a piano solo by Jessie. We then discussed the philosophy of Emerson and Thoreau, dealing [mainly] with the principle of compensation."'

At the October General Conference, N. Eldon Tanner was called to fill the vacancy in the Twelve caused by the death of George Q. Morris, who had died in April. Elder Tanner had served for two years as an assistant to the Twelve prior to this last call. And the following year, in October, he would be called as a counselor to President David O. McKay in the First Presidency, illustrating again the shifting nature of primacy among the hierarchy of the Mormon Church. From October 1963, when he became a member of the First Presidency, until 1970, N. Eldon Tanner had supervisory responsibilities over President Smith, even though he had had General Authority status only since 1960. Then, at the death of President McKay, Brother Tanner again became subordinate to President Smith, serving as his second counselor.

At the time of the call of Elder Tanner to the Twelve, there were other members of that quorum who had been called after Joseph Fielding Smith became its president—

Marion G. Romney, LeGrand Richards, Richard L. Evans, Howard W. Hunter, and Gordon B. Hinckley. In addition, Adam S. Bennion and George Q. Morris had been called afterward but had passed away before Elder Tanner joined the quorum. Moreover, Hugh B. Brown had also been called afterward, but at the time of Elder Tanner's call he was serving as a member of the First Presidency. This means, of course, that during a period of only eleven years, there had been nine changes in the membership of the Twelve, more changes than during any comparable period of Church history. Yet President Smith took these many changes in stride, patiently giving counsel and training to the new brethren as they joined the other apostles. By contrast, during the seven years between 1963 and 1970, there were no changes in the personnel of the Twelve.

There was a year's hiatus after the October 1962 General Conference before President Smith decided on another international tour. This one would take him to Australia again. Except for his short trip to Manchester, England, in 1971, it was to be his last. Undoubtedly a strong inducement for him and Jessie to make this trip was the presence in Melbourne, Australia, of Bruce and Amelia, as Elder McConkie presided over the Southern Australia Mission. They timed their departure on November 20, 1963, to coincide with the refulgence of spring in the southern hemisphere. Two days before leaving, Elder Smith went to the LDS Hospital to visit President David O. McKay, who had been "confined" for several days. "I found him cheerful," noted the President of the Twelve, "and was informed that he was to return to his home soon." President McKay's confinement resulted from a mild stroke he had suffered. This and other ailments would, within two years, bring about a historic change in the First Presidency.

The travelers changed planes at the San Francisco International Airport for the long flight to Australia. With an intermediate stop in Honolulu, they arrived at Sydney on the 21st. Waiting to meet them at Sydney was the mission president, Morgan Coombs, who took them immediately to the mission home. There they spent a relaxed day adjusting their internal time clocks and preparing for the coming weekend. They were met here by President Harry Brooks, who had been assigned to participate with President Smith in stake conferences scheduled in Brisbane, Sydney, and Melbourne. On Saturday the 23rd, the three of them flew to Brisbane, where, over the weekend, they held a stake conference with the usual crowded schedule of meetings, interviews, and settings apart. Elder Brooks gave special instruction about stake missionary work and home teaching while President Smith was the main speaker at all meetings, always delivering solid doctrinal sermons. Jessie sang, to the delight of all. She was also called on to speak briefly sometimes, peppering her remarks with amusing anecdotes about herself and President Smith, which, as always, had the tendency to soften the image projected by her husband's somewhat stern and somber pulpit presence. That transition always became complete when she would playfully persuade him to join her in one of their famous "do its."

The following day was spent in all-day missionary report and testimony meetings, where the apostle gave wise counsel to the missionaries and, as was his custom, responded to their doctrinal and historical questions. That night, he counseled the stake leaders.

Returning to Sydney on Tuesday, the travelers spent the rest of the week there, enjoying a Thanksgiving Day feast on Thursday with the Coombs family and holding meetings with the missionaries and with local leaders. A stake conference was held in Sydney over the following weekend.

On Monday, December 2, the travelers arrived in Melbourne, where they were met enthusiastically by the McConkies and their children. Here President and Sister Smith settled in for ten delightful days with the members of their family. Of course, there were intermittent meetings with missionaries and local leaders, and over the weekend a stake conference was held. But this left time for visiting in order to post each other on the news of the family. The apostle also spent leisure hours during several days browsing in the McConkie library, where he took a special interest in a volume on Australian history. Though nearing ninety, Joseph Fielding Smith retained an avid curiosity toward books in general, although a few, chiefly the scriptures and history, took precedence with him.

The Smiths flew out of Melbourne on Thursday evening, December 12, and, with an overnight stop in Honolulu where they cleared customs, arrived in Salt Lake City Saturday morning. There they were met by their son Douglas and the Church's travel agent, Franklin J. Murdock, and were driven to their apartment in the Eagle Gate. The following summer, shortly before President Smith's eighty-eighth birthday, he was privileged to ordain this son a Bishop to preside over the Bonneville Ward in the Bonneville Stake, where the apostle had lived for so long. As he had never served as a bishop himself and since Douglas was the first of his sons to serve in that capacity, the father was particularly interested in his son's service there and never missed an opportunity to attend meetings in the Bonneville Ward.

Chapter Twenty-three

Counselor in the First Presidency

J oseph Fielding Smith's extensive travels as president of the Quorum of the Twelve Apostles had given him an insight into the international character of the Church second to none, not excluding President David O. McKay. President McKay, of course, had spent an entire year in the early 1920s traveling around the world with Hugh J. Cannon, visiting Church members and units in many lands. At the time, however, the Church had gained no real foothold in the international areas, except in Great Britain and Europe. Even there, however, because of the concept of gathering to the United States, which had siphoned off large numbers of the more able and dedicated members, the Church units were weak, often being led by missionaries from the United States and housed, for the most part, in rented, substandard buildings. Also, President McKay had traveled extensively to many parts of the world after becoming the president of the Church. Most often, however, these were essentially ceremonial visits for the purpose of dedicating temples or chapels or performing other symbolic acts. On the other hand, President Smith's visits to Europe, the Far East, the Pacific, and South America were lengthy tours, occupying weeks or months during which he held numerous meetings in small branches, visited the members in their homes, and counseled and instructed missionaries about their work.

Viewing these tours in retrospect, they seem almost to have been arranged deliberately to help prepare Elder Smith for the time when he would become president of the Church. An event that occurred in 1965 could also be interpreted in this way. On October 29 of that year, Joseph Fielding Smith was set apart as a third counselor to President David O. McKay, whose incumbent counselors were Hugh B. Brown and N. Eldon Tanner. At the same time, Thorpe B. Isaacson was set apart as a fourth counselor to the Prophet. In the summer of 1963, President McKay had suffered an accident at his Huntsville farm that had triggered a series of health problems. As he was preparing to mount his favorite horse, Sonny Boy, something spooked the animal, causing it to bolt and run. The Prophet clung to the reins and was dragged for some distance before the horse was brought to a halt. Not long afterward, President McKay suffered a stroke. These circumstances required that he be hospitalized in November 1963, with a slight impairment of speech and some paralysis in his legs. During the two years that followed, prior to the call of the additional counselors, the Prophet's condition worsened. This, added to the increasing burden of the First Presidency as the Church continued its rapid growth, dictated the need for President McKay to seek additional help.

At the first meeting of the enlarged First Presidency on November 9, 1965, President David O. McKay elaborated on the reasons and the historical precedent for calling the additional counselors: "I welcome you as counselors in the First Presidency," he recorded in his diary on that date, "and acknowledge with hesitancy that I am not so well as I used to be and called you brethren as counselors in the First Presidency to help carry the work. I pray the Lord's blessings to attend us in this quorum of the First

Presidency. It is nothing new in the Church. The Prophet Joseph Smith had several counselors; President Brigham Young had seven at one time, I think; and this will constitute the quorum of the First Presidency. I should like to meet regularly with you and to take up matters . . . as the occasion requires."

Because it was decided that President Smith would continue his active roles as president of the Twelve and as Church historian, his duties in the First Presidency were necessarily limited. However, he attended all of the meetings of the First Presidency when he was in Salt Lake City, as also the council meetings held regularly in the temple, where he provided important insights into decisions that needed to be made. He was therefore privy to all official matters pertaining to the Church at the highest levels.

Thorpe B. Isaacson's intended role was to provide assistance in various financial and business matters. Regrettably, his ability to help with the work was destroyed when in early February, 1966, less than four months after his call as a counselor, President Isaacson suffered a massive stroke. Two years after that, in April 1968, Alvin R. Dyer was called as a fifth counselor in the First Presidency to fill the role originally intended for Elder Isaacson.

The four years and three months President Smith served as a counselor in the First Presidency provided important additional training for his ultimate service as president of the Church. Here he gained a perception of the work of the Church he had never had before. Previously, he had seen only bits and pieces of it. But here, at the pinnacle of Church leadership, he was able to see with clarity how the various aspects of the work were fitted together into a consistent, unified whole. The work of the Presiding Bishopric, especially, came into clearer focus for President Smith as he filled this new niche. Previously, his relationship with these brethren had been minimal, consisting chiefly of the few occasions during the year when all the General Authorities were brought together for spiritual refreshment and for the annual meeting of the

Council on Disposition of the Tithes. But these meetings provided no real insight into the vast scope of the work of the Presiding Bishopric in temporal affairs. As a member of the First Presidency, however, Elder Smith participated in lengthy, weekly meetings where the Presiding Bishopric reported on every aspect of their work and where policies and procedures designed to govern the temporal affairs of the Church were formulated. This opened up to President Smith a whole new vista of Church mechanisms and functions.

Part of this awakening to the temporal side of the Church also came from President Smith's new exposure to the extensive business holdings of the Church. Over the years, he had served on the board of directors of a few of the corporations owned or controlled by the Church. But he had never before seen the full scope of the Church's involvement in these.

Finally, Elder Smith's elevation to the presiding quorum of the Church brought home the extensive power vested in that quorum, and especially in its presiding officer, the Prophet. Here existed, then, the final earthly authority as to all executive, legislative, or judicial matters affecting the Church in its worldwide operations. And routinely the meetings of the First Presidency entailed the exercise of all these vast and varied powers. So, in a given meeting, the Brethren might at one point exercise their executive authority as they decided matters involving the announcement of policies or procedures previously decided upon. They might then don their legislative hats as they formulated plans for the future. And, finally, they might turn to an appeal from the judgment of a stake disciplinary council and exercise final judicial authority.

During the first months of Elder Smith's service in the First Presidency, most of the meetings were held in the First Presidency's Council Room in the north end of the main floor of the Administration Building at 47 East South Temple in Salt Lake City. While, as indicated, President McKay had suffered some physical impairment as a result

439

of his stroke, he could still move about with assistance. Here the members of the First Presidency would gather around their council table and, with their secretary, Joseph Anderson, taking minutes, handle the matters that had accumulated since they last met. These meetings were held almost daily during the work week. The separate, private offices of President McKay and his counselors Hugh B. Brown, N. Eldon Tanner, and Thorpe B. Isaacson were located in the corners of the main floor of the Administration Building, while President Smith retained his private office on the third floor in the Historical Department. All, however, had ready access to the council room that they shared as a quorum.

As President McKay's physical condition began to deteriorate, it became necessary to hold most of the First Presidency meetings in the Prophet's apartment in the Hotel Utah. The Brethren would walk there from the Church Administration Building next door, carrying in their briefcases any documents to be considered. Sometimes they would travel to Huntsville, Utah, during mild weather to meet in the small bungalow that the McKays had had constructed there.

In addition to attending the meetings of the First Presidency, President Smith participated in other ways in helping to carry on the work of the First Presidency. He followed through on matters relating to the aspects of the work with which he was most familiar — temple and missionary work and matters pertaining to the Historical Department and to the Twelve. He also represented the First Presidency at various ceremonial functions and participated with the others in conducting and speaking at the general conferences. For instance, at the October General Conference in 1966, the year following his call to the First Presidency, Brother Smith was the concluding speaker at the third session and gave the keynote address at the general priesthood meeting. He also conducted the fourth and the final sessions of the conference.

The change in his status effected no change whatsoever

in President Smith's focus as a speaker. The Saints who attended the third session Saturday afternoon heard a powerful sermon on the second principle of the gospel. "From the observations that we make as we travel from one place to another," said President Smith in his discourse, "and from what we read in the public press, we are of necessity forced to the conclusion that repentance from sin is extremely essential throughout the world today." (*Conference Report*, October 1966, p. 60.) From that premise, the speaker, using extensive scriptural references, portrayed mortality as a time of testing, emphasized that redemption from sin comes only through the Savior, and warned of judgments that would fall on the unrepentant. "And thus we might quote indefinitely from the ancient prophets," he said in conclusion, "in relation to the troubles, destructions, wars, and plagues which are to come upon the inhabititants of the earth—yea, even Zion also—unless the people repent." (Ibid., p. 61.) In his keynote address at the general priesthood meeting, President Smith traced the origin and chain of priesthood authority and then gave emphasis to one of his favored themes: priesthood responsibility. "The world today is torn asunder," he said. "Evil is rampant upon the face of the earth. The members of the Church need to be humble and prayerful and diligent. We who have been called to these positions in the priesthood have the responsibility upon our shoulders to teach and direct the members of the Church in righteousness." (Ibid., p. 84.)

The opening address of the October 1966 General Conference was given by President David O. McKay. Because of the weakness in his legs, he was unable to stand at the pulpit unaided. So a tall stool was provided for him, and he sat while delivering the talk. It was the last time he ever spoke in the Salt Lake Tabernacle. His remaining talks this conference were read by his son, Robert McKay. And at all subsequent general conferences until the time of his death, President McKay's talks were read by Robert or someone else. The Prophet's disabilities, of course, imposed heavier burdens upon President Smith and the other counselors.

Four months before the October 1966 General Conference, while President McKay was still fairly mobile, he and President Smith took a trip to Missouri to visit Adam-ondi-Ahman and other historic sites nearby. During sixty years of service as a General Authority, President McKay had never visited these places. In going there for the first time, the Prophet was anxious to have with him the Church historian, who was also his counselor and longtime apostolic associate.

The two old friends, ages ninety-three and and ninety, left the Salt Lake City airport the first week in June 1966. With them were the Prophet's eldest son, David Lawrence McKay, and Elder Alvin R. Dyer, assistant to the Twelve. At Kansas City, the party was met by several local leaders who served as guides and hosts. The visitors were driven to Independence, Missouri, where, before beginning the tour, they were taken to the mission home to freshen up.

The first stop was on River Boulevard in front of a small frame chapel owned by the Hedrikite Church. This is the high point of a sixty-three-acre tract that, in the 1830s, the Prophet Joseph Smith designated as the site for the temple of the New Jerusalem. The visitors then passed the nearby auditorium of the Reorganized Church, east of which is a twenty-three-acre site, owned by The Church of Jesus Christ of Latter-day Saints, that is part of the temple property.

Crossing the Missouri River, the visitors were driven north to Liberty. Here the party paused to visit the famed Liberty Jail, where, during the winter of 1838–39, the Prophet Joseph Smith, his brother Hyrum, and some of their associates were imprisoned for four months. As the group examined the crude and cramped dungeon, President Smith explained that in 1963, he had dedicated this historic structure and the modern rotunda that encloses it. President Smith also explained that it was in this unlikely place that Hyrum Smith, his grandfather, had first laid eyes on his father, Joseph F. Smith. The infant, who had been born at Far West on November 13, 1838, was soon after brought to the prison by his mother, Mary Fielding Smith, so the father could see and hold him.

The visitors were then driven further north through the pleasant, rolling countryside typical of the area, covered with a blanket of green — trees, hedges, and intermittent corn fields that, in early June, had not yet reached their full growth. Passing through Gallatin, the seat of Daviess County, the party crossed the Grand River, which makes its way through the valley of Adam-ondi-Ahman, and drove upward over an ungraded road to Tower Hill, which overlooks the valley. Here the visitors examined some ruins reported to have been identified by the Prophet Joseph Smith as an ancient prayer altar. Driving down a narrow, winding, unsurfaced road into the valley, the party passed the remains of the old Lyman Wight home, one of the few visible evidences of a Mormon community that had been established there in the 1830s, presided over by bishop pro-tem Vinson Knight. In the valley the visitors had a good view of a bluff area called Spring Hill, where many homes of the Latter-day Saints were built. Also in the valley, President Smith and others rehearsed the extraordinary events that the Prophet Joseph Smith had predicted would occur there in the future.

The visitors then turned southward, traveling to Far West in Caldwell County. Here they found no physical evidence of the thriving Mormon community that had once existed, except the four cornerstones of the old temple site that had been dedicated there. Joseph Fielding pointed out to President McKay the area west of the temple site where his father had been born, as also the approximate location of the old town square where, following their arrest, the Prophet Joseph Smith and Hyrum had been loaded into a wagon for the trip south, where, it was feared, they would be executed.

Because of time limitations, the party was unable to visit other places of historic interest in Missouri. But the trip, short though it was, had been sufficient to provide President McKay with an overview of significant events that had occurred there. This formed the basis for a later decision of the First Presidency to construct commemorative monuments at the Far West temple site and a visitors' center near the temple lot in Independence.

Two years later, President Smith returned to Missouri with several of the General Authorities. At the direction of President McKay, whose deteriorating health made it impossible for him to go there, President Smith first went to Far West, where he dedicated the monuments that had been constructed at the temple site during the two-year interval. These contained excerpts from revelations in the Doctrine and Covenants about Far West and significant events that had taken place there. From there, the party went to Independence, where President Smith broke ground for a visitors' center to be constructed near the temple lot that had been designated by the Prophet Joseph Smith.

The day chosen for the groundbreaking had been carefully selected. It was August 3, 1968, the 137th anniversary of the date when the Prophet Joseph Smith first dedicated the area. The printed program for the event contained the following statement made by the Prophet Joseph Smith on August 3, 1831: "I now pronounce this land consecrated and dedicated unto the Lord for the possession and inheritance for the saints, and for all the faithful servants of the Lord to the remotest ages of time, in the name of Jesus Christ, having authority from him." The program also contained a lengthy statement of President Joseph Fielding Smith that alluded to the Prophet's statement and to the apparent concern of some members of the Church about it: "Some of the members of the Church seem to be fearful lest the word of the Lord should fail. Others have tried to convince themselves that the original plan has been changed and that the Lord does not require at our hands this mighty work which has been predicted by the prophets of ancient time." President Smith then assured the audi-

Joseph Fielding Smith breaking ground at Independence, Missouri

ence, "We have not been released from this responsibility, nor shall we be. The word of the Lord will not fail. . . . The release from the building of the temple in 1833 did not . . . cancel the responsibility of building the city and the house of the Lord at some future time. When the Lord is ready for it to be accomplished, he will command his people, and the work will be done."

Because of President McKay's declining health, President Smith performed other ceremonial functions that ordinarily would have been handled by the president of the Church. So, three days after the exercises in Independence, President Smith went to New York, where he represented the First Presidency at the annual Hill Cumorah pageant. It was the first time he had seen this drama, and he was duly impressed. "It was excellent, magnificent," he wrote. "We heard every word, and the lighting was perfect. It brought tears to our eyes."

The participation of the First Presidency in events such as this was an essential part of the work. Because of the wide publicity given to them, they helped focus the attention of the members on themes and doctrines central to the mission of the Church. These are the things of which traditions are made, things that, in a sense take on a life of their own, helping to propel the Church toward its destination.

Behind the scenes, however, away from the view of the public, the First Presidency, day after day, performed the detailed work necessary to maintain the Church in proper order and aimed in the right direction. From the time of his call as a counselor, Elder Smith was intimately involved in the discussions and decisions of the First Presidency that marked the onward progress of the Church. A nagging issue of the day, which heavily influenced Elder Smith's dual roles as a member of the First Presidency and the president of the Twelve, was the restrictions imposed by the war in Viet Nam. A month before Brother Smith became a member of the First Presidency, the Church adopted a missionary quota of two per ward per year in order to comply with the requirements of selective service. This fueled many adjustments in proselyting activities because of reduced numbers of missionaries and increased shepherding concerns as more Latter-day Saints were siphoned off into military service. Steps were taken to obtain more LDS Chaplains, to furnish service personnel with the scriptures and other Church materials, and to instruct local leaders how to prepare young people for the moral challenges of military service. And as casualties mounted in the war, the local Church leaders were instructed in how to provide nurturing care for the wounded and for the families of those who had been killed. President Smith's participation in deciding issues arising out of the Viet Nam War was always colored by his own experiences as a father who had sent sons to war and who had suffered the anguish of losing one of them.

Shortly after Elder Smith's call to the First Presidency,

discussions were commenced about organizing a stake in São Paulo, Brazil. It was a matter of first importance, as there were then no stakes in all of South America. President Smith's ideas about this issue were important because of the insights he had gained during his extensive tour of South America a few years before. He had seen the potential of the area, had met the leaders, and was confident that creating a stake would securely anchor the Church there and would provide a stronger foundation for future growth. Once the decision had been made, Elder Spencer W. Kimball of the Twelve and Elder Franklin D. Richards, assistant to the Twelve, were assigned to effect the organization of the stake, which took place on May 1, 1966. Soon after, the international outreach of the Church was demonstrated again when the First Presidency approved the creation of a branch in Debnica Kaszub, Poland. This action, which was finalized in October 1966, was of special significance to President Smith as it revived memories of an October twenty-seven years before when he and Jessie sailed home from the Netherlands, the month after Germany invaded Poland. And in March 1967, further evidence of the rapid internationalization of the Church appeared when the First Presidency authorized a unified Church magazine that was to be published in nine different languages.

The general conference that convened the following month, April 1967, was one of historic significance. It marked the one-hundredth anniversary of the completion of the Salt Lake Tabernacle. As President Joseph Fielding Smith rose to conduct the afternoon session on Thursday, April 6, he stood at the pulpit that had been occupied by every president of the Church except Joseph Smith. Brigham Young had spoken there many times, admonishing, encouraging, and cajoling the Saints as they sat upon the building's hard, wooden benches, said in jest to have been deliberately made uncomfortable by Brother Brigham to ensure that his audiences remain awake and attentive. Through the intervening century, this extraordinary structure, with its vaulted dome and its mighty organ, was a constant reminder of the discipline and diligence of the pioneers who had built it in the wilderness during the years of their poverty. Of the General Authorities present on the stand of the Tabernacle at this session, Joseph Fielding Smith was the only living link to Brigham Young. President David O. McKay, of course, was also alive when President Young passed away in August 1877. However, he was fatigued from attending the morning session and so remained in his apartment in the afternoon, watching the proceedings on television.

Among the speakers introduced by President Smith at this session of the conference was Victor L. Brown, second counselor in the Presiding Bishopric, who provided the Saints with further insight into the rapid internationalization of the Church. Bishop Brown noted that several months before, the First Presidency had directed the Presiding Bishopric "to establish a translation, publishing and distribution organization, with the charge that Spanish speaking members of the Church in Mexico, Central America and South America were to receive the literature and materials of the Church in their own language and that they were to receive them at the same time they were received by the members of the Church in the center stakes." (*Conference Report,* April 1967, p. 35.) The bishop also said that soon after, the Portuguese, Finnish, Swedish, Norwegian, Danish, Dutch, German, French, Italian, Samoan, Tahitian, and Tongan languages had been added to this mandate. He then traced the process by which a vast organization had been put into place to carry out the simple directive of the First Presidency. Without attempting to label it as such, Bishop Brown, by his report, taught the rank and file of the Church an important lesson in the principles of authority, delegation, and accountability. And in the process, he parted the curtain far enough to partially reveal the vast power vested in the First Presidency, the presiding quorum of the Church. This quorum, of which President Smith was a member and over which he would later preside, could, as in this case, in a sentence set in motion a chain of events whose ripple effect would extend around the world and into the indefinite future. Being keenly aware of the vast consequences of their decisions, these men were careful about what they said and did so that a directive like this one, to organize a translation department, would ordinarily be preceded by a series of discussions during which the matter would be carefully analyzed and its impact weighed and calculated. Yet there were times when the Prophet, infused with revelatory light, might speak and act without premeditation or counsel, giving instructions with far-reaching effect. Such was the manner in which the whole system of international proselyting was begun when the Prophet Joseph Smith, without any preliminaries, whispered to Heber C. Kimball in the Kirtland Temple that he should open the door to the preaching of the gospel in England. The consequences of that whispered instruction are well known.

The semi-annual conference in October 1967 marked another centennial event. A hundred years before, Joseph F. Smith was sustained as a member of the Twelve. Joseph Fielding's father had actually been ordained an apostle the year before as the result of an action reminiscent of the instruction Joseph Smith whispered to Heber C. Kimball. Following a meeting of some of the brethren attended by twenty-nine-year-old Joseph F. Smith, President Brigham Young, without prior consultation, was prompted to ordain the young man to the apostleship. The results of that action are also well known. And well known, too, is an action taken at the semi-annual conference in 1967 that illustrates a prophetic initiative based upon consultation and analysis. At this conference the First Presidency called sixty-nine men to serve as regional representatives of the Twelve. The rapid growth of the Church had placed an almost impossible burden of administration and supervision upon the General Authorities. After long deliberation by the First Presidency and the Twelve, this action was taken to help lighten that load. However, since Joseph

Fielding Smith continued to serve as president of the Twelve, the action also tended to increase his personal burden, since the activities of these sixty-nine men would be subject to his overall supervision.

The decisions made by the First Presidency, like the call of regional representatives of the Twelve, ordinarily affected only the internal operations of the Church. Occasionally, however, an issue came before that body with implications not only for the Church and its members but also for the general public. Such was the issue of liquor by the drink, which surfaced in Utah in 1968. A group of citizens, spearheaded by local business people and strongly supported by a major Salt Lake City newspaper, had begun campaigning to amend Utah's strict liquor laws to permit the sale of liquor by the drink at licensed restaurants and taverns. Their argument was that the existing laws, which allowed the sale of liquor only by the bottle at state liquor stores, was a major deterrent to tourism and to the scheduling of national conventions in Utah. Because of the moral implications of the issue as far as the Church was concerned and because of fear that a change in the laws would alter the social ambience of the community and increase the likelihood of use of liquor by young people, the First Presidency officially opposed the proposed amendments to the laws in May 1968. At the same time, the Brethren openly authorized priesthood officers and quorums to distribute literature and to circulate petitions on the subject. Aside from his official involvement in this campaign as a member of the First Presidency, President Smith, at a strictly personal level, aggressively opposed the legislation because of a deeply held belief that liquor was one of the scourges of civilization. He attributed many of the sexual sins, against which he had spoken so openly and persistently over the years, to the use of alcohol. And he deplored the loss of health, much marital discord, and the increase in crime and public funding that could be traced to the use of liquor. These were the major considerations that, on this rare occasion, caused President

Smith and his brethren to abandon their customary policy against official Church involvement in public issues.

Meanwhile, the First Presidency continued to decide a myriad of issues involving the on-rolling work of the Church. President Smith had more than the customary interest when, in December 1968, approval was given to begin the microfilming of public and private records in both Poland and Korea. These would be added to the mounting accumulation of genealogical records from around the world safely stored in the Church's mountain vault east of Salt Lake City. President Smith's direct involvement in the beginning of microfilming by the Church and his extensive experience in vicarious temple work gave special personal significance to such a decision. The scope of the Church's involvement in gathering and preserving family records had given it international prominence among archivists and genealogists. It was that prominence that caused the First Presidency to authorize the genealogical department to spearhead the organization of a world conference on records that convened in Salt Lake City in August 1969.

Meanwhile, other facets of the work increased the international exposure of the Church. One was the continuing expansion of missionary work, marked by the inauguration of a two-month language training period for missionaries assigned to labor in foreign lands, and by the introduction of Mormon missionaries in Spain in January 1969. Another was the authorization given by the First Presidency for the Tabernacle Choir to sing at the International Exposition in Montreal, Canada, in August 1967. Four months later, on December 17, the choir presented its 2,000th broadcast. By this time, the performances of the choir, with the accompanying narrative and sermonettes by Elder Richard L. Evans, had become such a fixture of Sunday radio and television programming that to many these broadcasts had become their "church." The choir's reputation and public exposure were further enhanced when, in January 1969, it was invited to perform at the

451

inauguration of President Richard M. Nixon. Aside from his official involvement in the activities of the choir, President Smith took a personal interest because of his wife's role as one of its soloists. He never tired of hearing her sing, nor did he ever fail to laud her performances or to express pride in her talent.

Chapter Twenty-four

President of the Church

F
rom the time he was ordained to the apostleship and inducted into the Twelve at age thirty-four, Joseph Fielding Smith knew there was a possibility he might one day become president of the Church. At his ordination on April 7, 1910, his father had given him every key and authority necessary to lead the Church. At the time, however, these were in a suspended state, to become effectual only if he survived to become the senior, living apostle and to be ordained as the president of the Church by the other living apostles. But while this was a possibility from the day of his ordination, the likelihood of it becoming a reality was shrouded with uncertainty. Elder Smith was sufficiently mature then to know that life was tenuous at best and that there was no guarantee he would live long enough for the possibility to become reality. And eight years later when his brother Hyrum died unexpectedly while still a young man, the uncertainty about the length of his own life was undoubtedly increased. However, when he reached age ninety in comparatively good health, and with President David O.

McKay in a state of poor health, Joseph Fielding, perhaps for the first time, probably began to face up to the likelihood that he would one day become president of the Church, with all of the unrelenting responsibilities that position entails. In such circumstances, perhaps no one prayed more consistently and fervently for the continued health and well-being of President David O. McKay than did his counselor and longtime friend and associate, Joseph Fielding Smith. And Joseph's prayers were matched by his frequent gestures of love and concern for the ailing Prophet, including impromptu visits when he and Jessie would give the president and his wife little delicacies like some of Jessie's homemade jelly or when President Smith and others would call to give the Prophet priesthood blessings.

The unsought-for moment came on Sunday, January 18, 1970, when President David O. McKay quietly passed away, ending a notable career. At the moment of President McKay's death, Joseph Fielding Smith became, in fact, the head of the Church by reason of his position as president of the Twelve. President Smith was notified immediately of President McKay's death. He went first to the McKay apartment in the Hotel Utah, where he offered his condolences to Emma Ray McKay, the deceased Prophet's widow. Then, with members of his quorum, President Smith cooperated in working with the McKay family to make funeral arrangements.

The Salt Lake Tabernacle was filled to capacity when Joseph Fielding Smith stood at its pulpit to eulogize and pay last respects to his departed friend. Theirs had been a long and pleasant association. During the sixty years they had shared the apostleship, cross words had never been spoken between them. Of course they had had differences of opinion, but these had been expressed courteously, without rancor or bitterness. As a result, a great reservoir of mutual respect and trust had been built up between them that effectively absorbed any lingering residue of controversy.

The vast and complicated network of Church interests,

commitments, and responsibilities dictated the need that the office of Church president not be vacant for too long. While, as indicated, President Smith functioned as the de facto president of the Church from the moment of President McKay's death, to have continued that arrangement indefinitely would have created needless procedural complications and delays. Therefore, President Smith and his brethren of the Twelve decided to meet soon after the funeral to formally consider the question of reorganizing the First Presidency. The meeting was held in the upper room of the Salt Lake Temple on January 23, 1970. Fourteen apostles were present on that occasion: the twelve members of the Quorum of the Twelve as it existed at the death of President McKay, and elders Hugh B. Brown and N. Eldon Tanner who, at that time, were serving as counselors in the First Presidency. Also present was Joseph Anderson, secretary to the First Presidency.

The agendum for this meeting was short in form but long in duration and importance. The single issue before the Brethren was whether the First Presidency should be reorganized. If that issue were decided in the affirmative, there were procedural steps that would follow automatically. Ample time was taken to discuss the issue and all of its ramifications in detail. Each member of the quorum expressed his views, taking whatever time he wanted. All agreed that the reorganization ought not to be postponed; too many complications would be created by delay. And there were no detriments to going forward. So, after everyone had had his say, Elder Harold B. Lee moved that Joseph Fielding Smith be ordained as the tenth president of The Church of Jesus Christ of Latter-day Saints. That motion was seconded by Elder Spencer W. Kimball and carried unanimously. Joseph Fielding Smith then sat on a chair in the center of the room, and the other thirteen apostles surrounded him, each placing his right hand on the head of President Smith and his other hand on the shoulder of the one standing to his left. Elder Lee acted as voice in ordaining President Smith and in setting him apart as the

The First Presidency: Harold B. Lee, Joseph Fielding Smith, and N. Eldon Tanner

president, Prophet, seer and revelator of the Church. This formality was completed, satisfying the preordained requirements for fully investing President Joseph Fielding Smith with all the keys, powers, and authority necessary to direct the Church.

At this point, President Smith took his place alone in the center chair behind the desk in the west end of the council room. There he announced that after prayerful consideration, he had been impressed to nominate Harold B. Lee as his first counselor and N. Eldon Tanner as his second counselor. On motion duly seconded, these nominations were approved unanimously. The settings apart of the counselors were then performed. Since he was then second in apostolic seniority, Brother Lee was also sustained and set apart as president of the Quorum of the Twelve Apostles. And because Elder Lee's duties in the

First Presidency would make it impossible to lead out in administering the affairs of the Twelve, Elder Spencer W. Kimball was sustained and set apart as the acting president of the Twelve.

Certain sensitivities were connected with this reorganization. Elder Hugh B. Brown, who had served faithfully for several years as a counselor to President David O. McKay, was not called into the new First Presidency. Elder Brown, who was then eighty-seven years old, was not in good health. And because President Smith was even older and was not in the vigor of youth, he understandably felt the need for younger and more active counselors. Elder Brown willingly took his place in the Twelve, where he served until the time of his death. While Elder Brown undoubtedly understood the logic and the wisdom of President Smith's decision, he may also have felt some pangs of regret at having to sever associations and prerogatives he had enjoyed for so long. And the failure of President Smith to retain either Elder Alvin R. Dyer or Elder Thorpe B. Isaacson in the First Presidency perhaps involved similar sensitivities, although not in the same degree as with Elder Brown, and especially not with Elder Isaacson, whose physical disabilities had made it impossible for him to serve at all during the last four years of President McKay's tenure.

With these formalities behind them, the new First Presidency were prepared to go forward with their work. Because President Smith and President Tanner had both served in the previous First Presidency, they were fully aware of what had gone on before and about unfulfilled plans that had already been laid. Moreover, President Lee, who by this time had been a member of the Twelve for almost thirty years, understood most aspects of the work and required little time to become fully conversant with all the duties of the First Presidency.

Because President Smith's advanced age made it impossible for him to carry a heavy administrative load, he delegated broadly to his counselors from the outset. He relied most heavily on President Lee on ecclesiastical matters, while President Tanner was looked to for counsel on financial and business matters, a role he had played in the previous First Presidency. President Smith reserved to himself all final decision-making authority, whether in the ecclesiastical or the temporal field.

There was an excellent rapport among the members of the new presiding quorum. During all the time President Harold B. Lee had served in the Twelve, President Smith had had a personal affection for him and an admiration for his doctrinal soundness, administrative ability, and deep spirituality. And while President Tanner had served as a General Authority only a few years, President Smith had seen him function long enough in the First Presidency to have confidence in his ability and trustworthiness.

The day following the temple meeting, President Smith held his first press conference. It convened in the Church Administration Building, where representatives of the news media were in attendance. In addition to local newspeople, representatives of the national wire services were also present because of the widespread influence of the Church, because of the oddity that some people in the twentieth century believed in living prophets, and because the newly ordained prophet was almost ninety-four years old. President Smith was assisted by his counselors, who, with him, responded to a variety of questions about the Church and its policies past and future. Because the new presidency had been in place for such a short time, there was no attempt to sketch the future direction the Church might take, other than to affirm that all would be done in accordance with divine inspiration.

The installation of the new First Presidency entailed numerous staff and physical adjustments at Church headquarters. Over a period of weeks, President Smith moved into the presidential suite that had been occupied by President David O. McKay in the northeast corner of the main floor of the Church Administration Building. This move was tinged with much nostalgia for President Smith as it

*President Joseph
Fielding Smith*

required that he vacate offices in the Historical Department that he had occupied for many years. We must assume his comfort level in the new quarters was raised considerably when he brought with him a rolltop desk that had been used by his father, assorted knickknacks and mementoes he had accumulated over the years, and a large safe in which were stored many historic documents and sacred artifacts that had been under his exclusive control for many years. This safe was placed in the First Presidency's large vault on the main floor of the Administration Building. Its contents, in the years ahead, would provide grist for numerous unfounded rumors and speculations and, in some instances, would evoke demands that its contents be inventoried and made available for public scrutiny.

Concurrent with President Smith's move, President Harold B. Lee moved from offices upstairs to a suite in the southeast corner of the main floor of the Administration Building formerly occupied by President Hugh B. Brown.

459

President Tanner remained in the suite he had previously occupied across the foyer west of President Lee's office.

President Smith retained the services of his faithful secretary, Ruby Egbert, who had been with him for many years. However, because of his new, more visible role and the increased responsibilities that accompanied it, all agreed President Smith needed an executive secretary who could handle his correspondence, help plan his agenda, assist with routine procedural matters, serve as a buffer against unscheduled intrusions, and be available on call to assist the president in any other way. The person selected for this job was D. Arthur Haycock, who had performed a similar service for President George Albert Smith.

The need for an executive secretary was soon illustrated when President Smith's office was flooded with correspondence from well-wishers, from persons inviting him to speak, or from those offering advice or seeking personal interviews. Of the latter, one of the first persons of international prominence to seek an audience with President Smith was General William C. Westmoreland, U. S. Army chief of staff, who had played a key role in military operations in Viet Nam. He was accompanied to the interview by Major General Maurice L. Watts, Utah adjutant general, and by Elder Marion D. Hanks, assistant to the Twelve, who served on the Church Military Relations Committee and had personal knowledge of conditions in Southeast Asia, having visited LDS service personnel there to counsel and to encourage them. Visitors who sought an audience with the Prophet often wanted to serve some personal or public purpose by having their photograph taken with him and by having the visit publicized in the press. Because the distinguished visitor, and indeed the entire United States military establishment, had had a bad press during the Viet Nam War, General Westmoreland, regardless of the reasons that had prompted him to seek the interview, was undoubtedly pleased to have his picture appear in the newspapers at the side of the benign Prophet.

Not long after the visit of General Westmoreland, President Smith prepared to make his first trip out of Utah in his prophetic role. His purpose was to install Myrthus W. Evans as the new president of the Los Angeles Temple. While it was fortuitous that this was his first official act performed away from Salt Lake City, it was symbolic of the preferential status temples and temple work occupied in President Smith's priorities. Especially as he grew older, the importance of temples loomed larger in President Smith's thinking, coloring his attitudes and his sermons.

Back in Salt Lake City, the Prophet worked with his counselors to complete arrangements for the April General Conference, the keystone of which would be the Solemn Assembly. It was at this meeting, scheduled for April 6, 1970, the 140th anniversary of the organization of the Church, that Joseph Fielding Smith would be presented to the general membership for sustaining vote as tenth president of the Church. And other significant matters would be presented that required careful and prayerful consideration. Chief among these was the action of filling the vacancy in the Twelve caused by the elevation of Elder Harold B. Lee to the First Presidency. This was an action fraught with the most far-reaching consequences and not to be taken lightly. Considering that Joseph Fielding Smith's call to the Twelve was actually the trigger that propelled him into the prophetic office sixty years later was enough to give him serious pause before making the decision, a decision that, through inspiration, only he could make. Of course, in making that decision, he had the assistance of his counselors and the Quorum of the Twelve Apostles. So he used them in the way they were customarily used in making decisions of such importance. Each of them was asked to submit a list of three names of men whom they considered worthy and able to serve as a member of the Twelve. These individual lists were then consolidated by the counselors into a single list containing fifteen names that was then presented to President Smith. After carefully scanning the list, the Prophet, without hesitation or discussion, identified forty-six-year-old Boyd K.

461

Packer, an assistant to the Twelve, as the one to be called. This prophetic decision did not signal any purely personal preference on the part of President Smith. Still less did it signal any predominant superiority of the one selected over the others on the list. What it did signal was that the Lord had identified the one to be called for reasons best known to Him. The aptitudes, training, and temperament of Elder Packer would be significant as his ministry unfolded, affording opportunity for the full play of his qualities of character in a way that only the Lord could have foreseen.

In preparing for the conference, and in looking ahead to the future leadership needs of the Church, President Smith and his brethren decided to call three additional assistants to the Twelve: Joseph Anderson, longtime secretary to the First Presidency; David B. Haight, prominent California businessman and church and civic leader, who at the time was serving as a special assistant to the president of Brigham Young University; and William H. Bennett, well-known educator. At the same time, it was also decided that elders Thorpe B. Isaacson and Alvin R. Dyer would also be sustained as assistants to the Twelve, positions they had occupied before being called as counselors in the First Presidency. The action with respect to Elder Dyer was wrenching, both for him and for President Smith and his brethren. That Elder Dyer had been ordained an apostle by President McKay seems to have planted in his mind the idea that he might be called to fill the vacancy in the Twelve. And President Smith, being conscious of that, did not want to wound the feelings of one with whom he had served in the First Presidency. Yet personal feelings could not be allowed to enter into the decision. Time, the eternal healer, soon salved over these feelings, leaving no scar.

The sixth general session of the conference held on Monday morning, April 6, 1970, was the Solemn Assembly. President N. Eldon Tanner conducted the session and President Harold B. Lee presented the Prophet and the other General Authorities for sustaining vote, using the elaborate procedure of voting by quorums, priesthood holders, and the general Church membership. Immediately afterward, President Smith was called on to respond. He first expressed humility at the call, gratitude for his many blessings, and appreciation for the inspired leadership of his predecessor, President David O. McKay. The Prophet then expressed what proved to be the keynote of his administration. Said he, "And since we know that the Lord giveth no commandments unto the children of men, save he shall prepare a way that they may accomplish the thing which he commandeth them (1 Nephi 3:7), we are most humbly confident that this work will continue to prosper." (*Conference Report,* April 1970, p. 113.) The Prophet then acknowledged our Savior as the head of the Church, testified of the divinity of the work, and expressed appreciation for his counselors and the other General Authorities. He characterized President Harold B. Lee as "a pillar of truth and righteousness, a true seer who has great spiritual strength and insight and wisdom, and whose knowledge and understanding of the Church and its needs is not surpassed by any man." (Ibid., p. 114.) And he called President N. Eldon Tanner a man "of perfect integrity, of devotion to the truth, who is endowed with that administrative ability and spiritual capacity which enables him to lead and counsel and direct aright." (Ibid.)

His prior ordination as the head of the Church having been sustained by the members at the general conference, President Joseph Fielding Smith was fully and finally prepared to launch his prophetic administration. His work was divided into four general categories: counseling and planning with the inner core of leaders; ceremonial functions and administrative work at Church headquarters; performance of ecclesiastical duties at home and elsewhere; and speaking at various public functions. As to the latter, the Prophet was in such great demand that it was impossible to accommodate everyone. So, he had to pick and choose among the many invitations he received. The ones he accepted reveal his special interests and concerns.

Typical of these was one on May 2 when he addressed some two hundred handicapped seminary students who had gathered in Salt Lake City from Utah and several adjoining states. The following day found him in the Salt Lake Tabernacle, where he spoke to an overflow audience of University of Utah students who had gathered for their annual spring fireside. In early June, he spoke at a banquet that culminated a successful effort to help raise funds to assist a Salt Lake black congregation construct their chapel. And later in the month, he addressed a capacity crowd of MIA leaders assembled in the Salt Lake Tabernacle for the annual June Conference. Ceremonial functions during this period included visits from Felix Schnyder, Swiss ambassador to the United States; Afioga Afoafouvale Misimoa, Samoan secretary general of the South Pacific Commission; and G. Homer Durham, Utah commissioner of education. And behind the scenes, the Prophet counseled with his brethren about many things, some of which resulted in decisions with far-reaching consequences or that indicated new trends of President Smith's administration. In May, for instance, the brethren began to invite staff personnel to attend the first Thursday meeting of all General Authorities where they reported on various aspects of the work. So, on May 7, Antone Romney and Daniel Ludlow were present in the upper room of the temple to report on the status of the correlation program. The following month, Rex Skidmore attended that meeting to report on the teacher training program. Later, Wendell J. Ashton and Hugh W. Pinnock came to discuss a handbook for new bishops, and Doyle Green discussed the plans for the three new Church magazines, the *Ensign* (which replaced the *Improvement Era*), the *New Era,* and the *Friend*. These plans included the elimination of all advertising from the Church magazines. Still later, staff personnel from the Presiding Bishop's office came to explain new policies and procedures governing the construction of Church buildings.

Coincidental with this effort of the new administration to keep all of the General Authorities up to date on new developments in Church administration was the effort to involve the Quorum of the Twelve more directly in the decision-making process. So, the new First Presidency began to take to the temple meetings on Thursday for information and discussion most matters of importance that had been previously discussed in the meetings of the First Presidency.

Such a matter surfaced in early June when the Brethren discussed at length whether the position of Church commissioner of education should be reinstated. When that issue was decided in the affirmative, there was extended discussion about who should be appointed to fill it. Out of the several able men discussed, Neal A. Maxwell was selected. The call was extended to him at a meeting of the First Presidency on June 19, 1970, where he willingly accepted. Soon after, the new commissioner, with the aid of a search committee and the approval of the Brethren, selected Dallin H. Oaks as the president of Brigham Young University; later, Henry B. Eyring was selected as president of Ricks College.

Another such matter entailed the appointment of several brethren of the Twelve to monitor political actions and attitudes and proposed or existing legislation that could benefit or injure the Church. This group, whose functions extended worldwide, evolved into what was later called the Special Affairs Committee. Its purpose was not to exert political influence or to support or oppose political candidates but merely to assess the political environment and its trends that could affect the Church. Later, when political issues arose that had moral implications about which the Brethren felt impelled to speak out officially, it was this committee that spearheaded the action taken.

In mid-July, President Smith made his first trip outside the United States as president of the Church when he and President Tanner traveled to Mexico City. There special meetings were held with members and missionaries, and courtesy calls were made on government and civic leaders. This trip coincided with extended discussions and study about having separate Spanish-speaking units of the Church in the United States. There were advocates on both sides of this issue among the Brethren. Some felt that separate units allowed the minority members wider opportunities for participation and growth; others felt that separation tended toward fragmentation and created an undesirable "two church" image. The issue, which became more urgent as the number of minority language groups increased, was ultimately resolved by allowing separation while encouraging consolidation as soon as language and cultural barriers would allow it.

On returning from Mexico, President and Sister Smith went to Laguna Beach for a few days. There they enjoyed the quiet and serenity of the cottage on the bluff overlooking the sea. Back in Salt Lake City, the Prophet was involved with the Brethren in preparing for the planned visit of President Richard Nixon on the evening of July 24. President Nixon had sought the interview as an obvious means of promoting the candidacy of Republican senatorial candidate Laurence J. Burton in his attempt to unseat incumbent Democratic Senator Frank Ted Moss. While President Smith and the other General Authorities were well aware of the political motivations behind the visit, they agreed to it because it was the settled policy to grant audiences to distinguished visitors, regardless of their political affiliations.

There were special sensitivities about the planned visit, which had been widely publicized in advance, because of the unpopularity of President Nixon among a large and vocal minority. That unpopularity had lingered from the days almost twenty-five years before when Mr. Nixon, as a young congressman, had been a key player in the work of the House Unamerican Activities Committee that resulted in the perjury conviction of prominent Democrat Alger Hiss, an accused Communist conspirator. Nor had his reputation among Democrats been enhanced when, in a campaign against Helen Gahagan Douglas, he had persisted in referring to her as "the Pink Lady," implying that she had Communist ties or sympathies. And more recently, his unpopularity had ballooned because of his policies governing the involvement of the United States in the Viet Nam War. The depth of the antagonisms toward the nation's chief executive was illustrated by the threat of a radical element of the opposition party to stage a "nude-in" in front of the Church Administration Building to disrupt the photo opportunity for candidate Burton.

All this created concern among the Brethren because of the possibility that the visit would offend some faithful members who opposed Mr. Nixon politically, as they also opposed the chief beneficiary of his visit, Laurence Burton. There was concern also that the volatile feelings of the radical element could erupt into an embarrassing or even dangerous confrontation at the doorstep of the Church Administration Building.

Against that background the president of the United States arrived at the Salt Lake City Airport the evening of July 24. (Earlier in the day, President Smith had led the traditional Pioneer Day Parade down Main Street.) Among the presidential party were Mrs. Nixon, daughter Tricia, and George Romney, a Latter-day Saint and member of the president's cabinet. David Kennedy, another LDS member of the cabinet, was already in Utah, having participated in the Pioneer Day Parade in the little town of Randolph, Utah, his birthplace. A snafu in protocol created an embarrassing situation at the airport. Because this was intended to be a strictly Republican show, Utah's Democratic governor, Calvin Rampton, was not invited to join the welcoming party at plane side. He went there anyway, either to show respect to the president as Utah's chief executive or to make sure that the Democrats were not completely aced out of the pageantry. Whatever his motivation, the governor almost had to force his way into the receiving line. He was unable, however, to join the motorcade that accompanied President Nixon to the Church Administration Building.

A crowd of several thousand had assembled in front

*Joseph Fielding and
Jessie Evans Smith in
the Days of '47 parade*

of 47 East South Temple to welcome the distinguished visitor. Awaiting at curb side to greet him was President Smith and his counselors. After the usual formalities, members of Mr. Nixon's staff efficiently arranged everyone on the steps of the building for the event that had brought the president of the United States to Utah. Standing at the side of the First Presidency, President Nixon made a few remarks extolling the virtues of the Latter-day Saints while behind him and a few steps above, in full view of the television and the still cameras, stood candidate Laurence Burton. Those pictures, of course, appeared on all the local television stations and were splashed on the front pages of newspapers across the state. The intended implication, as far as the politicians were concerned, was that such close proximity to the First Presidency meant Church endorsement of Laurence Burton's candidacy. Once that photo-op had taken place, the politicians had obtained what they had come for.

President Smith and his counselors were aware of all this. They were wise men, experienced in the ways of the world and of politicians. And so they treated them all alike, without favor or discrimination. They hoped, however, that the Latter-day Saints would be astute enough to separate common courtesy and diplomacy on their part from opportunism on the part of the politicians.

Leaving the front steps of the Administration Building, the Brethren could see a gaggle of noisy dissenters carrying provocative signs and dressed in nondescript clothing. Ignoring the group, the First Presidency and their guest retired to the council room for a historic meeting. Assembled there were all members of the Twelve (except Elder Howard W. Hunter, who was in Tonga) along with George Romney and David Kennedy, members of President Nixon's cabinet, and members of the First Presidency's staff. This was the first time in the history of the Church that the Council of the First Presidency and the Quorum of the Twelve had been briefed in private by a president of the United States. On entering the room, Mr. Nixon circled the council table to shake hands with each one present. These included Elder Ezra Taft Benson, a future president of the Church, with whom the chief executive had been closely associated in Washington, D.C., for eight years while he had served as vice-president and Elder Benson had served as a member of the cabinet of President Dwight D. Eisenhower. Mr. Nixon then took his seat at the head of the council table to the right of President Joseph Fielding Smith. To Mr. Nixon's right sat President Harold B. Lee, another future president of the Church. To President Smith's left sat his counselor, N. Eldon Tanner. And to President Tanner's left sat still another future president of the Church, Elder Spencer W. Kimball. After all were seated, members of the press were allowed to enter the council room for five minutes of picture-taking, following which the room was cleared except for those seated at the table.

For a half hour, the president of the United States gave the governing hierarchy of the Mormon Church an intimate, off-the-record briefing about the major national and international issues facing the nation. This was preceded by several brief comments when the president made complimentary remarks about George Romney and David Kennedy, saying that he had been criticized for giving undue recognition to such a small group as the Latter-day Saints (who then comprised only about 1 percent of the total population). He defended his selections on the ground that they were the ablest and most experienced men in their particular fields. He also lauded the Church and its members, mentioning especially the favorable impression made by the missionaries at the Mormon exhibit at Expo 70 in Tokyo. He said that according to his daughter Julie and her husband, David Eisenhower, the LDS missionaries were the finest American ambassadors in Japan.

The president then launched into an extemporaneous discussion of the major issues facing his administration. On the domestic side, he commented on the nagging problems of housing, pollution, and unemployment. And at the international level, he was most concerned about the Viet Nam War, the turmoil in the Middle East, and the treaty discussions then in progress for the control of nuclear weaponry. In concluding his remarks, Mr. Nixon, who was reared in a Quaker family, said that since entering the White House, he had made a study of the presidents of the United States that revealed that while they came from diverse religious backgrounds, they all had this in common: as they assumed their duties and felt the weight of the burdens resting upon them, they became more prayerful and more dependent upon divine guidance. In response, Mr. Nixon was told that the members of the Church sustained each president of the United States, in turn, regardless of political affiliation, and offered prayers for their support.

After this briefing, President Nixon, surrounded as always by Secret Service personnel who accompanied him everywhere, went immediately to the Salt Palace to see the traditional Pioneer Day Rodeo and to be seen again in public with Laurence Burton, the man whom he sought to usher into the United States Senate. It didn't work.

Laurence Burton didn't make it, and Ted Moss was re-elected. The photo-op apparently made no difference, a fact most politicians seemed to know deep down. But this did not deter them from trying for it. And whenever they tried, they succeeded because the Church was as anxious to preserve good relations with all political parties as the parties were to get their candidates elected. So it was a harmless exercise, advantageous to the Church as it helped to create a friendly environment in which the Church could go its own way without undue interference from government. And if ever it became necessary to go to the government for help, as in cases involving foreign visas, it was always good to have friends in court, regardless of their political affiliation. So the unspoken maxim of President Smith and those who had preceded him was to be cordial to politicians without in any way endorsing their actions and policies.

Two issues not discussed by Mr. Nixon were of special concern to President Smith and his Brethren during this period—pornography and crime. Convinced that the increase in pornographic films and literature was a chief cause of a corresponding increase in sexual immorality in the Church, the Brethren had spoken out strongly against it from the pulpit and in editorials in the *Deseret News,* which was wholly owned by the Church. Because the *Deseret News* was advertising X-rated films, considered by the Brethren to be pornographic in nature, it was decided in August 1970 to ask the *News* to discontinue these ads. When the *Salt Lake Tribune,* which with the *Deseret News* jointly owned the NAC, the agency that handled the advertising for both papers, learned of this, it threatened to bring legal action. Nevertheless, the *Deseret News,* through its board of directors, discontinued running these ads. The Brethren also gave substantial monetary support to an organization called Morality in Media, whose purpose was to try to stem the tide of pornography throughout the nation, and otherwise used Church influence and resources toward this end.

471

In the summer of 1970, President Smith and his Brethren were also troubled by the rising tide of criminal activity in the United States and abroad. This was of special importance to the Church leaders because of threats of physical harm made by apostate groups and because of concern that the perceived wealth of the Church would make General Authorities and other Church representatives traveling abroad special targets for attempts at kidnapping or extortion. These concerns resulted in a significant increase in the number of full-time Church security personnel who gave special attention to the protection of the Prophet. Also, steps were taken to increase security mechanisms and facilities at the Church Administration Building and at the buildings on Temple Square.

In the months following the visit of President Nixon, President Smith was heavily involved in temple matters. In addition to presiding at ground-breaking ceremonies for the Ogden and Provo temples, he traveled to Mesa, Arizona, where he installed C. Bryant Whiting as the new temple president, and to Idaho Falls and St. George, where he installed Cecil E. Hart and Reed Whipple as the new presidents of those temples. Between these events, the Prophet published his twenty-fifth book, *Seek Ye Earnestly;* traveled to Hawaii, where he presided at ceremonies commemorating the fifteenth anniversary of the Church College of Hawaii; and presided at the 140th Semiannual Conference of the Church. In his keynote address, delivered at the Friday morning session, October 2, President Smith capsulized the essence of his apostolic teaching. "For more than sixty years," he said, "I have preached the gospel in the stakes and missions of the Church — pleading with the Saints to keep the commandments, inviting our Father's other children to accept the truth of salvation which has come to us by revelation in this present dispensation." The Prophet then reiterated the subordinate role he had played during all these years, while defining his concept of that role. "As agents of the Lord," he told the audience, "we are not called or authorized to teach the

President Joseph Fielding Smith at general conference

philosophies of the world or the speculative theories of our scientific age. Our mission is to preach the doctrines of salvation in plainness and simplicity as they are revealed and recorded in the scriptures." (*Conference Report,* October 1970, p. 5.) Having laid that foundation, President Smith then delivered a solid doctrinal sermon, emphasizing that salvation comes only through the atonement of Christ; explaining the role of Joseph Smith as the prophet of the restoration; tracing the rapid expansion of the work; defining the basic principles of faith, repentance, baptism, and the gift of the Holy Ghost; inviting the Saints to become more actively involved in the work and the nonmembers to come into the fold; and, finally, admonishing all to keep the commandments and endure to the end. In conclusion, the Prophet bore solemn testimony of "the truth and divinity of this great latter-day work," declaring as a matter of knowledge, not belief, that "God lives and that Jesus Christ is his Son." As to the mission of the Prophet Joseph Smith, he added, "I have a perfect knowledge that the

473

Father and the Son appeared to Joseph Smith in the spring of 1820 and gave him commandments to usher in the dispensation of the fulness of times."(Ibid., p. 8.)

The day before delivering this keynote address, President Smith and his counselors received a visit from the vice-president of the United States, Spiro Agnew, who was in Utah to promote the senatorial candidacy of Laurence Burton. Significantly, the vice-president, who had gained widespread notoriety by calling reporters "nattering nabobs of negativism," blamed the press and the neglect of parents for the spirit of permissiveness that had crept into society.

That the candidacy of Mr. Burton was in serious trouble is indicated by the fact that later in the month President Richard M. Nixon returned to Utah and on October 31 delivered a campaign speech in his behalf in the Salt Lake Tabernacle. As already indicated, that effort failed too as Mr. Burton was swamped a few days later by the incumbent, Frank Ted Moss.

In successive weeks following the election, the Prophet was the main speaker at the funerals of two prominent Latter-day Saints, Elder Thorpe B. Isaacson and Sister Emma Ray McKay, the widow of President David O. McKay. Neither service was a sad affair. Elder Isaacson's death was a welcome release from the physical imprisonment caused by the massive stroke he had suffered a few years before. And Sister McKay, who had lived a long and productive life, was undoubtedly joyous to be reunited with her husband who had preceded her in death only ten months before.

Not long before the death of Sister McKay, the Church's ninety-four-year-old Prophet, in obvious good health and spirits, was walking with his brethren toward the temple through the underground tunnel from the Administration Building. Noting the briskness of his pace, President N. Eldon Tanner said to him, "You certainly move along in a spry manner, President." Without breaking stride, President Smith answered, "I should — I've had plenty of practice." On another walk to the temple about the same time, the Prophet reminisced about watching the temple being built when he was a boy. He and his friends used to watch the stonecutters at work on Temple Square. And during the summer, they would go to the quarry in the mouth of Little Cottonwood Canyon to watch as the huge, rough stones were loaded onto flat cars for transport to Temple Square. There amid clutter and clanging confusion, the final act was performed by the stonemasons, who, with hammer and chisel, fashioned the unwieldy granite blocks into shape before they were hoisted onto the walls of the temple to be carefully fitted into place. This tedious process of erecting the sacred building stone by stone could not have failed to make an impression on the mind of the sensitive boy, Joseph Fielding Smith, who thereby learned of the slow, incremental means by which extraordinary results are brought to pass.

President Smith had certainly seen this process at work in his own life. Each phase, beginning as a son and brother in his father's large polygamous family and extending through the years of physical toil, missionary service, marriage, fatherhood and work as a student, researcher, author, and apostle, had been fitted together to produce the man who had become the Prophet, Seer, and Revelator of The Church of Jesus Christ of Latter-day Saints.

Through the myriad experiences President Smith had enjoyed during more than ninety-four years of life, there was one that had completely escaped him. He had never had a serious illness, nor had he ever been in a hospital as a patient. That remarkable record ended on December 8, 1970. On that day, a Tuesday, President Smith joined his Brethren for their usual First Presidency meeting, which, as usual, convened promptly at 8:00 A.M. With them that morning were Elder Howard W. Hunter of the Twelve and Elder Theodore M. Burton, assistant to the Twelve. These visitors had been invited to make a presentation about proposed organizational changes affecting the Historical Department, the Genealogical Department, and the

Presiding Bishop's office, something in which the Prophet was vitally interested. Suddenly during the presentation, President Smith became pale and nauseous, and, complaining of severe abdominal pains, left the council room with President Harold B. Lee. In his private lavatory, the Prophet was terribly ill, and because of this and the continued abdominal pains, President Lee was prompted to call an ambulance. With the sirens blaring loudly, President Smith was taken to the LDS Hospital, where he was checked into a private room. A series of tests revealed that the pain and nausea were caused by gallstones. After receiving treatment and spending two nights at the hospital, he was back at the office on Thursday the tenth. There he attended the usual meeting with the First Presidency and later with the Twelve in the temple. These occupied him continuously from 8:00 A.M. until 3:45 P.M. When someone expressed concern about the Prophet's going to the hospital, he downplayed it, saying, "Not many people die at age ninety-four."

During these lengthy meetings, it was reported that the Church had been successful in purchasing expensive property in Manhattan across the street from the Lincoln Center. There a combination church-residential-commercial building would be constructed, giving the Church an important presence in New York City. The meetings this day were unusually long because of lengthy discussion about the procedures followed in performing vicarious ordinances in the temples, another subject of special interest and concern to President Smith.

Two days later, all of the General Authorities and regional representatives assembled in the Salt Lake Temple Annex to receive special instruction from the First Presidency. There the Brethren were counseled about their ministries and their personal conduct. They were admonished to seek spiritual direction in speaking to the Saints—not to prepare speeches but to prepare to give speeches. They were also instructed to read the scriptures daily, to pray individually and with their families, and to hold family home evenings regularly. They were warned against false teachers and false prophets and were urged to cultivate the spirit of discernment. And, the brethren were counseled against trying to answer all questions put to them and, wherever possible, to encourage the questioners to seek answers from the scriptures or through the Holy Spirit. This meeting enabled the First Presidency to imbue the principal leaders of the Church with increased spirituality and dedication and to brief them about things they wanted them to emphasize.

A special initiative of the new First Presidency had its beginnings about this time when it was decided to hold area general conferences in different parts of the world. The purpose of these was to emphasize the international character of the Church, to encourage the Saints to remain in their native lands, to train and motivate local leaders, and to expose the members in outlying areas to the General Authorities. Once the general concept had been approved, the Brethren considered where the first such conference would be held. The issue was not difficult to decide; England was chosen because it was there the Church first commenced international proselyting. And Manchester, England, was selected as the host city because of key events in early Church history that had occurred there. There the *Millennial Star* was initially published, its first issue of May 1840 having on its front page Parley P. Pratt's poem "The Morning Breaks, The Shadows Flee." It was at Carpenters Hall in Manchester in the early 1840s that five special conferences were attended by members from the surrounding areas. And it was there that the nine members of the Twelve, led by Brigham Young, had held the only formal meeting of the Twelve that convened outside the United States. These decisions having been made, Elder Boyd K. Packer of the Twelve, who then had special responsibilities in the British Isles, was sent to Manchester in January 1971 to determine whether suitable physical facilities were available to house the conference.

Meanwhile, significant events were maturing at

Church headquarters. In early February, the last piece of structural steel was placed on the new Church Office Building. And about the same time, a major controversy erupted over the plans to raze an old Church building, the tabernacle in Coalville, Utah, to make way for a new stake center. The controversy, which became loud and bitter, pitted the stake leaders, who wanted a new, functional center, against a vocal and determined minority who were anxious to preserve this example of pioneer architecture. President Smith and his Brethren were caught in the cross-fire. Operating within established guidelines, the General Authorities gave wide latitude to local leaders in the construction of stake and ward buildings. There had been previous instances where old buildings had been razed to make way for new ones with no issue being raised. So the Brethren were amazed at the furor created at Coalville. They sought to mediate the dispute but failed. The local leaders were adamant in wanting a new building that would help them better serve the members, arguing that the tabernacle had become an expensive, useless museum piece. Their opponents were equally adamant, arguing persuasively that the tabernacle, as a physical symbol of pioneer aspirations, had much to teach the present and future generations. These opponents, knowing that local leaders had satisfied the building guidelines and were authorized to go ahead, obtained a temporary restraining order to prevent them from doing so. When they failed to have the restraining order made permanent, the local leaders immediately ordered the bulldozers to begin the demolition. They made a minor concession to the protesters by having portraits of early Church leaders cut from the ceiling for possible use in a future structure.

It was a no-win situation for everyone. Even the local leaders who won the tug-of-war lost much in the dissension the incident created among their members. And President Smith and his Brethren were troubled by criticism for failure to intervene and order that the tabernacle be preserved. They could have done this, and it was that knowledge which raised the ire and the criticism of those who opposed the demolition. But what the critics did not understand was that intervention by the General Authorities at that stage would have violated a policy of decentralization they had initiated. That policy was reflected again later in the year when the traditional June conference was discontinued in favor of smaller, local conferences and when the first general area conference was held in Manchester, England. The critics had not, therefore, become aware of the powerful thrust toward the internationalization of the Church and the loosening of the reins of control by the General Authorities at Church headquarters.

During the interval between the Coalville Tabernacle incident and the Manchester Area Conference, President Smith addressed the students of five universities or colleges, attended five stake conferences where he was the featured speaker, traveled to Southern California to speak to thirteen thousand young people, dedicated a ward chapel, presided and spoke several times at the April General Conference, traveled to Independence to dedicate a new visitors' center, presided and spoke at the annual mission presidents' seminar, presided and spoke at the MIA June conference, and was grand marshal at the traditional Days of '47 Parade. Amid these ceremonial and shepherding events, the Prophet continued to counsel regularly with his Brethren as they gave overall direction to the work.

A major project that occupied much time was a restructuring of several Church headquarters departments to meet the demands of a rapidly expanding international church. This resulted in the creation of two umbrella organizations, the Department of Internal Communications and the Department of Public Communications. The Brethren were aided in this undertaking by a group of prominent LDS business executives, chiefly Lee Bickmore, chairman of the board of Nabisco; James Conkling, a retired executive from the broadcast industry; and by a management consulting firm from the East. The Department of Internal

479

Communications was structured to facilitate the production, translation, and distribution of Church instructional and other printed materials around the world, while Public Communications was designed to improve the Church's public image, smooth and facilitate relations with the public media, and enable the Brethren to speak and act affirmatively rather than defensively on public issues that affected the Church. Chosen to head these two new departments were J. Thomas Fyans, who later became a General Authority, and Wendell J. Ashton, who later became publisher of the *Deseret News*.

On a personal level, this was a difficult period for President Smith. The attack of gallstones that had hospitalized him earlier weakened him physically so that his energy level was significantly lowered. On May 18, he suffered another serious attack that was very painful for him and troubling for his Brethren and family. But he stubbornly refused to go to the hospital. Once in a lifetime was enough! He elected to tough it out at home with such medication as the doctors prescribed and he was willing to take. These attacks were apparently sapping his strength, for he began to ride to and from the Thursday temple meetings rather than to walk as he had done routinely over the years.

Soon after this attack, Jessie began to have difficulties with her own health. When summer came, she had to be hospitalized. President Smith spent many hours at her bedside, comforting and encouraging her. July 19, 1971, the Prophet's ninety-fifth birthday, found him at the hospital with Jessie rather than at Liberty Park, where for so many years he had celebrated with his family. Because Jessie was not yet sixty-nine years old and had been in good health, President Smith seemingly had never considered that her illness might be terminal. It therefore came as a great shock to him when she quietly passed away on Tuesday, August 3, 1971. Her funeral was held two days later in the Salt Lake Tabernacle. At age ninety-five, President Smith had laid his third wife to rest and was a widower once again.

At the time of Jessie's passing, plans were being finalized for the trip to Manchester, England, for the area conference. The depth of the Prophet's mourning is suggested by his emphatic statement shortly after the burial that he had no intention of going to England under the circumstances. However, later counsel and reflection convinced him that he had to go. The expectation of the British Saints that the Prophet would be at Manchester had been built to such a high pitch that he really had no alternative. So, in the midst of his anguish at having buried his friend and sweetheart, President Smith began preparing for his last trip abroad.

The Prophet's traveling companions would be his son Douglas, his secretary D. Arthur Haycock, and a cousin, Donald E. Smith, a medical doctor. On Thursday, August 26, 1971, the four of them arrived in Manchester, where they checked into the Picadilly Hotel. That evening, President Smith and his first counselor, President Harold B. Lee, who had traveled separately to England, decided to call together the other General Authorities in a prayer meeting to help them prepare for the conference, which was to begin the next day. A conference room at the hotel was obtained for this purpose. The General Authorities present on this historic occasion, in addition to President Smith and President Lee, were elders Spencer W. Kimball, Marion G. Romney, Richard L. Evans, Howard W. Hunter, Gordon B. Hinckley, Thomas S. Monson, and Boyd K. Packer of the Twelve; Henry D. Taylor and Marion D. Hanks, assistants to the Twelve; Paul H. Dunn and Loren C. Dunn of the First Council of the Seventy; and Victor L. Brown of the Presiding Bishopric. In addition to these General Authorities, W. Jay Eldredge, general president of the YMMIA; Russell M. Nelson, general superintendent of the Sunday School; Joe J. Christensen, associate commissioner of education; D. Arthur Haycock; and the author were present. Because two members of the First Presidency and seven members of the Twelve were in attendance, this constituted an official meeting of the

Council of the First Presidency and Quorum of the Twelve, the first ever held outside the United States. At the request of the Prophet, President Lee conducted the meeting. It consisted of reports about the arrangements for the conference, a review of the agenda for the various meetings, and testimonies of the Brethren. The latter were highly spiritual, dwelling chiefly on the divinity and the restoration of the gospel, the beginnings of the Church in England, the ancestral ties of the Brethren to the British Isles, and the purpose and significance of the area conference.

The general meetings were held in the Bell-Vue Centre, a municipal park in Manchester. Kings Hall, an arena in the park, had been altered as much as possible to simulate the appearance of the Tabernacle in Salt Lake City. Special red chairs had been prepared for the General Authorities, the stand had been carpeted, and technicians had been sent over in advance to set up and check the sound system. Under the direction of regional representative Derek Cuthbert, ushers had been trained and all other physical arrangements had been made to ensure that the conference would proceed as smoothly as the general conferences in Salt Lake City.

President Smith delivered the keynote address at a session in Kings Hall on Friday, August 27, 1971. In it he emphasized that the Church is a worldwide organization, that it had grown to the extent that area general conferences were necessary, and that there was no better place to begin them than in England. He noted that all the presidents of the Church, except the Prophet Joseph Smith, had served as missionaries in the British Isles, and he commented on his own missionary service in England as a young man more than seventy years before. The Prophet also declared that the gospel is for all people, that it contains the answers to the world's pressing problems, and that, if followed, it would lead all people to exaltation. Other speakers at this session included Belle S. Spafford, general president of the Relief Society, and President Smith's niece, Florence S. Jacobsen, the president of the YWMIA. These sisters later participated in a special women's session where local auxiliary leaders were counseled and trained.

Approximately fifteen thousand Latter-day Saints attended this conference from all over Great Britain. It was the first time they had ever gained insight into the collective strength of the Church in their islands. This and the repeated statements from the pulpit at Kings Hall that they were an integral yet separate part of an international community of Saints seemed to imbue them with a new sense of identity and a determination to remain and build the Church in their own land. This was best illustrated by the concluding musical number of the conference, composed by a local member, entitled "This Is Our Place." In remarks preceding that number, President Smith had underscored this idea and capsulized the main message he and the other leaders had intended to convey during the conference. Said the Prophet, "We have attained the status and strength that are enabling us to fulfill the commission given by the Lord through the Prophet Joseph Smith, that we should carry the glad tidings of the restoration to every nation and to all people. And not only shall we preach the gospel in every nation before the second coming of the Son of Man, but we shall make converts and establish congregations of Saints among them. We are and shall be a world church. This is our destiny. It is part of the Lord's program."

As President Smith left the arena after the benediction at the last session, the audience rose as one and stood in silence until he was out of sight. Unlike most gatherings of the Saints, there was then no moving about or handshaking or visiting. The congregation merely stood as if transfixed and as if they were loathe to leave. Then, without announcement or accompaniment, they began to sing "We Thank Thee O God for a Prophet." When they had finished singing all three verses, they continued to stand, no one moving or speaking. After another interval of silence, and without any central direction, the congregation began to sing "God Be with You Till We Meet Again."

When all the verses had been sung, the audience still remained in place, seemingly not wanting the meeting and the sweet spirit that had attended it to end. Following yet another period of silence, the audience broke into applause, showing their appreciation by clapping their hands long and loud. Only then did they begin to move about and to speak. There were few dry eyes among them.

President Smith remained in England for two days after the conference to take care of some administrative work at the London Temple. He was also persuaded to drive to Wales to satisfy the urgent requests of members there. Originally he did not want to go. He was still in mourning over Jessie's death. And now that the conference had ended, he wanted to return home. He was strongly urged to go to Wales, however, if for no other reason than that it could be honestly reported that he went there during his visit to Great Britain. He finally decided to go but gave instructions that he was to be informed immediately upon crossing the border. When they entered Wales, he instructed the driver to stop, stepped out of the car onto the ground, got back in, and told the driver to turn around and go back, explaining, "Now you can say I was in Wales."

President Smith's plane was delayed in leaving Heathrow. As he and his companions sat waiting in the airport, the others were talking shop to while away the time. Anxious to be on his way, the Prophet told them he was ready to leave any time they had finished visiting. Douglas explained that their flight hadn't been called yet and that if the Prophet wanted to leave for home then, the only alternative was to walk. President Smith said he did not think they were quite ready for that yet.

On arriving in Salt Lake City, the Prophet was surprised that instead of being taken to the Eagle Gate, he was driven to Bruce and Amelia's home. In his absence, some of his favorite things had been moved from the apartment to a private room in the McConkies' house so that he would be close to members of the family who could prepare his meals and help with other needs. In addition, the other children came regularly in rotation to take him for rides and to visit and eat in their homes. While it hardly compensated for the loss of his sweetheart and did not provide the freedom he had once enjoyed, it was the best possible arrangement under the circumstances. As far as his family was concerned, it gave the children and the grandchildren the opportunity to have the Prophet in their homes regularly to enjoy his company and counsel.

The combination of Jessie's death, the strenuous trip to Manchester, and the upset in his living arrangements had a wearing effect on the Prophet's health. On Thursday, September 16, 1971, President Smith fainted during the First Presidency meeting, suddenly slumping over in his chair. He was taken to his office, where he soon revived. Over the protests of the Brethren, he insisted on going to the temple meeting. Afterward, he seemed perfectly normal.

As part of the October General Conference, a special meeting of General Authorities, regional representatives, and their wives was held in the Assembly Room of the Salt Lake Temple. The First Presidency, dressed in their white suits, gave timely counsel, urging those present to put on the whole armor of God and to live exemplary lives worthy of emulation by the members of the Church. Selected ones were then called on to bear their testimonies. It was a time of spiritual refreshment that prepared the hearts and minds of all for the conference sessions that would commence the next morning.

In his keynote address, President Smith alluded to the recent area conference in Manchester, saying that the Church had "come of age" in Great Britain and that the Saints there were "prepared and ready to administer the gospel to those of their nation." Stressing again the international character of the Church, the Prophet added: "And as it is among them, so it is or will be in other nations. The gospel is for all people, and the Lord expects those who receive it and its truths to offer them to their own nations and tongues." He then invited all to "come unto Christ and be perfected in Him," bore testimony of the Savior's divinity, and added his oft-repeated prayer that he would "remain faithful and true to the end." Finally, the Prophet, in a veiled, touching reference to Jessie's passing, said, "And as I join my testimony with that of Job, may I also unite with him in thanksgiving, for the cry, uttered out of the anguish and sorrow of his soul,' . . . The Lord gave, and the Lord hath taken away; blessed be the name of the Lord! '" (*Conference Report,* October 1971, pp. 6–7.)

While President Smith was quite vigorous during the conference, he later showed signs of diminishing strength. On Thursday, October 21, he became ill during the First Presidency's meeting and had to be helped from the council room. He complained of abdominal pains and seemed to be suffering from shortness of breath. He did not feel well enough to go to the temple afterward for the weekly council meeting. However, he was back at his desk the following Tuesday. Ironically, on that day his good friend Richard L. Evans, thirty years his junior, lay critically ill in the hospital. Elder Evans had become ill the previous Friday. He later showed signs of having suffered a stroke. Then he was hospitalized and lapsed into unconsciousness. Despite the fervent prayers of his family and friends and the administrations of his Brethren, he never regained consciousness. He passed away in the early morning hours of November 1, only nine days after he was stricken. Ninety-five-year-old Joseph Fielding Smith presided and spoke at the funeral, which was held in the Tabernacle on Thursday, November 4. His remarks and those of the other speakers betrayed a sense of disbelief at what had happened so suddenly. Since Richard L. Evans was only sixty-five years old and was one of the senior members of the Twelve, many had speculated that he would one day become president of the Church. It was not to be.

Elder Evans's death created a great void. He had been the Church's most visible ambassador to the nonmember

world. His weekly sermonettes while hosting the Tabernacle Choir broadcasts had given him a public exposure
not enjoyed by any other General Authority. This was
greatly enhanced by his election as the president of Rotary
International, which gave him an acquaintance with business and professional leaders around the world. And behind the scenes at Church headquarters, Elder Evans's
quiet and thoughtful demeanor, his incisive insights, and
his ability to express complicated thoughts in clear, concise
language had enabled him to exert a powerful influence
in shaping Church policies. Indeed, at the time of his death
he was playing a key role in restructuring various headquarters organizations into the umbrella departments of
Internal and Public Communications. Because of this and
other important initiatives under way, it was decided there
should be no delay in filling the vacancy in the Twelve
caused by Elder Evans's death. So, on Thursday, December
2, 1971, the Council of the First Presidency and Quorum
of the Twelve, while assembled in the upper room of the
temple for their weekly meeting, unanimously approved
Marvin J. Ashton for that purpose. He was immediately
invited to the temple, where he was called, given the apostolic charge, and ordained and set apart. Elder Ashton's
rich background as an assistant to the Twelve, a youth
leader and civic booster, a successful business executive,
and a former Utah State senator added important skills
and qualities to President Smith's inner leadership circle.

Shortly before Elder Ashton's call to the Twelve, President Smith and his counselors took another step to increase the sense of unity and commitment among the General Authorities and at the same time to instruct and
motivate local leaders. On Friday, November 12, 1971, the
General Authorities traveled by chartered bus to St.
George, Utah. In the evening, they were hosted at a banquet in one of the ward chapels by local priesthood leaders.
Early the next morning, they assembled in the upper room
of the St. George Temple, where Bishop Gordon Affleck
gave instructions about the procedure to be followed in

administering and passing the sacrament. When all was in readiness, the local leaders from the stakes in the temple district, numbering almost a thousand, were admitted to the temple. Following the congregational singing, prayers, and participation in the sacrament, the First Presidency and selected members of the Twelve gave instructions to the local brethren about matters of current interest and concern. These included gambling, racing, liquor by the drink, prostitution, apostates, family solidarity, counseling, Church disciplinary procedures, and worthiness interviews, especially those for temple recommends. President Smith was the concluding speaker, discussing the historical background of the St. George Temple, the first one built by the Latter-day Saints following the exodus, and the purpose and importance of the temple ordinances.

Aside from its training and motivational aspects, this gathering had special personal significance for President Smith. As already noted, he had been brought to St. George by his parents as a nine-month-old baby for the dedication of the temple in April 1877 when Brigham Young presided. Now, ninety-five years later, he returned, wearing the prophetic mantle as predicted by the inspired patriarch.

Back in Salt Lake City a month later, President Smith began to feel his age. On December 8, he fell, injuring his shoulder; and a week later, he fell twice more, fracturing three of his ribs and a hip. These last incidents required for a while that he be moved about in a wheelchair; and at home and in the office, he had to use a wheeled, stand-up push cart to keep his balance. He tolerated these aids only as long as absolutely necessary. In the midst of these adversities, his resiliency and sense of humor continued to show through. During the week when he first fell, President Smith conferred the sealing power on several brethren to be exercised in the Ogden Temple. One of them, whose wife was present, reminded the Prophet that he had performed their temple marriage fifty years before. Cupping his hand and whispering loudly in an aside to the man's wife, he said, "Can you ever forgive me?"

January of 1972, which opened President Smith's last year of mortality, found the Prophet and his Brethren involved in major organizational changes. The personnel to direct the newly created Department of Internal Communications were finally put in place with J. Thomas Fyans as the managing director, Doyle Green as editor of Church magazines, Daniel Ludlow as director of instructional materials, James Paramore as director of administrative services, and John Carr as director of translations and distribution. There were also major changes in the Historical Department. With the release of Elder Howard W. Hunter, the traditional duties of the Church historian were divided among three people. Elder Alvin R. Dyer was appointed as managing director of the Historical Department. Under him were historian Leonard J. Arrington and archivist Earl Olsen.

On January 18, the new temple in Ogden was dedicated. President Smith spoke and offered the dedicatory prayer at the opening session Tuesday morning. Because of the injuries he had suffered in December, the Prophet became quite weak as he stood at the pulpit and had to cut his speech short. As a result, others read the dedicatory prayer at the succeeding five sessions. Three weeks later, on Wednesday, February 9, 1972, the new Provo Temple was dedicated. Only two dedicatory sessions were held there with overflow seating in the Marriott Center, the George Albert Smith Fieldhouse, the Joseph Smith Auditorium, the Wilkinson Center, and the De Jong Social Center. President Smith gave the keynote address at both sessions but did not feel strong enough to read the dedicatory prayer at either one of them.

During this period, President Smith and the Brethren devoted many hours to discussing the creation of a new position called mission representatives of the Twelve and the First Council of Seventy. The concept was that these officials would function in mission districts in the same way regional representatives functioned in stakes, and that they would have joint accountability to the Twelve and the

First Council of Seventy. This organizational change was approved at a meeting of all General Authorities on June 2, 1972, and authorization was given to call twenty-nine mission representatives of the Twelve and the Seventy. Subsequent organizational changes resulted in the elimination of this office.

The Presiding Bishopric was reorganized at the April General Conference. Presiding Bishop John H. Vandenburg and his counselors, Robert L. Simpson and Victor L. Brown, who had served together since 1961, were released. Called to replace them were Victor L. Brown as presiding bishop and H. Burke Peterson and Vaughn J. Featherstone as counselors. The calls of these counselors again demonstrated the revelatory process by which such vacancies are filled. Long before the calls were extended to them, each had learned, by a revelatory prompting or a vivid dream, of his call to the bishopric.

At the same conference, John H. Vandenburg and Robert L. Simpson were called as assistants to the Twelve. Elder Vandenburg was then appointed as managing director of the Physical Facilities Department while Elder Simpson was appointed to serve as managing director of the Social Services Department, filling the vacancy created when Elder Marvin J. Ashton was called to the Twelve.

During this period, President Smith and his Brethren were gravely concerned about the physical condition of President Spencer W. Kimball, the acting president of the Twelve. Job-like, President Kimball was then suffering from serious heart problems, adding to the extraordinary series of illnesses with which he had been afflicted over the years. Elder Kimball's doctors had concluded that there was some chance he might not survive surgery, although they believed his chances of survival and a productive life thereafter were good. In making the decision whether to submit to surgery, Elder and Sister Kimball and members of the First Presidency, joined by the lead surgeon, Dr. Russell M. Nelson, later a member of the Twelve, counseled together. When the decision was made to go forward with the surgery, both President Kimball and Dr. Nelson received special blessings from the Brethren. The surgery was performed on Wednesday, April 12. Contrary to the usual practice, the temple meeting was held on that day instead of Thursday because of the departure of President Tanner the next day on an assignment. During the meeting, President Lee was called from the council room to take a telephone call and, returning, said with emotion, "The Lord has heard and answered our prayers." He reported that the surgery had been successful and that the prognosis was that "Spencer" would survive and be able to continue with his ministry.

It was also during this period that President Smith and his Brethren began to lay plans for the second area general conference, scheduled to be held in Mexico City in August. A committee consisting of members of the Twelve and other General Authorities, assisted by local leaders, had been appointed to study the alternatives and make recommendations. A key element in the planning, of course, was the assumption that President Smith would attend and play the featured role. There was nothing then to imply that he would not participate. Only his date with death on July 2 prevented him from doing so.

Meanwhile, there were several important events that would take place, along with the usual flow of activities, before that day. There was the annual meeting of the Council on the Disposition of the Tithes, which was held on Thursday afternoon, June 22, following the weekly council meeting in the temple. At that time, it was announced that the Church had its "year's supply" of surplus liquid assets so that it could function in the usual way for a year, even though there might be no income from tithes and offerings or other sources.

During the following week, the new mission presidents were instructed at the seminar prior to their departure for their fields of labor around the world. The final event of the seminar was a banquet and testimony meeting held Friday night, June 30. The international character of the

Church, a thing President Smith had repeatedly emphasized during his administration, was underscored by some
of the testimonies borne by the new mission presidents.
George Aposian Jr., for instance, told of the conversion of
his Armenian grandparents and of how in migrating to the
United States they had become separated from their three
older children. Brother Parra, who had to speak through
an interpreter, related faith-promoting experiences he had
had while serving as a young missionary in his native
country of Mexico. And Brother Ploeger, a German national, told of the remarkable circumstances surrounding
his release from a communist prisoner-of-war camp. The
brief remarks President Smith made to cap this special
evening were the last he would make in his prophetic
capacity.

Chapter Twenty-five

Death and Burial

President Joseph Fielding Smith spent a quiet, relaxing weekend with the McConkies and was looking forward to another Independence Day celebration. On Sunday afternoon, Amelia drove him to his own ward, the Eighteenth, for sacrament meeting. As always, the members gathered around to shake his hand and greet him as he entered and left the chapel. He was pleased to respond to the request of a young mother to touch her baby. On leaving, he joked with a young man who had taken his arm to help him down the two steps to the sidewalk, wondering aloud whether he could "jump" them. Later, son Reynolds came to take his father for a ride. They drove north to Bountiful to visit the Prophet's eldest daughter, Josephine Reinhardt, who had been a widow for many years. There plans were laid for a family gathering to be held at Josephine's home the following evening. After enjoying a visit with his daughter, who served him refreshments in her garden, the Prophet was driven back to the McConkies' home, where he shared a light supper with the family. Later, as he sat relaxing in a

Joseph Fielding Smith

President Joseph Fielding Smith

comfortable chair, which had been brought from the Eagle Gate, he chatted companionably with Amelia, who was seated nearby writing a letter. She left the room momentarily and on returning found him slumped forward in his chair, apparently unconscious. She summoned Bruce from a nearby room, and he promptly administered oxygen to the Prophet from a cylinder kept in the home for emergencies. It failed to revive him. Joseph Fielding Smith was dead seventeen days before his ninety-sixth birthday. He had reached "a good old age," had become "a mighty man in Israel," and had lived "to preside among the people," exactly as the patriarch had foretold.

Amelia's first call was to her brother Joseph, the eldest son, who, upon the Prophet's death, became the one to whom the family looked for leadership. Joseph phoned Reynolds, the next eldest living brother, and, asking his wife, Zella, to call the other children, left immediately for the McConkie home with his son, Lane, a physician. It was a solemn but not necessarily sad scene when the body of the aged Prophet was gently lifted from the chair to a nearby couch. The expectation that at such an advanced age their father might go at any time had steeled the children to the imminence of his death. His life had been full and meaningful, without regrets or recriminations. So, they talked quietly and reverently without any outward show of emotion, comforted by the strength and integrity of their father's life.

From their earliest remembrance, the Smith children knew that their father belonged not only to them but to the entire Church as well. That knowledge was powerfully reinforced when he became the Prophet, the one to whom members from around the world looked for leadership and direction. So, when they had conversed and counseled briefly as a family, they knew that their next move was to involve the Church in whatever arrangements were to be made for their father's funeral and burial. It was then that Joseph telephoned President Harold B. Lee to inform him of the Prophet's death. Within a half hour, President Lee and President Tanner were at the McConkie home to express their condolences. By that time, other members of the family had arrived. On entering the room where the Prophet lay, President Lee, who was then, in fact, the head of the Church, walked quietly to the couch, and, kneeling, took one of the Prophet's hands in his. He remained in that position for some time, not speaking, in prayer or meditation. He then arose to express his condolences to the family, his admiration for their father, and his admonition to them that they honor President Smith by living worthily.

Before arriving at the McConkie home, President Lee had triggered the publicity about the Prophet's death by calling a member of the First Presidency's staff, who, in turn, alerted the General Authorities and the Church press officer. Because of President Smith's age, appropriate summaries of his life had been prepared in advance, except for the circumstances immediately surrounding his passing. These were immediately made available to the news media so that soon the word that the Mormon Prophet was dead had flashed around the world.

Joseph Fielding Smith and his family

Later, President Lee appointed elders Ezra Taft Benson, Mark E. Petersen, and Delbert L. Stapley as a committee to work with the family in arranging for the funeral and burial. It was decided that the services would be held in the Salt Lake Tabernacle the following Thursday. The body lay in state in the foyer of the Church Administration Building all day Wednesday and Thursday prior to the funeral. Thousands passed by the open casket to pay their last respects to the great man. These included many nonmembers. The *Salt Lake Tribune,* which had attacked President Smith and his father so bitterly sixty years before, reflected on the vast change in attitude nonmembers had toward him. In noting his death, the *Tribune* editorialized: "Joseph Fielding Smith, a man stern in devotion to his creed, yet tender in regard for essential needs of people everywhere, gave wise counsel to his associates, loving care to his family and exalted leadership to his Church responsibilities. He will be missed, but remembered with special esteem."

The speakers at the funeral extolled other aspects of President Smith's character and ministry. They included presidents Lee and Tanner and Elder Bruce R. McConkie. The thread that ran throughout all of the talks was that the deceased Prophet's life and works provided the best and most fitting eulogy to be offered at his passing.

President Smith was lovingly laid to rest in the Salt Lake City Cemetery, high on the avenues overlooking the valley. Nearby were the graves of members of his family, including his three wives, his son Lewis, and his parents. One can imagine the joy with which they welcomed this son, husband, and father who had not only lived so as to realize the prophetic blessing pronounced upon him but had also lived up to his own life's credo, to be true and faithful to the end.

Bibliography

Primary Sources

Brewster, Hoyt W. Jr., Amelia S. McConkie, and Douglas A. Smith. Responses to questionnaire. Copies in possession of author.

Gibbons, Francis M. Diaries, 1970–1972.

Official Reports of the General Conferences of The Church of Jesus Christ of Latter-day Saints, 1910–1972.

Smith, Joseph Fielding. Journals, 1903–1972. Archives of The Church of Jesus Christ of Latter-day Saints, Salt Lake City, Utah.

———. Manuscripts. Archives of The Church of Jesus Christ of Latter-day Saints, Salt Lake City, Utah.

Newspapers

Church News, Salt Lake City, Utah, 1910–1972.

Deseret News, Salt Lake City, Utah, 1910–1972.

Salt Lake Tribune, Salt Lake City, Utah, 1910–1972

Periodicals

Articles about Joseph Fielding Smith from the Improvement Era

July 1970. "Portrait of a Prophet," a tribute in verse to Joseph Fielding Smith on his 94th birthday by S. Dilworth Young.

October 1970. "The Church Moves On" mentions Joseph Fielding Smith

499

in the Days of '47 Parade and a visit to him of President Richard M. Nixon.

Articles by or about Joseph Fielding Smith from the Ensign

July 1971. "A Modern Prophet at Ninety Five," by Albert L. Zobell Jr.

November 1971. Cover picture and description of Joseph Fielding Smith and Elder Derek A. Cuthbert during Manchester Conference.

July 1972. "A Day in the Life of President Joseph Fielding Smith," commentary by Jay M. Todd.

August 1972. "Joseph Fielding Smith—Apostle, Prophet, Father in Israel," by Bruce R. McConkie.

August 1972. "A Man Without Guile," by N. Eldon Tanner.

August 1972. "The President—Prophet, Seer and Revelator," by President Harold B. Lee.

August 1972. "A Review of the Administration of President Joseph Fielding Smith, January 23, 1970 to July 2, 1972," by Gordon Irving.

August 1972. "The Soul of a Prophet: Stories and Anecdotes of the life of President Joseph Fielding Smith," including "Thy Faith Hath Made Thee Whole," by Richard D. Proctor; "Let's Duet," by Ruth Christensen; "The View From the Family and Neighbors"; "Fascinated by Airplanes," by Albert L. Zobell Jr.; "Oldest President"; "Does the Journey Seem Long?" "President Smith's Last Two addresses."

August 1972. "Tributes and Messages of Condolence."

October 1976. "Joseph Fielding Smith, a Short Biographical Sketch."

April 1981. "Wartime Mission in Sweden," by C. Fritz Johansson.

May 1981. Comments about Joseph Fielding Smith by Loren C. Dunn.

November 1981. Comments about Joseph Fielding Smith by Boyd K. Packer.

August 1984. "Story of Joseph Fielding Smith from D. Arthur Haycock, Aide to Four Presidents," by Jack Walsh.

June 1985. "Story of Joseph Fielding Smith from Eduardo Balderas," by John E. Carr.

Articles from the Friend

July 1970. "President Joseph Fielding Smith," by Edith S. Patrick.

July 1971. "Friend to Friend," birthday wishes to President Joseph Fielding Smith.

October 1980. "Joseph Fielding Smith, 1876–1972."

Article from the New Era

August 1972. "President Joseph Fielding Smith, a Tithing Child," by William B. Smart.

Bibliography

Unpublished Talks and Papers in Possession of the Author

Talks given by Elder Howard W. Hunter and President N. Eldon Tanner with response by President Joseph Fielding Smith at dinner and tribute given at the Lion House, June 1970.

Talks of D. Arthur Haycock, and Jesse Evans Smith with response by President Joseph Fielding Smith given at multi-stake fireside, November 1, 1970.

Excerpts from talk of Belle S. Spafford entitled "Prophets I Have Known"

Paper entitled "Ethel Reynolds Smith, Wife of the President Joseph Fielding Smith," by Irene C. Jacobsen, April 1974.

Tributes of Joseph Fielding Smith given by Milton E. Smith, Joseph Fielding Smith Jr., and Douglas A. Smith with a taped message from Joseph Fielding Smith given at University of Utah Institute Devotional, October 8, 1971.

Books

Allen, James B., and Glen M. Leonard. *The Story of the Latter-day Saints.* Salt Lake City: Deseret Book Company, 1976.

Anderson, Joseph. *Prophets I have Known.* Salt Lake City: Deseret Book Company, 1973.

Arrington, Leonard J., and Davis Bitton. *The Mormon Experience.* New York: Alfred Knopf, 1979.

Berrett, William E. *The Restored Church.* Salt Lake City: Deseret Book Company, 12th edition.

Campbell, Eugene E., and Richard D. Poll. *Hugh B. Brown, His Life and Thought.* Salt Lake City, Utah: Bookcraft, 1975.

Cowan, Richard O. *The Church in the Twentieth Century.* Salt Lake City: Bookcraft, 1985.

Goates, L. Brent. *Harold B. Lee, Prophet and Seer.* Salt Lake City: Bookcraft, 1985.

Heslop, J. M., and Dell R. Van Orden. *A Prophet Among the People.* Salt Lake City: Deseret Book Company, 1971.

Kimball, Edward L., and Andrew E. Kimball. *Biography of Spencer W. Kimball.* Salt Lake City: Bookcraft, 1977.

McConkie, Joseph F. *True and Faithful.* Salt Lake City: Bookcraft, 1971.

Smith, Joseph F. Jr., and John J. Stewart. *The Life of Joseph Fielding Smith.* Salt Lake City: Deseret Book Company, 1972.

Smith, Joseph Fielding. The following books written by him were published in Salt Lake City by Deseret Book Company in the years indicated:

501

Bibliography

Essentials in Church History, 1922.
Seeking After Our Dead, 1928.
The Way to Perfection, 1931.
The Progress of Man, 1936.
The Life of Joseph F. Smith, 1938.
Teachings of the Prophet Joseph Smith, 1938.
Signs of the Times, 1942.
The Restoration of All Things, 1944.
Church History and Modern Revelation, volume 1 1953.
Church History and Modern Revelation, volume 2, 1953.
Man, His Origin and Destiny, 1954.
Doctrines of Salvation, volume 1, 1954.
Doctrines of Salvation, volume 2, 1955.
Doctrines of Salvation, volume 3, 1956.
Answers to Gospel Questions, volume 1, 1957.
Elijah the Prophet and His Mission and Salvation Universal, 1957.
Answers to Gospel Questions, volume 2, 1958.
Answers to Gospel Questions, volume 3, 1960.
Answers to Gospel Questions, volume 4, 1963.
Answers to Gospel Questions, volume 5, 1966.
Take Heed to Yourselves, 1966.
Seek Ye Earnestly, 1970.

Also, the three pamphlets written by President Joseph Fielding Smith:

Asael Smith of Topsfield, 1901.
Blood Atonement and the Origin of Plural Marriage, 1905.
Origin of the Reorganized Church and the Question of Succession, 1909.

Index

503

Index